THE UNITED STATES AND PANCHO VILLA:

A Study in Unconventional Diplomacy

Pancho Villa at the height of his power. It has been suggested that the head on the pommel of the saddle looks somewhat like Porfirio Díaz. (From a post card circulated in Mexico; photograph probably taken in 1914.)

THE UNITED STATES
AND PANCHO VILLA:

A STUDY IN
UNCONVENTIONAL DIPLOMACY

BY CLARENCE C. CLENDENEN, Ph.D.

Colonel, U.S. Army, Retired

KENNIKAT PRESS
Port Washington, N. Y./London

Preface

HISTORIANS of the Wilson era have concentrated so heavily on the major issues of neutrality and final participation in World War I that they have tended to neglect the problems presented by the prolonged civil strife and revolution in Mexico. These problems confronted President Wilson from the day of his inauguration, and they continued to plague him through both of his terms. His efforts to help bring a just peace and a constitutional government in Mexico led the United States into complex and strange diplomatic byways, some of which scholars have neglected.

In slighting the effects upon the United States of the situation in Mexico, American historians have also failed to evaluate the importance to American policy of the leading personalities of the Mexican Revolution. Thus General Francisco Villa remains merely a colorful and romantic figure, rather than a revolutionary leader whose actions and policies affected the American people. In the hope of placing him in his proper perspective in United States history, I have undertaken this study of the relations between him and the United States and of the complications that resulted.

I first became interested in the personality, character, and life of Pancho Villa when I went to the Mexican border as a newly commissioned second lieutenant of cavalry and served there from 1921 to 1924. Later tours of border duty increased my interest and curiosity. I became acquainted with men who had known Villa personally. I had the privilege of serving with soldiers who were veterans of the Punitive Expedition, who were in the tragic and unnecessary Carrizal clash, and who had fought in numerous small engagements with Villistas, Carranzistas, and Yaqui Indians.

My objectives are strictly limited to what is expressed in the title of this book. I am attempting to trace, in a more or less chronological order, the events of an obscure phase of United States diplomatic history. The greater part of my narrative is concurrent with what President Wilson called "watchful waiting." I am not, in any way, attempting a new history of the Mexican Revolution or a new interpretation of that momentous development. Therefore much that is of primary importance in any study of the Revolution is being omitted. Only those details that seem to have some bearing, direct or indirect, upon my subject are included. Such important issues as the position of the Church in Mexican politics and the program and activities of Zapata in the south are not pertinent in the relationships that developed between the United States and Pancho Villa. Likewise, in view of my purposes, I do not feel called upon to draw any comparison between Villa and Carranza as revolutionary leaders or to evaluate their respective stands upon purely Mexican issues. The only comparisons between them that I am consciously making are based solely upon how they appeared to the United States and how they affected Washington's policy. If, upon this basis, my conclusions, either expressed or implied, differ from those of scholars who are recognized authorities on the Mexican Revolution, I can only say that my conclusions seem to be supported by contemporary evidence. Such conclusions do not mean that I underestimate Carranza as a statesman and Mexican patriot or that I am personally sympathetic toward Villa.

For my material I have gone, as far as possible, to original and contemporary sources. President Wilson's Mexican policies and the American attitude toward the factions and leaders in Mexico were determined by the information available at the time. This information came from a wide variety of sources, such as consular and diplomatic officers, newspaper correspondents, the President's personal agents, and private individuals, many of whom had an axe to grind. But regardless of whether such information was biased or impartial, accurate or inaccurate, complete or fragmentary, it was the foundation upon which American policy was based. It led directly to the favor shown toward Villa during the months of "watchful waiting," to the undeclared war of the Punitive Expedition, and to American intervention in Villa's last battle.

C. C. C.

Menlo Park, California
February 1961

Acknowledgments

UNLIKE the payment of material debts, the obligation to acknowledge my indebtedness to the many people who have assisted and encouraged me is a particularly pleasant one to discharge. First and foremost, I must express my gratitude to Dr. Thomas A. Bailey, of Stanford University, who was willing to take a chance on a candidate somewhat past the usual age for new adventures and who was unsparing of his time and unstinting in his helpful criticism. It is difficult for me to acknowledge adequately the debt I owe to the Committee on the Albert J. Beveridge Award of the American Historical Association. I am deeply indebted to Dr. John J. Johnson, of Stanford University, for invaluable suggestions and for incisive and constructive criticism. Dr. Charles A. Gauld, formerly of Stanford University, was keenly interested in my project from its inception and called my attention to sources of information that otherwise I would probably have missed. I am heavily indebted, also, to Mrs. Edith Bolling Wilson for making available to me President Wilson's papers and to Mr. Warren Pershing for permission to examine and use the papers of his father, the late General of the Armies John J. Pershing.

Among others whom I must mention and thank are Mr. Gunther Lessing, vice-president of Walt Disney Productions, formerly the attorney in the United States for Villa's Division of the North. Mr. Lessing, busy as he is, took time and trouble to answer my questions in detail and gave me permission to use the information he furnished. I must not fail to thank Señorita Nellie Campobello, historian, novelist, *artiste,* director of the Mexican National School of the Dance, who graciously answered innumerable questions and took pains to obtain for me information that I could not have obtained otherwise. Dr. Alberto Rembao, editor of *La Nueva Democracia,* who knew Pancho Villa personally, cordially placed his knowledge at my disposal and permitted me to quote from our correspondence.

The personnel of the Manuscript Division, Library of Congress, and the archivists in the National Archives were all helpful far beyond their required duties. I am grateful for the numerous—almost innumerable—courtesies I received in the Bancroft Library of the University of California. Far from least among my creditors are the personnel of Stanford University Library, who were tireless in their assistance. It is scarcely necessary for me to say that the Stanford Library was the backbone of my research.

There are many others, failure to mention whom would be an act of ingratitude. Among those whose suggestions and assistance have been invaluable are Miss Aurora Hunt, Whittier, California; Mr. Eugene Weston, Los Angeles, California; Dr. Charles C. Cumberland, Michigan State University; the United States Army attachés at Mexico City and Bonn, Germany; the United States consul general at Mexico City; the United States consul at Juárez, Chihuahua; the United States commercial attaché, London; the cultural and commercial attachés of the German Embassy, Washington, D.C.; General Alberto Salinas Carranza, Mexico City; the Chief of the Department of Military History, Department of the Army, Washington, D.C.

In addition to those already mentioned, it is a sincere pleasure to thank and acknowledge my indebtedness to the following publishing firms and people for permission to use material to which they hold the rights:

The Caxton Printers, Caldwell, Idaho, for *Gringo Doctor,* by Dr. Ira Jefferson Bush.

The Christian Science Publishing Society, for permission to cite material in the *Christian Science Monitor.*

Doubleday and Company, for *Woodrow Wilson: Life and Letters,* by Ray Stannard Baker.

Dr. Martín Luis Guzmán, for *Memorias de Pancho Villa.*

Harcourt, Brace and Company, for *The Autobiography of Lincoln Steffens,* for *The Letters of Lincoln Steffens,* edited by Ella Winter and Granville Hicks, and for *Viva Villa! A Recovery of the Real Pancho Villa, Peon, Bandit, Soldier, Patriot,* by Edgcumb Pinchon.

Mr. Larry A. Harris, for *Pancho Villa and the Columbus Raid.*

Dr. Ives Hendrick, for *The Life and Letters of Walter Hines Page,* by Burton J. Hendrick.

Librería Patria, Mexico City, for *Pancho Villa,* by Pere Foix.

El Libro Español, Mexico City, for *Vida y hazañas de Pancho Villa,* by Ingeniero Elias L. Torres.

J. B. Lippincott and Company, for *Here Comes Pancho Villa: The Anecdotal History of a Genial Killer,* by Louis Stevens.

Methuen and Company, Ltd., London, for *The Eyes of the Navy: A Biographical Study of Admiral Sir Reginald Hall, K.C.M.G., C.B., LL.D., D.C.L.,* by Admiral Sir William James, G.C.B.

Dr. J. Fred Rippy, for permission to use a map in his book, *United States and Mexico.*

Carl Schünemann Verlag, Bremen, Germany, for *Bestie ich in Mexiko,* by Ernst Löhndorff.

The Stackpole Company, Harrisburg, Pennsylvania, for *Chasing Villa,* by Colonel Frank Tompkins.

Colonel H. A. Toulmin, Jr., for permission to use a map and material in his book, *With Pershing in Mexico.*

The United Press International Newspictures, for permission to reproduce the picture of Villa facing the firing squad.

The University of Minnesota Press, for *John Lind of Minnesota,* by George M. Stephenson.

The University of North Carolina Press, for *The Wilson Era: Years of Peace,* by Josephus Daniels.

Contents

Illustrations

Maps

THE UNITED STATES AND PANCHO VILLA:

A Study in Unconventional Diplomacy

Raids and Reprisals, 1850-1890

FOR three-quarters of a century after the Mexican War, the frontier region between Mexico and the United States was a half-explored wilderness. It was a haven for desperados, both American and Mexican, and for savage Indian tribes that were still unsubdued by either country. Both outlaws and Indians found it convenient to loot and murder in one country and take immediate refuge in the other. Thus, the border region became a prime source of friction between the two nations. Mexico was deeply suspicious of the United States, and Americans were bitterly resentful of the inability, or unwillingness, of Mexico to control the turbulent elements of the border population. Raids and reprisals, each with diplomatic complications, were almost commonplace. When Villa's raiders killed bewildered citizens in Columbus, New Mexico, on March 9, 1916, it was not the first time that such an incident had occurred, nor was General Pershing's expedition in pursuit of Villa's band the first time that United States forces had crossed the international line on the trail of marauders.

Citizens of both nations were guilty of lawless forays into the territory of the other. Until Porfirio Díaz imposed his ironfisted rule on Mexico, the continual civil wars of that country were a direct invitation to soldiers of fortune and unscrupulous adventurers. To mention only one, William Walker, "the gray-eyed man of destiny," in 1853 invaded Mexico and proclaimed the independence of the "Republic of Lower California," with himself as president.[1]

On the Mexican side, and somewhat comparable to Walker, was a flamboyant character named Juan Nepomuceno Cortina (or Cortinas). In the early morning of September 28, 1859, the people of the little frontier town of Brownsville, Texas, were awakened by wild shouts of "Viva Cortina! Mueran los gringos!" There was a brief fight at the jail, in which the jailer and one attacker were killed and the prisoners, most of whom were Mexicans, released. Several other Americans were killed in the town, and Cortina made an unsuccessful search for the marshal, who had once arrested him. There were no United States troops at Brownsville, and the citizens were terrorized until Mexican troops from Matamoros crossed the Rio Grande and drove the raiders away.[2]

Several months passed before a small force of United States regulars and Texas Rangers could be assembled, under the command of Major Samuel P. Heintzelman. Cortina, meanwhile, had established a fortified camp on United States soil and twice defeated local forces sent against him. He became a hero among the Mexican population, and it was predicted that he would drive the gringos back to the Nueces, or possibly even to the Sabine.[3] On Christmas Day, 1859, Heintzelman attacked Cortina's camp, killing several of the band and driving the remainder, including Cortina himself, across the Rio Grande. Parts of Heintzelman's force entered Mexico several times, bringing indignant cries of "invasion" from the local Mexican officials in spite of their failure to put a stop to Cortina's activities.[4]

During the next few years the normally turbulent condition of the border was rendered anarchic by French intervention in Mexico and civil war in the United States. Instances of both American and Mexican troops crossing the frontier were numerous. In March, 1863,

---

[1] William V. Wells, *Walker's Expedition to Nicaragua; a History of the Central American War; and the Sonora and Finney Expeditions, Including All the Diplomatic Correspondence, Together with a New and Accurate Map of Central America and a Memoir and Portrait of General William Walker* (New York, 1856), pp. 23–37.

[2] *House Reports*, 45 Cong., 2 sess., no. 701, Appendix B, p. 76.

[3] *Ibid.*, p. 77. Cf. also J. Fred Rippy, "Border Troubles along the Rio Grande, 1848–1860," *Southwestern Historical Quarterly*, XXIII (1919), 91–111.

[4] *House Reports*, 45 Cong., 2 sess., no. 701, Appendix B, p. 80.

Confederates crossed from Brownsville to Matamoros and seized a Union officer in that city.[5] A year later, Union troops having occupied Brownsville meanwhile, Major General F. J. Herron found it necessary to send four companies of Union infantry to Matamoros to rescue the United States consul, who was in danger because of the battle taking place there between the Mexican factions.[6] In New Mexico the local Union commander, Major General James H. Carleton, invited the governor of Chihuahua, Don Luis Terrazas, to send Mexican troops into the United States to dispose of outlaws who were raiding into Mexico. "Should Your Excellency desire to send [troops] across the river and seize by force the ruffians alluded to," he said, "this shall be your authority for so doing." [7]

The end of the Civil War in the United States and the final victory of the Juárez government failed to bring peace, law, and order to the frontier between the two countries. The decades following did not, it is true, produce any bandits who operated on Cortina's magnificent scale, but there were plenty of lesser gentry who found banditry more profitable and agreeable than peaceful industry.[8]

A military and diplomatic problem even more serious than that of outlaws was furnished by the tribes of Indians on both sides of the international boundary. The Indians, of course, recognized no boundary, but they knew that once across the Rio Grande, or across an imaginary line on the ground, they were fairly safe from pursuit. Bands of Comanches, Lipans, and other tribes harried the Texas frontier and disappeared with their prisoners and loot into Mexico. The worst offenders in the years immediately following the Civil War were the small but aggressive and warlike tribe of the Kickapoos.

During the Civil War a considerable portion of the Kickapoos, originally a Great Plains tribe living in Kansas, had migrated southward and found refuge in the Mexican State of Tamaulipas, near Remolino, about forty miles below the Rio Grande.[9] The local Mexican

[5] *Official Records of the Union and Confederate Armies in the War of the Rebellion*, 1st ser., XV, 1130–1132.

[6] *Ibid.*, XXXIV, 81–84.   [7] *Ibid.*, XV, 687.

[8] *House Reports*, 45 Cong., 2 sess., Misc. Doc. no. 64, Jan. 12, 1878. This document cites dozens of instances of bandit raids into the United States from Mexico. It is only fair to add that the Mexicans charged, probably with truth, that there were numerous lawless raids from the United States.

[9] *Ibid.*, p. 143.

population and officials soon came to regard them with great favor. They conducted themselves peacefully in Mexico, their presence was a deterrent to tribes hostile to the Mexicans, and their raids into Texas brought a profitable stream of cheap horses, cattle, and other loot.[10]

To put a stop to this particular nuisance, the Washington government was anxious to have the Kickapoos returned to United States control. The Mexican government agreed in principle, but the practical problem of returning the Kickapoos to the United States was not easy to solve. Neither the Indians nor the local Mexican officials were disposed to be co-operative. The diplomatic correspondence between the two governments dragged wearily along from 1870 to 1873, with the Kickapoos, in the meantime, crossing and recrossing the Rio Grande and robbing and murdering at will.[11]

The problem was brought into sharp focus, and an acrimonious diplomatic correspondence started in the spring of 1873. After a vicious Kickapoo raid into Texas, Colonel Ranald S. Mackenzie, at the head of four companies of his regiment, the 4th United States Cavalry, crossed the Rio Grande at night, made a forced march, and struck the Kickapoo village shortly after daybreak. A score of Indians were killed and a large number of prisoners taken, including one chief. Mackenzie burned the village and "had recrossed the Rio Grande before the militia of the Mexican Towns could be assembled to avenge this audacious violation of Mexican territory." [12]

Significant for the future was the almost hysterical indignation displayed by the Mexican press and officials because of the raid. The Kickapoos were successfully removed to the United States in the following year, but the unhappy situation on the border continued to be a source of friction and disagreement between the two countries. Small detachments of United States troops crossed the international

---

[10] *Papers Relating to the Foreign Relations of the United States, 1873*, p. 143. Hereafter referred to as *Foreign Relations*.

[11] *Ibid.*, pp. 198–231. The writer recalls seeing numerous headstones in the post cemetery at Fort Clark, Texas, inscribed "Killed in Battle with Kickapoo Indians." The old hospital records of the same post record large numbers of soldiers wounded in action with the Kickapoos.

[12] *Report of the Committee of Investigation Sent in 1873 by the Mexican Government to the Frontier of Texas, Translated from the Official Edition Made in Mexico* (New York, 1875), pp. 424–425. The Mackenzie expedition is also covered in *House Reports*, 45 Cong., 2 sess., Misc. Doc. no. 64, pp. 187–188.

boundary at frequent intervals in pursuit of hostile Indians, while movements of Mexican troops into the United States were not unknown.[13] There was, however, no agreement or mutual understanding in these affairs. By 1877, when the new dictator, Porfirio Díaz, seated himself firmly in the presidential chair of Mexico, relations between Mexico and the United States had become so strained because of the border situation that newspapers of both countries were speaking ominously of war.[14]

The dictator was faced with the simultaneous problems of consolidating his own power and of gaining the support of the powerful country to the north—support without which his regime probably could not survive. Like Venustiano Carranza almost forty years later, Díaz found that he could strengthen his position with his own people by taking a strong—even truculent—stand against the United States, while mollifying the United States by making a gesture toward cooperation.[15]

Bandit and Indian raids in the valley of the Rio Grande gradually ceased to be a serious international problem. At the western end of the border region another problem became acute, as settlers and miners began to move into the areas in which the various groups of Apaches had lived for centuries without serious interference. Restless bands of Apache warriors carried terror and death among the still sparse, but rapidly increasing, white population of Arizona and New Mexico. When pursuit became pressing, it was easy for them to disappear into the almost unexplored fastnesses of the Sierra Madre of Chihuahua and Sonora. The problem was similar to that presented by the Kickapoos but with one important difference. The Apaches murdered both Americans and Mexicans with complete impartiality, and there were few, if any, Mexicans who regarded them with favor. Consequently, it was easy for the two governments to reach, in 1882, an informal agreement whereby the troops of either country could cross the international boundary in close pursuit of hostile Apaches.[16]

The agreement was effective for one year, but because small bands of Apache warriors, under the leadership of such chiefs as Geronimo, were past masters in evading pursuit, it was necessary to renew the

[13] *House Reports*, 45 Cong., 2 sess., no. 701, pp. 8–9, 176.
[14] *Ibid.*, Appendix B, pp. 241, 244–250.   [15] *Ibid.*, no. 701, pp. 294–295.
[16] *Foreign Relations, 1882*, pp. 396–397.

pact annually for the next several years. In 1896, because of the depredations of the last of the noteworthy Apache leaders, The Kid (or El Chico), the agreement was amended so as to remain in effect until The Kid's band was either exterminated or subjected to the authority of one of the two governments.[17]

In accordance with this agreement, several American expeditions entered Mexico, achieving varying degrees of success. There were numerous sharp fights with Apaches, and considerable numbers of prisoners, mostly women and children, were brought back to the United States. American troops appearing in regions terrorized by Apaches were hailed as deliverers, except upon one tragic occasion.[18] In 1886 an expedition composed almost entirely of Indian scouts, led by Captain Emmet Crawford, of the 3d United States Cavalry, was attacked by local Mexican militia, apparently convinced that the expedition was an Apache war party. Before the misunderstanding was cleared up, Crawford was killed, and this gave rise to another international incident.[19]

The foregoing résumé of the relations between the United States and Mexico along their mutual frontier necessarily omits innumerable incidents and details that are interesting in themselves. The broad outlines of a pattern that was to become apparent in the twentieth century, when the border was again the scene of raid and counterraid, are clearly visible. The inability, or unwillingness, of the local Mexican authorities to prevent incursions into the United States and their failure to capture and punish raiders made it necessary for the United States frequently to take drastic action.[20] The patriotic resentment felt by Mexicans when United States troops crossed the international line and the glorification as national heroes of bandits such as Cortina, who defied the United States, were phenomena to be repeated during the years of the Mexican Revolution.

[17] *Ibid.*, *1896*, pp. 438–439. The Kid was never killed or captured. His fate is a mystery, but there were vague rumors in the 1920's that he was still living, still untamed, in the remote Sierra Madre.

[18] Britton Davis, *The Truth about Geronimo* (New Haven, Conn., 1929), pp. 165–166. Davis was an officer of several of the expeditions. Cf. Capt. John Gregory Bourke, *An Apache Campaign in the Sierra Madre* (New York, 1886).

[19] *Foreign Relations*, 1886, pp. 575–650.

[20] Chester Lloyd Jones, *Mexico and Its Reconstruction* (New York, 1921), pp. 279–283.

৯ II ৫

Villa and the Fall of
the Díaz Regime

THE opening decade of the twentieth century found Mexico, to all outward appearances, peaceful and prosperous under the strict rule of Porfirio Díaz, who had been in power, with one brief interruption, since 1877. The credit of the Mexican government stood high with the bankers of New York and London. Foreign capital poured into the country in a seemingly never-ending golden stream. Since the early days of Díaz' power there had not been a serious attempt at revolution, and most observers took it for granted that Mexico had completely outgrown the Latin American habit of governmental change by force instead of by peaceful election. In 1911, only a few short months before Díaz left his homeland for an exile from which he would never return, an admiring biographer wrote:

It is preposterous to talk about a reversion of the Mexican people to the old revolutionary habit. Diaz has done his work well. He has held his country-men still . . . until . . . all the thousand productive results of continued peace have made civil war unattractive to any important or numerous part of the nation.

The Mexican people are too busy to fight each other now.[1]

[1] James Creelman, *Diaz, Master of Mexico* (New York, 1911), pp. 416–417. It is ironical that the Revolution which overthrew Díaz was well under way when this book appeared from the press.

7

There were countless Mexicans, however, who were not included in the writer's "important or numerous part of the nation." Among them were the wealthy visionary, Francisco Madero, the saturnine Morelian, Emiliano Zapata, and an earthy, hard-bitten bandit of Durango and Chihuahua, Francisco Villa, whom the Díaz government had been unable to suppress.

Although the Mexico of Porfirio Díaz seemed to be progressing rapidly along the same paths as the more advanced nations of America and Europe, the mass of the people had gained little from the apparent prosperity and development. Socially, in fact, the Mexican people were retrogressing under the Díaz regime. Since the days of the Spanish conquest Mexico had been a country of baronial estates, but even under Spanish rule the communal holdings of the Indians and numerous small properties had given a certain measure of security to the lower classes. Under the rule of Díaz the communal Indian properties disappeared, the small landholder became a figure of the past, and the already vast estates of the wealthy *hacendados* expanded into feudal principalities. There was an important difference between the medieval feudal lord and the rich Mexican *hacendado*—the feudal lord was under recognized and customary obligations for the welfare of his vassals, whereas the owner of a Mexican hacienda was guided only by profits and his own conscience. Chattel slavery, as it existed in the United States, never flourished in Mexico and was formally abolished in the early years of Mexican independence, but peonage furnished an even cheaper form of labor.[2]

Since Mexico lacked the necessary capital for its own development, Díaz' policy from the first was to encourage foreign investors. Assured of rich profits, foreign capitalists poured money into Mexican mines, smelters, plantations, factories, and railroads. Most of the enormous estates were owned by Mexicans, but many foreigners were included among the holders of princely domains. William Randolph Hearst and General Harrison Gray Otis (owner of the Los Angeles *Times*), to mention only two, owned millions of acres of Mexican land. Mexican

[2] A temperate, and all the more damning for being temperate, estimate of peonage in Mexico is given in *Labor Conditions in Mexico* (U.S. Department of Labor Bulletin no. 38; 902), pp. 27–44. For a completely hostile picture, see John Kenneth Turner, *Barbarous Mexico* (Chicago, 1910). Cf. Edward Alsworth Ross, *The Social Revolution in Mexico* (New York, 1923), pp. 68–79, and Nathan L. Whetten, *Rural Mexico* (Chicago, 1948), pp. 101–107.

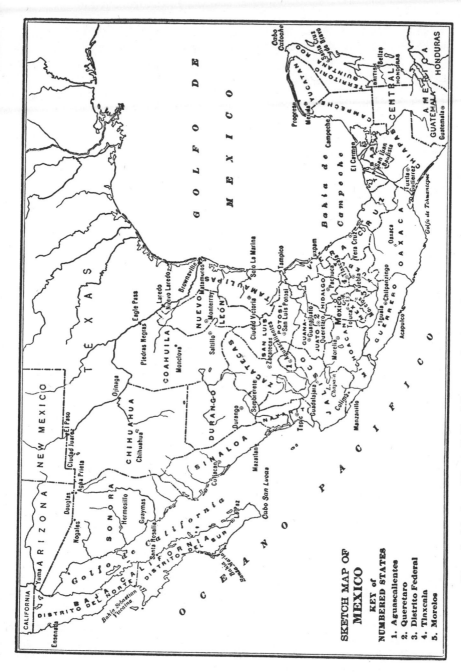

Map 1. Mexico. (From J. Fred Rippy, *The United States and Mexico*, by permission.)

industry was so completely dominated by foreigners and foreigners bulked so large in the ownership of Mexican land that one American commentator remarked: "The country in reality belongs to outsiders— to people who have never seen it, or visit it only occasionally." [3]

The internal peace which Díaz imposed upon a country that had been turbulent for half a century was maintained by force and terror. The famous corps of Rurales, originally recruited from among bandits who were given their choice between the firing squad and joining the force, made banditry and revolution unsafe. A believer in direct action, the dictator made no objection when the Rurales found it less trouble to apply the *ley fuga* than to hale malefactors into court.[4] Evidence is overwhelming that the Rurales were very loose in their interpretation of what constituted a malefactor. Runaway peons, strikers, personal enemies, and rivals of the local political boss—the *jefe político*—all were dealt with as ruthlessly and remorselessly as the most brutal murderer.

The number of Rurales was relatively small, but in upholding the dictator and the propertied classes they were reinforced by the army and the spiritual powers of the Church. Any disorder or threat too great for the strength of the Rurales was suppressed by the army. The loyalty of the army was assured by various expedients, not the least of which lay in special privileges for the officers, particularly the generals and officers of field grade. The Church, in theory, had lost the special position it enjoyed under Spain, but it was one of the greatest landowners of the country; its tremendous wealth was constantly increasing, and its influence permeated all phases and aspects of Mexican life.

Along with increasing resentment against the regime of Porfirio Díaz, a growing nationalism was beginning to be felt in all social and economic classes. It was not quite a feeling of national unity or of national pride, but manifested itself in a certain degree of antiforeign sentiment.

This was the Mexico into which Doroteo Arango, better known to

[3] James Middleton, "Mexico, Land of Concessions," *World's Work*, XXVI (Jan., 1915), 290.

[4] The *ley fuga* (law of flight) is the practice whereby guards have the right and duty to kill a prisoner to prevent his escape or rescue. The simple statement that the prisoner tried to escape is usually the only proof required.

history as Francisco Villa, was born shortly after Porfirio Díaz became President for the first time. It was a Mexico of unbelievable contrasts—a country of men who were rich and of men who struggled for a bare existence, a country of immense resources exploited for the benefit of a small minority.

In modern history there are very few men about whom legends have gathered as thickly as about Doroteo Arango. A peon who rose from banditry to power and influence, he became the embodiment of the hopes and aspirations of countless numbers of his countrymen, finally to die under a blast of gunfire from political assassins. The "rags-to-riches" theme, in all its variations, has always had a tremendous popular appeal; the political leader who is of humble origin usually has a glamour that captures the imagination in a way impossible for a person of higher social origin. His admirable qualities and good deeds are remembered, his weaknesses are forgotten, and the impracticability and failure of his program are overlooked. His life becomes the basis for myths that are repeated and exaggerated—and believed implicitly by many.

To innumerable Mexicans during the agonizing years of the Mexican Revolution, Francisco Villa was almost a Messiah; he was the devoted leader who would guide the forgotten man of Mexico—the peon—to comfort and plenty. He was the incarnation of Mexican patriotism and of fearless defiance of the hated gringo. To Americans, at the same time, Villa became a dual figure. To some he was the modern counterpart of Attila; to others he was a modern Robin Hood. The latter is a concept that now seems to be firmly imbedded in our folklore.[5]

Villa's early life is obscure, but most authorities agree upon certain details. He was born in 1878 in the village of Río Grande, municipality of San Juan del Río, in the State of Durango. Both legend and biographers agree that his parents were of the humblest class—*los de abajo*. His father was known as Agustín Arango, and his mother's maiden name was María Micaela Arámbula.[6] It is not clear whether

[5] Cf. John Reed, *Insurgent Mexico* (New York, 1914), and Edgcumb Pinchon, *Viva Villa! A Recovery of the Real Pancho Villa, Peon, Bandit, Soldier, Patriot* (New York, 1933).

[6] Elias L. Torres, *Vida y hazañas de Pancho Villa* (Mexico City, n.d.), p. 8. Torres was the principal representative of the Constitutionalist government in arranging for Villa's final surrender. He knew Villa intimately, and his statements are based upon information furnished by Villa himself.

Agustín Arango was a small, independent farmer or a peon in virtual slavery at the time of the birth of his first child, who was given the baptismal name of Doroteo.[7]

The year 1895, Agustín Arango having died meanwhile, found the seventeen-year-old Doroteo Arango living, with his mother and brothers and sisters, on a rancho which was part of the estate of the immensely wealthy Negrete family.[8] Young Doroteo had acquired a reputation as a hard and dependable worker who was respected by the other peasants of the rancho. By this time it seems that he had already had his first brush with Porfirian law and justice. He had formed a youthful friendship with a man named Francisco Benítez, who was a member of a gang of cattle thieves and was suspected of being a murderer as well. Doroteo, arrested as an accomplice, spent several months in prison before he was released through the friendly intervention of a neighboring *hacendado*, Pablo Valenzuela, a relative of the revolutionary writer of the same name.[9]

This story, whether true or not, later became significant by influencing the opinion of Villa held by various people of importance in the United States and Great Britain. Senator Henry Cabot Lodge, for instance, found it in a copy of the London *Daily Telegram* which someone sent to him and used it in a speech before the Senate on May 5, 1914, to blast President Wilson's judgment and policies.[10]

The hard-working peon boy became Francisco Villa, the bandit, while still in his teens. Legends cluster thickly about this crucial change in his life, but all have a common basis: avenging an insult to his young sister, he killed or wounded a son of the *hacendado* upon whose rancho Villa lived and worked.[11] In Porfirian Mexico there could be only one result when a peon made a murderous assault upon a member of the ruling aristocracy, and young Villa had to take to the mountains without delay. By some chance he managed to join a small band

[7] Early in his career as an outlaw, Doroteo Arango adopted the alias of Francisco Villa. Since this is the name under which he became famous, it will be used in this book. Pancho is a familiar nickname for Francisco.

[8] Martín Luis Guzmán, *Memorias de Pancho Villa* (Mexico City, 1934–1938), I, 8. Cf. Pere Foix, *Pancho Villa* (Mexico City, 1950), pp. 14–15.

[9] Torres, *Vida y hazañas de Pancho Villa,* pp. 8–9, and Pere Foix, *Pancho Villa,* p. 15.

[10] *Cong. Record,* 63 Cong., 2 sess., p. 7727.

[11] Ramón Puente, *Vida de Francisco Villa contada por él mismo* (Los Angeles, Calif., 1919), pp. 8–9. Cf. Guzmán, *Memorias,* I, 6–7.

of outlaws that was operating in Durango and southern Chihuahua, provided himself with a good horse by simply riding it away while the owner was in a nearby barroom, and was thenceforth a full-fledged bandit.[12]

Villa's adventures and misadventures during the next few years are outside the scope of this narrative. There is no reason to doubt the essential truth of Guzmán's account, which pictures him as a young man whose force of character and natural abilities soon made him leader of his band. He gradually became inured to violence and bloodshed but balked at killing from pure wantonness or sadism, as his companions apparently did at times. Likewise, there is no reason to doubt that he had longings for a more peaceful and unadventurous life and made attempts to establish himself as a law-abiding member of society. We may believe or regard with skepticism the views put into his speech by various writers during and after the Revolution that he found an honest life impossible in a society dominated by and run for the benefit of the rich.[13]

There is no record of when or where Francisco Villa first came into contact with Americans, but it is certain that he became acquainted with several during his career as a bandit. No American, as far as is known, has accused Villa of robbing him during this period of Villa's life, and at least one American who knew him during his bandit days regarded him very favorably.[14] It is possible that he spent some time in the United States, working as a laborer in California, Arizona, and New Mexico.[15] There is even an improbable rumor that he gained his first formal military experience as a trooper in the Roughriders, during the Spanish-American War.[16]

[12] Guzmán, *Memorias*, I, 17.

[13] *Ibid.*, pp. 5–61. This contains a full narrative of the phase of Villa's life covered in the last few paragraphs. Guzmán's account is based upon Villa's papers and personal acquaintance. It is accepted by Mexican historians of the revolutionary period as being authoritative.

[14] Dr. Ira Jefferson Bush, *Gringo Doctor* (Caldwell, Idaho, 1939), pp. 233–241.

[15] Larry A. Harris, *Pancho Villa and the Columbus Raid* (El Paso, Texas, 1949), p. 27.

[16] Anita Brenner, *Idols behind Altars* (New York, 1929), p. 201. A careful study of the muster rolls of the 1st United States Volunteer Cavalry (the Roughriders) fails to substantiate this rumor in any way. The entire regiment included little over a dozen men with Spanish names and only one man (with an Anglo-Saxon name) who signed by making a mark. This evidence is not conclusive but indicates the extreme improbability that Villa was a member of the regiment.

Regardless of possible interludes in which he attempted to make an honest living, Francisco Villa, until the outbreak of the Mexican Revolution, always returned to the life of a bandit. No other course was possible for him. In Porfirian Mexico, once a bandit, always a bandit. The forces that drove him into a life of violence were the same forces that erupted into the Revolution and catapulted him into a position of importance, making him a major factor in the policies of the United States and affecting the lives of countless Americans who had never heard his name before.

In the year 1910 those forces were not apparent. That year was the centennial of Mexican independence, and so firmly was it believed Mexico had outgrown political violence that the last thing the world expected was a violent change in regime in that country. There was a widespread belief, also, that the world was entering a happy era in which violence between nations and political parties would be as outmoded as the duel between individuals. The era of world peace was beginning. All political disputes would soon be settled by arbitration and election, not by "blood and iron."

The optimistic reporters on Mexico who found that the idea of civil war was "unattractive to any important or numerous part of the nation" or that "the Mexican people are too busy to fight each other" did not penetrate below the surface.[17] Among the dispossessed Indians and among the slave peons of the haciendas, the discontent was deep and dangerous. A spark would cause an explosion.

Those who hoped for a change were encouraged by an interview which Díaz gave in 1908 to a visiting American journalist, James Creelman. Díaz hinted that he might soon relax his iron control and permit a free election.[18] Shortly afterward, an opposition party began to appear. The prompt suppression of this incipient opposition, together with Díaz' renewed candidacy in 1910, showed that the only way a new regime could reach power in Mexico was by the traditional path of revolution.

In the election of 1910 Díaz was, of course, re-elected without any difficulty, especially as the opposition candidate, Francisco I. Madero, was securely lodged in jail at the time. Released from jail, Madero led

[17] Creelman, *Diaz, Master of Mexico,* p. 416.
[18] James Creelman, "President Diaz, Hero of the Americas," *Pearson's Magazine,* XIX (1908), 231–277.

the uprising that soon followed, and on May 10, 1911, to the surprise of the world, his followers captured the important border city of Ciudad Juárez—a victory that proved to be decisive.[19]

The details of the capture of Juárez by Madero's revolutionary army are obscure and are the subject of much controversy, but there is no question that the success was largely due to the energy and initiative of Colonel Francisco Villa, who suddenly found himself a soldier, rather than a hunted outlaw. In the first few weeks of the Mexican Revolution the peon-bandit had already traveled far.

Villa had become a member of the revolutionary army through the influence of Don Abrán González, one of the leaders of the movement to oust the dictator.[20] González was candidate for the vice-presidency with Madero and had found it necessary to flee to the United States to avoid arrest. Just when or where he and Villa first met is entirely unknown. One may conjecture that González, realizing that Díaz could be overthrown only by force, had previously noted Villa as a man who might be useful when the fighting started. This, admittedly, is only a guess, but it is not an unreasonable guess. In the middle of July, 1910, when Madero came to Chihuahua on his ill-starred electoral campaign, Villa was living in the city openly, in spite of having recently killed a man in the streets. He had a discreet interview with Madero and received confirmation of offers which González had already tendered him.[21] On November 15, 1910, Francisco Villa, at the head of fifteen men, took to the mountains, this time as an officer of the revolutionary army.[22]

The first weeks of the Revolution were unsuccessful for the Maderistas. On November 18, three days after Villa had taken the field, the American ambassador to Mexico, Henry Lane Wilson, reported that the "conspiracy" was widespread but that "it lacks coherence and the Government will easily suppress it." A week later he optimistically referred to "the recent revolutionary outbreaks" and to the "lack of

[19] Charles Curtis Cumberland, *The Mexican Revolution: Genesis under Madero* (Austin, Texas, 1952), pp. 116, 139–141. This is a scholarly and concise account of the confused events of the period.

[20] Guzmán, *Memorias*, I, 64–65. See also Puente, *Vida de Francisco Villa*, pp. 30–32.

[21] Ramón Puente, *Hombres de la Revolución: Villa* (Los Angeles, Calif., 1931), pp. 68–69.

[22] Guzmán, *Memorias*, I, 74–75.

intelligent leadership and organization [which] enabled the Govern-ment to suppress the rebellion." [23]

During the remainder of 1910 and the opening weeks of 1911 it seemed that Ambassador Wilson's use of the past tense was justified. Minor skirmishes occurred here and there, but the centers of popula-tion, the seaports, and the border cities remained firmly in the govern-ment's possession. The correspondent of the New York *Herald,* bored with the whole thing, reported in March, 1911, that the Revolution was a complete failure: "Nothing has been accomplished by the in-surgent forces outside of the columns of the El Paso press. . . . It is now possible to view the future of the revolution in Chihuahua in the light of what has passed, and it can be taken for granted that there will be no insurgent victories of any importance to chronicle." [24]

At about the time that this was written, the rebel forces suffered a heavy defeat near Casas Grandes, Chihuahua, in which Madero him-self was wounded and narrowly escaped capture. To all appearances, the revolt was crushed, but, paradoxically, the defeat served to strengthen the revolutionists. The fact that Madero had conducted himself with conspicuous bravery, in spite of his wound, enhanced his prestige and authority. The fainthearted deserted, leaving a hard core of the more determined. When, immediately after the defeat, Madero assembled all the scattered bands that would obey him, these depend-able forces included eight hundred men under Francisco Villa. Two months later the sudden capture of Ciudad Juárez by the insurgents, added to the pressure upon the government by Zapata in the south, sped the end of the Díaz dictatorship.[25]

During the campaign Villa's exploits as a revolutionary commander did not attract any particular attention in the United States—or in Mexico either, for that matter. There is no evidence that when his name first appeared in the records of the United States Department of State it attracted any attention at all. In a dispatch signed by General Pascual Orozco, which was intercepted by the government and a copy of which was sent to the State Department by the Mexican Embassy in Washington, Villa's name first appears: "I expect 85 companions

[23] *Foreign Relations, 1911,* pp. 363, 367–368.
[24] *Literary Digest,* XLII (1911), 489–491.
[25] Cumberland, *Mexican Revolution,* pp. 149–151.

from Carichic, and Mr. Villa with 50 more."[26] Pascual Orozco was the central military figure of the Revolution and was given full credit by the press for the final success of the campaign. Villa, if mentioned at all, was merely another more or less self-appointed Mexican "general"—and popular imagination in the United States pictured a Mexican army as being composed almost entirely of generals.

Shortly after the capture of Juárez, Villa managed to bring himself to the attention of the local American authorities. He had a violent quarrel with Giuseppe Garibaldi, grandson of the Italian liberator and a volunteer with the revolutionary army, and followed him across the Rio Grande into El Paso to kill him. Villa suffered the humiliation of being disarmed and hustled back across the boundary into Mexico. As to who had the temerity to disarm the formidable bandit-soldier, no two versions agree.[27]

Some of Villa's contacts with Americans were more agreeable than this. During the campaign he became acquainted with several prominent citizens of El Paso. He slipped across the border after midnight one night with Madero to be a guest of Captain Juan Hart, wealthy descendant of a famous El Paso pioneer. After the capture of Juárez, Villa and Abrán González spent several days resting at Hart's summer home at Cloudcroft, high in the mountains of New Mexico.[28]

Madero's hand was so strengthened by the capture of Juárez that he was able immediately to organize his provisional government. In Mexico City, Porfirio Díaz finally yielded to pressure and resigned ("abdicated" is probably a more appropriate word). Sadly he left the country where, for so many years, his slightest whim had been the law. The old dictator was escorted to Veracruz by a taciturn Indian general named Victoriano Huerta, whose loyalty to him was above doubt.

It was hoped and believed that the disorders in Mexico were near their end, that Mexico was about to settle down again to "industry and progress." Unfortunately there were already signs of the rift

[26] *Foreign Relations, 1911*, p. 412.

[27] Nellie Campobello, *Apuntes sobre la vida militar de Francisco Villa* (Mexico City, 1940), p. 18; Giuseppe Garibaldi, *A Toast to Rebellion* (Garden City, N.Y., 1939), pp. 301–302; Edward S. O'Reilly, *Roving and Fighting: Adventures under Four Flags* (London, 1918), pp. 284–286.

[28] Ernest Otto Schuster, *Pancho Villa's Shadow* (New York, 1949), pp. 71–73.

that was to keep the country split wide open for years to come. General Pascual Orozco was deeply disappointed because he was not made Minister of War in Madero's cabinet. The office went instead to Venustiano Carranza. Madero, whose humanity and lack of ruthlessness were weaknesses in a revolutionary leader, refused Orozco's demand for the execution of General Navarro, the Federal commander at Juárez. Three days after the capture of the city, Orozco, backed by a detachment of Villa's soldiers, with Villa present, attempted to arrest the Provisional President. Madero's firmness and personal courage quelled the incipient mutiny and aroused Villa's deepest admiration.[29]

The affair ended with all parties apparently reconciled, but it had later repercussions of the utmost importance. From that moment, Villa had an almost doglike devotion for Madero. Believing that Orozco had plotted so as to make him seem to be the instigator, Villa conceived a violent hatred for Orozco. Men whom Villa hated usually had reason for regretting it.

Villa left the revolutionary army within a few days and returned to Chihuahua. For several months he was engaged in the meat business—one of the few periods of his adult life during which he was peacefully occupied.[30] He had attracted very little attention from the world during the campaign, and his departure went unnoticed. He was not fated, however, to continue long as a businessman. The Revolution had hardly begun.

[29] Stanley R. Ross, *Francisco I. Madero, Apostle of Mexican Democracy* (New York, 1955), pp. 167–168.
[30] Guzmán, *Memorias,* Vol. 1, pp. 165–173.

❧ III ❦

Villa and the Orozco Rebellion

WHEN a nation has passed through a convulsion such as that which shook Mexico in 1911, the ways of peace do not return easily or quickly. A political change had taken place, but social and economic evils were still unchanged. Hopes for the stability and permanence of the Madero regime were strengthened by the failure, in December, 1911, of an abortive revolution staged by General Bernardo Reyes. Reyes, who had hoped to be Díaz' successor, was a veteran politician. As the election of 1910 approached, a diplomatic mission in Europe had been conveniently found for him, so that he had taken no part either in the election or in the subsequent uprising. Arrested in the United States in November, 1911, for violation of the neutrality laws, he managed to escape and proclaim a revolution a few days later. The popular support he had expected was conspicuously absent, and, entirely alone, he was captured by a detachment of Rurales on Christmas Day. Under the Díaz regime he would probably have been shot at once, but Madero merely confined him to prison.[1]

Meanwhile, General Pascual Orozco had been relegated to the relatively unimportant position of military commander in the State of Chihuahua. He was disappointed and embittered by Madero's failure to give him a cabinet position, and it is probable, too, that he

[1] Cumberland, *Mexican Revolution,* pp. 189–190.

19

had expected a substantial reward in other ways.[2] His position as military commander in Chihuahua made him an important figure locally, and within a short time he was associating on terms of intimacy with the wealthy landowners and the businessmen of the state. The United States consul at Chihuahua reported: "The well-groomed gentlemen of the wealthy Chihuahua clubs, who would not have touched the hand of this person but little above the rank of peon a year previously, began to flatter him with all kinds of social attentions, and it required a bare two months . . . for Orozco to become their servant, body and soul." [3] In record time Pascual Orozco was converted from being a revolutionary to being a main support of the counter-revolution.

Villa was watching the situation closely. He was summoned to the capital twice and questioned by Madero as to Orozco's activities. In early February, 1912, when Orozco declared against the government, Villa quietly slipped out of the city of Chihuahua with eleven followers and again headed into the mountains. Within a few days he was joined by five hundred men, most of them former members of his old command.[4]

The officials of the State Department in Washington could not have been altogether surprised at the outbreak of another revolution in Mexico, for Ambassador Henry Lane Wilson had been sending in a series of pessimistic reports, predicting trouble. The average American citizen was unpleasantly surprised but not too deeply interested. Latin American revolutions were widely regarded as merely squabbles for office and power, not to be taken too seriously. The *Review of Reviews,* expressing this point of view, dismissed the new outbreak in Mexico with a brief paragraph, characterizing it as a "petty revolutionary movement," which indicated only that Mexico had not yet had sufficient time to settle down.[5] The principal concern of Americans who gave any thought or attention to Mexico was for the safety of the large number of Americans in the country. Even that did not compete in interest with the noisy feud between President Taft and ex-President Roosevelt, a subject which really rocked the nation.

[2] Ernest Gruening, *Mexico and Its Heritage* (New York, 1928), p. 302. Cf. S. R. Ross, *Francisco I. Madero*, p. 168.
[3] Consul Marion Letcher to the Secretary of State, Oct. 17, 1913, National Archives, State Department File no. 812.00/9484.
[4] Guzmán, *Memorias*, I, 179–189.   [5] *Review of Reviews*, XLV (1912), 281.

Outside of the limited number of officials who kept Washington informed as to daily events, there was little, or no, interest in Francisco Villa. To most of the world he was completely unknown, and even those who were aware of him were uncertain of his position in Mexican politics. On February 23, the commanding officer of the United States forces at El Paso informed the War Department that "Pancheo Villa" had been entrusted with recruiting fifteen hundred men for Madero, but the American consul at Ciudad Juárez had other information.[6] On February 28, reporting the seizure of the city by the Orozquistas, the consul said: "It is rumored that General Villa, with his command of five hundred men, sent out by the Government to quiet the disturbances, have declared against Madero and will in a few days join those now in this city and march against Chihuahua."[7] Villa's position was clarified a few days later, when the American consul at Chihuahua reported him as attacking the Orozco forces near that city.[8]

For several weeks Villa conducted a singlehanded campaign against the rebels. He was victorious in several petty skirmishes and captured the important city of Parral, but after a stubborn defense of three days against a superior encircling force of rebels, he was forced to evacuate.

Villa's troops at Parral included an American soldier of fortune named Thomas Fountain—a valuable man because he could operate a machine gun. When Villa's forces evacuated Parral, Fountain was cut off and captured by the enemy. Neither side in Mexican civil wars was punctilious about the treatment of prisoners, and Fountain was killed the next morning. Possibly because he was an American citizen, the Orozquistas did not execute him formally. Rather, they invoked the traditional *ley fuga,* shooting him in the street.[9]

The killing of Thomas Fountain became a minor diplomatic issue at once. The idea which developed later, that under no circumstances may an American citizen become a soldier in a foreign army and that any American who does so has forfeited all claims to his government's interest and protection, was not yet prevalent. Consul Marion Letcher, at Chihuahua, on hearing of Fountain's capture and expected execution, protested to the Orozco authorities, but his protests were

[6] Secretary of War Stimson to the Attorney General, Feb. 23, 1912, National Archives, Department of Justice File no. 90755–1324.
[7] *Foreign Relations, 1912,* p. 729.   [8] *Ibid.,* p. 734.
[9] Edward S. O'Reilly, *Roving and Fighting,* p. 288.

ignored. Letcher learned of Fountain's death through the newspapers. Ambassador Wilson was directed by the Secretary of State to notify the Mexican government that any American who was taken as a prisoner of war must be treated "in accordance with the principles of international law." Letcher was instructed to deliver the same warning to Orozco and to add that Orozco's conduct would arouse the deep resentment of the American people.[10]

On the following day, April 15, 1912, a remarkable communication from General Pascual Orozco was telegraphed from El Paso, Texas, to the President of the United States:

Fountain was executed because he was fighting us, handling a rapid firing machine [gun] in Villa ranks. It was done without consideration what nationality he was. We want the strongest possible friendship with your wonderful people and have no prejudices against them. We mail you full explanation in the matter and feel confident you would approve it.[11]

Protesting to the Madero government about the execution of American prisoners captured by the rebels was obviously a futile diplomatic gesture. Letcher's warning to Orozco probably fell on deaf ears, for Letcher had previously reported that "the rebel authorities [are] insolent toward this office and Americans generally." He added later his opinion that Fountain was killed because of his nationality.[12] The one person who was in a position to give a warning that the rebels would heed was their bitter enemy, Francisco Villa—he promptly announced that he would execute immediately any Americans from the Orozco forces who might fall into his hands. Since such an act would have been directly contrary to the warning from Washington, Ambassador Wilson protested at once, but there is no indication that Villa ever received any orders on the subject.[13]

It may seem that the foregoing account of the death of a forgotten American adventurer in a forgotten campaign is a digression from the basic theme of this discussion. Yet within a short time, by some strange transposition, rumor had it that Fountain was murdered by Villa himself. Ambassador Wilson, as will be seen, believed fully that Villa killed Fountain, and the belief undoubtedly influenced Wilson's attitude.

In spite of Villa's efforts in Chihuahua, the campaign in the north,

---

[10] *Foreign Relations, 1912*, pp. 787–788.   [11] *Ibid.*, p. 790.
[12] *Ibid.*, pp. 777–778, 792.   [13] *Ibid.*, pp. 794–795.

meanwhile, had gone steadily against Madero. In March a Federal army was disastrously defeated at Telleno, in the State of Chihuahua. The unfortunate Federal commander, General José González Sala, committed suicide, leaving the remnants of the Federal force leaderless. Ambassador Wilson reported that Chihuahua had passed entirely out of the government's control, and he saw no possibility of the Madero regime re-establishing its authority in that important state.[14]

In the emergency, Madero turned to Victoriano Huerta. Madero and Huerta had had some differences while the latter was directing operations against the Zapatistas, but since Huerta was a professional soldier of long service, it was undoubtedly hoped that his basic loyalty was for Mexico and the established government, rather than to any particular party or individual.

Huerta arrived at Torreón on April 12 and assumed command of all the Federal forces operating against Orozco. Among the troops thus coming under his orders were Villa's irregulars. By the middle of May, Huerta had massed a powerful force and, with Villa's horsemen screening his movements and keeping the rebels off balance, on May 23 smashed Orozco's army in a second battle of Telleno. From then on, it was a simple matter of "mopping up" the remnants of resistance.

At the beginning of their association, relations between Villa and Huerta were outwardly cordial, but there was a definite clash of personalities and ideas. Villa, whose rank in the army was "honorary general," found himself addressed ironically as "Su señoría" or "Mi general honorario." His unprepossessing appearance, his rough clothes, his uncouth manners, made him the butt of sarcasm that he deeply resented. With his long background of violence and complete freedom from any sort of control, Villa would have been a difficult subordinate for the most tactful commander, and Huerta was anything but tactful. A rupture occurred on June 4, when Villa was suddenly arrested and placed in confinement, charged with insubordination. Huerta ordered his immediate execution, and Francisco Villa came as close to death as is possible for a man to do and survive. He was actually standing before the firing squad, when he was reprieved through the efforts of Raúl Madero, the President's brother, and Colonel Ribio Navarrete.[15]

[14] *Ibid.*, p. 281.

[15] See Guzmán, *Memorias*, I, 245–263; Pere Foix, *Pancho Villa*, pp. 143–149; Puente, *Hombres de la Revolución: Villa*, pp. 85–88; O'Reilly, *Roving and Fighting*, pp. 289–290. O'Reilly claims to have been nearby during these events, although not an eyewitness.

Instead of being executed, Villa was transferred to the military prison of Tlaltelolco, at Mexico City, where General Bernardo Reyes was confined.

There is a version of the reasons for Huerta's arrest and near execution of Villa that is so different from the generally accepted account, as given above, that it is worth quoting at length. Ambassador Henry Lane Wilson said:

After Huerta was placed in command of Madero's army and sent north to engage Orozco . . . a number of border chieftains were given commissions and ordered to report to Huerta. Among these chieftains was Francisco Villa, who had been leading the life of a bandit in the mountains of Durango, a fugitive from justice in the time of Diaz, but early gaining the confidence of Madero. Villa reported to Huerta but afterward led his followers on marauding expeditions against the civil population in the region through which they were passing. At that time many of the great estates in the north were owned by Americans who, suffering injury to person and property through the uniformed bandits of Villa, communicated through consuls and directly with the embassy, asking for protection. I immediately brought the complaints to the attention of the President [of Mexico] in a personal interview. He questioned the reliability of my information, saying that Villa was a "patriot and an honourable gentleman." I then, in compliance with the President's wish, made a second investigation, which confirmed the reports that had inspired my representations in the first instance. Armed with this information I went a second time to the President and gave him full and conclusive information. To my astonishment he again impugned the character of the testimony which had been given me and seemed inclined to maintain his position. I then quietly but formally requested him to "arrest Villa and have him tried by court-martial." When he demurred to my request, I said to him that he was forcing me to the unpleasant course of asking my own government to send troops to furnish protection to American citizens which he declined to give. The President then observed that this would mean war. I said to him that "when soldiers in the uniform of a government attacked the persons and property of a friendly government and reparation was denied by the offending government, an act of war had been committed." As I announced this dictum a perceptible change took place in his manner and he said, "Very well, Mr. Ambassador, I will have the man arrested and tried." This promise was carried out. Villa was arrested and tried by a court-martial over which General Huerta presided. He was found guilty of the crimes charged and sentenced to be shot at daybreak the following day. Madero, however, interfered and commuted his sentence to imprisonment in the military peniten-

Villa faces Huerta's firing squad. This purports to be an actual photograph taken an instant before Villa was reprieved through the intercession of one of President Madero's brothers. (By permission of United Press International Newspictures.)

tiary at Mexico City. From this prison Villa finally escaped and was in arms against Madero when Madero was overthrown.[16]

It is possible, of course, that Henry Lane Wilson was responsible for Villa's arrest, but except for Wilson's own statement, evidence is lacking. It is improbable that the Mexican historians who have scanned his diplomatic career in Mexico with deeply hostile motives would have overlooked this incident if there were any indication whatever to verify it. Several glaring discrepancies are immediately apparent in the statement. Villa was commissioned and in the field against Orozco *before* Huerta assumed command. Villa's irregulars were *not* in uniform, and Villa was *not* in arms against Madero at the time of the latter's overthrow. The reports of the several American consuls in the theater of operations include numerous complaints about outrages and insolence by the Orozquistas but are singularly lacking in complaints about the Federals. Wilson testified before the Fall Committee and wrote his memoirs several years after the events he described, and his memory may well have been faulty.

As mentioned, Villa was transferred to the military penitentiary of Tlaltelolco. His confinement was not onerous, and during this period of enforced idleness he tried to make up some of the arrears in his education. In the following December, in broad daylight and disguised only by a pair of dark glasses, he walked out of the prison. He escaped with such ease that there is a strong presumption that the authorities were not at all averse to having him free. Following a devious route, he made his way to the United States, entering upon a term of exile that was to end when his enemy, Victoriano Huerta, seized the government.[17]

The Orozco campaign had made Villa sufficiently important that his arrest and his subsequent escape were matters of some diplomatic interest. Oddly enough, the first American official to learn of Villa's arrest was apparently Consul Alonzo Garrett, at Nuevo Laredo, hundreds of miles from the scene of the incident. Garrett notified the State Depart-

---

[16] Henry Lane Wilson, *Diplomatic Episodes in Mexico, Belgium, and Chile* (Garden City, N.Y., 1927), pp. 293–294. Wilson made subtantially the same statement in his testimony before the Fall Committee, on April 16, 1920. Cf. *Investigation of Mexican Affairs: Hearing before a Subcommittee of the Committee on Foreign Affairs, United States Senate*, 66 Cong., 2 sess., pp. 2274–2275. Hereafter cited as *Fall Committee Report*.

[17] Guzmán, *Memorias*, I, 312.

ment on June 5, within a few hours after the arrest had occurred.[18]

The news of Villa's escape to the United States was not widely publicized, but it could not be kept secret. On January 11, 1913, Ambassador Wilson reported that according to the Mexico City newspapers Villa was in El Paso, Texas. In case the State Department might not know just who Francisco Villa might be, Wilson added: "Villa was a former Federal leader and ex-bandit who has been in prison in Mexico City for the murder of Fountain and for other anti-American activities, as a result of the Embassy's representations last spring." [19]

Temporarily calling himself Jesús José Martínez, Villa had stepped across the street from Nogales, Sonora, to Nogales, Arizona, early on January 2, 1913, leaving behind a Mexico that again was apparently on the road to peace and order. But he knew that more trouble was brewing. While in prison he had been visited by an acquaintance, Licenciado Antonio Tamayo, who had made certain propositions on behalf of General Bernardo Reyes. Tamayo did not require an immediate answer, suggesting that Villa consider the matter for a few days. Before he could return for an answer, Villa had vanished.[20]

As soon as possible after arriving in the United States, Villa sent information to the Mexican President and to Don Abrán González, who was now the governor of Chihuahua. President Madero could not reply, but Don Abrán responded by forwarding Villa fifteen hundred pesos, at the same time advising him that if he returned to Mexico he would compromise the friends who were working on his behalf.[21]

In El Paso, Villa took a room in an obscure part of the city. For obvious reasons he had no desire for publicity, and his presence in El Paso, although already reported in newspapers in Mexico, was not confirmed until he was ferreted out by an enterprising reporter for the El Paso *Times:*

All doubts as to the whereabouts of Colonel Pancho Villa, the federal volunteer officer who recently escaped from prison in Mexico City, where he had been placed for insubordination on orders from General V. Huerta, were re-

[18] *Foreign Relations, 1912,* p. 814.   [19] *Ibid., 1913,* p. 693.
[20] Guzmán, *Memorias,* I, 285–289. Cf. Puente, *Vida de Francisco Villa,* pp. 53–54. *Licenciado* is an academic grade, corresponding approximately to the master's degree in the United States. In Mexico the term is customarily used as a personal title by lawyers.
[21] Guzmán, *Memorias,* I, 313–315.

moved last night [January 12, 1913] when he was located in a South El Paso Street rooming house by a Times reporter.

Villa would not talk for publication. He said he did not care to discuss his escape from the penitentiary, nor would he tell how he crossed the border. At his room in the hotel were four bodyguards. . . . When seen by the Times representative, Villa was armed with two revolvers and a large dirk.[22]

Of Villa's life in El Paso, very little is known. He was joined by a few of his old companions and was a frequent visitor at the Mexican Club, the center of the social life of "Little Chihuahua." He received a few visitors, but nothing suggests any great activity on his part at this time.[23] There seems to be no basis for the legend that he went out only at night because he was warned by the police not to show himself on the streets. Nor is there any reason to suppose, as one of his American biographers has said, that "Villa was *persona non grata* to President Taft, and was constantly watched while in El Paso."[24] It is unlikely that President Taft gave any personal attention to a relatively obscure Mexican revolutionary general who was a refugee in the United States. Villa was not the first one, or the only one. That he was kept under surveillance as a guarantee against violation of the neutrality laws can reasonably be taken for granted. He moved circumspectly at all times. There were men who would not hesitate to kill him, even though he was in the United States, and Villa was not a man to take unnecessary chances on assassination.

Villa's exile was not of long duration. He had been in El Paso less than two months when the news arrived of the uprising in Mexico City —*La Decena Trágica*—and the murder of President Madero and Vice-President José Pino Suárez.

A brief résumé of the tragic events in Mexico City is necessary. The circumstances under which Victoriano Huerta became Provisional President of Mexico affected President Wilson's attitude and policies and thus contributed to the favor which Villa later enjoyed with the United States. Likewise, President Wilson's patent hostility with regard to Huerta strengthened Villa's friendliness for Americans and toward the United States.

The revolt, which had been planned for some time, broke on the

[22] El Paso *Times,* Jan. 13, 1913, quoted in Larry A. Harris, *Pancho Villa and the Columbus Raid* (El Paso, Texas, 1941), p. 49.

[23] Pinchon, *Viva Villa!* pp. 219–220.   [24] *Ibid.*, p. 220.

morning of February 9, 1913, when disaffected forces released General Felix Díaz and General Bernardo Reyes from prison. Within a few hours, Reyes was killed while leading an attack upon the National Palace, but unfortunately for Madero, General Lauro Villar, who was directing the defense, was seriously wounded. Madero, thereupon, gave the command to General Huerta. For more than a week the fighting seesawed through the city, with artillery and machine guns making the place a shambles.

In the midst of the confusion, obscure movements were taking place, the mystery of which has never been clarified. Late in the afternoon of February 17, Ambassador Wilson cabled to the Secretary of State that General Huerta had notified him to expect the removal of President Madero at any moment. Twenty-four hours later he informed Washington that Madero and Pino Suárez had been removed from office and imprisoned. At the same time Huerta sent a personal message to President Taft, saying: "I have the honor to inform you that I have overthrown this Government. The forces are with me, and from now on peace and prosperity will reign." [25]

Within a week the deposed President and Vice-President were murdered under circumstances that seemed to place the responsibility squarely upon Victoriano Huerta, in spite of official excuses and explanations. The world was horrified, and even Francisco Villa, hardened killer though he was, professed to be shocked.[26]

Far from bringing "peace and prosperity" to Mexico, Huerta found himself headed for trouble as soon as the news of his seizure of the presidency became known. In Chihuahua, Emilio Vásquez Gómez, a perennial candidate for the presidency, announced the formation of a provisional government, with himself as Provisional President. Much more important, as the future was to show, was the proclamation by Governor Venustiano Carranza, of the State of Coahuila, of the secession of his state from the Mexican union. On February 21, 1913, Carranza told Philip E. Holland, the American consul at Saltillo, the state capital, that Mexico now faced a revolution much greater than any that had occurred before.[27] On March 26, Carranza issued the

[25] *Foreign Relations, 1913*, pp. 720–721.
[26] Puente, *Vida de Francisco Villa*, p. 57.
[27] *Foreign Relations, 1913*, pp. 721, 727–728.

Plan of Guadalupe, under which he assumed the title and position of "First Chief of the Constitutionalist Army and Depository of the Executive Power of the Republic of Mexico." [28] In view of the crucial role which Carranza played in Mexico the next few years, it is interesting to note that Consul Holland described him as "a man of force and no mean ability. . . . One of Mexico's ablest officials, and . . . a man of strict integrity." [29]

Apparently Villa had made no specific plans for his return to Mexico until the news arrived of the events in Mexico City. He was enraged at the murder of Madero and the usurpation of the government by his bitter enemy, Huerta. Information also reached him from some unknown source that the new regime intended to demand his extradition from the United States.[30] Action of some sort was obviously now necessary. With such funds as he had, plus some money he obtained from his brother, Villa bought rifles and ammunition, saddle equipment, and a few horses. Receiving word that Don Abrán González was sending additional funds through Governor Maytorena, of Sonora, Villa made a hurried trip to Tucson, Arizona, to which Maytorena had fled. On arriving at Tucson, Villa learned that his old and trusted friend, Don Abrán, had been brutally murdered by the Huertistas. Maytorena advanced Villa a thousand pesos from his own pocket and urged him to start a campaign in Chihuahua, where he was well known and familiar with the country.[31]

On returning to El Paso, Villa found that because of the vigilance of the local Huertista officials the horses he had purchased could not be brought in from Juárez. Since a campaign in the vast reaches of Chihuahua would be impossible without horses, Villa resorted to a subterfuge to mount himself and his "army." Daily, for several days, they hired horses from an El Paso livery stable, making it a point to return the animals promptly and in good condition. After several days, when the same group of Mexicans hired horses late in the afternoon, the stable owner thought nothing of it. They failed to return, and the nucleus of the Villista army of the future had disappeared into the

[28] *Ibid., 1914*, p. 630. Cf. also Gruening, *Mexico and Its Heritage*, pp. 98–99.
[29] *Foreign Relations, 1913*, p. 727.　　　　　[30] Guzmán, *Memorias*, II, 7.
[31] Puente, *Vida de Francisco Villa*, p. 57. See also Guzmán, *Memorias*, I, 315–316. González was tied, hand and foot, and thrust down between the cars of a moving railroad train.

darkness before he discovered his loss. It was not the first time that Villa had acquired horses by somewhat irregular means.[32]

Naturally, Villa did not broadcast his plans, but he took at least one American into his confidence. Dr. Ira J. Bush, the veteran American physician who had known Villa as a bandit, met him on the street in El Paso:

We walked to my office together. He said that he was entering Mexico that night to begin his campaign against Huerta, and asked me to go with him. I explained that I could not personally accompany him, but would aid him in any other way that I could. There were eight men ready to cross into Mexico with him—not a very pretentious following, but I knew that as soon as he entered Mexico his old command would rally around him.[33]

The nine men slipped silently across the Rio Grande into Chihuahua on a night in early April, 1913. It was not, indeed, an impressive force, but they were filled with hatred and hope—a dangerous combination— and were led by a determined man who had fought superior forces and eluded capture for twenty years.

[32] Guzmán, *Memorias*, I, 317. John Reed (*Insurgent Mexico*, p. 121) says that Villa's first act, upon capturing Juárez later in the year, was to pay the stable owner twice the value of the horses.

[33] Bush, *Gringo Doctor*, p. 233.

⪢ IV ⪡

Emergence of Villa as a Power

BY the time Villa and his little group crossed the boundary, the revolt against Huerta had gained considerable headway in northern Mexico. In Sonora, Colonel Alvaro Obregón had driven the Huertista garrison of Nogales across the line into the United States. A few days later he captured the border village of Naco, which was important as a railway junction and port of entry.[1] The Huertista governor of Villa's native state, Durango, asked the American consul, in alarm, if the Americans living in the capital would be willing to assist in defending the city against the "bandits" who were menacing it.[2]

Villa moved rapidly deep into the interior of Chihuahua, and in a few days was in a region where his reputation was well known. His band increased as new men joined and old followers hurried to rejoin. By May 11 his force had grown to the point that the New York *Times*, in a paragraph on the capture of Parral by the insurgents, noted that "Gen. Villa, who has recruited 400 men in the Guerrera [sic] district, is hurrying overland to assist other groups of insurgents in cutting off the retreating Federals." [3]

At the start of the revolt there was no bond between the various revolutionary leaders in northern Mexico except their common hatred

[1] Alfonso Taracena, *Mi vida en el vértigo de la Revolución Mexicana* (*Anales sintéticos, 1900–1930*) (Mexico City, 1936), pp. 203, 210.
[2] *Foreign Relations, 1913*, p. 793.
[3] New York *Times*, Sunday, May 11, 1913, 3:7.

for Huerta. "There was no agreement binding the revolutionaries. There was only a common enemy . . . and a common drive to get a satisfactory place in life." [4] Thus, Villa's band was not the only one fighting against the Huertistas, but in the short space of a month he had become probably the most powerful individual rebel leader in Chihuahua. Since the Huertistas were stronger than any one of the rebel groups, several chiefs, such as Maclovio Herrera, Manuel Chao, and Tomás Urbina, put their forces under Villa's command, in order to present a united front. [5] They probably intended their subordination to be only temporary, but in fact, from that time on, their bands were permanent parts of Villa's army.

The nominal recognition of Carranza as First Chief and acceptance of his Plan of Guadalupe by most of the rebel chiefs gave the insurgents a small degree of political unity, but Carranza's actual authority was shadowy. [6] Villa was visited at Ascensión, after several weeks of campaigning, by two emissaries who urged him to acknowledge Carranza as head of the revolutionary government and to accept the Plan of Guadalupe as the basis for action. Villa was quickly persuaded but stipulated that no other general should ever be placed over him and that no generals should be nominated in his force without the consent of the senior officers. "Nobody has taught us to fight and to comply with our duty, nor will any man command us whom we have not chosen." [7]

Carranza accepted Villa's reservations and designated him as commander of all revolutionary forces in Chihuahua, thus giving formal recognition to what was already an actual fact. Recognizing Carranza as the head of the revolutionary government made no real difference to Villa. His nature made it impossible for him to be subordinate to anyone, and he remained, as he had been from the beginning, an independent commander—a *caudillo* at the head of his private army.

Villa stayed at Ascensión for several weeks, awaiting arms and ammunition from the United States. The responsibilities that now rested upon his shoulders were not entirely new, but they were on a vaster scale than in his previous experiences. Food and forage were a minor

[4] Anita Brenner and George R. Leighton, *The Wind That Swept Mexico: The History of the Mexican Revolution, 1910–1942* (New York and London, 1943), p. 39.

[5] Puente, *Vida de Francisco Villa*, p. 61.	[6] *Ibid.*, pp. 66–68.

[7] Guzmán, *Memorias*, II, 15–18.

problem, for his men were accustomed to living off the country, but equipment, arms, and ammunition constituted a problem that had to be solved continually, if the force were to survive. Northern Mexico produced none of these necessities. Almost the only source of supply was the United States, Americans who were willing to take the chance of getting into trouble with their own government for violation of the neutrality laws expected to be paid promptly and well.

Supplies and equipment do not flow of their own accord. There must be planning and organization. That Villa had already established such an organization is beyond doubt. He had laid the necessary foundations while still in exile, and his army was a future hope, as proved by the statement he made to Ramón Puente, that at Ascensión he was awaiting supplies to be forwarded by the agents whom he had left in El Paso.[8]

To know just who these agents were, with exactly whom they conducted their business, and how the transactions were accomplished would be interesting, but such activities were necessarily clandestine. Since March 14, 1912, the export of arms and ammunition from the United States to Mexico had been forbidden, under an executive order issued by President Taft and continued by President Wilson. There were heavy penalties for violation of the order. Neither vendors nor purchasers desired any attention from agents of the Department of Justice and were careful to maintain no records that might be used as evidence against them. It probably would not be far from the truth if one visualized agents and sellers meeting surreptitiously in out-of-the-way places and pack animals splashing through the shallows of the Rio Grande at night as armed men kept a vigilant watch.

One illustrative incident has come to light. While still in El Paso, Villa had promised Dr. Ira J. Bush that he would, as soon as possible, look into the case of an American physician named Harle, who had been unjustly sentenced to prison in Chihuahua before the Revolution. Dr. Harle's grateful mother, on being informed that Villa needed ammunition badly, telegraphed five hundred dollars to Dr. Bush. With the money he bought a large quantity of cartridges from an El Paso firm and arranged for their delivery to a Colonel Ortega, a Villista officer with whom he was in contact.[9]

[8] Puente, *Vida de Francisco Villa*, p. 62: "Me quede . . . mientras me llegaba parque conducto de los amigos que había dejado en El Paso como mis agentes."
[9] Bush, *Gringo Doctor*, p. 234.

Mrs. Harle's contribution bought a mere fraction of the ammunition being smuggled across the border in spite of neutrality laws and presidential proclamations. By July, Villa's force was sufficiently supplied and reorganized to be able to move again. On July 11, 1913, Consul Thomas Edwards, at Ciudad Juárez, reported that Villa, with twelve hundred men, was three days' march distant and would undoubtedly attack the city. On July 23 Edwards informed the State Department that Juárez was completely isolated, with Villa on the west and Colonel Toribio Ortega threatening it from the east. The two were awaiting reinforcements from Sonora before attacking. The expected attack, however, failed to occur, and northern Mexico lapsed into relative quiet for several weeks.[10]

By this time the American public as a whole had lost interest in what was happening south of the border. The average American of the early years of the twentieth century felt little concern, except sporadically, toward events outside the United States and could not conceive of any way in which he could be affected personally by a civil war in Mexico. The situation in Mexico was, moreover, so vague and obscure that one nationally distributed journal included Villa among the revolutionary chiefs who "have offered their adherence to the provisional government." [11] An anonymous journalist summarized the attitude of the average American as looking "at the headlines with languid curiosity" and then turning "to the more diverting debate on our tariff or our currency." [12]

No important military operations took place in northern Mexico during the summer of 1913, but in the diplomatic field there were events of deep significance. President Woodrow Wilson, who had been inaugurated within a few days after Huerta's *coup d'état,* had immediately issued a public statement, making it abundantly clear that he could have "no sympathy with those who seek to seize the power of government to advance their own personal interests or ambitions." [13]

[10] National Archives, State Department File nos. 812.00/8022, July 11, 1913, and 8122, July 23, 1913. The Ortega mentioned is presumably the one to whom Dr. Bush delivered the ammunition.
[11] *Current Opinion,* LV (July, 1913), 12.
[12] In Rafael Zayas Enriquez, *The Case of Mexico and the Policy of President Wilson* (New York, 1914), p. 143.
[13] In Edgar E. Robinson and Victor J. West, *The Foreign Policy of Woodrow Wilson, 1913–1917* (New York, 1917), p. 180.

This statement was, in effect, a positive refusal to recognize the Huerta government.

Meanwhile, Henry Lane Wilson continued to hold the position of American ambassador to Mexico. His social and political philosophy was as far apart as the poles from that of President Wilson, and he was a strong supporter of Huerta from the very first. In his dispatches he never ceased to predict that Huerta was about to bring the turmoil in Mexico to an end and to urge Huerta's immediate recognition. Clearly he did not represent the views of the administration in Washington, and in July he was recalled and his resignation accepted. To accredit another ambassador in his place would, in diplomatic practice, have constituted *de facto* recognition, and this President Wilson refused to do. Instead, the President decided to send as a personal representative and "advisor to the embassy" former Governor John Lind, of Minnesota.

In Chihuahua, as the summer drew to its close, there was a revival of activity. On August 25, 1913, Consul Edwards telegraphed to the State Department from Juárez that Villa's forces had not been heard from and that they might have moved south.[14] They had, for three days later Villa, acting upon information given him by some American railway employees whom he had intercepted pumping a handcar toward Madera, smashed into San Andrés, west of the city of Chihuahua, surprising and completely destroying a large Federal force. Only a handful of the Federals escaped, and the spoil left in Villa's hands included supplies and equipment, several loaded railway trains, and even some artillery—the first that Villa had obtained.[15] The American consul at the city of Chihuahua informed the State Department of Villa's sudden reappearance on August 28, 1913, adding that his force consisted of twelve hundred cavalry and that the captured artillery totaled four field guns and six mountain guns.[16] A few days later, on September 8, Edwards telegraphed from Juárez that Villa, with his forces greatly strengthened, was approaching the city, but again Villa dropped from sight. Edwards reported a week later that all contact with Villa had been lost.[17]

[14] National Archives, State Department File no. 812.00/8545, Aug. 25, 1913.

[15] Puente, *Vida de Francisco Villa,* pp. 63–64.

[16] National Archives, State Department File no. 812.00/8623, Aug. 28, 1913. In his statement to Dr. Puente, Villa mentioned only two "heavy guns."

[17] National Archives, State Department File nos. 812.00/8743 and 8892, Sept. 16, 1913.

It is possible, although a pure guess, that the rumors of Villa's approach toward Juárez were carefully fostered by Villa himself. While the alarmed Federals in the northern part of Chihuahua were looking to their defenses, Villa was actually bypassing the strongly held city of Chihuahua and marching rapidly to the southeast, toward the important railway junction of Torreón. The Constitutionalists had recently been defeated in an attack upon Torreón, and the Federals, as long as they held the place, could reinforce Chihuahua and other critical points, almost at will.

During the march, Villa's forces continued to increase in strength, as numerous local bands joined him. A meeting of the generals and colonels, called by Villa himself while on the march, confirmed his supreme authority over the entire force and adopted the name "División del Norte"—Division of the North—the name by which Villa's army was subsequently known. By the time the Division of the North reached the vicinity of Torreón, with the revolutionary forces from Durango added, it had grown to the respectable total of almost ten thousand officers and men [18]—a much more impressive command than the eight men who had followed him across the Rio Grande less than five months before!

The fighting in Villa's first battle at Torreón was close. For twenty-four hours there was no decisive gain by either side, with Villa, according to his own later admission, seriously considering a withdrawal.[19] Late in the evening of October 1, the Federals began destroying their ammunition, and a final desperate assault by the Villistas carried them into the heart of the city.[20]

The victory at Torreón was decisive in more ways than one. From an obscure insurgent leader, Francisco Villa suddenly became a man to be reckoned with in the affairs of Mexico. He was now a commander who had demonstrated in battle his ability to win victories, and the Division of the North was the most powerful single force on the insurgent side. Its fighting effectiveness was tremendously increased by the spoil taken at Torreón, which included artillery, vast amounts of ammunition, an armored railway car, several railway trains, and some forty locomotives.[21] Above all, Villa had won the devoted confidence of

[18] Puente, *Vida de Francisco Villa*, pp. 66–68.   [19] *Ibid.*, p. 70.
[20] Guzmán, *Memorias*, II, 38–39.   [21] *Ibid.*, p. 39.

his troops. The victory at Torreón imbued them with the *esprit* which wins battles in spite of odds.

Americans who had considered a Mexican revolution as nothing more than a rather gaudy spectacle were horrified at what followed the captured of Torreón. The captured Federal officers were promptly shot —a fact which caused the *Review of Reviews,* forgetting that the execution of prisoners was a common practice in Mexico, to state solemnly that the "Constitutionalists disgraced their cause." The *Review of Reviews* also furnished the information that a number of American and German residents of Torreón had been "massacred"—a rumor that proved to be untrue.[22] Mrs. Edith O'Shaughnessy, the wife of the American chargé d'affaires, strongly sympathetic toward Huerta, wrote to her mother: "Yesterday, Torreón fell into the hands of the rebels, and many atrocities were committed against Spanish subjects." [23]

At this time, there was a deep popular prejudice against Spaniards in Mexico. Spaniards were the traditional enemies and oppressors in Mexican history. Unfortunately, many of the Spanish who lived in Mexico in the early years of the present century had done nothing to endear themselves to the Mexican people. As Mrs. O'Shaughnessy said further: "They [the Spaniards] keep the countless pawn-shops; they are the usurers and money lenders of all kinds; they are the overseers on the *haciendas* and, incidentally, they keep all the grocery shops." [24]

Such people are usually disliked, wherever they may be. Villa shared the popular prejudice against Spaniards, and in addition, he believed that all Spaniards were Huertistas at heart. A short time later he told a representative of the State Department that he knew "very well that the Spaniards throughout Mexico are in sympathy with Huerta." [25] He suspected also that the Spaniards at Torreón were responsible for the arrest and execution of numerous Constitutionalists among the population of the city.

As a result, immediately after the capture of the city, Villa issued an order giving Spaniards only a few hours to leave, confiscating their property, and promising death for any who did not comply. Forced

[22] *Review of Reviews,* XLVIII (Nov., 1913), 540.
[23] Edith O'Shaughnessy, *A Diplomat's Wife in Mexico* (New York and London, 1916), p. 6.
[24] *Ibid.,* p. 94.   [25] *Foreign Relations, 1913,* p. 910.

from their homes, these unfortunate people were herded ruthlessly out of Torreón. Few were as lucky as one individual who was supposed to have convinced Villa that, as a native of the Canary Islands, he was not a Spaniard and was therefore allowed to remain.[26]

Early reports of the capture of Torreón indicated that a large number of Spaniards had been executed. The Spanish minister in Mexico City received unconfirmed information that "one or two" had been killed, in addition to several who were murdered earlier in the campaign.[27] Summarizing the week's news, the *Independent* for October 16, 1913, noted that it was both reported and denied that Villa's man had slaughtered one hundred and seventy-five Spanish residents of Torreón.[28]

Nor were the Spaniards the only foreigners to feel the weight of Villa's hand at this time. On October 18, Nelson O'Shaughnessy, the American chargé d'affaires, reported that Villa was detaining forty Germans, seven Englishmen, forty French, and a large number of Italians. He was permitting Americans to depart from Torreón freely, but the Europeans were being held as hostages against a counterattack by Federal forces.[29]

There was a widespread belief that it was up to the United States to take action of some sort. There were many, in both the United States and Europe, who believed that the United States was morally bound to take positive measures, since, under the Monroe Doctrine, it would not permit European intervention. Early in 1913 the London *Daily Chronicle* said flatly that the "effect of the Monroe Doctrine is to throw upon the United States the onus of acting, not only on her own behalf, but on behalf of civilization."[30] Only a few days before the fall of Torreón, the *World's Work* asserted: "The United States, having put a prohibition upon interference from Europe, assumes the responsibility of seeing that law and order take the place of tyranny, rebellion, and brigandage."[31]

No European power had ever admitted the validity of the Monroe

---

[26] Gen. Francisco L. Urquizo, *"Recuerdo que . . .": Visiones aisladas de la Revolución* (Mexico City, 1934), pp. 266–267.

[27] *Foreign Relations, 1913*, p. 900.

[28] *Independent* (New York), Oct. 16, 1913, p. 111.

[29] *Foreign Relations, 1913*, pp. 898–899.

[30] London *Daily Chronicle*, quoted in the *Literary Digest*, XLVI (March 15, 1913), 566.

[31] *World's Work*, XXVI (1913), 497.

Doctrine, but they were more than willing for the United States to take the full responsibility for the safety of their nationals in Mexico. During the terrible ten days of fighting in Mexico City, the Secretary of State instructed Ambassador Henry Lane Wilson to extend protection to imperiled foreigners without regard to their nationality, and similar instructions were sent to the commanders of American naval vessels in Mexican waters.[32] Since Wilson's departure from Mexico, the chargé d'affaires, O'Shaughnessy, had made it his personal policy to encourage his diplomatic colleagues to seek assistance at the American Embassy when their compatriots were involved in difficulties.[33]

After Villa's occupation of Torreón, the first diplomatic representative in Mexico City to hurry to O'Shaughnessy was the German minister. Late in the afternoon of October 18, O'Shaughnessy cabled to the Secretary of State:

The German Minister requests me to make urgent representations to my Government regarding the 40 Germans detained in Torreón by Francisco Villa, who he states is permitting American citizens to depart. . . . The Minister states that he has been sure that the United States Government can and will use its unofficial good offices with the rebel leaders.[34]

The Secretary of State, William Jennings Bryan, promptly directed the American consular agent at Torreón, George C. Carothers, "to make clear to the rebel authorities that all foreigners desiring to leave should be permitted to do so unmolested," adding that the agent should extend to all foreigners the same protection given to Americans.[35]

Although Villa was holding the Germans, Frenchmen, Englishmen, and Italians as hostages, he felt no resentment against them as he did against Spaniards. The Spanish minister, Señor B. J. de Colgan, had a conference with O'Shaughnessy on the night of October 19, 1913, following which O'Shaughnessy forwarded to the State Department two formal letters which De Colgan gave him. The letters recounted various murders and other outrages committed by Villistas against Spaniards and included the information that "Francisco Villa demanded from the merchants in general, excepting the American citizens, a forced loan of three million pesos in cash or in drafts on New York." Villa had made it

[32] *Foreign Relations, 1913*, pp. 897–898.
[33] Edith O'Shaughnessy, *A Diplomat's Wife in Mexico*, p. 86.
[34] *Foreign Relations, 1913*, pp. 898–899.   [35] *Ibid.*, p. 899.

very clear just what would happen to these merchants if the money were not forthcoming promptly.[36]

De Colgan's letters did not reach Washington for several days. Villa left Torreón meanwhile and could not be reached. The State Department decided, under the circumstances, to take up the matter with Carranza, the official head of the Constitutionalist government, who had established his temporary capital at Hermosillo, Sonora. Accordingly, on November 5, 1913, Consul Louis Hostetter, at Hermosillo, was instructed to say informally to Carranza that "if he exercises the control over Villa's forces which he is reported to have . . . he will immediately order adequate punishment of the authors of these outrages, and that no more such outrages will be perpetrated." [37]

The peculiar wording of this telegram indicates that the State Department strongly suspected what later proved to be a fact—Carranza's authority over Villa was more theoretical than real. There is no evidence that Carranza ever gave any orders on this matter to his formidable "subordinate." If he did, Villa chose to ignore them.

In spite of early rumors that a number of Americans had been killed at Torreón, Villa obviously favored Americans over other foreigners. The German minister, in his appeal to O'Shaughnessy, noted that, while Germans were being detained, Americans were allowed to depart freely. The Spanish minister remarked that American merchants were exempted from Villa's forced loan. Villa placed a strong guard to protect the office of the American consular agent, George C. Carothers. He suppressed disorders with a stern and heavy hand. The natural result was that any bad impression upon Americans caused by his maltreatment of Spaniards and his execution of captured Federal officers was largely counterbalanced.[38]

Had the administration in Washington been inclined to modify its attitude toward the Constitutionalists because of Villa's actions, such a temptation was speedily removed by Huerta himself. President Wilson's hostility toward Huerta grew out of the questionable means by which

[36] *Foreign Relations, 1913*, pp. 900–901. According to Guzmán (*Memorias*, II, 42, 46), the demand was made on the bankers, rather than the merchants, and was for three hundred thousand pesos, instead of three million.

[37] *Foreign Relations, 1913*, p. 901.

[38] William Carol, "The North and South War in Mexico," *World's Work*, XXVII (1914), 305; testimony of George C. Carothers, *Fall Committee Report*, pp. 1765–1766.

Huerta had obtained office. Wilson hoped that an orderly, constitutional government, in the American concept of that term, would develop in Mexico. Any lingering possibility that the United States would finally recognize Huerta was destroyed on October 10, 1913, when Huerta summarily imprisoned one hundred and ten members of the Chamber of Deputies, who had voted in favor of a resolution against him.[39] From then on, he ruled as an undisguised military dictator. The arrest of the deputies crowded Torreón and its aftermath from the columns of the American newspapers, and even the alleged mistreatment of foreigners seemed to be of lesser importance. The American public forgot Villa's supposed cruelty in their anger at the excesses of his bitterest enemy.

Whether or not Villa was impressed by American protests against his treatment of Spaniards is unknown. He was anxious for American good will and support, but he was too busy with preparations for the next campaign to worry over what must have seemed to him a very unimportant matter. In all probability he had no inkling that he had caused any diplomatic embarrassment for the United States. If he gave the matter any thought at all, he probably wondered why the United States should trouble itself over a few contemptible Spaniards. As for the unfortunate Spaniards, the United States had to be content with assurances from Carranza that if they had not mixed in Mexican politics they were guaranteed the same protection as all other foreigners.[40]

Leaving a strong garrison in Torreón, Villa moved his forces northward toward Chihuahua, again absorbing scattered revolutionary bands during the movement. His chief of staff, General Juan N. Medina, strongly urged him to leave General Tomás Urbina's troops behind. They had been charged with excesses and lack of discipline. Medina said: "Our Revolution will not be helped by any disgraceful act committed within view of the United States." Villa needed the men but, recognizing the possibilities of danger, persuaded Urbina himself to remain at Jiménez.[41]

Large amounts of arms and ammunition were captured at Torreón, but Villa foresaw the need for more. The only source for such necessities was the United States, where the clandestine supply organization

---

[39] *Foreign Relations, 1913*, pp. 836–838.   [40] *Ibid.*, pp. 913–914.
[41] Guzmán, *Memorias*, II, 51–52. Urbina's troops were accused of excesses and atrocities in the capture of Durango, earlier in the year.

was still functioning. Before starting the movement northward, Villa dispatched his brother Hipólito and a companion to the United States as purchasing agents. Provided with three hundred thousand pesos in cash, they crossed the Rio Grande near Ojinaga. The Presidential Proclamation of March 14, 1912, was still in effect; they moved so as to attract no attention. No record of their activities has come to light, a fact from which one can surmise that they were successful in their mission. At least, they were not caught.[42]

Villa's attack upon Chihuahua started on November 5, 1913. Fighting several days without any noteworthy gain, the Villista forces suffered heavy losses. To avoid defeat, Villa decided upon a stroke the pure audacity of which marks him as a truly brilliant field commander. With two thousand picked men, he slipped around the city to the north, late at night on November 13. Early the next day he ambushed a railway train and loaded his troops into the boxcars. Forestalling Federal suspicion by a series of skillfully faked telegrams, the Villistas rode brazenly into the heart of Ciudad Juárez at midnight, November 15. The dumfounded Federal garrison was so demoralized by the sudden irruption into their midst that the entire city was firmly in Villa's possession before daybreak.[43]

American newspapers gave a prominent place in their Sunday editions next day, November 16, 1913, to the astonishing exploit. Readers learned that Villa was deeply regretful that a lone American, a taxicab driver waiting for his fare in Juárez, had been killed in the confused street fighting. Mayor E. C. Kelly, of El Paso, conferred with Villa at the international bridge and then went to his headquarters at the customhouse. Villa assured Mayor Kelly that all Americans within his zone of authority would receive full protection and that he would meet the expected Federal counterattack far enough to the south so that there would be no danger of bullets striking in El Paso.[44]

Ironically, in the column of the New York *Times* paralleling the story of the capture of Juárez and Mayor Kelly's interview was a short, unsigned article characterizing Villa as a bully, braggart, and coward.

[42] *Ibid.*, p. 53.

[43] *Ibid.*, pp. 64–75. Cf. Puente, *Vida de Francisco Villa*, pp. 73–76, and Ernst F. Löhndorff, *Bestie ich in Mexiko* (Bremen, 1927), pp. 234–244. According to the latter, the train crew of the commandeered train was made up of Americans who were not unwilling to co-operate with the Villistas, especially as they were promised a substantial reward.

[44] New York *Times*, Sunday, Nov. 16, 1913, 2:3–4.

The article repeated the legend that Mayor Kelly disarmed and kicked Villa at the time of his quarrel with Giuseppe Garibaldi. The anonymous writer was positive that Villa was still a bandit, serving in the revolutionary army only for pay and loot.[45]

During the next few days the newspapers again told of the execution of Federal prisoners. The New York *Times* informed its readers that President Wilson was embarrassed and disturbed by the slaughter at Juárez.[46] There were rumors that the State Department was conducting an investigation, but Secretary Bryan denied that such an investigation was either being made or under consideration.[47] A few days later the *Independent*, summarizing the recent news, charged that one hundred and twenty-five Federal prisoners had been put to death and stated that "it is admitted that 95 were thus executed without trial," many of them being compelled to dig their own graves. This slaughter, the *Independent* added, was not relished at Washington.[48]

Villa, who appreciated fully the value of American good opinion, probably did not believe that his treatment of Federal prisoners at Juárez was unduly harsh. Both sides executed prisoners. Most of the unfortunates who faced firing squads in the Juárez cemetery were Orozquistas, whom the insurgents regarded as traitors and deserving of no consideration whatever. The relatively few regular soldiers who were captured were either released or taken into the Villista ranks, as were the musicians of the Federal bands.

Whether or not the stories of the slaughter at Juárez were true, they were widely repeated in American newspapers and, strangely, evoked little popular horror. Before a week had passed, the executions had vanished from the pages of the papers and were supplanted by more timely and more exciting items. It seems, in fact, that no great revulsion was felt by any Americans except those who sympathized with the Huerta regime. Americans taking any interest at all in Mexico felt somewhat as did the editor of *Harper's Weekly*, who remarked: "It is a sad thing, this death in warfare, but it is not the worst. The oppression of a people, such as Mexico has long known, is worse." [49]

The newspapers of the United States lost interest in Villa's alleged

[45] *Ibid.*   [46] *Ibid.*, Tuesday, Nov. 18, 1913, 2:1.
[47] *Ibid.*, Wednesday, Nov. 19, 1913, 2:1.
[48] *Independent*, LXXVI (Nov. 27, 1913), 385. The allegation that the victims were compelled to dig their own graves seems to be a feature of nearly all atrocity stories.
[49] *Harper's Weekly* (New York), Dec. 13, 1913, p. 4.

atrocities at Juárez, but he continued to be the most colorful figure who had captured the popular imagination. On the Sunday following the *coup de main* at Juárez, it was announced that Villa had dynamited a Federal troop train south of the city, with "enormous loss of life." [50] Only occasionally, and then with no particular emphasis, was the name of Venustiano Carranza, the presumptive head of the revolutionary government, brought to the attention of the American public. To most Americans, Villa had become the outstanding figure of the Mexican Revolution, the virtual head of the movement, until, a short time later, a normally well-informed American publication referred to "Villa's uprising" against the Huerta government.[51]

One of Villa's first acts after capturing Juárez was to designate a full complement of local officials, municipal, state, and Federal. Thus the basis was laid for a complete government, dominated by Villa himself, in the state of Chihuahua. Immediately, also, he took advantage of easy access to the stores and business houses of El Paso to place orders for clothing and for such equipment as could be lawfully exported from the United States.[52]

The anticipated Federal counterattack developed quickly. On November 20, information was received that the Federals were moving northward from Chihuahua. Villa kept his promise to Mayor Kelly that he would fight the Federals at such distance that bullets would not reach United States territory. On Monday, November 24, the newspapers announced that Villa was awaiting the Federal attack at Tierra Blanca some twenty-six miles south of Juárez. At the same time the New York *Times* informed its readers that "Washington watches Villa." [53]

Villa undoubtedly remembered, too, the international complications that arose in earlier battles at Juárez, when shots from Mexico killed and wounded spectators in El Paso. Aside from any friendliness he felt for the United States and toward Americans in general, he could not afford to take unnecessary chances on arousing the resentment of the United States or of provoking reprisals. In the capture of Juárez, the rapidity of his attack and his strict orders against firing toward Amer-

[50] New York *Times*, Sunday, Nov. 23, 1913, 2:8.
[51] *Collier's Magazine*, LIII (June 13, 1914), 17.
[52] Guzmán, *Memorias*, II, 74.
[53] New York *Times*, Monday, Nov. 24, 1913, 2:5.

ican territory had prevented any unpleasant incidents.[54] By deliberately moving his forces to a point out of range of the United States, he was ensuring against international complications that could seriously endanger the success of the Revolution.[55] There were other considerations as well. In a close defense of Juárez his dispositions and movements would be under observation from the United States, and it would be easy for the Federals to gain vital information. There would be enormous loss of life among noncombatants if the battle degenerated into a street fight.

Leaving General Medina in command at Juárez, Villa moved southward with the bulk of his fighting forces. The next day, Tuesday, November 25, 1913, the headlines announced that a great battle was in progress. Early in the day, General Medina's patrols quietly rounded up all Americans found in Juárez, escorted them to the international bridge, and politely, but firmly, made them leave Mexico. In reply to indignant protests, Medina explained that this measure was taken for their safety in case fighting occurred in the streets of the city.[56]

The battle of Tierra Blanca was a disaster for the Federals. The next day Villa jubilantly announced a victory, and in Juárez General Medina relaxed his restrictions so far as to permit the entry of Americans who had legitimate business in the city.[57]

The key city of Chihuahua, with its garrison depleted and demoralized, was now isolated from the rest of Huertista Mexico. Knowing that he could not resist a determined attack, the Federal commander decided to abandon the city and march to Ojinaga, on the border. This was the nearest place where there were other Federals and where he could not be completely surrounded. Leaving two hundred men to preserve order and arranging with the foreign consuls to see that these men were not executed, the Federals evacuated Chihuahua on the night of November 29, 1913. Consul Marion Letcher notified the State Department the next day, adding that Villa knew about the arrangement made with the consuls and that he, Letcher, was using his "good offices to the fullest extent in the interest of society and humanity." [58]

On the same day the State Department, realizing that Villa's power

[54] Puente, *Vida de Francisco Villa*, p. 76.   [55] *Ibid.*
[56] New York *Times*, Tuesday, Nov. 25, 1913, 1:8.
[57] *Ibid.*, Wednesday, Nov. 26, 1913, 1:8.
[58] *Foreign Relations, 1913*, p. 864.

was spreading and probably fearing further diplomatic complications from Villa's hatred of Spaniards, sent a telegram to the consul at Juárez. It directed him to impress upon Villa the importance of protection for the lives and property of all foreigners in the territory he controlled.[59]

The Federals from Chihuahua groped painfully across the desert, unpursued by any large force of Constitutionalists but harried all the way by small bands. Discouraged, tired, thirsty, hungry, hampered by the swarms of women and children that always accompanied a Mexican force, the Federals finally staggered into the fortified camp at Ojinaga on December 7. At least a hundred had been killed during the march, and an unknown number had died of exhaustion or had deserted.[60] Their presence at Ojinaga brought an additional problem to the United States—a problem caused indirectly, but nonetheless actually, by Villa's amazing successes. Sooner or later Villa would have to destroy this remaining pocket of Federal resistance, and again the United States would have to maintain its neutrality.

Villa moved promptly to seize Chihuahua, which fell into his hands like the proverbial ripe plum. Entering the city on December 8, he found the Federal detachment that had been left to preserve order. Soldiers who were willing to change sides and enroll in the Constitutionalist army were quickly enlisted; the remainder were sent on their way, safe and sound (*sano y salvo*).[61] There is no way of knowing how much influence the foreign consuls may have had in this matter, but their representations undoubtedly had some effect.

The capture of the city of Chihuahua made Villa supreme in the state. Although he was careful to observe constitutional forms, as shown when he appointed civil officials at Juárez, he was, *de facto,* the military dictator. He held power and authority as absolute as Porfirio Díaz at the height of his career. Only a few weeks earlier the pro-Huerta press of Mexico City had triumphantly declared that "Francisco Villa, the pertinacious guerilla of Chihuahua," had suffered a " terrible discomfiture" and was "fleeing in appalling rout," in search of a safe refuge in the mountains.[62] Villa's fame overshadowed that of his

[59] *Ibid.,* p. 899.   [60] *Independent,* LXXVI (Dec. 18, 1913), 536.
[61] Guzmán, *Memorias,* II, 121–122.
[62] *Independiente* (Mexico City), quoted in *Current Opinion,* LV (Sept., 1913), 149.

nominal chief, Venustiano Carranza. To the great majority of Americans, Villa had become the Mexican Revolution personified. To the United States government his status had changed. He was no longer merely another Mexican insurgent general but a factor to be reckoned with in the determination of major policies.

❧ V ❧

Beginning of Wilson's Interest in Villa

THE succession of dramatic victories in the autumn of 1913, culminating in the occupation of the city of Chihuahua, did more than make Villa front-page news in the United States. His sudden prominence, his known antecedents, and his ruthlessness, together with statements that were beginning to appear as to his political and social ideals, made him a highly controversial figure as well. Although few Americans understood the issues involved in the Mexican Revolution, there were many people who sincerely believed that the future peace and welfare of Mexico depended upon the victory of the "strong man," Victoriano Huerta. For such people Villa was anathema. To people whose views were the opposite, Villa had become the embodiment of the hopes and aspirations of the Mexicans who refused to accept another Porfirian dictatorship.

Shortly before the capture of Juárez, Mrs. Edith O'Shaughnessy, wife of the American chargé d'affaires and a friend and admirer of Huerta, was aghast at the possibility that John Lind might recommend lifting the embargo on arms for the rebels, thus assisting Villa. "Any measure tending to undermine the central authority, imperfect though it be, can only bring calamity." After the capture of Chihuahua, she remarked in a letter: "The women flee the towns that he [Villa] and his men enter.

I suppose there is no crime that he has not committed, no brutality toward wounded, sick, and prisoners and women." [1]

In Mexico City, Major Cassius E. Gillette, formerly of the United States Army, and Paul Hudson, electing themselves spokesmen for the Americans in Mexico, characterized the struggle as a fight between civilization and savagery, "with the United States . . . now ranged on the side of savagery." To these men, of course, Huerta represented civilization, while Villa was the epitome of savagery.[2] Probably the most vitriolic denunciation of Villa and the rebels against Huerta was voiced by the former ambassador, Henry Lane Wilson, a few months after the events which have just been related. Crediting Villa with being the real leader of the revolutionary party, Wilson charged that the Constitutionalist armies were merely large gangs of bandits. As for Villa himself, Wilson accused him of pillaging and looting the greater part of the State of Chihuahua; in his twenty-five years as a bandit he had committed more than a hundred murders and could be depended upon to murder and loot whenever he could do so with safety to himself.[3]

The opposite extreme in views of Villa was expressed by an American admirer in passages that are almost a panegyric:

He has come to know something of this land of his. . . . And for good or ill he is wedded to it. He is far too largely and simply constituted to know the itch of personal ambition; in its stead there emerges in him a fierce self-identification with his people. Henceforth their struggles are his struggles, their destiny his destiny. . . .

[The capture of Juárez] bursts like an arc-light upon the murk of Mexican affairs, revealing Pancho Villa as . . . the man that must be reckoned with. Overnight, his personality, views, plans and purposes become matters of international concern; for it now appears that tomorrow he easily may be the master of Mexico, and, thus, of the fate of vast foreign investments; and while Europe and American Big Business are backing Huerta, Woodrow Wilson and . . . American democracy clearly are disposed to support any outstand-

---

[1] Edith O'Shaughnessy, *A Diplomat's Wife in Mexico*, pp. 45, 90.

[2] *Current Opinion*, LV (Dec., 1913), 394. Paul Hudson was the editor of the *Mexican Herald* and was strongly pro-Huerta in his sympathies. Cassius E. Gillette was a former officer of the Corps of Engineers, United States Army, who had resigned from the army for the more lucrative calling of free-lance engineer. He was interested in various speculative mining enterprises in Mexico.

[3] Henry Lane Wilson, "Errors with Reference to Mexico," *Annals of the American Academy of Political Science*, LIV (July, 1914), 152–153.

ing and responsible antagonist who will oust the usurper and restore constitutional government. All eyes are on Pancho Villa.[4]

The worried man in the White House was watching developments in Mexico with close attention. His election was the climax of the "progressive" movement in the United States, and he was primarily interested in domestic reform. In spite of a lifetime of study and research in politics and government, Woodrow Wilson had given little heed to foreign affairs. He had, in fact, remarked to a close friend: "It would be the irony of fate if my administration had to deal chiefly with foreign affairs." [5] He was deeply moved by the chaos in Mexico and anxious to do whatever was possible, with justice and short of armed intervention, to bring peace to the country. He was horrified by the murder of Madero and Pino Suárez and by Huerta's cynical arrest of the opposition deputies. It became a cardinal point in President Wilson's Mexican policies that under no conceivable circumstances would he recognize Huerta. Any idea that he might eventually change his mind was effectively banished by a circular sent on November 7, 1913, to the principal American diplomatic missions. It stated, without mincing words, that the President felt it his duty to require Huerta's immediate retirement; the United States would not regard any act of Huerta or his dummy congress as binding upon the Mexican people.[6]

Woodrow Wilson's antipathy toward Huerta and all that Huerta represented was so deep-seated that he does not seem to have been unduly shocked by the reports of wholesale executions by the Constitutionalists or by Villa's rough treatment of Spaniards. On November 13, while the American press was still carrying stories about the executions and while the State Department was still corresponding about the mistreatment of Spaniards, Wilson was visited by Sir William Tyrrell, secretary to Sir Edward Grey, the British Foreign Minister. Sir William's mission on this occasion, apparently, was to sound out the President as to Mexico. To a remark by Sir William that he could see little difference between the leaders in Mexico, Wilson replied that "Carranza was the best of the three, and that Villa was not so bad as he had been painted." [7]

[4] Pinchon, *Viva Villa!* pp. 221, 245.
[5] Ray Stannard Baker, *Woodrow Wilson: Life and Letters*, IV (Garden City, N.Y., 1931), 55.
[6] *Foreign Relations, 1913*, p. 856.
[7] Burton J. Hendrick, *The Life and Letters of Walter H. Page*, I (Garden City, N.Y., 1925), 205.

John Lind, the President's personal representative in Mexico, disliked the Huerta regime as strongly as his chief, and his reports were distinctly favorable toward the insurgents. He later altered his opinions, but in the fall of 1913 Lind believed that Villa might be just the man to bring peace and reform to Mexico. On the very day on which Villa's troopers were hiding in freight cars for the dash into Juárez, Lind wrote to the Secretary of State: "Let this housecleaning be done by home talent. It will be a little rough and we must see to it that the walls are left intact, but I should not worry if some of the verandas and French windows are demolished. General Villa . . . would do the job satisfactorily." [8]

The capture of Chihuahua again brought into focus the plight of the Spaniards who lived within Constitutionalist areas. Villa decreed their immediate expulsion, as he had done at Torreón, and was completely unimpressed by efforts of the British consul on their behalf. "Tell them to begin to pack," he said sharply to the consul. "Any Spaniard caught within . . . this state after five days will be escorted to the nearest wall by a firing squad. . . . The Spaniards must go." [9]

In Madrid, on December 12, the Minister for Foreign Affairs sent a note to the American ambassador, urgently requesting that the American consul at Chihuahua intervene on behalf of the four hundred Spaniards of that city. The Spanish ambassador in Washington informed the State Department that he had received telegrams saying that Villa ordered all Spaniards to leave Chihuahua within ten days, under pain of death. The ambassador asked also that immediate instructions be sent to the consul at Chihuahua for the protection of "the lives and property of my compatriots which appear to be in grave danger." [10]

In a statement to the press, the Spanish ambassador was understandably bitter:

Villa promised to protect all foreigners, including Chinese, but excepting Spaniards. At Chihuahua he demanded $1,500,000 in gold, in exchange for revolutionary scrip. Consul Letcher attempted to send a code message to Washington about this, but Villa would not allow it. Villa looted all stores owned by Spaniards. [11]

[8] Lind to Bryan, Nov. 15, 1913, quoted in George M. Stephenson, *John Lind of Minnesota* (Minneapolis, 1935), p. 246.
[9] John Reed, *Insurgent Mexico*, p. 128.
[10] *Foreign Relations, 1913*, pp. 903–904.
[11] New York *Times*, Sunday, Dec. 14, 1913, 2:5.

Fortunately for Villa's favor with the State Department, the allegation that he had been discourteous toward the American consul was not confirmed. Letcher's messages were all in cipher, and Mrs. Letcher, arriving at El Paso a few days later, informed reporters who questioned her that if Villa had prevented her husband from sending messages in cipher she had never heard of it.[12]

Bryan acted promptly in response to the requests of the Spanish ambassador. Letcher was directed to see Villa at once. He must make it clear that inflicting the death penalty or enforcing the banishment order would horrify the whole civilized world.[13] Three days later Letcher was ordered to use his good offices to protect Spanish property and (significantly) to urge Villa to "remember that every act of cruelty is repeated and exaggerated, and they should therefore give as little opportunity as possible for such complaint even in their dealings with Mexicans." [14]

Letcher had anticipated his instructions and had seen Villa already. Villa was adamant; the expulsion of the Spaniards had saved them from being massacred by the population. Letcher believed that this was false, but when one recalls Mrs. O'Shaughnessy's remarks about the Spaniards in Mexico, it may not have been as farfetched as he believed. The only concession Letcher could obtain was a promise that Spaniards who could prove that they had taken no part in Mexican politics would be allowed to return.[15]

The problems growing out of Villa's hatred of Spaniards were not the only complications that arose after the capture of Chihuahua. Scarcely less than his hatred of Spaniards were his dislike and distrust of the wealthy *hacendados*. Luis Terrazas, the son of General Luis Terrazas, former governor of the state and reputedly the owner of two-thirds of it, had taken refuge in the British consulate, from which he was forcibly removed in spite of the consul's vehement protests. Newspapers in the United States reported that young Terrazas had been immediately executed. Oddly, the reports made no mention of Villa but merely referred to the invaders of the consulate as Constitutionalists.[16]

The report of Terrazas' death was untrue, but Brigadier General

[12] Sacramento *Union*, Wednesday, Dec. 17, 1913, 1:1.
[13] *Foreign Relations, 1913*, p. 904.   [14] *Ibid.*, pp. 907–908.
[15] *Ibid.*, pp. 902–903, 909.
[16] New York *Times*, Friday, Dec. 12, 1913, 2:1.

Hugh L. Scott, who was in command of the United States forces at El Paso, learned that he was being held in the Chihuahua penitentiary.[17] Luis Terrazas was a Mexican citizen, and the United States could not properly take any official action for him. In Mexico City, Nelson O'Shaughnessy, appealed to by a "Mr. C" [Creel?], promised that he would have brought to Villa's attention, by the "most indirect channels," the unfavorable impression that any harm to Terrazas would make in the United States.[18]

At this point, it should be stressed that the events just related took place *before* Sir William Tyrrell's interview with President Wilson. The President must have known about them, but he was still of the opinion that Villa was not as bad as he had been depicted.[19] Villa, as an avowed and powerful enemy of Huerta, held a position in the President's estimation that his blithe disregard of the accepted canons of civilized warfare could not entirely destroy.

Nor was the President alone in his opinion. Even the conservative New York *Times* found it not inconsistent to publish a photograph of Villa entitled "Villa, the Robin Hood of Mexico," in the same issue in which the seizure of Luis Terrazas was called "an act of brigandage." [20]

The Constitutionalist government, presided over by Venustiano Carranza as First Chief, meanwhile remained in the background. During the eventful days of November and early December, 1913, Carranza had not asserted himself, and the fact that in theory Villa was merely a subordinate was completely forgotten. As remarked before, Villa was actually a free agent, an independent *caudillo* with a private army.

This fact had been tacitly recognized by the United States government when Secretary Bryan, some time before the capture of Torreón, notified Villa that he would be held personally responsible for the safety of Americans and other foreigners.[21] Bryan, at this time, did not seem to have as much confidence in Villa as he had a little later.

Shortly after the first anxious messages were received from the Spanish ambassador about the plight of his compatriots in Chihuahua, the decision was made in Washington to send a special envoy to Villa, to reinforce the efforts of the consuls. The man selected for this important

[17] *Foreign Relations, 1913,* p. 905.
[18] Edith O'Shaughnessy, *A Diplomat's Wife in Mexico,* p. 90.
[19] Hendrick, *Life and Letters of Walter Hines Page,* I, 205.
[20] New York *Times,* Sunday, Dec. 14, 1913, 2:4, and rotogravure section.
[21] National Archives, State Department File no. 812.00/9275, Oct. 29, 1913.

and delicate mission was George C. Carothers, who had been in business in Mexico and had been an American consular agent for thirteen
years. He was in Torreón when Villa captured the city and had formed
a very favorable opinion of Villa at that time—an opinion based on
Villa's prompt suppression of looting and his action in furnishing a
guard for the American consular office.[22]

Carothers was at Texas City, Texas, when an urgent telegram was
dispatched, on December 9, directing him, "if your affairs are in such
shape that you can leave immediately, to go to Chihuahua to confer
with Villa." Carothers was told that Villa was disposed to protect all
foreigners who had been strictly neutral but that Huerta sympathizers
would have their property confiscated. Carothers' immediate mission
was to protect the lives and property of Americans and other foreigners.[23] Four days later an additional telegram informed him of the
instructions sent to Letcher and directed him to proceed immediately.
"If you should see Villa on the way, renew and reinforce Letcher's
representations." [24] This telegram was followed in turn, on December
15, by another instructing him to use his good offices with Villa, at the
first opportunity, for Luis Terrazas and for numerous wives of fugitives
who were reported as being held in Chihuahua by Villa's orders.[25]

Carothers arrived at Chihuahua on December 22 with two of Villa's
confidential advisers and two representatives of Carranza, whom he
had happened to meet at El Paso. Villa received Carothers with great
cordiality, inviting him to breakfast and giving him a full hour's interview. Villa was positive, Carothers reported, that the Spaniards of
Chihuahua were hand in glove with the Huertistas, but he had no intention of shooting any of them without positive proof of guilt. To a
suggestion that prisoners should be given a fair trial before being executed, Villa readily assented, assuring Carothers also that he was not
going to shoot Luis Terrazas, although he had confiscated all the
Terrazas holdings. Moreover, Carothers told the State Department, he
had been given full information about the important conference between Villa and the Carranza emissaries who had accompanied him
from El Paso.[26]

Disturbing information and rumors, meanwhile, continued to reach

[22] *Fall Committee Report*, pp. 1755, 1765–1766.
[23] *Foreign Relations, 1913*, pp. 902, 906.   [24] *Ibid.*   [25] *Ibid.*, p. 907.
[26] *Ibid.*, pp. 909–910.

Washington. The Constitutionalists, according to these reports, had taken large quantities of coal from the American Smelting and Refining Company. An American citizen had been mulcted of six thousand pesos. The German and Japanese residents of Chihuahua feared the same fate as the Spanish colony, and Villa was still refusing to allow the wives and children of refugees to leave Chihuahua.

Instructions were telegraphed to Letcher to include Japanese in his good offices, and on December 27, 1913, further orders were dispatched to Carothers:

Discreetly ascertain from Villa all possible details of the subjects mentioned. Represent to him that the world is watching with intense interest his every move and that his treatment of the Spaniards has already provoked much comment unfavorable to the Constitutionalists. Urge upon him the advisability of relieving this situation by permitting the departure of all who desire to leave, and of making a declaration that protection will be afforded to all foreigners and their property.[27]

Probably Carothers did not receive this message in time to act upon it during his trip to Chihuahua. In any event, he had already discussed most of the points mentioned in his interview with Villa on December 23. The really significant feature of the message was the overt anxiety displayed by the Secretary of State that Villa's acts and policies should not put the Constitutionalists before the world in an unfavorable light. The same anxiety was apparent in the earlier messages sent to Letcher. If Villa's ruthlessness and disregard of generally accepted conventions should cause loss of popular and international sympathy for the Constitutionalist cause, the difficulties of realizing President Wilson's hopes for Mexico would be increased manyfold.

The end of 1913 and the opening of the year 1914 found Villa's prestige high in the United States and continuing to rise. Very little, if any, revulsion was caused by the execution of numerous Federals, the expulsion of the Spaniards from Chihuahua, or the forcible removal of Luis Terrazas from the British consulate. The average American could not feel too much sympathy for a man as rich as Terrazas was reputed to be, and "twisting the British lion's tail" was an activity that was not altogether unpopular. Villa's spectacular succession of victories captured the imagination, and his activities as *de facto* dictator of

[27] *Ibid.*, pp. 909–910, 916.

Chihuahua excited a great amount of interest. The New York *Times,* calling him "the Robin Hood of Mexico," as mentioned before, condoned his ruthlessness with the opinion that his brutality was caused by the "lack of standards" resulting from his illiterate ignorance.[28] Even Mrs. Edith O'Shaughnessy, outspokenly sympathetic toward Huerta, grudgingly admitted in a letter written on January 6, 1914, that Villa had "shown himself clever about finding capable agents to whom he is willing to leave the gentler mysteries of the three R's" and that a man who had known Villa for a long time, and who had seen him recently, told her that "some mental, if not moral, evolution had been going on." [29]

Having become politically important and with the resources of the State of Chihuahua to spend on his army, the former bandit suddenly found himself socially acceptable. There was a stream of invitations from well-wishers and sycophants—probably, also, from hopeful merchants. It was about this time that General Hugh L. Scott, who had been following Villa's campaign with professional interest, gave him a pamphlet on the accepted practices of civilized nations in waging war, with the suggestion that he follow the rules.[30]

Villa lost no time in preparing his forces to renew the fight against the Federals, who had regained Torreón and maintained a tenuous position at Ojinaga. The embargo upon munitions from the United States was still in force, but nevertheless a river of weapons and ammunition flowed across the Rio Grande. "It was easy to get ammunition as long as the smugglers received the extortionate prices they demanded. It came in piano cases, buried in cars of coal and packed in cases of canned goods." [31] Weapons and ammunition were not the only items —the Tri-State Grocery Company, of El Paso, furnished a carload of lard; Endicott, Johnson and Company received an order for 27,624 pairs of shoes; a New York firm sold 2,500 army hats; canned goods and preserved meats rolled into Villa's supply depots in fantastic quantities. A certain Felix A. Sommerfeld (or Somerfelt), a somewhat

---

[28] New York *Times,* Sunday, Dec. 14, 1913, rotogravure section.

[29] Edith O'Shaughnessy, *A Diplomat's Wife in Mexico,* p. 159.

[30] Harris, *Pancho Villa and the Columbus Raid,* pp. 28–29, 71. Cf. also John Reed, *Insurgent Mexico,* pp. 142–143.

[31] O'Reilly, *Roving and Fighting,* p. 299.

shadowy figure, was paid almost two hundred thousand dollars in three weeks' time.[32]

After a few weeks of recruitment, rest, and organization, Villa's forces were ready for the elimination of the last fragments of Federal power in the north, the Federal garrison at Ojinaga. The morale of the Federals was low. The majority of the officers and men had made the terrible march across the desert from Chihuahua. They were outnumbered, completely cut off from the rest of Federal Mexico, and few of them had any desire to die as heroes in a last-ditch defense. The garrison included, also, a large proportion of Orozquista volunteers, who could expect no mercy.

Even with the odds so heavily in his favor that the final outcome could not be in doubt for a second, Villa's attack upon Ojinaga developed in a way that a later generation was to call a "blitzkrieg." On January 10, 1914, he rode triumphantly into the little border town as the last terrified Federals and *colorados* (Orozquistas) splashed frantically across the Rio Grande to the safety of the United States.

As a direct result of Villa's victory, United States authorities were presented with a new problem—what to do with the fugitive Federals who fled across the Rio Grande, happy to surrender to Major M. M. McNamee and to find themselves surrounded by a protective guard of United States soldiers. Refugees in small groups were nothing new, but this time there were five thousand in one miserable mass, including a thousand women and over five hundred children. In addition, the fugitives brought with them almost three thousand horses and mules. Quickly disarmed and organized into provisional companies and battalions, they were marched to the nearest point on the railroad and transported to Fort Bliss, at El Paso.[33]

At Fort Bliss a camp covering some sixty acres was prepared for them, strongly guarded and surrounded by wire. Every refugee was vaccinated and given antityphoid inoculations. A school for the numer-

[32] Harris, *Pancho Villa and the Columbus Raid*, pp. 71–72. Harris states that these, and many similar expenditures, are shown in Hipólito Villa's bankbook on the Guaranty Trust Company, of New York. The bankbook is in Harris' possession. Hipólito Villa acted as his brother's purchasing agent in New York. Felix Sommerfeld was Villa's principal agent in the United States for several years.

[33] Capt. George H. Estes, 20th Infantry, "The Internment of Mexican Troops in 1914," *United States Infantry Journal*, XI (July, 1914–June, 1915), 748–752.

ous children was established at once, and the men were put to work mixing adobe to build Mexican-style huts. Native arts and industries were encouraged, and the greater part of the fugitives settled down happily to being the guests of the United States. A few escaped, but it is alleged that the vast majority could not have been forced to leave. In the late spring of 1914, when war was seriously threatened, the internees were transferred to Fort Wingate, New Mexico. Eventually all were repatriated to Mexico or were released to remain in the United States, if guaranteed employment.[34]

It is difficult to see any other way in which the problem so unceremoniously dropped into the United States government's lap by Villa's whirlwind success could have been handled. President Wilson's opponents seized upon the refugee camp as a convenient, if somewhat puny, club with which to belabor his administration. A national magazine which was bitterly opposed to him published a full-page cartoon satirizing the camp. It pictured signs such as "Camp Dolce Far Niente," "Picnic Ground for Family Parties," and "If You're Tired of Revoluting, Try Our Rest Cure. Uncle Sam Foots the Bills!" [35]

Villa probably never dreamed that his victory at Ojinaga would cost the American taxpayer what then seemed the unbelievable sum of twenty-five hundred dollars a day or that the results of his victory would provide a weapon for President Wilson's political enemies. It was almost the first, but far from the last, occasion on which Villa and his actions would be used to reproach the administration in Washington.

Ojinaga was a final "mopping up" of Federal power in Chihuahua. Villa's authority was now even more absolute than before. The correspondent of the London *Times* remarked that the capture of Ojinaga marked Villa as the most prominent leader on the rebel side. He commented on Villa's effective intelligence service and the stern way in which order was maintained in Torreón after its capture. He believed that Villa's bold strokes were probably due to three Americans on his staff, who were veterans of the campaigns in Cuba and the Philippines.[36]

[34] *Ibid.*, XII (July, 1915–Feb., 1916), 38–57, 243–264. Cf. also Peter B. Kyne, "With the Border Patrol," *Collier's Magazine*, LIII (May 9, 1914), 20–22.

[35] *Collier's Magazine*, LIII (Aug. 1, 1914), 23.

[36] London *Times*, Jan. 13, 1914, 7:2. As far as can be ascertained, there were no Americans or other foreigners on Villa's staff at any time. The few American soldiers

The dictator in Mexico City hung grimly to his usurped office in spite of the series of Federal disasters in Chihuahua. The United States unwittingly strengthened his position by the embargo on exporting munitions. Huertistas held all the principal seaports, making it easy for them to import arms and ammunition from Europe. Events in Chihuahua visibly weakened Huerta's position, and it became apparent that if the Constitutionalists could obtain readily what they needed from the United States his final downfall would be accelerated. Consequently, on February 3, 1914, President Wilson proclaimed the embargo lifted.[37]

There is no way to determine whether or not the flow of weapons and ammunition across the border was increased. Since the Constitutionalists no longer had to purchase through smugglers and other shady characters, their supply problems must have been eased and the costs immeasurably decreased.

President Wilson's action was regarded very critically by certain influential people in Great Britain—people who believed that British interests in Mexico would be furthered most by a Huertista victory. An English writer who claimed authoritative knowledge of Mexico said:

I do not doubt for a moment that the American commercial and financial interests are endeavouring by unfair means to oust the long-established interests in Mexico. . . . It is . . . to General Villa that the Americans are turning for aid in their campaign against General Huerta, and in order to help him the embargo on rifles was . . . raised early in February. . . . In the event of a rebel success, it is to the tender mercies of Villa that we are to look for protection.[38]

The same indignant and apprehensive English writer considered it "extraordinary" that Villa sent a message expressing his gratitude to an unspecified New York newspaper. He quoted Villa as saying that raising the embargo was an act of justice by President Wilson, that this act would enable him to overwhelm Huerta and would establish a firm bond of friendship between the Mexican and American peoples. A

---

of fortune who served with him appear to have been mostly technical specialists, such as machine gunners, or were ordinary adventurers. Cf. John Reed, *Insurgent Mexico*, pp. 157–160.

[37] *Foreign Relations, 1913*, pp. 446–448.

[38] J. H. Kennedy, "The Real Trouble in Mexico," *Fortnightly Review*, XCV n.s. (Jan.–June, 1914), 1050.

further and final result would be the establishment of a constitutional government in Mexico.[39]

That Villa sent such a message to a New York newspaper in the words credited to him may be questioned, but there is no doubt that he was overjoyed at the lifting of the embargo and felt a full measure of gratitude for it. On being informed, he tossed his hat into the air, embraced his informant, and exclaimed: "The war will soon be over. I think that President Wilson is the most just man in the world. All Mexicans will love him, and we will look on the United States as our greatest friend!" [40]

By this time Villa's prestige was so high that, both to the American public and to the responsible officials of the State Department, he completely eclipsed Carranza. The *Literary Digest,* reflecting a segment of newspaper opinion in the United States, observed that the capture of Ojinaga not merely pointed to Huerta's imminent downfall but also pointed clearly to the fact that the man who would take Huerta's place was not Carranza, or Zapata, but Francisco Villa.[41]

With such a view prevailing, it was natural that the man himself and his every act were observed closely by all Americans who had any interest whatever in the situation in Mexico. The brutalities charged against him, the numerous executions for which he was responsible, his expulsion of the Spaniards from the places he captured, were all overshadowed by the glamour of his victories. It was possible at last that a man had appeared on the scene who had the necessary combination of strength and idealism to bring a just peace to Mexico.

Questioned as to the requirements for peace in Mexico, Villa gave a brief list, the most significant of which were (1) the complete elimination of Huerta and all his supporters, (2) a change in the land laws so that landownership would be more generally distributed, and (3) ratification of the confiscation by the Constitutionalists (i.e., by himself) of the huge Terrazas and Creel estates.[42] The first of these conditions was strictly in line with President Wilson's announced policy toward Mexico, and the other two were definitely not contrary to anything he had ever said.

At this time Villa probably had no political or social program beyond

[39] *Ibid.,* pp. 1051–1052.
[40] "Letting the Guns into Mexico," *Literary Digest,* XLVIII (1914), 303–304.
[41] *Ibid.*   [42] *Ibid.,* p. 145.

providing for the poor at the expense of the rich. As mentioned, he had confiscated the enormous Terrazas estates, and likewise he had exacted forced loans from the banks and businesses of the places he captured. In these measures he simply followed practices established in the long series of Mexican civil wars—practices followed as far back as the original revolt against Spain.[43]

Confiscation of the huge estates and forced loans from people supposed to be able to pay were not the only measures Villa took in Chihuahua. The Brooklyn *Eagle* referred to certain of the steps he took as "socialistic experiments [which] have compelled the attention of the world."[44]

Calling a public measure socialistic was not a complete condemnation in the minds of many people in 1914. In the United States the Socialist Party had just polled the largest number of popular votes it was ever to receive in a national election, and the movement appeared to be growing. Even people who had scant sympathy with socialistic philosophy favored many of the measures advocated by the socialists. A graduated income tax had recently been instituted; for years the public had been deeply concerned with ways and means of controlling "big business." There was serious discussion of the advisability of government ownership of railroads and public utilities. A large part of the public could hardly be shocked at what Villa was doing in Chihuahua. Rather, if anything, his "socialistic" measures increased his stature in the eyes of an appreciable part of the American people.

These measures were simple and direct. It is not at all probable that Villa gave any thought to their social and philosophic implications. His immediate purpose was to gain funds to equip his army for the recapture of Torreón. To finance the purchase of ammunition and other supplies it was necessary that such businesses and industries as Chihuahua supported should resume operation. Unhandicapped by any opposition, he ordered shops to reopen and industries to start work again. With true revolutionary directness and simplicity he "called together the workmen, placed experts at the head of the industries, and told them to go to work. . . . The heads of the industries pay running

[43] Nathaniel Weyl, "Mexico, European and Native," in Charles C. Griffin, ed., *Concerning Latin American Culture: Papers Read at Byrdcliffe, Woodstock, New York, August, 1939* (New York, 1940), p. 135.

[44] Quoted in the *Literary Digest*, XLVIII (1914), 145.

expenses and turn over the balance of the proceeds to the dictator." The tramway system, the electric-light plant, a brewery, a clothing factory, and the gambling casinos were all put into operation for the benefit of Villa's treasury. In addition, he planned to open a bank and a mint for coining the gold and silver bullion that his forces gathered in during the campaign.[45]

Such economic measures did not lower the general American estimate of Villa, and they tended to cause a favorable impression in the ranks of American liberals. When it became known that he was a total abstainer and seldom touched tobacco, even many of the godly in the United States were willing to overlook his years of banditry and the scores of murders which rumor said he had committed. The promise he seemed to offer as a possible future chief of the Mexican republic more than balanced the embarrassment which his treatment of the Spaniards of Chihuahua had caused the State Department.

[45] The correspondent of the New York *Sun*, quoted in the *Literary Digest*, XLVIII (1914), 170–174.

≫ VI ≪

Villa, Friend of the United States

WHILE Villa's star was rising, his primitive hatred of Spaniards and the callous greed of some of his followers continued to provide diplomatic vexations for the United States. Notwithstanding efforts of the American consular officers in northern Mexico to mitigate the unhappy lot of the Spanish residents, new offenses against them were reported. On January 2, 1914, the American ambassador at Madrid received a note from the Minister for Foreign Affairs, imploring the good offices of the United States on behalf of the Spaniards of the city of Parral.[1] A few days later, at a diplomatic reception, the king called the American ambassador aside and said that two of his subjects had recently been murdered in Chihuahua. The king requested that the United States take energetic measures for the protection of Spaniards in Mexico.[2]

Almost simultaneously, the Spanish ambassador in Washington informed the State Department that, under orders from Villa, the municipal chief of Guanaceví, Durango, was about to confiscate a mine which was only partly owned by Spaniards, the other owners being Mexicans and an American.[3] The State Department responded by telegraphing orders to Consul Louis Hostetter, at Hermosillo, Sonora, Carranza's temporary capital, to take up at once the matter of protection for

---

[1] *Foreign Relations, 1914,* pp. 784–785.　　　　[2] *Ibid.,* pp. 785–786.
[3] *Ibid.,* p. 786.

Spanish subjects in the parts of Mexico under Constitutionalist control. Hostetter was instructed to point out the adverse effect upon public opinion that such acts would inevitably produce.[4] At the same time Letcher, at Chihuahua, was directed to investigate the reported killing of the two Spaniards in that city and ascertain what action, if any, was being taken to discover and apprehend the guilty parties.[5]

The results were disappointing. Hostetter was given an obvious "brush-off." The Constitutionalist authorities informed him that there had been no complaints by the Spaniards of Parral—however, an investigation would be made "by telegraph." [6] As for Letcher, he learned that two Spaniards had been actually murdered in cold blood. The local authorities had promised the British vice-consul, who represented Spain, to make a full investigation.[7]

No one claimed that Villa was personally involved in this unfortunate incident, although it was perpetrated by his subordinates. He was in the midst of the expedition against Ojinaga and was not at Chihuahua at the time it occurred. Since he could not be reached during the campaign, the matter could not be taken up with him immediately.

The State Department kept the telegraph wires humming with instructions and demands for information. Carothers was told to see Villa about the mine that was to be confiscated, "if you can readily reach him," and was directed also to assist the secretary of the Spanish Legation at Havana, who was being sent to Mexico, to do whatever he could for the Spaniards of Chihuahua.[8] Letcher finally notified the department that the revolutionary authorities had made no investigation whatever of the murder of the two Spaniards at Chihuahua. Furthermore, they had no intention of making such an investigation. General Manuel Chao, the acting governor of the state, claimed that the two victims had been lawfully executed "by superior military order, meaning by order of Villa," under the Juárez decree of 1862.[9]

Carothers was unable to see Villa until he returned to Juárez. Consequently, Carothers was unable to prevent the confiscation of the Guanaceví mine by General Tomás Urbina. Urbina, who had been a bandit with Villa long before the Revolution, was a man with a reputation for sadistic cruelty, colossal greed, and utter unscrupulous-

[4] *Ibid.*, p. 785.   [5] *Ibid.*, p. 787.   [6] *Ibid.*, p. 788.
[7] *Ibid.*, pp. 789–790.   [8] *Ibid.*, pp. 787–789.   [9] *Ibid.*, pp. 791–792.

ness. It is worthy of note that he was finally killed, apparently by Villa himself, for his peculations and disloyalty.[10]

While the matter of the Guanaceví mine was still occupying the attention of the State Department, the newspapers suddenly provided a further issue. On February 4, 1914, a short article from the Associated Press appeared with a headline saying, "Villa Warns Spaniards." The article quoted Villa as announcing that all Spaniards captured in the coming Torreón campaign would be dealt with summarily and that he was now issuing this warning so that the Spaniards could leave Mexico before falling into his hands. According to the press, he added that seventy-one Spaniards taken at the previous capture of Torreón had all violated their pledge not to take up arms again. "Therefore I say they will be shot if captured. Those against whom I have no positive proof will be banished from the country, as other Spaniards were from Chihuahua." [11]

The Spanish ambassador in Washington lost no time in requesting immediate action by the United States. Byran telegraphed to Carothers, directing him to inform Villa that the United States could not believe the truth of the report. At the same time Hostetter, at Hermosillo, was ordered to take the matter up with Carranza.[12]

The replies from both Carothers and Hostetter were reassuring. Villa promised protection to all foreigners, including Spaniards, and the First Chief remarked that the Associated Press was not always to be trusted. In any event, he said, he had given strict orders that foreigners and their property were to be respected. Carothers was satisfied that Villa meant what he said and that the pledges were good.[13]

But diplomatic complications for the United States were not at an end. On Thursday, February 19, an inconspicuous item in the New York *Times* said that Gustave Brouch, an American citizen of German parentage, had been sentenced by Villa to be shot as a spy and that a British subject named William S. Benton had been arrested, suspected of being connected with a Federal filibustering plot.[14] The following

[10] *Ibid.*, p. 793. Cf. Pastor Rouaix, *Diccionario geográfico, histórico y biográfico del Estado de Durango* (Mexico City, 1946), pp. 473–474. John Reed, who admired Villa deeply, gives an unflattering picture of Urbina in *Insurgent Mexico*, pp. 25–33.

[11] New York *Times*, Wednesday, Feb. 4, 1914, 2:3.

[12] *Foreign Relations, 1914*, pp. 790–791.   [13] *Ibid.*, pp. 791–792.

[14] New York *Times*, Thursday, Feb. 19, 1914, 2:3–5.

day the London *Times* noted briefly that there was some question as to the whereabouts of William S. Benton, "believed to be a British subject." Villa, according to the *Times,* said that Benton had threatened him. Next day the *Times* added cautiously that Benton was believed to be a brother of Sir John Benton, K.C.I.E., and that it was reported that he had been executed following a court-martial.[15]

As soon as Benton disappeared, his wife, who was a Mexican, telegraphed frantically to Sir Cecil Spring-Rice, the British ambassador in Washington. Sir Cecil hurried to the Secretary of State, who sent orders posthaste to Carothers, to Consul Thomas Edwards at Juárez, and to Vice-Consul Frederick Simpich at Nogales, Sonora, where Carranza had just established his headquarters. They were all directed to make inquiries and to endeavor to obtain Benton's release.[16]

Carothers had acted before receiving the Secretary's telegram. Informed in El Paso that Benton had gone to Juárez for the "declared purpose of telling Villa what he thought of him," Carothers had gone to see Villa, at the request of some of the British residents of El Paso. Villa asked Carothers if his inquiry was official. On being informed that it was not, Villa refused to say anything further, except that "Benton was all right, that nothing had happened to him." [17]

The telegraphic orders for both Carothers and Edwards arrived while Carothers was in Juárez. Edwards thereupon went to Villa and was told in strict confidence that Benton had used very abusive and threatening language to Villa, finally reaching for his gun. He was overpowered, disarmed, and later killed by Rodolfo Fierro.[18] Carothers, relying on Villa's word and not knowing of Villa's admission of Benton's death, telegraphed to the State Department that Benton would probably be released the next day.[19] When he was not released and Edwards' report was received in Washington, an international crisis occurred.

Benton's death brought out sharply the highly debatable matter of

[15] London *Times,* Friday, Feb. 20, 1914, 5:9; Saturday, Feb. 21, 1914, 5:1.
[16] *Foreign Relations, 1914,* pp. 842–843.
[17] Statement of George C. Carothers, *Fall Committee Report,* pp. 1784–1785.
[18] *Ibid.* Benton quarreled with Villa as early as 1912, when Villa threatened to shoot him. This fact, previously unknown, was ascertained by the present writer. Cf. Memorandum from the Secretary of War to the Attorney General, National Archives, Department of Justice File no. 90755–1324, Feb. 23, 1912.
[19] *Foreign Relations, 1914,* p. 843.

the responsibility of the United States for Mexico. There was widespread acceptance of the belief that since the United States under the Monroe Doctrine would not allow any European intervention in the Western Hemisphere it was morally responsible for the conduct of the nations of the hemisphere. As mentioned before, the London *Daily Chronicle,* early in 1913, probably representing general British opinion, said that the Monroe Doctrine threw upon the United States the entire onus of acting in the Mexican situation. In this opinion the *World's Work* concurred thoroughly.[20] The idea was further strengthened by the willingness of the United States to have its diplomatic and consular officers use their "good offices" on behalf of foreigners in Mexico. To a certain extent American responsibility had been tacitly accepted at one time by the Secretary of State himself. Following the capture of Torreón in October, 1913, Bryan personally drafted a telegram on the retention of foreigners against their will. Boaz Long, chief of the State Department's Latin American Division, sent Bryan a memorandum with the dry comment, "It hardly seems that the Monroe Doctrine could be construed to impose upon us an 'obligation to extend to other nationals the same protection we extend to American citizens' throughout America." Long pointed out that warning Villa that he would be held "personally responsible" for the safety of Americans and other foreigners in Mexico might mean intervention.[21]

To interpret the Monroe Doctrine as making the United States fully responsible for the acts of any faction in Mexico was not intended at any time, nor was it so understood by responsible officials in Great Britain. Sir Edward Grey, on being questioned in Parliament as to the government's action in the Benton case, replied that Great Britain had no means of communication with Villa except through the United States. The United States had undertaken the mission of representing Great Britain only because of friendship and good will. Great Britain, Sir Edward added positively, did not hold the United States responsible in any way.[22]

In spite of all denials that the United States was accountable for anything occurring in Mexico, the idea would not down. The London

[20] Cf. pp. 38–39 *supra.*

[21] National Archives, State Department File no. 812.00/9275.

[22] *Parliamentary Debates,* 30 Parl. of the United Kingdom of Great Britain and Ireland, 4 sess., 5th ser., 4 George V, LVIII, 1410; LIX, 247–250. Hereafter referred to as *Parliamentary Debates.*

Sunday Times said: "The nation which demands respect for the Monroe Doctrine has a particular obligation to the other Powers." The London *Daily Mail* sneered that "the bandit Villa" was a particular protégé of the United States and editorially demanded to know how long the President proposed to allow Mexico to "flounder in her present morass of anarchy." [23] In Parliament, Sir John D. Rees, a member of the Opposition, said: "It is made clear in the communications with Washington that this country must hold the United States responsible." A few days later he asked if representations had been made to the United States concerning the reported confiscation of the property of certain British subjects "by the forces of Villa and Carranza." [24] Mr. John R. P. Newman wanted to know if all of Mexico, or only the northern part, was in the United States sphere of influence in the same degree that southern Persia was in the British sphere of influence. He also demanded to know if Washington was not responsible for the protection of British interests in Mexico.[25] In France the future Premier, Georges Clemenceau, the "Tiger," remarked in *L'Homme Libre* that the United States was responsible for the murder of Benton and for the anarchy in Mexico because it would not allow England or any other power to intervene.[26]

In the United States the Benton affair provided a perfect opportunity for President Wilson's opponents to attack both his policies and himself, not realizing, or possibly not caring, that they were implicitly admitting that the United States must be responsible for Mexico and for the acts of Francisco Villa. Congressman James R. Mann, of Illinois, a conservative Republican, was patriotically indignant that the government had taken no action when Americans were molested in Mexico, but he asked rhetorically, "Can you kill an Englishman without trouble?" Congressman Frank W. Mondell, of Wyoming, likewise a staunch member of the "Old Guard," fumed: "The death of one Englishman seems to have stirred up the administration more than all the outrages committed against Americans for months." [27]

Notwithstanding the indignation of President Wilson's political opponents, the United States did not make a greater effort in the Benton

[23] "The British Press on Benton's Fate," *Literary Digest*, XLVIII (1914), 481.
[24] *Parliamentary Debates*, LIX, 207, 1635. [25] *Ibid.*, p. 5.
[26] "French Criticism of Our Mexican Methods," *Literary Digest*, XLVIII (1914), 546.
[27] *Cong. Record*, 63 Cong., 2 sess., p. 4245.

case than it did in previous and less well publicized cases. In every instance the United States had made all possible effort, short of threatening force, to protect everyone who was entangled in the turmoil of the Revolution. Immediately after Consul Edwards confirmed Benton's death, Secretary Bryan ordered him to obtain and forward a copy of the court proceedings under which Benton was sentenced. This order was followed a few hours later by instructions to get full information about the quarrel between Benton and Villa and to obtain the release of Benton's body to his wife. The British government felt "confident that the Secretary of State will cause a full and impartial inquiry to be made" and ordered the British consul at Galveston to go at once to El Paso, to co-operate with the American officials and be in a position to receive firsthand information.[28]

Throughout the whole confused affair Villa was uniformly courteous to Carothers, Edwards, and Letcher, but at the same time he never yielded to a single one of their requests. To Edwards he said that "he could not let the body go now, but would do so later." He promised to have the grave well marked, so that later identification would be easy. He told Carothers that he was very sorry that he could not deliver Benton's body at that time, and to Letcher he promised to order the exhumation of the body for examination but stipulated that it must be reinterred in the same place. On being informed that the United States proposed to send a special commission, composed of both American and British representatives, to investigate the killing, he offered a special train for the commission's use.[29]

At about the same time, urgent inquiries from the State Department about the German-American, Gustave Brouch (or Bauch), who had been reported as sentenced to death, disclosed that he had been released before the inquiries were received.[30]

A further complication was about to be injected into the situation. Before the international furor over Benton's death had really got under way, Villa sent a telegram to Carranza, giving his own version of the case, "so that you will not be surprised by false reports."[31] On February 24, 1914, remembering that Carranza was supposed to be

[28] *Foreign Relations, 1914*, pp. 843–845, 846–852.
[29] *Ibid.*, pp. 847, 849, 850, 855.
[30] Secretaría de Relaciones Exteriores, *Labor internacional de la Revolución Constitucionalista de México* (Mexico City, n.d.), pp. 43–45.
[31] *Ibid.*, p. 37.

the head of the Constitutional government and Villa's superior, Bryan directed Vice-Consul Simpich, at Nogales, to request that Carranza order the delivery of Benton's body to his relatives.[32] Simpich was unable to see Carranza for three days, during which Bryan sent a second telegram. Before he could see Carranza, Simpich was informed that the First Chief was extremely dissatisfied: representations about the Benton affair should come through a British official and not an American; all such communications should be addressed to the head of the government, not to a subordinate, such as General Villa. In his written reply, on February 28, Carranza rather curtly reaffirmed these principles and reminded the Secretary of State: "I am the First Chief of the Constitutionalist Army, and it is to me, as I have informed you on repeated occasions, that governments should address themselves in international matters." [33]

Having thus asserted himself and defended the dignity of the Constitutionalist government, Carranza proceeded to emphasize his position by ordering Villa not to discuss the Benton case with either Americans or British; there should be no further investigation except what he himself might order.[34] Since Villa found, probably to his own surprise, that he had stirred up a hornet's nest, he was glad to obey the First Chief's order. An American correspondent who discussed the case with him later noted that "he was evidently worried by the excitement the affair had caused and [was] anxious to hush it up as quickly as possible." [35]

Although the Benton affair dropped out of public interest and discussion rather quickly, echoes continued to be heard until they were drowned out by the explosion of war in Europe, six months later. As late as July 23, 1914, Mr. F. Hall, Member of Parliament for Dulwich, asked truculently if any assurance had been received from the United States that it would refuse to recognize any government in Mexico that did not guarantee punishment of Benton's murderers. Sir Edward Grey refused to demand such an assurance.[36]

It would be too strong to say that Benton's death deeply affected

[32] *Foreign Relations, 1914*, pp. 849–850.
[33] *Ibid.*, pp. 853, 856–857. Cf. also *Labor internacional*, pp. 37–40.
[34] *Foreign Relations, 1914*, p. 859.
[35] Joseph Rogers Taylor, "Pancho Villa at First Hand," *World's Work*, XXVIII (1914), 265.
[36] *Parliamentary Debates*, LXVI, 613.

relations between the United States and Great Britain, but it is not incorrect to say that discussion and negotiation between the two countries became more difficult. The American ambassador in London, Walter Hines Page, found "the fact that the murder had been committed by the faction that was more or less under the protection of the American Government was especially embarrassing." [37] Later in the spring, in a personal letter to the President, Page reported that everybody, from Sir Edward on down, looked on Villa as an unprincipled scourge—a brigand and murderer.[38] Sir Edward Grey himself recorded that conversations with the American ambassador were not always sympathetic. "I could not be enthusiastic when I heard . . . Villa . . . spoken of as the 'Sword of Revolution' in Mexico. Villa shot a British subject in cold blood, and it was impossible to feel that morality was really to be secured by substituting him . . . for Huerta." [39]

In Washington the determination to strengthen the Constitutionalists as the quickest means of ridding the world of the Huerta regime was as strong as ever—and Villa was the outstanding man on the Constitutionalist side. Hence, not even the difficulties and embarrassment he had caused by killing Benton made the administration in Washington lose faith in him entirely. Late in March, 1914, a full month after the Benton case became front-page news, Carothers was told to use his influence with Villa to prevent any harsh treatment of British subjects or other improper actions by Villa. "It would embarrass us and greatly injure the Constitutionalist cause if anything were done that could arouse additional criticism of Constitutionalist methods." [40]

In spite of the unexpected storm which the Benton affair caused, Villa continued his preparations for the next step in the campaign—the recovery of Torreón. Carload after carload of war material moved across the boundary into Mexico. The shipments even included a few airplanes. It is not certain whether Villa had any aviation before the Torreón campaign, but he was quick to recognize the advantage such weapons would give him.

Since there were almost no Mexican aviators at that time, the pilots were foreigners, mostly Americans. All of them were self-taught

[37] Henderson, *Life and Letters of Walter H. Page*, III, 106–107.
[38] *Ibid.*, p. 96.
[39] Viscount Edward Grey of Fallodon, *Twenty-five Years, 1892–1916* (New York, 1925), II, 99.
[40] *Foreign Relations, 1914*, p. 862.

"barnstormers," using crude bombs made from metal pipe filled with dynamite. The moral effect of the strange machines piloted by American adventurers is graphically described by a surgeon in Villa's army:

They're like great big birds that don't even seem to move sometimes. . . . The god-damn things have got some American fellow inside with hand-grenades by the thousand. . . . You know how a farmer feeds corn to his chickens, huh? Well, the American throws his lead bombs at the enemy just like that. Pretty soon the whole damn field is nothing but a graveyard.[41]

Villa's preparations for the coming campaign showed foresight and an administrative consciousness that made a most favorable impression upon correspondents and other observers. The preparations included converting a railway train into a modern and well-equipped hospital train, capable of transporting and caring for fourteen hundred patients. It was staffed by a group of surgeons headed by Dr. Andrés Villareal, who was a graduate of Johns Hopkins University.[42]

Villa's concern for the care of the wounded, apparently something new in Mexican internecine warfare, may have been partly due to the influence of Brigadier General Hugh L. Scott. On February 19, 1914, Villa and Scott, who was then in command of the United States forces at El Paso, met at the international bridge for a formal inter-view and conference.[43] Scott, a professional soldier of long service, a former superintendent of the United States Military Academy, and governor of one of the Moro provinces in the Philippines, took an immediate liking to the Mexican. Villa, for his part, conceived an admiration for General Scott which he never lost.[44] Speaking Spanish fluently, Scott told Villa plainly the effect upon American and European opinion of the executions and other barbarities with which Villa was charged. He pointed out emphatically that Villa was prejudicing any hopes of foreign assistance at some future time when he might really need it. Further, Scott read at some length from a recently published

[41] Mariano Azuela, *The Under Dogs,* trans. by E. Munguía (New York, 1929), pp. 109–110.

[42] George Marvin, "Villa," *World's Work,* XXVIII (1914), 280, 283. Cf. the New York *Times,* Friday, May 15, 1914, 4:5.

[43] New York *Times,* Friday, May 20, 1914, 1:4.

[44] Gen. Hugh Lenox Scott, *Some Memories of a Soldier* (New York, 1928), p. 518; Josephus Daniels, *The Wilson Era: Years of Peace, 1910–1917* (Chapel Hill, N.C., 1944), p. 203.

pamphlet embodying the recognized conventions by which the civilized nations sought to make war somewhat less hideous. Villa was impressed and shortly afterward sent a messenger to General Scott's headquarters requesting a copy of the pamphlet, which he proposed to have translated into Spanish for distribution among his officers. To reciprocate, he sent Scott a bundle of finely woven ponchos.[45]

While preparing for the attack upon Torreón, Villa received an important accession to his staff. Through the capture of numerous guns, his artillery branch had grown, and he needed badly a qualified artilleryman to command it. Its performance in battle had not been satisfactory, and there was no one in Villa's forces competent to handle it properly. In response to Villa's requests, Carranza detailed General Felipe Angeles to the Division of the North. Angeles was one of the few professional soldiers in the Constitutionalist forces. He was a graduate of the Military Academy at Chapultepec and had studied at the French artillery school. He speedily gained Villa's full confidence, and from the time he joined until his death before a Carranzista firing squad in 1919, he was unswerving in his devotion and loyalty to his bandit chief. Angeles' influence over Villa was profound, although it is not always easy to specify in just what ways he exercised it.[46]

Simultaneously with preparations for the coming campaign went reconstruction in Villa's zone of control. The battered railroad between Juárez and Chihuahua was repaired and kept in operation. The repairs extemporized by Villa's self-taught engineers were crude but effective, and trains were kept running on a more or less regular schedule.[47] Villa co-operated with American officials in efforts to suppress the drug traffic, but at the same time the cabarets, barrooms, and brothels of Juárez were a fruitful source of revenue for his treasury.[48] Under his guarantees, the American Smelting and Refining Company under-

---

[45] Louis Stevens, *Here Comes Pancho Villa: The Anecdotal History of a Genial Killer* (New York, 1930), p. 131; George Marvin, "Villa," *World's Work*, XXVIII (1914), 272–273.

[46] Bernardo Mena Brito, *El lugarteniente gris de Pancho Villa (Felipe Angeles)* (Mexico City, 1938), *passim*. The author, who was a Carranzista general, was violently anti-Villa and believed that Angeles was the evil genius behind Villa.

[47] Gregory Mason, "The Mexican Man of the Hour," *Outlook*, CVII (May–Aug., 1914), 292–301.

[48] Owen P. White, *Out of the Desert* (El Paso, Texas, 1923), p. 257; Harris, *Pancho Villa and the Columbus Raid*, p. 71.

took to reconstruct its smelter at Chihuahua. In return for the protection of the smelter and for guarding shipments of lead to El Paso, the company kept his railway trains supplied with coal. It has been alleged, also, that the American Smelting and Refining Company made substantial contributions to his exchequer.[49]

Preparations finally completed, Villa began moving his forces toward Torreón during the last days of March. The Federal garrison of the city had been greatly strengthened and was commanded by General José R. Velasco, a man whom Villa respected and who was considered one of the ablest of the Federal generals. For eleven days and nights the fighting was close and deadly, casualties on both sides mounting to figures that completely belied the popular idea that a Mexican battle was a rather noisy spectacle in which almost nobody got hurt. At last, on April 3, 1914, the Villistas penetrated into the last defensive lines of the city, and the shattered remnants of Velasco's garrison fled toward Saltillo.

The capture of Torreón after the hardest-fought battle of the Mexican Revolution and the relatively tight discipline maintained in the Villista army after the battle confirmed the opinion of Americans who believed that Francisco Villa was the man of the future in Mexico. Favorable opinion was strengthened in the next few weeks by reports indicating that Villa had taken to heart General Scott's advice as to the civilized treatment of wounded and prisoners. It was true that the *colorados*—Orozquista volunteers—were promptly shot as traitors, but the Federal regulars were spared and put to work cleaning up the debris of battle. The foreigners of the city, including many Spaniards, were unharmed. An American physician, Dr. A. N. Carr, the only doctor remaining in Torreón after the Federals left, on reporting to Villa was directed to continue his work in the hospital.[50] The American counsul, Theodore C. Hamm, granted an interview immediately after Villa entered the city, on April 3, reported: "General Villa was very anxious that I should bring to the attention of my Government that he was scrupulously complying with the usages of civilized warfare in regard to his treatment of prisoners and wounded of the enemy." [51]

[49] Harvey O'Connor, *The Guggenheims: The Making of an American Dynasty* (New York, 1937), pp. 335–336.
[50] New York *Times*, Saturday, April 4, 1914, 1:8; Sunday, April 5, 1914, 2:4.
[51] National Archives, State Department File no. 812.00/11703.

A correspondent characterized Villa's treatment of the captured Federals as being the first instance, on the rebel side, in which humanitarian principles had prevailed.[52]

Ignorant though he may have been, Villa was fully sensible from the earliest period of his military career of the value of the good will of the United States. He understood well the part that the newspapers could play in forming a public opinion in the United States favorable to himself and his cause.[53] Newspaper correspondents were granted interviews freely, and it was rumored that he paid a liberal sum monthly to an El Paso newspaper for publicity.[54] Within a short time after the capture of Juárez he became aware of a new and important medium by which he and his troops could be presented in a most favorable light. The American public was given an inkling in a rumor that was published in February, 1914:

In a darkened office room in a New York skyscraper a fortnight ago a dozen men sat watching some motion pictures. . . . Three of the little group of spectators were members of the Madero family. The others were magazine men, newspaper reporters and directors of an American motion picture corporation in which General Pancho Villa recently became a partner. In return for granting this corporation "exclusive motion picture rights" of his campaign, the General is to share in the profits from the films. The "movie show" in the skyscraper was a private exhibition of the first two reels of a cinematograph history of Villa's proposed march from the Rio Grande to the City of Mexico.[55]

The rumor that Pancho Villa was a partner or stockholder in an American motion-picture concern received wide circulation. In a caustically hostile statement the special staff correspondent of the San Francisco *Examiner* remarked that Villa was said to be financially interested in the news films being taken of his field operations.[56] In Mexico City, Mrs. Edith O'Shaughnessy, equally hostile, recorded stories that while the fighting at Torreón was in progress Villa had deliberately delayed an attack until after daybreak so that the motion-picture cameras could be used.[57] The same stories, in even more

[52] George Marvin, "Villa," *World's Work*, XXVIII (1914), 272.
[53] Guzmán, *Memorias*, II, 106.
[54] Harris, *Pancho Villa and the Columbus Raid*, p. 73.
[55] *Collier's Magazine*, LII (Feb. 7, 1914), 13.
[56] San Francisco *Examiner*, Friday, May 1, 1914, 1:7.
[57] Edith O'Shaughnessy, *A Diplomat's Wife in Mexico*, p. 243.

specific form, have been repeated and believed in recent years, taking their place in the Pancho Villa legend, even though in the absence of any trustworthy evidence they must be regarded as highly apocryphal.[58]

With all his faults Villa was too good a field commander to allow his desire for publicity to jeopardize an attack, so that the rumors mentioned may have been essentially a form of hostile propaganda. There is no question that the motion-picture cameramen were given every opportunity to see and photograph every phase of the fighting at Torreón. They took full advantage of their opportunities and happily reported after the battle that they were all safe and sound, in spite of the dangers they had faced. And within a few weeks advertisements in American newspapers proclaimed: "Absolutely Authentic in Every Detail. General Villa in Battle. Photographed under Fire at Chihuahua, Juárez, Torreón, Including the Tragic History of His Life." [59]

It is impossible to determine whether public opinion in the United States was influenced either for or against Villa by the display of films. To anyone who favored Huerta, the motion pictures of Villa in battle were evidence of his childish vanity. Conversely, a person favoring the other side would very likely feel that the pictures were proof of Villa's courage, energy, and military ability. The greatest probability is that most Americans who viewed the films regarded them purely as entertainment, without any particular political implications.

As mentioned earlier in this chapter, after the Torreón campaign increasing numbers of Americans sympathetic toward the Constitutionalists came to believe that Villa was definitely the man of the future in Mexico. Not all Americans, by any means, favored the Constitutionalists. The editor of *Harper's Weekly* aptly quoted "a man who travels constantly through the West" as saying: "I find just two classes that object to Wilson's Mexican policy. One is the politicians, who always disapprove what the other party does. The other consists of those to whom property is the most sacred idea in the world." The editor added: "The second class is numerous. Its horror is genuine over the disorder of Villa and his disregard for certain 'rights.'" [60] Americans

[58] Terry Ramsaye, *A Million and One Nights: A History of the Motion Picture* (New York, 1926), II, 670–673.

[59] Advertisement in the theater section of the New York *Times*, Friday, May 13, 1914, p. 24.

[60] "One Experience," *Harper's Weekly*, LVIII (June 27, 1914), 4.

who disliked President Wilson and his policies could feel nothing but aversion at the obvious favor which the administration felt toward Villa. Typifying this attitude, Senator Albert Fall, of New Mexico, on April 21, 1914, made a long, rambling, and almost violent speech in the Senate, denouncing Villa. On several previous occasions Fall had attacked Huerta, but on this occasion he completely reversed himself.[61]

Strangely, Americans who regarded Villa as a calamity do not seem to have taken advantage of the ammunition he offered them in his intransigent hatred and persecution of Spaniards. After the capture of Torreón the unfortunate Spaniards who fell into his power again posed a diplomatic problem for the United States. It was true that he did not keep the chilling threat to shoot them out of hand (if he really made such a threat), but his attitude and policy were as ruthless and vindictive as before.[62]

Consul Theodore C. Hamm reported to the State Department after his interview on April 3:

As far as General Villa is concerned all foreigners are divided into three classes; the Americans being the most favored with absolutely no restrictions placed upon their business transactions; foreigners other than Spaniards, who must pay moderately for the privilege of transacting business; Spaniards, who are beyond the pale.[63]

Still lurking in the background was the question of the responsibility of the United States. Certain European powers, unlike Great Britain, insisted that, since they could not act, the United States must accept full responsibility for their nationals in Mexico. During March, while Villa was completing his preparations for the southward movement, two unnamed European powers (presumably Germany and France) served notice that they would hold the United States fully responsible for what was likely to happen after Villa and Zapata entered Mexico City and demanded to know if the United States was prepared for eventualities.[64]

On the morning of April 6, three days after Villa entered Torreón,

[61] *Cong. Record*, 63 Cong., 2 sess., p. 6993.

[62] *Foreign Relations, 1913*, p. 910.

[63] National Archives, State Department File no. 812.00/11703.

[64] Anne Wintermute Lane and Louise Herrick Hall, eds., *The Letters of Franklin K. Lane, Personal and Political* (Boston and New York, 1922), Lane to Dr. Benjamin Ide Wheeler, March 13, 1914, p. 147.

the newspapers carried the now familiar news that the Spaniards were ordered deported.[65] The Spanish ambassador in Washington immediately called at the State Department and placed the problem in the hands of the United States. The Secretary of State had already sent a telegram to Carothers, who was at Carranza's headquarters. The Secretary of State hoped that the newspaper report was not true, but if it proved to be true, Carothers was to take the matter up with Carranza, "courteously but in the most impressive manner." Once again Carothers was to stress the unfavorable impression that the mistreatment of the Spaniards would make upon the world.[66]

Carothers sent a telegraphic report on the Spaniards of Torreón before the Secretary's instructions reached him. He had been in Torreón on April 3 and was an eyewitness of Villa's visit to the place where most of the Spaniards had been assembled. Carothers listened while Villa made a violent speech, accusing the Spaniards of aiding the Federals and shouting that he would be justified in shooting them all. Other nations might misunderstand his motives and call him an assassin if he killed them; therefore he would be content with expelling them from Mexico. Carothers and several members of Villa's own staff tried to dissuade him, but he refused to listen.[67]

From Torreón, Carothers went to Carranza's headquarters. The First Chief gave him an immediate interview, but was completely unsympathetic. Carranza refused to interfere with Villa's orders, saying that it was also his own desire to get all Spaniards out of Mexico. He had positive proof, he informed Carothers, that the Spaniards of Mexico were giving financial support to the Huerta regime, and if they did not leave the country before he got to Mexico City, he would have to order many of them executed.[68]

Baffled by Carranza's support of Villa, which was probably unexpected, the Secretary of State next wired to Carothers to suggest "discreetly" to Carranza the desirability of suspending the deportation order—and this Carranza did not choose to do. The following day a trainload of seven hundred unfortunate Spaniards arrived at El Paso. The Secretary of State hoped that "the Red Cross will . . . be able to extend some assistance to destitute Spanish refugees from Torreón." [69]

[65] New York *Times,* Monday, April 6, 1914, 1:1.
[66] *Foreign Relations, 1914,* pp. 795–797.   [67] *Ibid.,* p. 797.
[68] *Ibid.,* p. 798.   [69] *Ibid.,* pp. 798–799.

Unable to save the Torreón Spaniards from expulsion, the United States bent its efforts to prevent the confiscation of Spanish property. Carranza made a public statement that such property would not be confiscated, but local commanders did as they pleased. Hamm telegraphed from Torreón that many cases of outright confiscation occurred after the First Chief's announcement was made. Letcher was immediately ordered to ascertain from Carranza just what steps would be taken to protect abandoned Spanish property and 'to punish those who were responsible for looting and confiscation.[70]

Assistance by American consular officials was suddenly handicapped by Carranza's insistence that he could receive representations only from accredited representatives of the countries directly concerned. This was obviously an attempt to force the recognition of his government and may have had an additional motive in the embarrassment caused him by continual appeals of Americans on behalf of other foreigners. After considerable discussion and some apparent misunderstanding, the matter was finally compromised by Carranza's agreement that American officials could speak for other foreigners if such assistance was formally requested—a hairsplitting solution which "saved face" for everybody.[71]

Carloads of cotton confiscated from the Spanish planters of the area around Torreón were beginning, meanwhile, to arrive at El Paso for sale, although Villa had ordered that no Spanish property was to be touched without his personal approval. Presumably he authorized the seizure of this cotton, since the proceeds from its sale seem to have gone into his war chest. Efforts to obtain compensation for the despoiled owners, who were of several nationalities, caused diplomatic correspondence that lasted for several weeks.[72]

After the capture of Torreón, and until events suddenly took an ominous turn, Villa's treatment of Spaniards occupied a disproportionate part of the time and attention of the State Department and its representatives in Mexico. In the mass of telegrams and reports there are two salient features that strike the reader at once. First, the United States was anxious that the Constitutionalists should do nothing that might prejudice their cause in the world's opinion. A telegram from the Secretary of State on April 7 told Carothers to stress that

[70] *Ibid.*, pp. 802–803, 808.   [71] *Ibid.*, pp. 803–808.
[72] *Ibid.*, pp. 802, 813.

"indiscriminate deportation of foreigners will produce a most unfavorable impression." [73] The United States was consistently following the policy which had been set by President Wilson's determination not to recognize the Huerta regime under any circumstances, a policy from which he had not deviated.

Second, and equally salient, is the fact that Villa held the United States, and Americans in general, in the highest regard. This is specifically shown in numerous reports and statements by the American consular officers in Villa's zone of authority. In spite of his supposedly uncontrollable temper and impatience of opposition, Villa allowed Carothers to expostulate with him over his order expelling the Spaniards.[74] Consul Theodore C. Hamm, reporting his interview after Villa's entry into the captured city, said: "Generalissimo Villa . . . was in a most communicative frame of mind, discussing future plans with me with entire freedom." Even more indicative was Villa's apparently voluntary promise to Hamm that Americans shipping merchandise out of Mexico would not be charged the export tax which everyone else was required to pay.[75] And finally, on April 11, at the end of a report in which he discussed various Constitutionalist officials, Carothers informed the Secretary of Sate in categorical terms: "He [Villa] is not only friendly, but extremely grateful, to the United States." [76]

Only a few months before, Villa and eight companions slipped secretly across the border on stolen horses. Now he not merely enjoyed the favor of the United States, but his own favor was courted. His attitude, his views, his policies, were of direct interest and importance to the United States in determining its own policies.

[73] *Ibid.*, p. 796.   [74] *Ibid.*, p. 798.   [75] *Ibid.*, pp. 807–808.
[76] *Ibid.*, p. 804.

≈ VII ≈

Villa and Veracruz

DURING the time in which the attention of the State Department was devoted to the plight of the Spaniards of Torreón, other events complicated further the already confused situation in Mexico. Disorder was not confined to the states held by the Constitutionalists but extended over the whole country. In Mexico City, Victoriano Huerta contemptuously ignored suggestions from Washington that he bow himself out. His stiff-necked attitude, together with danger for Americans and other foreigners, had caused the concentration of a strong American naval force in Mexican waters. From this fact grew the next complication.

The largest foreign investments, and probably the greatest foreign colony in Mexico, were at Tampico, a city which the oil industry had made a place of particular importance and sensitiveness. In April, 1914, Tampico was held by the Federals, but was threatened by the Constitutionalists. On the morning of April 9 a party from the U.S.S. *Dolphin* went ashore to obtain gasoline. The boat was flying the United States flag and the men were in uniform and unarmed, but the Huertistas arrested them and paraded them through the streets of the city. Although they were released immediately, Rear Admiral Henry C. Mayo, commander of the naval forces at Tampico, regarded the arrest as a direct and intentional insult to the United States. He demanded that the act be formally disavowed and that the Federals hoist the American flag and salute it with twenty-one guns.[1]

Taking a serious view of the matter, President Wilson approved Admiral Mayo's action. Thus the affair was transformed from a squabble between two local commanders into an international issue. For several days the cables between the two capitals hummed. Huerta was willing to give in partially, but he refused to agree that his government should salute the American flag first. He suggested submitting the whole controversy to the Hague Tribunal (which would have been tantamount to recognition) and was willing to salute if the Americans returned the salute simultaneously. This, in the view of the United States, would have destroyed the entire value of the salute. To break the impasse thus reached, President Wilson addressed a joint session of Congress on April 20, 1914. He reviewed the matter from its start and added other instances of contempt or insolence displayed by the Federals toward the United States. By an overwhelming majority, Congress authorized the President to employ the armed forces to obtain from Huerta "the fullest recognition of the rights and dignity of the United States." [2]

The necessity for using the armed forces arose immediately. On the very day on which President Wilson addressed Congress, the American consul at Veracruz informed the State Department of the imminent arrival at that port of the German ship *Ypiranga,* with a cargo of arms and munitions for Huerta.[3] In the small hours of the next morning, orders went out to Rear Admiral Frank F. Fletcher, who was in command of all American naval forces in Mexican waters, to seize the customhouse at Veracruz and prevent the delivery of the *Ypiranga's* cargo.[4] By the evening of April 22, after two days of street fighting, American forces were in possession of the entire city of Veracruz, and Chargé d'Affaires Nelson O'Shaughnessy had been handed his passports.[5]

War was in the air. Probably most Americans believed that the seizure of Veracruz was merely the first step toward full-scale intervention. The ease with which Veracruz was taken led to the idea that the Mexican power of resistance was not to be taken seriously.

[1] *Foreign Relations, 1914,* pp. 448–449.
[2] *Ibid.,* pp. 449–476. Cf. Baker,' *Woodrow Wilson,* IV, 316–324.
[3] *Foreign Relations, 1914,* p. 477.   [4] *Ibid.*   [5] *Ibid.,* pp. 481, 484.

Yet there was the possibility that Huerta might suddenly become the leader behind whom all patriotic Mexicans would rally to oppose the invader.

The danger of this was indeed very grave. On April 21, while the street fighting in Veracruz was still going on, Carothers was directed to see Carranza at once to make clear the President's position—that he was not making war on Mexico but was obtaining redress for an indignity committed by Huerta's Federals. "[The President] has been careful to distinguish between General Huerta and his supporters and the rest of the Mexican people." [6] But in spite of President Wilson's good intentions and his careful differentiation between Huertistas and other Mexicans, Carranza's reply was not reassuring. "The invasion of our territory . . . violating the rights that constitute our existence as a free and independent sovereign entity, may indeed drag us into an unequal war . . . which until today we have desired to avoid." [7]

On the same day, April 22, Consul Marion Letcher telegraphed that Carranza was forced by his military leaders to take a strong and almost defiant stand.[8] From Sinaloa, General Alvaro Obregón, the most trusted and next to Villa the most prominent of Carranza's generals, advised joining forces with Huerta in an immediate declaration of war against the United States.[9]

On the American side of the border there was real apprehension. At El Paso the garrison consisted of only about fifteen hundred troops, while there were many more than that number of Mexican internees. The population of the city was overwhelmingly Mexican, and a stone's throw distant lay the completely Mexican city of Juárez. Hysterical rumors began to circulate that there was a conspiracy among the Mexican servants in El Paso to poison their employers. Once the slaughter started, the odds in favor of the Mexicans would be twenty to one, and Americans could expect no mercy.[10] Farther west on the border, people were alarmed by equally extravagant rumors that Obregón was preparing to invade Arizona.[11]

[6] *Ibid.*, p. 480. [7] *Ibid.*, pp. 483–484. [8] *Ibid.*
[9] Guzmán, *Memorias*, III, 54.
[10] Alice M. Williamson, "My Attempt to Be a War Correspondent," *McClure's Magazine*, XLIII (1914), 73.
[11] George Creel, *The People Next Door: An Interpretive History of Mexico and the Mexicans* (New York, 1926), pp. 332–333.

The almost unanimous voice with which, according to Letcher, the Constitutionalist generals advised a strong stand against the United States did not include Villa's. Before the Americans landed at Veracruz, Villa was reported to have remarked curtly that it was "Huerta's bull that was being gored." [12] On April 21, as soon as news of the landing became known, Carothers informed Washington that there was a strong feeling of resentment at Juárez, but the Villista officials were taking precautions to prevent any disturbance. Villa was expected to arrive at Juárez the next afternoon, and Carothers hoped to obtain his views immediately.[13]

Carothers' interview with Villa was more than satisfactory. Francisco Villa had no intention of being stampeded into a war against the United States. Indeed, he was so cordial that Carothers' report of the interview is worth quoting at length:

I have just returned from interview with Villa. I dined with him. He said there would be no war between the United States and the Constitutionalists; that he is too good a friend . . . and considered us too good friends of theirs for us to engage in a war; . . . that as far as he was concerned we could keep Vera Cruz and hold it so tight that not even water could get in to Huerta. . . . He said that no drunkard, meaning Huerta, was going to draw him into a war with his friend; that he had come to Juárez to restore confidence between us. . . . As indicative of his frame of mind he handed me a beautiful blanket with the request that I forward it to General Scott with his compliments.[14]

Carothers added that he hoped, through Villa, to keep the Constitutionalists neutral. Unfortunately the Carranzista censors, through whose hands newspaper accounts passed, were interested in making it appear that Villa was in full accord with the First Chief's antagonistic views.

Secretary Bryan was, of course, extremely gratified at Villa's stand and authorized Carothers to say that any action by the United States would be determined entirely by the attitude of "General Carranza, General Villa and their associates." Villa's statement to Carothers, Bryan felt, indicated a breadth of view and understanding of the

[12] New York *Times*, April 19, 1914, 1:6.
[13] National Archives, State Department File nos. 812.00/11587 and 11596, April 21, 1914.
[14] *Foreign Relations, 1914*, pp. 485–486. The published version of this report differs in a few unimportant details from the original in the State Department files.

situation which were greatly to his credit. "We sincerely hope," Bryan concluded, "that he represents the views of the Constitutionalists." [15]

Villa may not have represented the views of the majority of the Constitutionalists, but he was in a position to determine their action. On April 25 he sent a personal message to President Wilson, in which he reaffirmed what he had said to Carothers. Specifically, he disavowed the attitude Carranza had expressed and was somewhat apologetic because the situation had been aggravated by the form of the note which the First Chief sent to Washington. Carranza's note, Villa said, "was entirely personal, and the attitude of one person, whatever his momentary authority, cannot carry such weight as to bring on a war between two countries desiring to continue at peace." Villa believed, so he said, that Carranza was endeavoring to uphold the dignity of his country but did not intend that his pronouncement should be considered as hostile toward the United States. [16]

Evidently believing that Villa supported Carranza's stand, the Huertista General Maas wrote to him, urging that all patriotic Mexicans join Huerta to repel the invader. Villa returned a tart reply that left no doubt as to whom he considered the real enemies of Mexico. [17]

In just what way Villa persuaded Carranza to modify his truculent stand remains a mystery. There is some reason to believe that he sent Carranza a message that was actually an ultimatum. [18] An American correspondent related that

when the test of mastery came between Villa and Carranza over the question of the attitude of the Constitutionalists toward the United States, Villa took Carranza aside. . . . "See here," said Villa, bluntly waving his big hands like an angry bear; "I and my men put you where you are, up in the clouds. Don't forget we can pull you back to earth again." [19]

Whatever the means of persuasion may have been, the result was that Carranza found it no longer expedient to express his hostility toward

[15] *Ibid.*, pp. 486–487. In the original document, in the State Department files, the sentence just quoted is in Bryan's own handwriting.

[16] *Ibid.*, p. 488. Carothers transmitted this letter, which was addressed to President Wilson and marked "Personal and Confidential," to the Secretary of State.

[17] San Francisco *Examiner*, May 6, 1914, 2:1.

[18] Mena Brito, *El lugarteniente gris de Pancho Villa*, pp. 69–70. Cf. Francisco Bulnes, *The Whole Truth about Mexico* (New York, 1916), p. 382.

[19] Gregory Mason, "Campaigning in Coahuila," *Outlook*, CVII (June 20, 1914), 397.

the action of the United States, although he never formally retracted his first statement.[20]

Direct pressure on the First Chief was not the only effort made by Villa to prevent Mexicans uniting under Huerta's leadership. Edwin Emerson, the staff correspondent of the New York *World*, learned that a special envoy from Villa, Colonel Fabio de la Garza, had persuaded Zapata to turn a deaf ear to a Huerta emissary who came preaching a holy war of all Mexicans against the invader.[21]

After the first tension died down, Americans who were familiar with the situation felt a glow of gratitude toward the ex-bandit who was credited with preventing all of Mexico from uniting to fight the United States. Alarming reports were circulated that the forces under General Frederick Funston, which had replaced the navy at Veracruz, were in grave danger from General Maas's surrounding Mexican troops. Fear for the safety of the Americans in Veracruz was tempered by the knowledge that Maas would not be reinforced by Villa's veterans.[22] A new picture of Pancho Villa began to form in the vision of the American public—a picture well presented by the *Outlook*'s correspondent:

No one who was present at a dinner given to Villa and his staff by the war correspondents a few days before the start for Saltillo could have come away with the impression that the man is insincere. . . . When the big athlete [Villa] stood up to speak, his huge chest bulging beneath a soft silk shirt, opening to expose his bull neck, he was positively embarrassed. After stammering that he was no speaker and preferred fighting to talking, he forgot his self-consciousness and fairly bellowed out an exhortation for his followers and Americans to practice mutual forbearance and to stand together for the elimination of Huerta. As he spoke his eyes blazed and he hammered the table with his fists, looking not so much like a great general whose name spells terror to his enemies as like a big, earnest boy—the captain of a football team, if you will—urging his companions to fight harder.[23]

[20] *Foreign Relations, 1914*, p. 494.

[21] *Literary Digest*, XLVIII (May 23, 1914), 1236.

[22] San Francisco *Examiner*, May 4, 1914, 1:7. Army forces replaced the navy landing force at Veracruz on April 30. It is very probable that General Funston himself felt no alarm whatever.

[23] Gregory Mason, "The Mexican Man of the Hour," *Outlook*, CVII (June 6, 1914), 305–306.

At the conclusion of his unrehearsed speech, Villa proposed a toast to President Wilson—the only occasion recorded on which Villa was seen to drink anything alcoholic. After the toast, the glasses were smashed on the floor.[24]

To many Americans the image of a big athlete, possibly uncouth in his manners but comparable to an American schoolboy, essentially sincere and in dead earnest, was a picture which they could understand and with which they could sympathize. Immediately forgotten were the stories of Villa's ruthlessness, the killing of Benton and the slaughter of prisoners after each victory. The only thing remembered was the "diamond in the rough" who was a friend of the United States and, lone-handed, had prevented all Mexico from rising against the United States. Rumors in the press that Villa was holding up his advance against Saltillo until the arrival of motion-picture cameras evoked no caustic comment but only sympathetic amusement.[25]

Admiration for the picturesque ex-bandit and self-taught soldier was not completely unanimous among the American people, in spite of widespread gratitude for his stand. President Wilson's political opponents, and particularly those classes and groups who were dissatisfied with his measures for economic and financial reform, saw nothing at all admirable in Villa. Villa's lurid past made him a handy bludgeon with which to belabor the President and his policies. In the Senate, on May 5, 1914, while the situation in Mexico was still doubtful, Senator Henry Cabot Lodge started a speech on Panama Canal tolls, but switched to Mexico. Remarking that the government of Mexico was of supreme interest to the United States, he said: "One of the leading candidates is that general who has distinguished himself so much in northern Mexico lately—Francisco Villa." With this introduction, he then proceeded to read an article which had appeared on April 15 in the London *Daily Telegraph*, entitled "Francisco Villa —A Frightful Career of Murder and Torture." [26]

On the same day Senator Henry F. Lippitt, of Rhode Island, with

[24] John W. Roberts, special correspondent, in the New York *American*, Sunday, May 17, 1914, 2:6.

[25] Harris, *Pancho Villa and the Columbus Raid*, p. 73. Cf. the San Francisco *Examiner*, May 1, 1914, 2:5.

[26] *Cong. Record*, 63 Cong., 2 sess., p. 7727.

the obvious intention of embarrassing the President, introduced a resolution demanding that "the Senate [be informed] whether there is any foundation for the following statement . . . in the Washington *Post* of May the 5th: 'President May Aid Gen. Villa to Become Next Ruler of Mexico.'" [27] The resolution was tabled but not until after acrimonious argument between the President's supporters and the "Old Guard" Republicans.

Many newspapers and magazines became violently pro- or anti-Villa. *Collier's Magazine* devoted an editorial page to quotations from an article by John Reed, whose views had recently appeared in another magazine. *Collier's* concluded with the comment, "It is grotesque that President Wilson, after revolting at Huerta, should find himself giving aid and comfort to, and practically in alliance with, such a leader and such an uprising as Villa's." [28]

If a journal that had supported President Wilson in the past was as caustic as *Collier's*, it is not surprising that editors who were hostile to the administration were even more unrestrained in their remarks. In *Leslie's Illustrated Weekly Newspaper,* Villa was picturesquely presented as "the wolf of the Sierras set to guard the Mexican sheepfold." As if this were not sufficiently horrifying, he was further characterized as "a robber, a murderer, a rapist." By contrast, Huerta was presented as a man who, "with all his faults . . . is a trained soldier, a natural diplomat, who has stood for law and order, the security of life and property." [29]

The correspondent who wrote these words had been with the Huerta forces and was prejudiced in Huerta's favor. The tone of his article was fully in accord with the policy of his journal, as attested by its editorial columns. In the issue for the preceding week the editor had advised that the United States stay out of Mexican affairs because the constitutional President, General Huerta, was perfectly capable of handling the situation. This was written when the United

[27] *Ibid.,* pp. 7720–7721, 8155. Senator Lippitt was the successor of Senator Nelson Aldrich and was a strong proponent of the latter's conservative economic and political ideas.

[28] "Wilson and Mexico," *Collier's Magazine,* LIII (June 13, 1914), 17. It is noteworthy that the editors of *Collier's,* normally well informed and accurate, evidently believed that Villa had started the revolution against Huerta. Farther on in the article cited, reference is made to "Villa's bloody uprising."

[29] F. J. Splitstone, "Looking Ahead in Mexico—A Forecast," *Leslie's Illustrated Weekly Newspaper,* CXIX (July 9, 1914), 33.

States was, to all intents and purposes, at war with Huerta. The same editorial page, revealing other possible motives for disagreement with Wilson's Mexican policy, carried articles headed "Hostility to Business Must Cease" and "The Muckrakers Must Go." [30]

The Hearst papers, though not quite so violent in their objections to association with a bandit, missed no opportunity to use Villa as a weapon against the administration. The New York *American,* for example, printed a large cartoon that showed a benign William Jennings Bryan with his arm about the shoulder of a particularly repulsive caricature of Villa and saying, "He's good enough for me." [31] The same journal was deeply disturbed by a report that the State Department had authorized the delivery of one million dollars' worth of ammunition to Villa and Carranza, because it would probably be used in a few days to "shoot down American boys." [32]

In the noisy war of words, Villa's friends were as vocal as his enemies and likewise included numbers of responsible public men and periodicals of recognized standing. Replying to an attack by Congressman Frank Mondell, Representative William Kent of California, an Independent who had been an insurgent Republican, declared that Villa had proved himself to be a great leader—a brave man who kept his word. "He has, in a crucial time, had the courage . . . to believe our protestations of disinterestedness, and seems to possess such a marvelous power of leadership as to hold his people in leash." [33] The correspondent of *Harper's Weekly* remarked sharply: "Villa may be as cruel and unprincipled as a Nero, but it is about time for sensible Americans to stop referring to him and his generals as mere bandits. He has displayed martial courage and military genius of the highest order." [34]

In general, those who favored Villa in the critical weeks following the seizure of Veracruz seem to have been in the majority. They also had the advantage of including the President himself and the Secretary of State. William Jennings Bryan was quoted as having referred to Villa as "a Sir Galahad." [35] President Wilson told an interviewer that

[30] *Ibid.* (June 25, 1914), p. 14.   [31] New York *American,* May 5, 1914, ed. page.
[32] *Ibid.,* May 10, 1914, 2:2.   [33] *Cong. Record,* 63 Cong., 2 sess., pp. 7339–7340.
[34] McGregor, *Harper's Weekly,* LVIII (May 9, 1914), 10. This correspondent never signed himself otherwise than as indicated here.
[35] Howard F. Cline, *The United States and Mexico* (Cambridge, Mass., 1953), p. 190.

he was much impressed with the consular reports after Villa's capture of Torreón—how the Villistas treated their prisoners with humanity and tried to follow the rules of civilized warfare, so as not to incur "the stigma of being barbarians." [36] The President also, in a private letter to Ambassador Walter Hines Page, in London, observed that it was "most important . . . that people over there should get a more just and correct view of Villa." [37]

Actually, the emotions expressed by the spokesmen in the controversy were too violent to be explained by mere disagreement over the expediency or propriety of favor shown an ex-bandit. The dispute was an extension into the field of foreign affairs of an embittered quarrel that had been going on in the United States for years. With a few exceptions, the people who supported the President and favored Villa were proud to be considered as liberals or progressives. The conservative elements—especially "Old Guard" Republicans—generally opposed everything President Wilson advocated, including his Mexican policy. Speaking strictly from the "progressive" point of view, the editor of *Harper's Weekly* expressed the matter succinctly in his comments on the debate between Representatives Mondell and Kent, to which reference has been made:

The British Tory still regards Charles Stuart a martyr and Cromwell a murderer. The French Royalist still longs for the man on horseback. . . . In America, now that the Mexican question has been so vividly brought to our attention, you will find the Tory denouncing "that murderous and illiterate bandit, Villa," and the Liberal characterizing Huerta as a traitor and a bloody tyrant.[38]

An essential part of the intellectual climate which produced the emotional controversy over Villa was the tendency of the time to see the evil hand of "big business" in all international disputes. To many, the Revolution in Mexico was not an uprising of the Mexican people against intolerable conditions but rather a brawl for supremacy among rival groups of predatory capitalists. "Lurking in the background of

---

[36] Samuel G. Blythe, "Mexico: The Record of a Conversation with President Wilson," *Saturday Evening Post*, May 23, 1914, quoted in full in the *Cong. Record*, 63 Cong., 2 sess., pp. 9095–9097.

[37] Baker, *Woodrow Wilson*, IV, 347.

[38] Editorial in *Harper's Weekly*, LVIII (May 16, 1914), 3.

every discussion of any phase of the chaos in Mexico," said the *Review of Reviews*, "is the general assumption that, in some way, 'Big Business,' operating through the banking houses of London and New York, is the real, but invisible force that is dominating things south of the Rio Grande." [39]

It was generally believed that Huerta was favored by "the interests," but charges were not lacking that Villa was merely a tool to further the machinations of "Wall Street." In New York, shortly after the seizure of Veracruz, Bouck White, a socialistically inclined clergyman, proclaimed that President Wilson was nothing but a puppet in the hands of the corporate interests that wanted war.[40] The editor of *Collier's Magazine* claimed to "know all about the connection between the rebel junta at Washington and certain American oil interests." [41] No elaboration was given of the innuendo, but the inference was unmistakable.

But such allegations did not seem to attract much popular interest, and the controversy over Villa soon died down. The attention of that small segment of the public that was really interested in Mexican affairs was diverted to the Niagara Falls Conference and its unsuccessful efforts to mediate between the Mexican parties. Before the summer of 1914 was over, the situation in Mexico was all but forgotten in the shadow of the clouds that arose over Europe.

One can reasonably conclude that, but for the former bandit, Francisco Villa, the results of the occupation of Veracruz would have been far different from what they actually were. Hostility to the United States was almost an integral part of the Mexican national tradition, suspicion of American motives a certainty in the thinking of even educated Mexicans. With the nominal head of the Constitutionalist Party openly resentful, with the Constitutionalist general who was next to Villa himself in prominence frankly advocating war with the United States, one word from Villa could have precipitated disaster. That word was not spoken. Instead, the whole weight of his influence was thrown toward maintaining peace with the United States. This was

[39] *Review of Reviews*, XLIX (1914), 279.

[40] New York *Times*, May 4, 1914, 2:5. It is interesting to note that Bouck White was arrested a few days later for creating a disturbance in church by "heckling" John D. Rockefeller.

[41] "Wilson and Mexico," *Collier's Magazine*, LIII (1914), 17.

a point that did not receive due attention from those critics of President Wilson and his policies who were horrified at the thought of diplomatic association with a bandit and who were shocked at the bandit's disregard of property and life.

While the furor over the propriety of association with Villa was going on in the United States, the war in Mexico continued its tragic course. The border, however, was quiet as the fighting moved southward. In the vicinity of El Paso, Villista patrols along the Rio Grande were accompanied by American cavalry patrols on their own side of the river because there had been a disagreeable incident when a Huertista sympathizer fired on the Villistas from the American side.[42] Carranza somewhat curtly rejected the well-meant efforts of the commissioners at Niagara Falls to impose an armistice. Meanwhile, the Constitutionalist armies steadily pressed their advantage.[43] Constitutionalist forces under General Pablo González occupied Tampico on May 14, 1914. The Federals made no attempt to defend Saltillo, where a fierce fight had been anticipated, and on May 20 Villa moved into the city.

The smoothness of the Constitutionalist advance southward was interrupted by the defeat of General Natera in his attempt to storm Zacatecas, but the interruption was only temporary. Villa's forces moved toward the city, and on June 23, after four days of stiff fighting, they swept over the Federal defenses and chalked up one more spectacular victory. Preparations were made for the usual execution of the captured Federal officers, but Villa, in high good humor, unexpectedly spared their lives.[44]

To all appearances, the ordeal through which Mexico was passing had nearly run its course. The capture of Zacatecas destroyed the last hope of Huerta and his sympathizers. At the same time, news dispatches carried the information that the Niagara Falls Conference had reached a workable solution for the problems of the unhappy country. After a conference with the Secretary of State on June 25, President Wilson authorized a statement that the Mexican situation was more promising than it had ever been before.[45] One more push by the combined insurgent armies in the north would seemingly end the war.

[42] Peter B. Kyne, "With the Border Patrol," *Collier's Magazine,* LIII (1914), 10–11.

[43] *Foreign Relations, 1914,* pp. 514–515.

[44] *Independent,* LXXIX (July 6, 1914), 8.

[45] New York *Times,* Friday, June 26, 1914, 5:1.

The world was consequently mystified by a lengthy statement issued to the press by Captain Alfredo Breceda, Carranza's private secretary, who arrived at Washington late on the night of June 26. Breceda accused General Felipe Angeles, Villa's chief of artillery and reputedly the most brilliant professional soldier in Mexico, of fomenting discord between Carranza and Villa. The mystery was intensified a few days later when it became known that Villa was moving the greater part of his forces northward, instead of grouping them for the final and decisive blow.

Trouble was obviously brewing between Villa and the First Chief, although the details of the disagreement and the underlying reasons for it were entirely unknown. A rift between the two had been rumored for a long time. In November of the previous year, Mrs. Edith O'Shaughnessy, strongly pro-Huerta, noted rumors in Mexico City that Villa had proclaimed himself the head of the revolutionary forces because of Carranza's inaction. This, she believed, signified the imminent rise of a second party in the north. It was probably the same rumor that caused Francisco Escudero, the acting Foreign Minister in Carranza's cabinet, to inform the press that there was no possibility of a break between Carranza and Villa.[46]

The rumor Mrs. O'Shaughnessy noted was baseless, but stories of disagreement persisted. Commenting on Villa's capture of Ojinaga, the *Review of Reviews* remarked, in February, 1914, that as far as was known Villa still recognized Carranza as the head of the Constitutionalist government, although little had been heard of Carranza recently. There were even rumors that he was dead.[47] In a midnight interview with General Hugh L. Scott, on the international bridge at El Paso, in February, 1914, Villa stressed his unswerving loyalty to Carranza, adding that he would give up his command on Carranza's order.[48] The capture of Torreón gave rise to a new crop of rumors that Villa was about to oust Carranza—rumors that Villa's continued protestations of loyalty did not entirely dispel. That Villa did not always see eye to eye with the First Chief and was capable of forcing his own views upon Carranza was clearly shown at the time of the Veracruz affair. In spite

[46] Edith O'Shaughnessy, *A Diplomat's Wife in Mexico*, p. 63. Cf. the New York *Times*, Monday, Dec. 1, 1913, 1:8.
[47] *Review of Reviews*, XLIX (1914), 152.
[48] Scott to his wife, Feb. 14, 1914, Hugh Lenox Scott Papers, Library of Congress.

of the open disagreement at that time, Villa denied any but the most cordial relations between himself and Carranza.[49]

Coming at the moment when President Wilson's policies toward Mexico seemed to be reaching full success, the rift threatened to be disastrous. Huerta could be trusted to take full advantage of any discord among his enemies, and the efforts of the United States to bring peace to Mexico by eliminating him would be totally wasted. The State Department therefore stirred itself, as the rumors became thicker, to reconcile the two revolutionary chiefs. Secretary Bryan sent an urgent telegram to Carothers, directing him to emphasize to both Villa and Carranza how disastrous it would be if they were to fall out at this time. "They must have confidence in each other and work together until they secure the reforms necessary for the restoration of permanent peace and prosperity."[50] On the same day, July 3, John R. Silliman, who had been the American vice-consul at Saltillo and who was well acquainted with Carranza, was sent posthaste from Washington to Mexico to confer with him.[51]

The published accounts of the disagreement between the two Constitutionalist leaders were vague. From the moment when the first reports leaked out that all was not well between Villa and Carranza, fantastic stories began to circulate. On July 1 newspapers in the United States carried the startling information that General Felipe Angeles had been executed the preceding day by Villa's personal order.[52] Felix Sommerfeld, credited with being Villa's "chief personal agent" in the United States, informed the press that he did not believe the report; Villa was neither disloyal to Carranza nor planning a new uprising.[53] Villa himself promptly sent a telegram flatly denying that Angeles had been executed, although by some strange quirk this telegram was published as a denial by Villa that Angeles had been executed by Carranza.[54]

In such an atmosphere of confusion and uncertainty, the American public was ready to believe almost anything. When, within a few days, an explanation appeared that presented the matter in terms of "big

[49] San Francisco *Examiner*, Saturday, May 2, 1914, 2:1.
[50] *Foreign Relations, 1914*, pp. 556–557.
[51] *Ibid*. Cf. the New York *Times*, Friday, July 3, 1914, 3:4.
[52] New York *Tribune*, Wednesday, July 1, 1914, 1:7–8.
[53] New York *Times*, Wednesday, July 1, 1914, 2:2.
[54] New York *Tribune*, Thursday, July 2, 1914, 2:1.

business" and "Wall Street," the mystery seemed to be solved. In circumstances that have never been explained, some correspondence was stolen from "Captain" Sherburne G. Hopkins, a Washington attorney. Hopkins' principal client was Henry Clay Pierce, a millionaire oil magnate with large interests in Mexico. The letters, published in a New York newspaper, seemed to indicate that Hopkins was promoting a reorganization of the Mexican railways in a way from which his client would profit immensely. Hopkins, it appeared, had so far insinuated himself into Carranza's confidence as to be a close adviser and had managed to get an old friend, Alberto J. Pani, named as manager of the railroads under Constitutionalist control. The scheme had been foiled by Villa, who refused to allow Pani to take charge of the railroads in territory under his authority. Over this, a sordid matter by which rich Americans expected to profit, the two leaders had quarreled, according to the interpretation of the New York *Herald*, in which the stolen letters were published.[55]

Such a simple and facile explanation was readily accepted by Americans who saw in Mexico's troubles merely an extension of the issues that had agitated the United States during the early years of the century. Intrigues in Wall Street and selfish lust for wealth by unscrupulous and predatory capitalists formed a satisfying explanation for any disagreeable and obscure occurrence. The *Herald* said: "The real cradle of Mexican liberty has been revealed—it is Wall Street." [56]

There was probably no real substance behind this oversimplified explanation, despite the fact that Pani was subsequently designated as the director-general of the railways under Carranza's control.[57] A definite effect of the report was to present Villa as a champion who opposed the underhanded schemes of foreign capitalists as courageously as he opposed the soldiers of Victoriano Huerta. In the eyes of his admirers, his stature as a potential statesman increased.

While American newspaper readers were being informed that Villa and Carranza were merely puppets moved by conflicting business interests, the representatives of the State Department were laboring to

[55] Quoted in the *Nation*, XCIX (July 2, 1914), 7. Cf. the *Literary Digest*, XLIX (July 11, 1914), 48. Sherburne G. Hopkins, a Washington attorney (always referred to as "Captain," for some unknown reason), is a shadowy figure whose activities were regarded with suspicion by several United States officials.

[56] *Nation*, Vol. XCIX (July 2, 1914), p. 7.

[57] Alberto J. Pani, *Mi contribución al nuevo régimen* (Mexico City, 1936), p. 212.

bring about a reconciliation between the two. Carothers was able to see Villa on July 5, shortly after receiving instructions from Washington. After the interview, he was extremely noncommittal with the newspaper correspondents, but he sent an optimistic telegram to the State Department. Villa was fully aware, he reported, of the disastrous possibilities involved in a break with the First Chief. Villa's attitude toward Carranza, nevertheless, was almost bitter. "Is it possible," he asked Carothers, "that a great nation like yours can not see what kind of a man Carranza is . . . ?" Carothers left the interview believing that Villa would patriotically make every effort to reach an understanding with Carranza and was even willing, if necessary, to eliminate himself.[58]

Silliman, appointed as special agent with Carranza, was unable to see him until the afternoon of July 9. By that time, to all appearances, the difficulties between the two chiefs had been reconciled. Consequently, Silliman made no effort to act as a peacemaker but confined himself to trying to persuade Carranza to accept the recommendations of the Niagara Falls Conference. In this he was unsuccessful, for Carranza, backed by his generals (presumably including Villa), was determined to accept nothing less than unconditional surrender by the Huertistas.[59]

On July 9, 1914, the day on which Silliman interviewed Carranza, Villa personally handed Carothers the text of an agreement which his representatives had reached with Carranza's agents after several days of conference at Torreón. Both Villa and Carranza accepted the agreement, and the breach appeared to be healed, with the Constitutionalists again presenting a united front to their enemies. In the agreement Carranza was recognized as the First Chief, while Villa himself continued as commander of the Division of the North. Villa was granted control over the railroads in his zone and was permitted to retain General Felipe Angeles on his staff. A list of names was prepared from which Carranza agreed to choose his cabinet. Last was a brief declaration of the principles for which the Constitutionalists were fighting. Recognizing that the Revolution sprang from social and economic abuses, the agreement specified reform measures. Land would be reapportioned for the benefit of the peasantry, the welfare of labor assured, and laws enacted to "hold to their responsibilities such mem-

---

[58] *Foreign Relations, 1914*, p. 557.   [59] *Ibid.*, pp. 562–563.

bers of the Roman Catholic clergy as may have lent moral or physical support to the usurper." [60]

Next day, July 10, Carranza informed Consul General Philip Hanna, at Monterrey, that there was now a satisfactory understanding among all the revolutionary leaders. In spite of this, he requested at the same time that the United States keep the border closed to munitions but permit shipment of arms and ammunition to Tampico.[61] Since this would deny munitions to Villa while making them available to Carranza, it appeared that he had little confidence in the effectiveness of the agreement.

Concurrently with the friction between the two leaders came more trouble. On July 3 it became known that the Constitutionalists at Zacatecas—that is, the Villistas—had arrested Donald St. Clair Douglas, the British vice-consul, charging him with spying and operating a searchlight for the Federals during the battle. He was to be tried by court-martial, and if found guilty he would probably be shot. The Benton affair had not been entirely forgotten, and Benton was a private citizen. The execution, or even the mistreatment, of His Majesty's vice-consul would be infinitely more grave.[62]

Villa was at Juárez when the arrest occurred. He was not personally involved, although it was done under his authority. He telegraphed orders that there must be no hasty or summary action; the trial must be absolutely fair. Consul Theodore C. Hamm hurried to Zacatecas to prevent another Benton case. The Mexicans were no more anxious for such an affair than the British and Americans. Both Villista and Carranzista officials assured the British vice-consul at El Paso that no action would be taken before Hamm's arrival, and Villa himself promised full "consideration and justice." [63] The trial, which was prompt, resulted in acquittal, but Douglas was ordered to leave Mexico immediately. The chancelleries of Great Britain and the United States were greatly relieved.[64]

[60] *Ibid.*, pp. 559–560. The list of names from which Carranza agreed to select his cabinet and which met with Villa's approval included Alberto J. Pani.

[61] *Ibid.*, pp. 560–561. Immediately after the seizure of Veracruz, the United States had reimposed the embargo upon shipment of arms and munitions to Mexico.

[62] New York *Times*, Saturday, July 4, 1914, 3:3.

[63] London *Times*, Monday, July 6, 1914, 8:3. American newspapers all referred to Douglas as a vice-consul, but the London *Times* made no mention of any official position.

[64] New York *Times*, Tuesday, July 7, 1914, 2:6.

Rumors, many of them completely absurd, continued to circulate. The flurry over Douglas had scarcely died down when a report appeared in Mexico City, repeated in the United States, that Villa had been killed by a woman in Torreón. The story, started in Mexico City, where Huerta was still firmly entrenched, may have been a bit of wishful thinking on the part of the Federals. Before the rumor could affect the political situation, it was promptly scotched by a telegram from Villa to the New York *Times,* saying that he was very much alive and anxious for the next blow against Huerta.[65]

The "next blow" against Huerta did not fall. The strong-willed old despot finally recognized that the odds against him were too great, with the United States implacably hostile, Zapata pressing from the south, and his northern enemies again united. Early in the second week of July, 1914, American newspapers were predicting his resignation, and on July 15, Cardoso de Oliveira, the Brazilian minister to Mexico, who had represented the United States since O'Shaughnessy's departure, notified the State Department that Huerta's resignation was expected that afternoon.[66]

The sensational news was emblazoned across the front pages of the newspapers the next day. President Wilson's policy had proved successful, and by encouraging the Constitutionalists, the United States had driven the "usurper" from the presidency of Mexico. Secretary Bryan jubilantly cabled to Cardoso that the resignation of Huerta would greatly simplify matters. All that remained to be done, Bryan believed, was for the new Provisional President, Licenciado Francisco Carbajal, to transfer the office peacefully to Carranza.[67]

Villa's reaction to the news of Huerta's resignation was one of skepticism. His first opinion was that Huerta had resigned the presidency so as to take the field in active command of his armies, and Villa looked forward to the opportunity to cross swords personally with his old enemy. Disappointed in this hope, he kept his own counsel and continued to recruit and strengthen his forces.

[65] New York *Times,* Thursday, July 9, 1914, 1:2; Saturday, July 11, 1914, 2:1.
[66] San Francisco *Chronicle,* Tuesday, July 14, 1914, 1:1. Cf. *Foreign Relations, 1914,* p. 563.
[67] *Foreign Relations, 1914,* p. 564.

❧ VIII ❧

Paul Fuller, Envoy to Villa

IN Washington there were high hopes of final and permanent peace in Mexico as soon as it became certain that Huerta was really eliminating himself from the scene. Secretary Bryan telegraphed to the Brazilian minister, who was representing the United States in Mexico, "We take it for granted that the new President will immediately enter into negotiations with Carranza for the peaceful transfer of authority," adding that the United States would use all its influence to bring all parties together. To Silliman, the special agent with Carranza, Bryan telegraphed instructions to remain until further orders, so that contact with Carranza would be assured. Bryan further directed Silliman to urge Carranza to send emissaries at once to Carbajal, for "the war would seem to be over and all that remains to be done can be done peacefully and a pacific entrance into Mexico City will greatly aid in assuring friendly intercourse with the outside world." [1]

The possibility that Carranza might be a mere figurehead, a front for Villa, found no expression in the instructions Bryan sent to Oliveira and Silliman. Rather, there is the unexpressed, but implicit, conviction that the final decision in matters of real importance rested with Carranza. At the same time the Secretary of State was not unaware of the possibility that Villa, who had so long dominated the daily headlines, was still a factor to be considered. Immediately after receiving informa-

[1] *Foreign Relations, 1914,* p. 564.

99

tion that Carranza was willing to receive emissaries from Carbajal—on the same day, in fact—Bryan telegraphed to Collector Zach Cobb, at El Paso, asking him to transmit a message to Carothers or if Villa happened to be at Juárez to give him the message directly. The message was that the President was very anxious that nothing should delay the reforms needed to restore justice to the Mexican people. The President was certain that General Villa would use his influence to preserve harmony and ensure co-operation among the Constitutionalists.[2]

The dispatch of identical messages of advice to both Carranza and Villa on July 23 further emphasized that the United States still regarded Villa as a power in Mexico, but one whose relationship to the First Chief was doubtful. The two leaders were reminded, rather obliquely, that recognition by the United States was vital for any Mexican government and that the conduct of the Constitutionalists at their moment of triumph would determine whether or not the United States would feel justified in recognizing the new regime. Specifically, they were advised that the new government must recognize the rights of foreigners, legitimate financial obligations incurred by Huerta must be settled, relations with the Church must be handled with due deference to the opinion of the outside world, and there must be no general proscription of political opponents.[3]

Carranza's reply, transmitted through Silliman, was extremely non-committal. The First Chief promised that the lives and property of foreigners would be protected "in the future as they have been in the past" and that obligations contracted by a legitimate Mexican government would be honored. As for the other points stressed by the American note, Carranza promised nothing more than to give them careful study.[4]

What Francisco Villa's reaction may have been to the identical note sent to him is conjectural. He and Carothers probably discussed the matter at length, and Villa certainly discussed it with his trusted advisers, but there is no record of his reply, if he made one.

Throughout the month of July, 1914, in spite of the apparent reconciliation between Carranza and Villa, rumors continued to filter to Washington that the rift between the two was not really healed. On July 18, General Hugh L. Scott, now stationed at Washington, wrote to his wife, who was away for the summer:

[2] *Ibid.*, p. 567.   [3] *Ibid.*, pp. 568–570.   [4] *Ibid.*, p. 575.

Villa telegraphed me six big pages of letter paper giving his reasons for coming north from Zacatecas & asked me to put it in the hands of the President. The State Dept. sent in here asking for it before I knew anything about it—& it came in shortly after—it seems that some of their people on the border telegraphed them that it was on the way it said in substance that Carranza was preventing him from getting coal and ammunition to go further into Mexico on account of jealousy of his division that had had the good fortune to distinguish itself—he protested his lack of personal ambition saying he was fighting for his country and would not fight Carranza unless attacked, then only in self defense. . . . I took it at once to the Sec'y War telling him the Constitutionalists [Villistas] did not want it to [get] to Mr. Bryan's hands because he would at once let the Carranza people have it & so widen the breach—the Asst Secy took it to the President who said he would not let it out.[5]

A few days later the chief surgeon of the American Smelting and Refining Company wrote to Scott, saying that matters between Villa and Carranza were only "patched up." [6] Innumerable straws in the wind indicated further trouble. Obregón continued toward Mexico City, but the Division of the North, the spearhead of the Revolution, remained in its billets. There were disquieting reports that Villa, with his division inactive and the war apparently almost over, was increasing his forces and accumulating reserves of arms and munitions.

The United States continued efforts to bring about a peaceful transfer of authority to the Constitutionalists. A meeting between representatives of Carranza and Carbajal to arrange for a conference on terms of surrender failed completely. Carranza grimly refused any terms except unconditional surrender, in spite of strong representations from Washington as to the necessity for reasonable concessions to the Federals.[7]

While efforts were being made to bring the factions together for a conference, the long-dreaded general war started in Europe. President Wilson, in addition to the problems of his internal program and the anxieties of the Mexican situation, now found himself confronted by the difficulties of safeguarding the neutrality of the United States in a world

[5] General Scott to his wife, July 18, 1914, Hugh Lenox Scott Papers, Library of Congress. Scott was made Assistant Chief of Staff of the Army on April 22, 1914. He became Chief of Staff on Nov. 17, 1914.

[6] Dr. Carlos Rusk to General Scott, July 27, 1914, *ibid*.

[7] *Foreign Relations, 1914*, pp. 564, 566, 567, 571, 573, 580.

at war. For days, in early August, 1914, he probably had little time for Mexico. The sudden eruption of the European war strengthened his hand in one particular. There was now no possibility of interference, or even serious objection, by any European power to any measures the United States might take in Mexico.

Carranza's stubborn refusal to consider suggestions made by the United States undoubtedly caused the President to think of Villa, whose status, as has been emphasized, was still uncertain. The administration's disappointment and irritation at Carranza were reflected in a rather sharp note for Carranza's personal attention, dispatched on July 21:

Our advice offered, and everything stated in our telegram of the 23d, cannot be modified, nor can we recede from it in the least without deep and perhaps fatal consequences to the cause of the present revolution which, if that advice is accepted in the spirit in which it is given, may now be made completely and gloriously successful. This Government is reluctant to contemplate the possible consequences to Mexico if it should be forced to withhold recognition from those who are now to succeed General Huerta.[8]

President Wilson and his Secretary of State both found it impossible to believe that the differences between Carranza and Villa were too deep, too fundamental, to be settled by negotiation. On August 11 Secretary Bryan sent messages to Carothers and Silliman, saying that the President believed that "the differences which are said to exist between Generals Carranza and Villa are not so grave as some would have them appear." The two special agents were directed to try to bring about a meeting between Carranza and Villa, "under favorable circumstances, free from partisan influence." Then the spirit of patriotism which motivated the two leaders would undoubtedly enable them to arrive at a workable solution.[9]

President Wilson was in a quandary. He was desperately anxious that the war in Mexico should not break out again, and he was sincerely, almost fanatically, anxious for the right to prevail. As to what constituted the right, and his role in bringing about a victory of the right, he had expressed a few days after the seizure of Veracruz:

My ideal is an orderly and righteous government in Mexico; but my passion is for the submerged eighty-five percent of the people of that Republic, who are now struggling toward liberty. . . . They [the special interests, the aris-

---

[8] *Ibid.*, pp. 578–579. Silliman delivered this message to Carranza on Aug. 2.
[9] *Ibid.*, p. 584.

tocracy, etc.] want order—the old order; but I say to you that the old order is dead. It is my part, as I see it, to aid in composing those differences so far as I may be able, that the new order, which will have its foundation on human liberty and human rights, shall prevail.[10]

To fulfill successfully such idealistic purposes, it was essential that the two revolutionary leaders be reconciled. Failing in that, the President must decide which of them was most deserving of his support. The information upon which to base so momentous a decision, he felt, was not yet sufficiently complete. In his own words, "In the Mexican matter there was a time when it did not appear who in Mexico was a sincere friend of the people." [11]

President Wilson held favorable views of both Carranza and Villa. He told Sir William Tyrrell that he had confidence in Carranza, and in April, 1914, when the first rumors of a rift began to circulate, he had written to General Scott that "General Villa certainly seems capable of some good things and often shows susceptibilities of the best influence." [12]

To determine as objectively as possible which of the two rival leaders was most likely to be a "sincere friend of the people," the President decided to send another personal representative to Mexico. By this means he hoped to get an unprejudiced and unbiased picture of the situation. Although the practice of sending personal representatives was regarded with some disfavor by the regular diplomatic and consular officers, it had the obvious advantage for the President of giving him information from a person whose judgment he trusted and who was responsible to him alone.

Consequently, on August 10, 1914, Collector Zach Cobb, at El Paso, was requested by the Secretary of State to inform General Villa that the President was sending a personal friend with a message.[13] The friend whom the President selected for this mission was Paul Fuller, a prominent New York attorney.[14]

[10] Samuel G. Blythe, "Mexico: The Record of a Conversation with President Wilson," *Saturday Evening Post*, CLXXXVI, pt. 2 (May 23, 1914), 3.

[11] Ida M. Tarbell, "A Talk with the President of the United States," *Collier's Magazine*, LVIII (Oct. 28, 1916), 6.

[12] President Wilson to General Scott, April 16, 1914, Hugh Lenox Scott Papers.

[13] National Archives, State Department File no. 812.00/12800, Aug. 10, 1914.

[14] No record has been found, either in the Woodrow Wilson Papers or the State Department files, of Fuller's instructions. It is possible that he received them orally from the President himself.

Fuller was received at Juárez by General Juan Medina, Villa's former chief of staff. He was now acting in the dual capacity of mayor of Juárez and Villa's personal representative, with instructions to accompany Fuller. A special car was attached to the train for Chihuahua, where Villa was supposed to be at the time. On Fuller's arrival at Chihuahua, General Felipe Angeles presented himself to pay his respects to the President's envoy. He and Fuller had a long conservation, during which Angeles remarked that Villa was still "incomplete" but was developing rapidly. Villa was willing, Angeles emphasized, to eliminate any military men from the new government which was to be formed.[15]

Villa had not remained at Chihuahua but had gone to Santa Rosalía, leaving another special car to carry Fuller to him. At Santa Rosalía, after several somewhat formal interviews, the two men had a long private conversation, during which Fuller gave Villa a personal letter from President Wilson and sounded him out on various subjects.[16]

Fuller was more than favorably impressed. He reported:

Villa is an unusually quiet man, gentle in manner, low-voiced, slow of speech, earnest and occasionally emotional in expression, but always subdued, with an undercurrent of sadness. He has no outward manifestation of vanity or self-sufficiency, is conscious of his own shortcomings and his lack of preparation for the task of reorganization.

During the talk, Villa told Fuller at length of his lifelong desire to see his people raised from virtual serfdom and become a democratic people without a specially privileged class.

Reminded that if the United States withheld recognition from the new government he would be responsible for peace and order in northern Mexico, Villa replied: "I will pledge myself to preserve the peace throughout the district under my command." He promised also to take immediate action in Sonora, where fighting between Governor Maytorena's Yaqui Indians and the Carranzistas was endangering Americans on the border. Fuller questioned Villa about a statement

---

[15] All details of Fuller's mission are taken from his report, "Memorandum for the President," National Archives, State Department File no. 812.00/15013, Aug. 20, 1914.

[16] No record copy of this letter could be located. It is quite likely that it was written by President Wilson personally, on his own typewriter, and no copy preserved.

that had appeared in the El Paso *Times* on August 14, in which Villa was quoted as saying that no military man should hold office in the new government and that the promised agrarian reforms should be accomplished in consonance with the Constitution and laws. Villa confirmed the statement unhesitatingly, adding that he desired no office at all for himself.

On the return journey, Villa accompanied Fuller as far as Chihuahua. Fuller again had a long private conversation with him. Villa related the story of his own life, describing how, at the age of fourteen and a half, he had shot the rich *hacendado* who attempted to seduce his sister and how he was compelled to become an outlaw. Fuller took this occasion to stress President Wilson's hope that there would be no vindictive treatment of political enemies and that the Church would not be persecuted for the misdeeds of a few individuals. Asked about a visit to Carranza by a personal representative of the President, Villa replied that such a visit might be worth while. After a crowded schedule, Fuller boarded the train at El Paso, bearing a personal letter from Villa to the President in reply to Wilson's message and carrying in his mind a picture of Francisco Villa as a man "of frankness and sincerity of purpose."

The letter which Fuller bore for the President was brief:

HONORED SIR:

Your valued letter of the ninth of the current month was handed to me by Mr. Paul Fuller, whom you were so kind as to introduce to me and whose acquaintance was most agreeable to me. Having had the opportunity of prolonged conversation with him upon various matters relating to the international problems of our country, which we desire to see resolved in a just manner and in accordance with the provisions of the Constitution of 1857 by which we are governed.

Mr. Fuller will give you full details of our interviews and advise you of our controlling desire for a pacific solution of our difficulties providing always that the aspirations of our people are satisfied.

I am sincerely grateful for the good wishes you express and I avail myself of this opportunity to subscribe myself

Your obedient and respectful servant
FRANCISCO VILLA [17]

[17] State Department translation, included as an enclosure with Fuller's report. See note 15, *supra.*

Just what took place on Fuller's arrival at Washington is not recorded, but it is a safe assumption that the President heard his favorable impressions. President Wilson now had firsthand information, but he was not yet compelled to make an irrevocable decision. Although, hour by hour, the situation in Mexico was becoming more critical and there was sharp fighting in Sonora, the two leaders had not yet openly broken with each other. There was still hope that they could be reconciled and that the victory over Huerta meant lasting peace for Mexico.

Actual events in Mexico, in the meanwhile, were by no means at a standstill. On the very day on which Fuller, en route from El Paso to Washington, was busily composing his "Memorandum for the President," Carranza triumphantly entered Mexico City. Five days earlier, on August 15, 1914, General Alvaro Obregón's forces quietly moved into the city. Carranza had stubbornly ignored all the well-meant suggestions and advice from Washington, and his victory now seemed to be complete. He was unhampered by any conditions of surrender. His authority over Mexico was admitted by both the United States and Great Britain, as evidenced by a request from London that the United States use its influence with Carranza to prevent further depredations against the property of the British-owned Mazapil Copper Company in states which were actually held by Villa.[18]

There was, unfortunately, still abundant reason to fear that the rift between the two leaders of the Constitutionalists was not entirely healed. It was noted that the troops which Obregón led into Mexico City—troops which formed the basis for Carranza's power and authority—were entirely of Obregón's personal following. A week before the entry of the Constitutionalists into the capital it became known that Carranza had not invited Villa to participate in the victory parade or even to be represented. All the troops having the honor of making the triumphal entry into the city and of guarding the First Chief came from Obregón's forces. The famous Division of the North was pointedly ignored, and this fact did not auger well for the immediate future of Mexico and President Wilson's hopes of a permanent and just peace.

There were other indications that did not look propitious. Early in August, Villa outlawed the Carranza fiat currency that was circulating in his territory. At the same time he appointed a commission, headed by General Felipe Angeles, to begin work upon dividing up the great

[18] National Archives, State Department File no. 312.115 M 451/12, July 31, 1914.

estates of "unfriendly" people. It was reported that already eighty families were quartered on the great ranch which had belonged to William S. Benton and that foreign property owners in the State of Chihuahua were being driven out by new taxes that amounted to virtual confiscation.[19]

Another complicating factor affecting the new government of Mexico, and consequently affecting the relations of the United States with both Carranza and Villa, was the presence in southern Mexico of another revolutionary party and another active rebel army. General Emiliano Zapata had been in rebellion since the days of Díaz. He had refused to acknowledge the Madero government and had never subscribed to the Constitutionalists' Plan of Guadalupe. Instead, he issued his own Plan of Ayala, calling for the immediate confiscation and division of all the great estates. During the war against Huerta he had been in *de facto* co-operation with the Constitutionalists simply because he was fighting the same enemy. The United States, in its efforts to bring about peace in Mexico and to eliminate Huerta, had never entirely lost sight of Zapata, but he was so far distant that there had been little, if any, contact with him. No attempt had ever been made to establish the quasi-diplomatic relations that had been maintained with Villa.

With peace seemingly assured, it now became of superlative importance to gain Zapata's adherence to the new government. The possibility of an open split between Villa and Carranza accentuated the necessity. Soon after entering Mexico City, the First Chief intimated to Silliman that possibly the good offices of the United States might be useful in promoting a conference and understanding with Zapata.[20]

The Secretary of State responded at once to this suggestion and named a certain Hall, said to be a personal friend of Zapata, as special representative to attempt to bring about an understanding between the southern general and the Constitutionalists.[21] Long before Hall could leave the United States—in fact, before Bryan could reply to Silliman's message—Silliman reported that Zapata was decidedly unfriendly in his attitude toward Carranza; he had disarmed and was holding two thousand Constitutionalist soldiers and was treating Villa emissaries at his headquarters with the highest consideration.[22]

[19] *Independent*, LXXIX (Aug. 17, 1914), 235. The latter statement is not confirmed by State Department records.
[20] *Foreign Relations, 1914*, p. 589.   [21] *Ibid.*, p. 592.   [22] *Ibid.*, p. 591.

Nor was this all. On September 1, a new special representative of the State Department, Leon J. Canova, who had been sent to Mexico to assist Carothers, reported that Carranza had not waited for the good offices of the United States but had sent delegates directly to treat with Zapata. The result was 100 per cent failure. Reflecting a determination as stubborn as that of Carranza himself, Zapata refused to yield one iota from his insistence upon his Plan of Ayala. He intimated that he had an understanding with Villa and said flatly that he would promise nothing without Villa's concurrence.[23]

In view of the strong suspicion that the breach between Villa and Carranza was not entirely healed, Zapata's attitude was of the utmost significance. It indicated that Villa was still distrustful of the First Chief and his motives, and it proved beyond doubt that Villa's influence extended far beyond the limits of his direct authority.

With all hopes gone of bringing about an understanding with Zapata, Carranza informed Silliman, on September 14, that matters had come to an open rupture. Two Zapata envoys were imprisoned, and Carranza declared that prison awaited any others who might come. Silliman, in reporting this unfortunate turn of events, added that Carothers believed that Villa would never approve an attack upon Zapata.[24]

A few days later further circumstantial proof appeared of the existence of a sympathetic understanding between Villa and Zapata. One Jenkinson, the American Red Cross representative in Mexico, visited Zapata. He was received very cordially and had a long conversation with the Morelian chief. On returning to Mexico City he informed Silliman that Zapata sharply criticized Carranza for making his triumphal entry into the capital without a Villa representative. Jenkinson confirmed the previous report that there were Villa agents at Zapata's headquarters, who were being treated with deference and great consideration.[25]

Although vitally interested in relations between Villa, Carranza, and Zapata, the immediate attention of the United States was suddenly focused far to the north, on the hamlet of Naco, lying sprawled astride the border between Arizona and Sonora. For several weeks the partisans of Villa and the forces loyal to Carranza in the State of Sonora had been in open conflict. A Carranzista force was besieged in Naco, Sonora, by

---

[23] *Ibid.*, pp. 592–593.   [24] *Ibid.*, p. 596.
[25] National Archives, State Department File no. 812.00/15013, Aug. 20, 1914.

the pro-Villa forces of Governor Maytorena. Shots from the Mexican side of the line wounded several people in the United States, and there was grave danger that the undisciplined Yaqui Indians, who formed a large part of Maytorena's army, would sooner or later cross the boundary, forcing the United States to take drastic action. There was serious danger, too, that the fighting in Sonora would spread to the rest of Mexico. This was the gist of the unfortunate situation to which Villa had promised Paul Fuller that he would give his immediate personal attention.

On August 16 General Obregón suggested to the First Chief that he be authorized to go to Chihuahua to confer with Villa face to face, in an effort to solve the Sonora difficulties. Carranza approved, and on August 24, 1914, Obregón arrived at Villa's headquarters. Villa received him with great friendliness, saying: "Look here, my friend—if you had come with troops, we would have received you with bullets, but since you come alone, you are perfectly safe; Francisco Villa is not treacherous. The destinies of our country are in your hands and mine." [26]

Next day, in Washington, General Scott received a telegram from Villa, saying that he and General Obregón had been "specially commissioned by Señor Carranza to go to Sonora" to put a stop to the troubles there. Villa requested that Scott obtain permission for him and Obregón to pass through United States territory with an armed bodyguard, in a special military train.[27] General Scott had the highest regard for Villa at this time, as ample evidence proves, but he was unable, or unwilling, to permit a body of armed Villista soldiers on United States soil. He told his wife, in his daily letter, that he was afraid that Villa might become quarrelsome. The State Department was arranging for the passage of Villa and Obregón through the United States to Sonora with an American, rather than a Mexican, escort.[28]

On August 26 Villa and Obregón, on the best possible terms with each other, crossed the border into the United States at El Paso. They were received, on behalf of the Department of State, by Collector Zach

[26] Alvaro Obregón, *Ocho mil kilómetros en campaña* (Mexico City, 1917), pp. 262–263, 266. This was written by Obregón some time after the event. The point of view expressed throughout the book is, naturally, very biased, but there is no reason to doubt Obregón's factual correctness.

[27] Villa to Scott, Aug. 25, 1914, Hugh Lenox Scott Papers.

[28] Scott to his wife, Aug. 27, 1914, *ibid.*

Cobb, who escorted them and acted as interpreter when they called informally to pay their respects to the commander of the local United States garrison, Brigadier General John J. Pershing. Pershing, who was relatively unknown outside of army circles at that time, had recently assumed command of the United States forces at El Paso and in the vicinity. Before the two Mexicans proceeded on their way to Sonora, the entire group was photographed together.[29]

The conference at Naco lasted only a few days. An agreement was reached by which it was hoped that the fighting at Naco would end, and thus there would be no more danger for Americans on their own soil. In substance, Villa agreed to withdraw his partisans to a considerable distance south of the town, and Obregón agreed that the Carranzista garrison would not advance southward. Actually, the agreement was a complete concession by Villa to the wishes of the United States, for in effect he agreed to give up the attempt to capture the town. At this time there is no doubt that both Villa and Obregón were sincerely anxious to prevent more serious trouble, and they were willing to listen to arguments by Carothers, who was present, and by General Scott, who was in telegraphic communication with Villa. Because of Scott's recognized influence over Villa, the Secretary of War had wished that he go to the border and take part in the conference, but Scott felt that he could accomplish as much by telegraph, and he was reluctant to leave his post of responsibility in Washington at such a critical time.[30]

The situation in Sonora being apparently relieved, Obregón returned to Mexico City, pausing at El Paso long enough to write a short letter to Secretary Bryan, to be transmitted through the Constitutionalist consular agent at El Paso and Collector Cobb. Referring to a letter written by Bryan on August 13, 1914, in which Bryan congratulated both Obregón and Villa on the success of their "pacifying mission," Obregón thanked him and added: "This auspicious opportunity affords me the satisfaction of saying to you that both General Villa and I, as well as the Mexican Republic in general, thankfully acknowledge the

[29] National Archives, State Department File no. 812.00/13013. This was the photograph, which is often shown, of Pershing, Obregón, and Villa in a smiling group.
[30] In his daily letter to his wife, on Aug. 27, 1914, Scott wrote that he had received a satisfactory reply from Villa and would not have to go to the border (Hugh Lenox Scott Papers).

efforts put forth and the attentions shown by the American Government in aiding us to achieve the end we are pursuing." [31]

Villa, after the conference, visited some of the United States garrisons on that part of the border and had a long conversation on night operations with Colonel Richard M. Blatchford, of the 12th United States Infantry. Villa was reputed to be the only Mexican revolutionary commander who would attack at night.[32]

The apparent concord and cordiality between the two outstanding Constitutionalist military leaders and the fact that they had reached an agreement on a very touchy question without too much difficulty gave hope that the peace which had been reached might be lasting. This hope was strengthened when it became known that their private discussions had ranged far beyond the immediate problem in Sonora. They had, in fact, arrived at an agreement regarding the cessation of military rule and the establishment of a civil government in Mexico. Paul Fuller, who went to Mexico City within a few days after his return to Washington from his mission to Villa, examined the joint program drawn up by the two and gave it his unqualified blessing. "United support of northern and northeastern divisions gives good prospect of acceptance either willing or enforced," he reported. "This union of forces increases chances of Zapata's submission." [33]

The renewed unity of purpose between Villa and the elements loyal to Carranza had an additional effect, of direct interest and importance to the United States. Obregón felt, like most Mexicans, that the continued occupation of Veracruz by the Americans was an intolerable affront to Mexican national honor. "It is very humiliating," he telegraphed to Villa on September 11, "that the flag of the Stars and Bars [*sic*] continues to wave over the port of Vera Cruz." Accordingly, he suggested that both he and Villa request Carranza to institute immediate measures to persuade the United States to evacuate.[34]

Villa replied the same day:

[31] *Foreign Relations, 1914,* p. 593. Since the letter of Aug. 13 referred to was written *before* Villa and Obregón went to Sonora, it is not certain just what "pacifying mission" was meant. Search of the National Archives by Mr. Carl L. Lobke, the archivist in charge, fails to disclose the letter.

[32] *Harper's Weekly,* LIX (Nov. 14, 1914), 59.

[33] *Foreign Relations, 1914,* pp. 594–595. Cf. Obregón, *Ocho mil kilómetros en campaña,* pp. 278–280.

[34] *Foreign Relations, 1914,* p. 595.

I accept with enthusiasm your patriotic idea that we should all together approach the President of the Republic to ask how to take up the matter of the departure of the American forces which are in Vera Cruz; for it is really humiliating and shameful for our beloved country that invading forces still remain in Vera Cruz when there exists no justification for it.[35]

Villa still desired the approval of the United States. Evidently doubtful as to how his vehement expression might be interpreted, he telegraphed at once to Felix Sommerfeld, directing him to assure General Scott that the joint request did not imply the least hostility toward the United States on his part.[36]

Just how much effect, if any, the request had in connection with President Wilson's decision to withdraw from Veracruz is impossible to say. On September 15 the Secretary of War received orders from the President to make immediate preparations for withdrawal.[37] The news was received in Mexico City the next day, September 16, which happened to be the Mexican Independence Day, and at the Independence Day celebration, with Carranza present, cheers went up for the President of the United States. Francisco Villa, from his headquarters at Chihuahua, sent a telegram to President Wilson, thanking him "in my name and that of the Mexican people" and expressing his gratification that the "American Government, of which you are the distinguished head . . . has so faithfully interpreted the sentiments and aspirations of the patriotic Mexican people." [38]

A few days later, Carothers was directed to inform Villa that the President had received the telegram and that it gave him much pleasure to receive it. The President, Carothers was told to say, hoped that the withdrawal from Veracruz would be recognized by the Mexican people as another proof of the strong desire of the United States to aid in the speedy establishment of a genuinely representative government.[39]

Thus the middle of September, 1914, found Mexico apparently well on the way to internal peace. President Wilson's policies seemed to have been abundantly successful. The Constitutionalists had won the long contest, and largely under persuasion from the United States the threat of a split by the strongest of the Constitutionalist generals ap-

---

[35] *Ibid.*, p. 296.
[36] Sommerfeld to Scott, Sept. 15, 1914, Hugh Lenox Scott Papers.
[37] *Foreign Relations, 1914*, p. 597.   [38] *Ibid.*, p. 599.
[39] *Ibid.*, pp. 602–603.

peared to be over. Villa and Obregón seemed to feel cordial friendship for each other, and Villa, as the United States had urged, was submissive to the authority of the First Chief, to whom he referred respectfully as the President. All that remained to be done was to hold elections and establish a democratic government.

≫ IX ≪

Villa's Breach with Carranza

THE hopes of the United States that the halcyon calm of mid-September foretold peace in Mexico were abruptly shattered on September 23 by urgent telegrams from both Silliman and Canova. Silliman reported: "Villa in telegram to Carranza yesterday disowns First Chief. . . . Carranza, thinking my presence might be of service . . . has urgently requested that I go immediately to Washington. . . . I assume all responsibility and am leaving Mexico tonight." [1] Canova telegraphed from Chihuahua on the same day that Villa had definitely decided to break with Carranza. "This afternoon he informed me he had stood all he intended to. . . . In the future will act independently." [2] Three days later Carothers confirmed and amplified Canova's information, forwarding a message which Villa had sent to various Constitutionalist generals. Villa stated his firm conviction that Carranza was incapable of establishing a democratic government and invited them to join him in delivering the provisional government to Don Fernando Iglesias Calderón. Villa solemnly avowed that he would accept neither the presidency nor the vice-presidency.[3]

In spite of the undoubted disappointment and dismay caused by the news, it is unlikely that the State Department was completely surprised

---

[1] *Foreign Relations, 1914,* p. 605.
[2] National Archives, State Department File no. 812.00/13275, Sept. 23, 1914.
[3] *Foreign Relations, 1914,* p. 605.

by the sudden explosion. The rumors of Villa's dissatisfaction, supported by almost innumerable items of circumstantial evidence, had persisted too long to be entirely dissipated by the apparent harmony following the mission of Villa and Obregón to Sonora. In the few days immediately preceding the rupture there were clear indications that violent discord was hidden beneath the deceptively calm surface. Accompanied by Carothers and an aide-de-camp, Obregón made a second journey to Chihuahua to confer with Villa, arriving there on September 16, 1914. The particular matter for discussion was Villa's participation in a convention of Constitutionalist leaders, which was to be called to determine the future government of the country. Carothers had a long interview with Villa the next day, September 17, and reported that Villa believed that Carranza would not permit an honest convention. On September 18 Villa remarked to Canova that Carranza had not yet instituted any of the promised reforms, nor had he shown the slightest disposition to do so. In fact, Villa intimated, Carranza was determined to be another dictator. Canova's frank opinion was that any real reconciliation between Villa and Carranza was impossible, and, anticipating events by a few days, Canova predicted that an open break would occur at any moment.[4]

Both Carothers and Canova heard Villa and Obregón quarreling violently during a private conference. Their voices were raised in anger to the point that a squad of soldiers from Villa's personal bodyguard surrounded his quarters at double time. The two Americans were unable to distinguish just what was said, but the rage in the voices in the inner room was unmistakable. Obregón later told Canova that Villa threatened to shoot him at once.[5]

The immediate cause of this quarrel was the situation in Sonora. Villa demanded that Obregón order the Carranzista forces out of the state, in accordance with what he asserted were the provisions of the pact made a few days earlier.[6] In the war of words which followed the break, the Carranzistas claimed that their side had followed the Pact of Sonora exactly but that Villa, determined to find an excuse to make trouble, placed his own strained interpretation upon it.[7] The embittered claims

[4] National Archives, State Department File no. 812.00/13227, Sept. 19, 1914.
[5] *Ibid.*, File nos. 812.00/13237 and 812.00/13323, Sept. 17 and 22, 1914, respectively.
[6] *Ibid.*
[7] Mexican Bureau of Information, *"Red Papers" of Mexico: An Exposé of the*

and counterclaims were of deep interest to the State Department in attempting to evaluate the rights and wrongs of the case, but such attempts, in the long run, were futile.

After the quarrel, Obregón and his aide, Colonel Serrano, were permitted to board a train to return to Mexico City, but at Torreón the train was stopped by orders from Villa. It seemed that the two men might be taken off and shot at any moment, a fate which they both expected. In this emergency Canova exerted himself. After speaking energetically to several of Villa's closest advisers,

I went to see General Villa. I did not intimate to him I felt any fear he might execute Obregón, but I asked him when General Obregón was going away, saying that I felt the sooner . . . [he] could get back to Mexico City and use his influence with General Carranza, the quicker the troubles of the country would be solved. . . . I do not believe General Villa had any intention of executing Obregón, unless some act of hostility on the part of General Carranza inflamed him.[8]

Statements as to what followed are so contradictory that any attempt to sift the truth from the embittered propaganda of a civil war would be hopeless, even if it were worth while to try. On receiving reports of Obregón's difficulties, Carranza suspended all railway movements north of Aguascalientes and ordered that any southward movement of Villa's forces be resisted.[9] Villa took this as a hostile act and notified Carranza: "I declare that you are not recognized as the First Chief of the Republic, remaining at liberty to proceed as may suit my convenience."[10]

From the perspective of half a century later, it is easy to see that one of the basic causes of the tragic split in the Constitutionalist party was a clash of the personalities of the two leaders. Carranza was aristocratic, cold, unemotional; Villa was earthy, ebullient, violent. They were both men of inflexible will; in their social beliefs they had much in common, but each believed himself to be the only one capable of implementing those beliefs, while he was equally convinced that his opponent was totally unfit. A head-on collision, sooner or later, was almost inevitable.

The immediate causes of the rupture, aside from Carranza's action in

---

Great Científico Conspiracy to Eliminate Don Venustiano Carranza; Documents Relating to the Imbroglio between Carranza and Villa (New York, 1914), p. 14. Hereafter referred to as Mexican Bureau of Information, *Red Papers.*

[8] National Archives, State Department File no. 812.00/13326, Sept. 25, 1914.

[9] Mexican Bureau of Information, *Red Papers*, p. 14.   [10] *Ibid.*, p. 15.

stopping rail traffic in and out of Villa's territory, was disagreement over the convention which was to frame a new government. Such a convention, to which Villa referred in his conversation with Carothers on September 17, was agreed upon in the Pact of Torreón, in July, when the dispute between Carranza and Villa was presumably settled. The pact provided that a convention would be held in Mexico City as soon as the Revolution had definitely triumphed. Delegates, one for each thousand soldiers, were to be elected by committees of senior officers, subject to approval by the respective division commanders.[11]

Carranza refused to concur in this method of selecting delegates and substituted a provision for their designation by the generals and the governors of the states. But this was not the only source of disagreement. The proposals submitted jointly by Villa and Obregón provided for the re-establishment of civil government, immediate elections, opening of the courts, and guarantees that no military man would be a candidate for the presidency or the governorship of any state. There was, moreover, specific provision that would prevent Carranza's candidacy.[12] Since the Villa-Obregón propositions had been approved by President Wilson's personal representative, Paul Fuller, the United States was directly interested in the matter.

As soon as the news of the break was received in Washington, the first concern of the State Department was to assure itself of representation in each camp and of regular communication with both sides. To this end, Theodore Belt, who was already in Mexico, was ordered to remain with Carranza while Silliman was in the United States. Carothers was directed to remain at Villa's headquarters at Chihuahua, while his assistant, Leon J. Canova, accompanied Villa in the field.[13]

On the afternoon in which Canova interceded to save the lives of Obregón and Serrano, Villa's secretary told him that they were going to Mexico City to "throw the dictator out," and a short time later Villa himself told Canova that he had just broken relations with Carranza. Villa was smiling, and "his eyes were dancing, apparently in delight over his decision." Canova remonstrated, pointing out the terrible consequences of taking the aggressive and the desirable moral effect of peaceful measures upon Mexico and the rest of the world. Villa agreed and promised that he would order immediate elections in the states

[11] *Ibid.*, p. 4.   [12] *Ibid.*, pp. 5–6.
[13] National Archives, State Department File no. 812.00/13279, Sept. 23, 1914.

under his control. But he did not stop the preparations that were going on with a rush—the loading of cars with guns, ammunition, forage, equipment, and supplies of all kinds.[14]

For a few days the situation remained static, although the southward movement of Villa's troops continued. Both leaders, with anxious eyes on the United States as well as on their own people, began what a later generation would call "psychological warfare." Carranza's initial pronouncement was the first to reach the United States, forwarded from Mexico City by Theodore Belt on September 29. Replying to demands that he resign, Carranza termed Villa's movement a "reaction" and referred to Villa himself as "the perhaps unconscious instrument of Porfirism and Cientificism." [15] This was a charge calculated to appeal to the deep hatred in Mexico for Porfirio Díaz and for the wealthy clique known as the Científicos; in addition, it was a direct appeal to President Wilson's well-known prejudice against the moneyed "interests."

Villa, for his part, issued a "Manifesto to the Mexican People" the next day at Chihuahua. He accused Carranza, among other offenses against the spirit of the Revolution, of refusing to call elections but rather leaving that decision to a convention which he would dominate. Under his domination, the convention, according to the manifesto, would never issue such a call. Villa accused Carranza further of attempting to prevent attendance of the delegates of the Division of the North by suspending railway traffic. Villa expressly repudiated the idea that he or any of his generals would be candidates for the presidency or the governorship of any state. He invited all Mexicans to join him in eliminating the dictator, promising them that as soon as Carranza was removed a civilian provisional president would be designated, who would call immediate elections and initiate social and economic reforms.[16]

Villa's manifesto, like Carranza's pronouncement, was intended to influence opinion in the United States, as well as to appeal to his own people. As propaganda it was probably more effective than Carranza's rather vague accusations of reaction, Porfirism, and Cientificism. Villa made very specific accusations of interference with the establishment

[14] *Ibid.,* File no. 812.00/13326, Sept. 23, 1914.
[15] *Foreign Relations, 1914,* p. 606.   [16] *Ibid.,* pp. 607–608.

of a democratic, representative government. The American prejudice against dictatorship and militarism was too well known, especially since the outbreak of the war in Europe, for the stress placed upon those allegations in the manifesto to be accidental.

Probably few Americans outside of the State Department read Villa's manifesto, but his conduct and his other public statements constituted extremely effective propaganda. His meteoric rise, the picturesqueness of his bandit background, his Robin Hood reputation, all combined to capture the popular imagination. These, together with his insistence upon constitutionalism, were not without their influence upon government officials who determined national policy—including, one may reasonably assume, President Wilson himself.

Early in September, 1914, before his journey to Sonora with Obregón, Villa told news correspondents that his aim was to prevent military rule, of which Mexico had had too much. The Constitution must not be trampled underfoot by the army. He was determined, he said, that Mexico should have good civil government, and he would "bring every bit of moral suasion to bear" in defense of the people's rights.[17] This statement, so thoroughly in accord with American beliefs and prejudices, received wide publicity, as did Villa's repeated assertions that no military man should hold the presidency of Mexico. The Indianapolis *News*, for instance, commented editorially on the fact that Carranza had not endorsed the stipulation that no military man should be a candidate, and optimistically, the paper "believed, however, that he will do so, for Villa is firm on this point." [18]

At about the same time as the public statement mentioned in the preceding paragraph, Villa telegraphed to General Scott concerning the Huertista internees, several hundred of whom were still at Fort Wingate, New Mexico. Villa guaranteed their safety and protection if they should be released in the sections of Mexico under his control. He added that he could provide work for most of them.[19] Since the Mexican internees had presented a disagreeable and onerous problem from the very start, this message did nothing to lower the esteem in

[17] *Independent,* LXXIX (Sept. 7, 1914), 332.

[18] Cited in the *Literary Digest,* XLIX (Sept. 26, 1914), 561.

[19] National Archives, State Department File no. 812.00/13237. In a letter to General Scott dated Sept. 8, 1914, Gen. Tasker H. Bliss mentioned such a telegram, and the Hugh Lenox Scott Papers include a copy of one dated Sept. 15, 1914.

which Villa was held by the War Department. Nor did his reputation suffer by an amending telegram, specifically requesting that five individuals, including one Máximo Castillo, be not released.[20]

Knowing well that the approval of the United States was essential to his success, Villa made haste, as soon as he decided to break with Carranza, to convince Washington of his good will. On September 23 Canova informed the State Department that "Villa says you may be assured that whatever happens, the rights of foreigners will be respected insofar as his control extended." [21]

By making an early bid for American favor and support, Villa took the lead over Carranza. Carranza's supposed tardiness in initiating the reforms promised by the revolution caused rumors that he felt no real enthusiasm for such reforms—that as a rich landed proprietor himself he was actually opposed to such measures as the partition of the huge haciendas.[22] In addition, in the critical days of the break, Carranza provoked antagonism in Washington as successfully as though he were doing so deliberately. Following the announcement of the pending withdrawal of the American forces from Veracruz, the State Department requested guarantees from Carranza that the inhabitants would not be required to pay a second time the local and municipal taxes, collected during the American occupation. Guarantees were also asked for the refugees, including many religious, who had flocked to Veracruz for safety since April. These requests were transmitted on September 22, through the Brazilian minister, Cardoso de Oliveira. A full week passed without any reply from Carranza. On October 1, 1914, Bryan cabled that the State Department was "anxiously awaiting" a reply, but still there was no answer. Not until October 5 was Cardoso able to send any information to Washington. On that date he received from Carranza's foreign office a note that amounted to a demand that the United States fix the date for the evacuation. No mention was made of the guarantees.[23] For several weeks Carranza stubbornly refused to give the guarantees, on the grounds of "inexpediency." Not until his

[20] Hugh Lenox Scott Papers. Castillo was supposed to be responsible for the Cumbres Tunnel disaster, in which a large number of people, including several Americans, were burned to death.
[21] National Archives, State Department File no. 812.00/13279, Sept. 23, 1914.
[22] *Review of Reviews*, L (Sept., 1914), 373.
[23] *Foreign Relations, 1914,* pp. 603, 608, 609.

hand was forced, under circumstances which will be discussed later, did he yield.

Comparison of the attitudes toward the United States shown by the two principal antagonists at this time leaves small cause for wonder that Villa was regarded in Washington with somewhat greater favor than Carranza. On Villa's part was openly expressed friendship—on Carranza's part was contemptuous silence or open flouting of American wishes. General Scott, in his daily letter to his wife on September 26, expressed not merely his private opinion, but the tacit official opinion of the time:

I must tell you the way I look on Villa—Carranza has climbed to what power he has on Villa's shoulders and is trying to kick him down—he has no real power of his own—Villa is the real force in Mexico and has caught Carranza by the neck each time he has broken his agreements and put him back on the track until now it has arrived at such a stage in the game that his falsity can be stood no longer—he was made to keep his agreement to call a convention Oct 1st in Mexico for the election of a Provisional President. Villa ordered his delegates south to the convention—Carranza cut the railroad at Aguas Calientes so Villa delegates could not go on—so that when the convention meets only his own delegates will take part & enable him to make himself another dictator of Mexico, which Villa is determined to prevent. . . . Villa seems to have taken a romantic regard for me & I send him word once in a while to keep him steady in his course. The last time I sent him word that if he continues on his course in insisting on constitutional government and putting his personal ambitions aside he will be considered as the "Washington" of Mexico—and so he will without any doubt.[24]

While everything seemed to indicate that Villa was the leader whom the United States would probably support, President Wilson was anxious to make an impartial decision based on complete information. Paul Fuller, having visited and formed an impression of Villa, was the logical envoy to report on Carranza. Thus the President could obtain a view of both sides from a man who was able to make unbiased comparisons. On August 26, 1914, immediately after reporting on his mission to Villa, Fuller left Washington again. Traveling "by devious means, intended to be direct," as he somewhat facetiously reported, he

[24] Hugh Lenox Scott Papers. General Scott was speaking modestly. There is ample evidence to prove the extraordinary influence he had over Villa at this time.

arrived at Veracruz on September 3 and at Mexico City the next day.[25] The following day, September 5, 1914, Fuller had his first interview with Carranza. Fuller moved and worked rapidly. Only six days later he had managed to converse with nearly all the principal officials of the Carranza government, including Foreign Minister Isidro Fabela, Alfredo Robles Dominguez, Miguel Díaz Lombardo, General Alvaro Obregón, and Carranza's private secretary.

The Carranzista officials, knowing that Fuller had previously visited Villa, were somewhat reserved in their attitude, probably being uncertain as to how he might feel toward the Carranza government. Fabela informed him that the difficulties with the Division of the North had been greatly exaggerated in the press (this was before the open rupture) and that most of Villa's generals had pledged their support to Carranza.

To Carranza himself, Fuller stressed President Wilson's strong wish to see the Constitutionalist Party fully reunited and the early establishment of a constitutional government in Mexico. The President was glad to see in the newspapers that the First Chief had issued a call for a convention to be held on October 1. Carranza, apparently, made no comment on this but discussed how he had been misrepresented in the United States. He had been pictured as unfriendly, he said, but "these statements are absolutely without foundation. I have not seen fit to defend myself." Carranza then charged that "pernicious American influence" was back of Zapata's intransigence and that "a like influence from American sources has been exercised on Villa." [26]

On September 7 Fuller was shown the program agreed upon between Villa and Obregón during their mission to Sonora, to which reference has been made.[27] Fuller noted that this program was substantially the same as that which Villa had outlined to him and of which President Wilson was informed. Fuller told Obregón that he was highly gratified at the program and hoped that it would be carried out fully. "He [Obregón] said he hoped that it would, but he was reticent as to any assured expectation of its acceptance."

[25] Paul Fuller, "Memorandum for the President," National Archives, State Department File no. 812.00/14236, Sept. 18, 1914. Except as otherwise noted, all details of Fuller's mission to Carranza are taken from this report.
[26] *Ibid.*
[27] Obregón, *Ocho mil kilómetros en campaña,* pp. 278–280. Cf. *Foreign Relations, 1914,* pp. 594–595.

Nor was expectation of the adoption of the program the only thing about which Obregón was reticent. Obregón's own account of the interview fails to mention any discussion of the program but indicates that he was somewhat doubtful about Fuller and believed that Fuller did not understand clearly the situation and issues. On receiving word that Fuller desired an interview, Obregón responded that he had nothing to discuss but that there was no reason why they should not meet informally. He specified that he would not have a conference with Fuller. During the course of the conversation Fuller inquired why Obregón did not have a personal representative in Washington, as Villa did. Obregón replied by explaining at some length that the First Chief was the only person entitled to such a representative. Fuller then "appeared to be about to go into this further, but as my answers began to be laconic [the interview ended.]" [28]

In his farewell call upon Carranza, Fuller took up the program agreed upon between Villa and Obregón, remarking that this program was fully in consonance with President Wilson's views and that its early adoption would assure the sympathy and approval of the American people. Carranza, as far as is known, made no comment on the inference that a scheme for the organization of the new Mexican government should be approved by the President of the United States. Nor was any remark made as to Fuller's implicit reflection upon Obregón's loyalty and Carranza's authority, when he asked why Obregón did not have a personal representative in Washington, as Villa did. Whether or not Fuller realized such inferences, they were undoubtedly noticed and silently resented. It is possible that Fuller thus unintentionally stiffened Carranza's attitude and caused Villa, by contrast, to appear the more reasonable of the two.

Fuller's final experiences in Mexico City confirmed his original belief in Villa. He was unfavorably impressed with the "spirit of hatred and proscription" toward the defeated Huertistas displayed by Isidro Fabela and Carranza's secretary. Against Fabela's assumption that all Huertista officers were accomplices in Madero's murder, Fuller contrasted a proposal by Villa to incorporate in the Constitutionalist army all who could prove good conduct and ability. Fuller's estimate of Carranza himself was far from favorable: "A man of good intentions but without any sufficient force to dominate his petty surroundings, and

[28] Obregón, *Ocho mil kilómetros en campaña*, 281–282.

greatly hampered by the fear of losing his prestige, which hampers him from adopting conciliating measures or correcting mistakes, and makes him adhere to mistaken courses, adopted under pressure." Such an opinion by the President's personal envoy did nothing to change the relative positions of Villa and Carranza in Washington's opinion.

During the next few weeks, while Carranza continued pointedly to ignore the demands for the Veracruz guarantees, the President and the Secretary of State had ample opportunity to reflect upon Fuller's estimate and compare Villa's friendliness and open co-operation with Carranza's resentful attitude.

The convention met on October 1, 1914, in the hall of the Chamber of Deputies. Carranza had previously announced that the purpose of the convention would be to "designate a new depository as trustee for the high authority with which I am invested." [29] Immediately after convening, the delegates decided to adjourn at Mexico City on October 5 and reconvene at Aguascalientes five days later.[30] This decision, which met with Carranza's approval, arose from the fact that there were no Villista delegates present. In his telegram of September 22, denouncing Carranza, Villa charged that there was a premeditated desire to place stumbling blocks in the way of any settlement; consequently the Division of the North would take no part in the convention. It was believed that if the convention were moved to a place closer to Villa's territory he might be induced to take part, and thus additional serious troubles for the country would be forestalled.[31]

On the evening of October 4 Carranza appeared before the convention and made a brief speech in which he charged that the social and political reforms for which the Revolution was fought were being frustrated by Villa's conduct. Again he accused Villa of being the tool of the Científicos and "those who have been refused public posts on account of cowardice and ineptitude." In a final, dramatic gesture, he tendered his resignation as First Chief, promising to abide faithfully by the convention's decisions. "I can only deliver over my authority, and I do deliver it at this moment to the Chiefs here united." [32]

Since there were neither Villa nor Zapata representatives in the convention at this time, and every general and every state governor present was an avowed Carranzista, it was hardly surprising that, by

[29] *Foreign Relations, 1914,* p. 606.   [30] *Ibid.,* p. 608.
[31] Mexican Bureau of Information, *Red Papers,* p. 15.   [32] *Ibid.*

unanimous vote, the convention refused to accept the resignation. Thus far, Villa's contention that Carranza would dominate the convention completely appeared to be true.

People who hoped that the convention would be the first step toward immediate constitutional government in Mexico were disillusioned by the speech made the next day by Luis Cabrera, a brilliant individual who had been for some time a member of Carranza's diplomatic mission in Washington. Cabrera spoke frankly against the immediate re-establishment of a constitutional regime, arguing that a period of dictatorship was necessary in which to effect the reforms promised by the Revolution. "Do you realize," he said, "that the greatest exertions made by a reactionary element against a revolution, have always consisted in the re-establishment of legality?" [33]

Cabrera spoke at length upon this theme and by his own mental processes came to the conclusion that the delegates at Aguascalientes would be subjected to pressure to avoid making any changes. The obvious inference was that the pressure would come from Villa. It was a subtle elaboration of Carranza's charge that Villa was a tool of the reactionaries. Although Cabrera's speech was propaganda aimed at his own countrymen, he cannot have been ignorant of the suspicion with which Americans regarded anyone who was believed to be an agent of "the interests" or "big business."

After adjourning at Mexico City on October 5, the convention reconvened at Aguascalientes and by the evening of October 15 had completed its permanent organization. It took the surprising step of proclaiming itself the sovereign power of Mexico and then voted to withhold action upon the status of the First Chief until after the arrival of delegates from Zapata. Since the original summons was made by Carranza, Zapata had not been invited to send delegates. Because it was obvious that nothing permanent could be accomplished without Zapata, a special committee was designated to visit him and extend a personal invitation to participate.[34]

The United States was, of course, deeply interested in the Aguascalientes convention but could not take any direct action to influence it. Canova went to Aguascalientes to observe, while Carothers remained

[33] Mexican Bureau of Information, *Speech by Luis Cabrera before the Convention, Mexico, D.F., October 5, 1914* (New York, 1914), p. 7.
[34] *Foreign Relations, 1914*, pp. 610–611.

with Villa's headquarters, then at Zacatecas. The fact that the American observer was one of the State Department's representatives with Villa may possibly have given rise to the idea that the United States was backing Villa's claims and policies—or even dictating them. Because of the favor which the United States had shown Villa in the past, such a conclusion would not be unnatural for Mexicans whose minds and hearts were filled with the traditional Mexican distrust of the Colossus of the North.

It seemed at first that the Carranza "steam roller" would be able to crush all opposition, in spite of the Villista delegates now present and the convention's independent action in declaring itself the sovereign power in Mexico. The Carranzistas were reported to have an overwhelming majority of eighty-nine votes to Villa's seventeen.[35] Villa himself felt that the situation was not too hopeful; he telegraphed to General Scott that the opening of the convention was unsuccessful.[36] Knowing that Scott was interested, Villa sent him a succession of telegrams during the convention, detailing events from his own point of view and stressing that Carranza must be eliminated.

Day after day the convention dragged on. Villa informed the State Department, through Canova, that he would support any provisional president who might be selected, except Carranza.[37] After heated discussion, the convention formally requested Carranza's resignation. He bluntly refused, saying that he would deliver the executive power only to a president elected by the people. This gave color to Villa's earlier contention that Carranza was willing to submit his resignation only to a convention so packed with his own delegates that its refusal was a foregone conclusion. Villa remarked to Carothers that as soon as a truly representative convention met in neutral territory Carranza's real ambitions toward despotism came to light.[38]

It soon became apparent, however, that Villa's fears that Carranza would be able to dominate the convention completely were without too firm a foundation. The convention's action in declaring itself sovereign and the request for Carranza's resignation clearly proved this. Away from the atmosphere of Mexico City, delegates who had

[35] *Independent,* LXXX (Oct. 12, 1914), 51.
[36] Hugh Lenox Scott Papers, Oct. 12, 1914.
[37] National Archives, State Department File no. 812.00/13531, Oct. 18, 1914.
[38] *Foreign Relations, 1914,* pp. 611–612.

been regarded as Carranza stalwarts began to show a degree of independence. Some of them began to share Villa's fear that Carranza planned to turn himself into another Porfirio Díaz.[39]

There is no evidence that the State Department was impressed with the danger of Carranza's becoming another irresponsible dictator, but there is indication that it was increasingly impatient with Carranza's failure to give guarantees for the people of Veracruz. The withdrawal of the occupation force had been suspended because of Carranza's obvious disinclination to give the guarantees.[40] Pressed for an answer, Carranza evaded the issue by referring the matter to the convention for a decision.[41] Several days later, after there had been ample time for the convention to take action, the Acting Secretary of State, Robert Lansing, telegraphed to Canova, directing him to ascertain if the convention had a copy of the demands. If not, the convention should ask Fabela for a copy.

Fabela, meanwhile, informed Silliman that Carranza considered it inexpedient to issue such a statement as the State Department desired. Fabela assured Silliman that no one in Veracruz would be molested for co-operating with the American forces during the occupation and that no back taxes would be collected. Since this was not an official statement or acknowledgment of the American demands, the United States refused to accept it.[42]

Finally, over a month after Washington had sent the demands, the Brazilian minister informed the State Department that although the convention had authorized Carranza to comply with the desires of the United States he still refused to do so. His reason this time was that General Aguilar, who was to take over Veracruz from the Americans, had already issued a proclamation embodying what the United States asked. Carranza, moreover, stated that he regarded the whole matter as a purely domestic affair; compliance with American desires would be a violation of Mexican sovereignty. In conclusion, Carranza again demanded that the United States fix the date for the evacuation.[43]

Such a reply, after an irritating delay of five weeks, did nothing to cause the United States to feel more friendly toward Carranza. The

[39] José C. Valades, *Las caballerías de la Revolución* (*Hazañas del General Buelna*) (Mexico City, 1937), p. 90. Buelna was a general from Tepic and was a delegate in the convention.

[40] *Foreign Relations, 1914*, pp. 603, 608–609. [41] *Ibid.*, p. 610.
[42] *Ibid.*, p. 611. [43] *Ibid.*, pp. 613–614.

reply of the Secretary of State, on November 1, contained a distinct note of asperity and was a virtual ultimatum:

In view of the fact that the convention acted favorably upon the Department's requests, it was hoped that there would be no further cause for delay on the part of General Carranza.

The Department does not consider that the proclamation issued by General Aguilar is in compliance with its requests, as the central government at Mexico City might feel justified in repudiating the guarantees promised by General Aguilar. General Carranza has not even stated that he endorsed or would regard as binding [General Aguilar's proclamation].

You may assure the Acting Secretary for Foreign Affairs that . . . as soon as General Carranza gives definite assurances in accordance with the requests contained in the Department's September 22, 9 p.m., the date for the evacuation will be fixed without further delay.[44]

On November 2 the convention named General Eulalio Gutiérrez, a Villa supporter, as Provisional President of Mexico. The next day he formally notified Carothers that the spirit of the convention was in favor of giving the guarantees that the United States wanted.[45]

Washington now found itself faced with the delicate problem of deciding to whom Veracruz should be surrendered. The State Department was also becoming increasingly impatient with Carranza's stubbornness and dilatoriness. On November 6 Lansing sent a "Strictly Confidential" message to Carothers, directing him to consult with Villa and "unofficially and confidentially" ask his opinion: Should Veracruz be turned over to General Aguilar, upon receipt of the assurances from the Provisional President, or should the United States delay until an officer was specially designated by the convention for the purpose?[46] Faced with the convention's open and probably successful bid for American support, Carranza grudgingly gave way and finally, on November 13, 1914, issued a proclamation containing the desired assurances.[47]

During the period when Carranza was exhibiting an almost studied contempt for the United States, Villa, as shown by his actions, indicated a real desire to maintain American favor. Early in October, Carothers spoke to Villa of heavy losses being suffered by an American mining

[44] *Ibid.*, p. 616.   [45] *Ibid.*, p. 617.
[46] National Archives, State Department File no. 812.00/13744a, Nov. 6, 1914. The writer was unable to locate any reply which Carothers may have sent to the Secretary of State in response to these instructions.
[47] *Foreign Relations, 1914*, pp. 621–622.

company operating in Sonora. Villa at once ordered Governor May-torena to furnish guards for the company's metal shipments and to give the company's properties full protection. At the same time Villa requested a *quid pro quo*—one of the few he ever requested. He told Carothers he "would view with satisfaction any action . . . of the Government of the United States tending toward the dissolving of the many revolutionary juntas now organizing in New Orleans, San Antonio, El Paso and other border towns . . . which can serve only as a means of retarding peace."[48] The State Department replied that if Villa or anybody else would furnish names and facts, the matter would be taken up at once with the Department of Justice.[49] Carothers also took up with Villa the case of the German vice-consul at Zacatecas, whose property had been seized when the Villistas captured the city. Villa ordered an immediate investigation and the return of the property to its owner.[50]

Still, Villa was not 100 per cent pliant in deference to the wishes of the United States. He had held Luis Terrazas as a prisoner ever since the capture of Chihuahua, months before. Washington had made many inquiries about Terrazas and on October 3, urged by his family, asked again for his release.[51] Villa's reply, through Carothers, was that he could not possibly release young Terrazas. Holding him was the only way to prevent the family from assisting filibusters.[52]

During the critical period of the convention there could be little doubt as to which of the principal antagonists seemed to promise fulfillment of President Wilson's hopes for Mexico. Carranza, according to all indications, stood for dictatorship. Villa stood for representative, constitutional government. In spite of his statement to Paul Fuller, Carranza was distinctly antagonistic toward the United States, while Villa had always been friendly and co-operative.

Before the announcement that General Eulalio Gutiérrez had been selected as Provisional President of Mexico was a period when it became increasingly evident that no compromise of the differences between Carranza and Villa was possible. On November 19 Villa himself suddenly appeared before the convention and made a speech which

[48] National Archives, State Department File no. 812.00/13412, Oct. 6, 1914.
[49] *Ibid.*, File no. 812.00/13417, Oct. 8, 1914.
[50] *Ibid.*, File no. 812.00/13745, Nov. 11, 1914.
[51] *Ibid.*, File no. 812.00/13351, Oct. 3, 1914.
[52] *Ibid.*, File no. 812.00/13745, Nov. 11, 1914.

hearers described as "eloquent." He pledged himself to support any provisional president chosen by the convention (Carranza excepted). Following his speech, he and all the delegates signed their names on a national flag, in proof of sincerity. The Zapata delegates finally arrived, accompanied, significantly, by General Felipe Angeles. En route, they had passed through Guadalupe, where Villa then had his headquarters and where he had received them with great honor.[53] Wild rumors circulated that Villa's escort had insulted and mistreated delegates—rumors which proved to be untrue and which may have been started deliberately by his enemies.[54] Villista troops finally moved into the city of Aguascalientes—to coerce the convention, said Villa's enemies; to protect the convention and enable it to deliberate without interference, said his supporters.[55] Villa delegates joined with the Zapatistas in endorsing Zapata's Plan of Ayala, and together the two groups elected Gutiérrez as Provisional President. Villa placed his army at the disposal of the convention and the new President, promising that if Carranza clung to office the Villistas would remove him by force.[56]

All hopes of a peaceful solution were now destroyed. The convention ordered Carranza to yield office to Gutiérrez by November 10. Carranza's reply was to order his delegates to leave the convention and all generals to return to their commands.[57] The convention retaliated by declaring Carranza in rebellion and naming Francisco Villa as its Commander in Chief.[58] It was apparent that another violent phase of the Mexican Revolution could not be delayed much longer.

[53] *Review of Reviews,* L (Nov., 1914), 522–523; *Independent,* LXXX (Nov. 2, 1914), 159.
[54] *Ibid.*   [55] *Review of Reviews,* L (Nov., 1914), 523.
[56] *Independent,* LXXX (Nov. 2, 1914), 159.
[57] *Foreign Relations, 1914,* p. 618.   [58] *Ibid.,* p. 620.

X

Villa, the Man of the Hour?

DURING the whole controversy, most Americans who were interested in Mexican affairs were nearly as confident as Villa himself regarding the final outcome. Americans knew Villa's military record; every newspaper told of his battles. General Alvaro Obregón and General Pablo González had attracted little attention in the United States, and it was taken for granted that their soldiers could not stand against the assault of Villa's tough veterans. Villa was known, also, to be well prepared. During the period of stormy debate he had been recruiting his forces and accumulating supplies and ammunition. Shortly before the Aguascalientes convention, Canova reported that Villa had 40,000 men, all well armed and equipped, a reserve supply of 240 carloads of coal, from 250 to 300 carloads of provisions, and an ample number of railroad cars and locomotives for transportation. The greater part of the coal had been purchased through American dealers in El Paso. With this source of supply, Villa was independent of the mines of Coahuila for fuel.[1]

Newspaper correspondents and readers were not the only ones who were impressed. On October 8, in a personal letter to General Scott, General John J. Pershing remarked: "Villa seems to be a strong man, and may be the man of the hour." [2] General Pershing was more re-

[1] National Archives, State Department File no. 812.00/13518, Oct. 6, 1914.
[2] John J. Pershing Papers, Library of Congress.

strained in his judgment and comments than General Scott, but at this time he had a high opinion of Villa. Pershing had never had Scott's opportunities to know Villa personally, and since July a positive order from the Secretary of War forbade army officers to hold any communication with Villa upon official matters without previous authority.[3] Pershing, doubtless, had followed Villa's campaigns with professional interest. He recorded that when he met Villa and Obregón, on their way to Sonora, "both Generals Villa and Obregón impressed me as being very strong and very sincere men."[4] Dr. Carlos Rusk sent Pershing a sketch of Villa's life, making no attempt to gloss over Villa's career as a bandit. Rusk remarked that it was impossible for one man to have committed all the crimes Villa was supposed to have perpetrated; it was customary in Chihuahua to blame all crimes on Villa. Pershing, replying, said that he intended soon to send Villa a photograph of himself.[5]

Pershing's restrained judgment, and even General Scott's more enthusiastic opinion, paled before other estimates comparing Villa and Carranza. The scholarly Albert Bushnell Hart, comparing Villa to a "train robber, a pickpocket and a New York gunman," characterized Carranza as "a badly carved figurehead, animated with Huerta's desperate determination that other men shall fight and die for him at a distance."[6] A rather well-known newspaper woman, while vainly trying to persuade both American and Mexican authorities to permit her to be a war correspondent, interviewed several refugees at El Paso:

I said that I had heard that Carranza was master . . . a stronger man than Villa and in every way more responsible.

"Nobody who's lived . . . in the interior of Mexico would have told you that," rather scornfully replied my refugee, who was a personal acquaintance of both generals. "Carranza is the flagstaff that is waved, the fine figurehead, but Villa is the man of Mexico. To my mind he has in him the making of a modern Napoleon. He is a genius. . . .

Now the world rings with the name of this peon. . . . Not merciful by

[3] National Archives, State Department File no. 812.00/12753, July, 1914. The order stated, also, that there was no objection to Villa's entering the United States unarmed and in civilian clothes. On such occasions he was to be treated with every courtesy.

[4] John J. Pershing Papers, Memorandum, Aug., 1914.

[5] *Ibid.*, Sept. 14, 1914.

[6] Albert Bushnell Hart, "The Postulates of the Mexican Situation," *Annals of the American Academy of Political Science*, LIV (July, 1914), 140–141.

nature, he is clever enough to become so, or to assume—no, to cultivate—any fine quality by which he can live up to his reputation, and make the world he well realizes is more enlightened than his own respect him. . . . Huerta could never rise to heights. Villa could, and may.[7]

The several opinions just cited were expressed before the Aguascalientes convention. Subsequently, the odds for Villa seemed to become more favorable every day. This was especially true when it was learned that, after a formal declaration of war by Obregón on November 19, Villa's army was moving southward.[8] Carranzista resistance seemed to be completely ineffectual, and Carranza himself lost no time in abandoning the capital. He moved, with his government, first to San Luis Potosí, then to Veracruz, arriving there on November 26, only three days after the American forces had sailed for home. Veracruz, he notified the American consul, would be the capital of Mexico until further notice.[9]

With Carranza's troops easily overcome, the allied forces of Villa and Zapata closed in quickly on Mexico City. Carothers accompanied Villa and reported that Villa stopped a day or two at each of the principal cities, installing civil officials and "putting things on a peace time basis." At Tacuba, Villa announced that he would wait for Zapata before entering Mexico City, so that they could enter together. The following day, December 2, 1914, he dispatched a mission to Zapata to arrange for the triumphal entry. It is evidence of Villa's attitude toward the United States at this time that the mission included George C. Carothers. "Our object," reported Carothers, "was to induce General Zapata to go to the City of Mexico and make a formal entry at General Villa's side." [10]

The delegation was cordially received by Zapata, and arrangements were made for the two chiefs to meet and confer at Xochimilco, before entering the capital. Both Carothers and Canova were eyewitnesses of the meeting. Canova reported: "Both of them fell to discussing a character neither liked—Carranza." The discussion was within the hearing of the two Americans, who were apparently as much a part of Villa's party as his Mexican staff officers and from whom there were no secrets.[11]

[7] Alice M. Williamson, "My Attempt to Be a War Correspondent," *McClure's Magazine*, XLIII (Sept., 1914), 71–72.

[8] *Foreign Relations, 1914*, pp. 624–625.   [9] *Ibid.*, pp. 626–627.

[10] National Archives, State Department File no. 812.00/14061, Dec. 20, 1914.

[11] *Ibid.*, File no. 812.00/14009a, Dec. 8, 1914.

Zapatista forces, moving closely on the heels of the departing Carranzistas, had entered Mexico City several days before this meeting. On December 1, Carothers went into the city alone and conferred with Cardoso de Oliveira, who informed him that the Zapatistas were maintaining excellent order contrary to all expectations.[12] For weeks past the inhabitants of the city, and especially the foreign colony, had been apprehensive. Zapata had been widely advertised as a monster of inhuman cruelty. Most of his soldiers were illiterate Indians who were supposed to be little better than outright savages and hated all foreigners and upper-class Mexicans. Nor had Villa's reputation been helped by the newspapers of the capital during the Huerta regime and the dispute with Carranza. To the surprise of everybody, the Villa-Zapata forces were under the strictest discipline and gave the city complete freedom from disorder. The Brazilian minister informed the State Department that "the general situation [is] surprisingly good." [13]

On December 6, 1914, Villa and his southern ally formally entered and took possession of the city. To a public that had become accustomed, since the preceding August, to the drabness and sordidness of modern war, the spectacle of the march into Mexico City was something out of another, and more colorful, world.

Soldiers afoot in khaki and felt or straw sombreros, mounted soldiers in the most original of charro suits, wearing hats that were large to the point of being caricatures. Wonderful hats, some gold or silver trimmed, which with the saddles divided the pride of the owners. . . .

A few hours earlier General Villa had passed us riding side by side with Zapata. A stern, heavy-bodied man, dressed in an elaborate suit of dark blue and gold, hardly recognizable as the Villa I had seen on the border.[14]

An estimated thirty thousand men marched into Mexico City that day, and Villa was reported to have some thirty thousand more within marching distance—troops newly recruited, whose discipline did not yet measure up to Villa's standards.[15] It was probably the greatest number of troops assembled at one time and place on the American con-

[12] National Archives, State Department File no. 812.00/14061, Dec. 20, 1914.
[13] *Foreign Relations, 1914*, p. 627.
[14] Allene Tupper Wilkes, "Villa Enters Mexico City," *Harper's Weekly*, LX (Jan. 16, 1914), 57. Villa seems to have been wearing the conventional uniform of a Mexican *general de división*.
[15] National Archives, State Department File no. 812.00/14061, Dec. 20, 1914.

tinent since the American Civil War and added to the impression that Villa's strength was overwhelming, as compared with Carranza's.

The conduct of the occupying forces in Mexico City continued to impress observers. The correspondent of *Harper's Weekly* remarked: "Though there was no enthusiastic demonstration, there was a sigh of relief from the fear that had held the people of the City for weeks. . . . Everywhere were heard expressions of hope and returning confidence . . . for Zapatistas and Villistas . . . alike behaved with justice and good sense." [16] In addition to maintaining public order and conducting themselves quietly, the forces of Villa and Zapata added to the good will they had gained by restoring to the owners vast quantities of loot abandoned by the Carranzistas.[17] In fact, the situation in Mexico City was so promising that President Wilson was said to be highly pleased, especially as he had counted on the generals who supported the convention to restore law and order.[18]

The two men who were now ruling in Mexico City were, moreover, openly favorable toward the United States. In contrast, the attitude displayed by Carranza and his group was not calculated to arouse confidence or sympathy in the United States. During Independence Day celebrations at Parral, General Maclovio Herrera and his brother, who had been Villistas but were now ardent Carranzistas, stood approvingly beside an orator who railed against the United States, urging all loyal Mexicans to fight against the traitor who was betraying his country to the gringo.[19] During the Aguascalientes convention there were clear indications that anti-American feeling was being deliberately encouraged and fostered by the Carranza government. There were even reports that an attack was being planned to drive the Americans out of Veracruz—a desperate attempt by Carranza to rally and unify the Mexican nation to his own support.[20]

Villa, on the other hand, showed such confidence in the United States that he included George Carothers, an official representative of the State Department, in the personal delegation he sent to treat with Zapata. During the conference at Xochimilco both Villa and Zapata "expressed very warm friendship for the United States and expressed

[16] Wilkes, "Villa Enters Mexico City," p. 57.
[17] *Independent*, LXXX (Dec. 28, 1914), 491.
[18] New York *Times*, Wednesday, Dec. 2, 1914, 1:1.
[19] National Archives, State Department File no. 812.00/13431, Oct. 1, 1914.
[20] *Independent*, LXXX (Nov. 16, 1914), 229.

their gratitude for the moral assistance they have received from us." [21]
General Felipe Angeles gave a practical demonstration of Villista
friendship by offering Silliman the use of the military telegraph lines
for any messages he might need to send.[22]

Cynics may have felt that the news coming from Mexico City was almost too good to be true, and certainly too good to last. In spite of all
the good reports, before many days dark and ugly stories began filter-
ing to the outside world from Mexico City. It appeared that the Villa-
Zapata regime, while maintaining good public order and apparently
observing a spirit of justice and fairness, was quietly "liquidating" its
enemies—and suspected enemies—in large numbers. Reports began
coming to the State Department of midnight arrests, mysterious disappearances, surreptitious firing squads, of a concealed reign of terror.
In 1914 the world was not accustomed to the extermination of political
enemies, as it has unfortunately become since that time, and the
United States was shocked. The State Department was particularly
disturbed to learn that General Eduardo N. Iturbide was included
among the proscribed and had gone into hiding. Iturbide had been
the governor of the Federal District under the Huerta regime but was
considered to be a disinterested patriot. It was he who arranged for
the Constitutionalists to enter the capital peacefully in August. He was
credited with being a friend of the United States and with having
assisted numerous Americans who needed help.[23]

On December 13, 1914, Secretary Bryan sent a telegram to Silliman,
who had remained in Mexico City, expressing disappointment and
distress at learning that political executions were taking place. Silliman
was ordered to "bring every influence on [the] authorities in behalf
of political prisoners" and to do everything in his power for Iturbide.
Bryan stressed the ill effect that such atrocities would have on the
opinion of the world.[24]

On December 13, probably ignorant of the telegram to Silliman,
Canova sent an urgent message, suggesting that Carothers bring the ill
effects of the executions to Villa's personal attention. (Villa, accompanied by Carothers, had left Mexico City for the north.) "In the
night another batch was executed." Canova believed that Villa's better

[21] National Archives, State Department File no. 812.00/14061, Dec. 20, 1914.
[22] New York *Times,* Wednesday, Dec. 2, 1914, 1:1.
[23] *Foreign Relations, 1914,* pp. 585–586.   [24] *Ibid.,* pp. 628–629.

advisers were not with him and that he was now under the influence of two members of his staff, Fierro and Almanza, who had sinister reputations as killers. The next day Canova forwarded a detailed list of those known to have been killed; he believed that many of the executions resulted from personal grudges, rather than real or fancied political offenses.[25]

Silliman telegraphed to the State Department on December 14 that the Zapatistas were in favor of stopping secret executions and of having public trials. Nevertheless, they were bitter against General Iturbide, whom they accused of numerous murders while he was governor of the Federal District. Silliman did not believe the accusation, as he considered Iturbide to be a man "incapable of murder." He was told, he added, that Villa had said that he had nothing at all against Iturbide.[26]

Whether or not it was due to his efforts, Silliman was able to report two days later that the executions seemed to have stopped.[27] This was confirmed by Canova on December 18. A large part of the mysterious disappearances that had been charged to Villa and Zapata, Canova added, were actually caused by reactionaries, deliberately trying to make trouble and satisfy their own private grudges. To stop this sort of thing, Villa and Zapata had formed a special unit to patrol the city and summarily execute anybody making unauthorized arrests.[28]

An unexpected and unfortunate outcome of the interest of the United States in General Iturbide was the sudden ending of Canova's usefulness in Mexico. Iturbide had taken refuge in the British Legation. At Silliman's urgent request, Provisional President Gutiérrez gave him a safe conduct to the United States, escorted by Canova. The Zapatistas were indignant, and Manuel Palafox, a Zapatista member of Gutiérrez' cabinet, publicly referred to Silliman and Canova as "knaves," charging that they had received a quarter of a million dollars for conniving at Iturbide's escape. Despite their wrath, the Zapatistas respected the safe conduct. But Villa, for unknown reasons, sent telegraphic orders to the north to intercept Iturbide. Iturbide and Canova learned of this,

[25] National Archives, State Department File nos. 812.00/14018, Dec. 15, 1914, and 14097, Dec. 16, 1914.
[26] *Ibid.*
[27] National Archives, State Department File no. 812.00/14010, Dec. 14, 1914.
[28] *Ibid.*, File no. 812.00/14043, Dec. 18, 1914.

left the train at Santa Rosalía, and made their way, with Iturbide in disguise, to Ojinaga and safety.[29] Although Canova was simply obeying his orders as a United States officer, Villa took a prejudiced view. He publicly denounced Canova, and Carothers advised the State Department that it would be unwise for Canova to return to Mexico. A curious sequel to this affair was that a certain member of Carranza's cabinet was as indignant as Villa or Zapata—declaring that the United States had no right to assist "this rich Mexican." [30]

It is impossible at present to determine whether the rumors and reports about the "blood bath" in Mexico City were true or merely products of bitter and vindictive civil-war propaganda. Statements that seem to have originated in Carranzista sources gave the numbers killed as running into the hundreds. According to these reports, the executions did not cease when Silliman and Canova so reported but instead were conducted with greater secrecy. The firing squads were said to be busy even on Christmas Day.[31]

To what extent Villa was personally responsible for the dark events supposed to have occurred in Mexico City was (and is) a disputed matter. As noted earlier, he was absent from the capital when the situation was at its worst, and immediately upon his return he announced that he had come to put a stop to the killings.[32] This, his enemies pointed out, he could have done by telegraph—his absence from Mexico City was very conveniently timed to enable him to deny responsibility.

The executions seemed to cost Villa very little of the regard in which he was held by the administration in Washington and by large numbers of the American people. The war in Europe was hardening the American public to tales of slaughter. In Villa's earlier career there were murders ascribed to him personally, but this time the reports were too vague, too nebulous and general, to cause any great amount of horror to become attached to him individually. There were, in addition, other factors and considerations which seemed to mitigate any guilt. In late December, Carranza issued a decree ordering the immediate execution, without trial, of any former Huertistas captured while serving in the forces of Villa and Zapata.[33] Offsetting any re-

---

[29] *Independent*, LXXXI (Jan. 4, 1915), 12.   [30] *Ibid.*   [31] *Ibid.*
[32] *Ibid.* (Jan. 11, 1915), p. 47.   [33] *Ibid.*, LXXX (Dec. 28, 1914), 491.

pugnance which might be felt for Villa because of events in Mexico City were reports that he had sent a large number of war orphans, whom he gathered out of the streets himself, to Chihuahua to be cared for and educated at his expense. For several months past, it was said, he had been supporting numerous orphans in Chihuahua and the United States.[34] Less appealing to sentiment and emotion, but of solid appeal to government officials and businessmen, was the effort of Villa and Zapata to put their finances on a sound basis, which included calling together a group of Mexico City bankers to advise and assist them.[35]

During December, 1914, the Carranza government established itself in Veracruz. The propaganda mills continued to work at high pressure; the realignment of parties and people proceeded apace, but there was little shooting. Confidence of Americans in Carranza went lower than before, because the few battles that were fought were Villa victories; even a battle near Tampico which was reported by the Veracruz government as a great victory turned out instead to be a defeat.[36]

Everywhere, and in all ways, the apparent odds favored an early and complete victory by the combined forces of Villa and Zapata. Mexico had not yet achieved the peace that was believed to be so near when Huerta fled the capital, but Francisco Villa seemed to be a man with the vision and power to lead the country to a just peace and enlightened government. As one editorial writer commented:

[Mexico] is unfit to govern itself on the democratic plan; and the firm but enlightened autocrat who can gain and hold mastery, as successor to Porfirio Díaz, has not yet been acknowledged.

This role of strong man may even yet have to be played by Francisco Villa. He is illiterate, of the humblest origin, and of very unpromising record. But he has developed into a military genius, and he seems to have the luck to be fighting on the side of destiny, of the common people, and the wise principle of keeping on good terms with the United States.[37]

[34] *Ibid.*, p. 492. This is partly confirmed by Taracena, in *Mi vida en el vértigo de la Revolución Mexicana*, p. 316.

[35] Walter F. McCaleb, *The Public Finances of Mexico* (New York, 1921), p. 232.

[36] *Literary Digest*, XLIX (Dec. 15, 1914), 1312. Cf. the New York *Times*, Thursday, Dec. 3, 1914, 1:1, and Taracena, *Mi vida en el vértigo de la Revolución Mexicana*, p. 318.

[37] *Review of Reviews*, LI (Jan., 1915), 9.

In spite of the gruesome reports of midnight executions in Mexico City, at the end of 1914 Villa appeared to be the man of destiny for Mexico. Friend of the United States and advocate of a program according with American ideals, he seemed thus by many circumstances the man to establish a government in Mexico that the United States could eventually recognize and support.

❧ XI ❧

Villa, Dictator of the North

MEANWHILE, events in Sonora, too, seemed to give evidence that Villa was the Mexican leader most deserving of the confidence of the United States. It will be recalled that, in August, Villa and Obregón had conferred about the situation that had developed at Naco. At that time, in deference to Washington's insistence that American citizens be no longer endangered, Villa had ordered his forces withdrawn to the south. The dispute seemed to be settled, but, in September, Governor Maytorena defeated General Benjamin Hill, the local Carranzista commander, driving him into Naco, which was again besieged.[1]

At the beginning of the siege, people on the American side of the border, forgetting the lessons of the past, were interested spectators, but wild and random shots soon dampened their curiosity. By the end of November the adobe houses of Naco, Arizona, were almost as deeply pitted and pocked by rifle and machine gun fire as the houses on the Mexican side. Several Americans, including a number of soldiers, had been killed and wounded, and it was widely feared that Maytorena's Yaqui Indians might get out of control and erupt across the border at any moment.[2]

[1] *Independent*, LXXX (Oct. 5, 1914), 10. Cf. Obregón, *Ocho mil kilómetros en campaña*, p. 335, and Manuel Ortigoza, *Ciento catorce días de sitio: La defensa de Naco* (Mexico City, 1916), p. 14.
[2] *Independent*, LXXX (Oct. 12, 1914), 51; (Oct. 19, 1914), 51; (Nov. 30, 1914), 312.

The situation became so critical that the United States forces at Naco were reinforced and General Tasker H. Bliss was detailed to take command. On December 9, 1914, the State Department sent identical notes to Carranza and Provisional President Gutiérrez, pointing out that the local commanders at Naco were failing entirely to control their subordinates. The conclusion was that unless corrective steps were taken at once, the United States would be compelled to "employ such forces as may be required." [3]

Guitérrez promptly telegraphed to Maytorena to take immediate measures to prevent trouble, even to breaking off the siege if necessary.[4] Carranza, on the other hand, was indignant at the possibility that United States forces might violate Mexican soil and at the suggestion that his followers might be partly responsible.[5]

This was the situation on December 16, 1914, when General Scott hurriedly left Washington for the border. He arrived at Naco on December 19. After issuing a sharp warning to both sides that no more firing across the border would be tolerated, he arranged for a series of conferences with the opposing Mexican commanders.[6]

Torrential rains made it difficult to keep engagements and hold conferences, but despite difficulties, an announcement came on the day after Christmas that an agreement had been reached.[7] The Carranzistas agreed to evacuate Naco, and both factions promised not to occupy the place again. The town would be open and neutral until there was a govenment in Mexico recognized by the United States or until one side or the other had gained undisputed supremacy in Sonora. The Carranzistas were to hold Agua Prieta, and Hill's force was to march to that place from Naco without interference by the Villistas. The latter, for their part, were to remain in possession of Nogales without being molested by the Carranzistas.[8]

Governor Maytorena, presumably, had consented to these arrangements, but he refused to sign the agreement, on the grounds that

[3] *Ibid.* (Dec. 21, 1914), p. 492; *Foreign Relations, 1914,* p. 649. It has always been suspected that many of the shots fired into the United States were far from accidental. The writer has been told by eyewitnesses of seeing Carranzista soldiers take deliberate aim toward the United States.

[4] *Foreign Relations, 1914,* pp. 649–650.   [5] *Ibid.,* pp. 651–652.

[6] New York *Times,* Sunday, Dec. 20, 1914, 16:1.

[7] *Ibid.,* Wednesday, Dec. 23, 1914, 8:2; Friday, Dec. 25, 1914, 5:1; *Foreign Relations, 1914,* pp. 653–654.

[8] *Ibid.*

he was without authority. He was obviously extremely reluctant to bind himself. On direct orders, telegraphed by Villa, his troops began to evacuate in front of Naco, but on December 30 the Yaquis were again in their trenches, and firing was resumed.[9] The solution of the difficulties at Naco seemed as far distant as before.

An urgent message was now sent to Villa, asking him to come north to confer with General Scott. Villa was willing but was unable to arrive for several days.[10] The conference, with Carothers present, took place on January 7, 1915, on the international bridge between El Paso and Juárez. Villa argued with Scott at length, asking for Scott's consent to stage a hurricane attack on both Agua Prieta and Naco. He guaranteed that he would capture both places in a single day and thus solve all difficulties finally. But Scott was adamant in his insistence that the agreement must be carried out exactly as it was drawn up. The discussion was carried over to the next day, and at last Scott's arguments and perseverance prevailed. On January 9 Villa telegraphed positive orders to Maytorena to sign the agreement and carry it out without further delay.[11]

Villa had again shown that he was willing to co-operate with the United States. Maytorena's prompt compliance with the last order evinced proof that Villa's authority in northern Mexico was beyond dispute. General Scott wrote to his wife: "He came up to Juarez announcing that he had come to meet my wishes. . . . I watched him. . . . with the greatest interest—his intelligence is most apparent— he looks you right in the eye." [12]

Meantime, while Villa was in the north conferring with General Scott, the situation in the capital was becoming more confusing than ever before. Upon adjourning at Aguascalientes, the convention voted to reconvene at Mexico City on the first day of 1915. Friction was developing between the Provisional President and Francisco Villa. Eulalio Gutiérrez was far from being a spineless nonentity, but in spite of the dignity of his position and his imposing title, he was powerless. His orders were obeyed only as far as his formidable lieutenants, Villa and Zapata, chose to obey them. On January 9, before Villa's re-

[9] New York *Times*, Sunday, Dec. 27, 1914, 6:1.

[10] Puente, *La vida de Francisco Villa*, pp. 98–99.

[11] Hugh Lenox Scott Papers. The order to Maytorena, signed by Villa personally, is included in General Scott's papers.

[12] *Ibid.*

turn to the capital, Gutiérrez confided to Silliman that both Villa and Zapata were becoming unbearable and that something important was about to happen.[13] What the "something important" might be, Gutiérrez gave no hint. The friction had not yet reached the public in definite form, and rumors were discounted because, to all appearances, Villa and Gutiérrez were in perfect accord.[14]

The convention assembled on New Year's Day. It promptly accepted a decision of the presiding officer that a majority of members who were loyal to the convention constituted a quorum. Carranzistas did not dare to be present, so that the convention, without any difficulty, qualified itself to do business. General Roque González Garza, a staunch Villista, was elected permanent chairman, whereupon the convention debated a plan for preconstitutional government which had been submitted by the Zapatistas.[15] Everything seemed to be going smoothly, with a reasonable prospect that an orderly government would be evolved.

On January 16 came the startling announcement that Provisional President Gutiérrez, with several members of his cabinet and a considerable part of the garrison, had disappeared during the night. González Garza immediately assumed charge of the capital and declared martial law, "in order that any person who commits atrocities or disturbs the public peace will be executed." Cardoso de Oliveira was notified, with the additional information that General Villa would arrive the same evening, accompanied by a force strong enough to sustain the convention.[16] To allay any fears as to the safety of Americans and other foreigners, a message was sent to the convention's agent in Washington, saying that the city was quiet and under complete control.[17]

The convention promptly deposed Gutiérrez and named González Garza as Provisional President in his stead—an act generally credited to Villa's influence. No one believed for an instant that the disappear-

[13] National Archives, State Department File nos. 812.00/14173, Jan. 9, 1915, and 14095, 14104, 14106, Dec. 29, 1914.

[14] *Independent*, LXXXI (Jan. 31, 1915), 46.

[15] *Foreign relations, 1915*, pp. 643–644.

[16] *Ibid.*, pp. 644–645. Cf. Frank Tannenbaum, *Peace by Revolution: An Interpretation of Mexico* (New York, 1933), p. 160.

[17] *Foreign Relations, 1915*, p. 646.

ance of Gutiérrez would make any difference at all in the real authority behind the conventionist government—it was Villa.[18]

This fact had been understood by the State Department for some time, as evidenced by the instructions sent to Cardoso on December 26: "Please call upon President Gutiérrez and General Villa at once." [19] With the Mexican situation suddenly reaching new heights of uncertainty, it became increasingly important that an American representative remain constantly with Villa. Canova having become *persona non grata*, additional instructions were sent to Carothers several days before Gutiérrez' flight from Mexico City.[20] He was directed to travel with Villa "until we can find someone to take your place." This was difficult, because few people had the necessary qualifications—loyalty to the administration, friendship with Villa, and fluency in Spanish.[21]

A few days earlier, Carothers received proof of his personal influence with Villa and of Villa's consistent regard for the rights of Americans. For a considerable length of time certain unnamed subordinates of Villa had been seizing large quantities of hides, some of which belonged to Americans. Carothers brought the matter to Villa's attention and on January 7 reported that Villa had promised immediate remedial action. Carothers was hopeful of obtaining the return of the hides to the owners.[22]

Carothers was not able at once to travel with Villa. Following his conference with General Scott, Villa had returned to Mexico City, while Carothers remained in the north. He informed the Secretary of State on January 18 that Villa had telegraphed him to remain at Aguascalientes, where he, Villa, would arrive during the night. Carothers further informed the department in the same dispatch that the "new movement" was possibly part of a plot by certain Carranzista generals to eliminate both Carranza and Villa. Villa's staff were advising him to operate against Tampico and the Coahuila coal fields. This would leave Mexico City entirely in the hands of the Zapatistas, who,

[18] E.g., "A Procession of Presidents," *World's Work*, CIX (Feb., 1915), 304, refers to "Roque Gonzalez Garza, *made by Villa Provisional President of Mexico*." (The present writer's italics.)

[19] *Foreign Relations, 1914*, pp. 653–654.

[20] *Independent*, LXXXI (Jan. 4, 1915), 12.

[21] National Archives, State Department File no. 125. 36582/123, Jan. 12, 1915.

[22] *Ibid.*, File no. 812.00/14160, Jan. 7, 1915.

Carothers feared, would be unable to hold the city by themselves.[23]

Carothers' fear was justified. The bulk of Villa's troops were moved north, and on January 27, 1915, Silliman reported that the Zapatista forces and the members of the convention had left the capital the preceding night. The new Provisional President and a few of his cabinet remained one more day, but they too left the next morning. In the afternoon of January 28 General Obregón, with some ten thousand Carranzista troops, reoccupied the city.[24]

The political and military situation in Mexico was changing with kaleidoscopic rapidity in which Villa, in his seemingly impregnable position, appeared to constitute the one stable factor. Not even the desertion of Gutiérrez or the loss of the capital by his allies, the Zapatistas, affected his prestige seriously. The occupation of Mexico City by Obregón hardly compensated the Carranzistas for the losses they had suffered since the first of the year. They had been defeated at Puebla, and there were reports that the garrison of Oaxaca, about eight thousand men, had suddenly declared for Villa.[25] In the north, the Carranzistas were forced out of the important city of Monterrey, in the First Chief's home state. Before leaving, on January 15, they burned the railroad station—an act of unnecessary vandalism. Villistas under General Felipe Angeles occupied Monterrey the next day. Consul General Hanna reported that "the best of order prevails and the officers and soldiers instead of looting have taken an . . . interest in assisting the people." [26]

Even if the ugly stories from Mexico City in December and the melodramatic flight of Gutiérrez had caused the United States to view Villa askance, Carranza again put him into the position of the lesser of two evils. For unknown reasons Carranza suddenly decreed that Veracruz would be the permanent capital of the country. Cardoso de Oliveira reported that Carranza was trying to force the Diplomatic Corps, which he had previously ignored, to move to Veracruz. Cardoso suggested that the United States "intimate to Carranza . . . in

[23] *Ibid.*, File no. 812.00/14238, Jan. 11, 1915. It is not clear whether Carothers was referring to Gutiérrez' flight or to a new revolutionary movement that was rumored at this time.

[24] *Foreign Relations, 1915*, pp. 648–649.

[25] *Independent*, LXXXI (Jan. 4, 1915), 12, and (Jan. 11, 1915), 47.

[26] National Archives, State Department File nos. 812.00/14222, Jan. 15, 1915, and 14228, Jan. 16, 1915.

a strong and decisive way the imperative necessity of leaving someone in the Foreign Office here . . . for the transaction of more important matters with himself or his Foreign Minister." [27] All the
other diplomats in Mexico City advised their governments that it
might be necessary to emulate the United States—to withdraw their
diplomatic personnel and be represented only by special agents.

Agreeing with Cardoso, Washington pointed out to Carranza that
the proposed transfer of the capital was creating an impression that
the Constitutionalists were unable to hold Mexico City. If the foreign
diplomats were withdrawn from Mexico, "a situation will be produced
the grave results of which it is believed Carranza has not duly estimated." [28]

After this, little more was heard of the proposed transfer. The
major effect, probably, was to increase Villa's relative favor with
the United States. Regardless of his undeniable faults, he did not
habitually take deliberate measures calculated to antagonize foreign
governments.

Concurrent with Carranza's ill-timed and tactless announcement
was the sudden and unanticipated clarification of Villa's political
position. The abandonment of Mexico City by the Zapatistas while
Villa was in the north cut him off completely from any communication
with what was left of the government established by the convention.
The new Provisional President had fled, the convention itself had
fled, and all railroads, telegraph lines, and roads were disrupted by
the enemy. Under these circumstances, Villa assumed governmental
powers openly. On February 4, 1915, he telegraphed to his agent in
Washington to notify the Secretary of State that he had "for the time
being, and only for the period during which communication is impossible, assumed political authority." For the transaction of public
business he created three cabinet positions: Foreign Relations and
Justice, Interior Affairs and Communication, Finance and Industry.
The cabinet so formed was to be attached to general headquarters, at
Chihuahua. Special attention was invited to the fact that the con-
vention, on January 18, had "ratified the appointment of General
Villa, all of whose acts will be regarded as those of the 'Provisional
Government.'" [29]

---

[27] *Foreign Relations, 1915*, pp. 649–650. [28] *Ibid.*, p. 651.
[29] *Ibid.*, pp. 650–651, 662–664.

Villa's assumption of political authority without a provisional president acting as a "front" was widely regarded in the United States as the actual assumption of the presidency.[30] According to Villa's own statement, he did not intend it as such. Uncontrolled circumstances caused him to become in actual fact a possibly unwilling, but undisguised, military dictator. Since the shadowy government of the conventon was never re-established, the State Department no longer had to deal with a puppet provisional president whose authority depended entirely upon his nominal subordinate.

Carranza hurled another barb before the tension resulting from his proposed transfer of the capital had died down. Aiming directly at the United States, which was represented in Mexico by special agents, Carranza suddenly forbade his officers and officials to have any dealings at all with "confidential or consular agents of foreign governments." His expressed reasons were so logical that reply was impossible—relations with foreign governments were his own exclusive prerogative as First Chief; in no other way could unity of policy and action be assured. Carranza "recommended" that military commanders refuse to permit any confidential agents with their commands.[31] Since the United States was the only country represented in Mexico by special agents, the inference was obvious, especially as the order mentioned the "defection of General Francisco Villa and other officers of the Northern Division" as showing the dangers from such agents.

For a considerable period after the Carranzistas reoccupied Mexico City, Villa was relatively inactive. It was surmised that he was hoarding his ammunition, which was supposed to be hard to get because of the war in Europe.[32] During this time there were wild rumors that Villa had been murdered by his lieutenant, Rodolfo Fierro, and the press discovered that an attempt had actually been made to assassinate him during the Aguascalientes convention.[33] The would-be assassin was captured and confessed that he had been hired by certain persons in Mexico City to suborn Villa's troops and eliminate Villa himself. Carothers was present during the interrogation and heard the confes-

[30] E.g., *Independent*, LXXXI (Feb. 15, 1915), 252.

[31] *Foreign Relations, 1915*, pp. 652–653.

[32] *Independent*, LXXXI (Feb. 8, 1915), 196. There is no evidence that the war in Europe made the slightest difference in the volume of munitions going to Mexico.

[33] *Ibid.*

sion. He was probably an eyewitness of the execution, which took place immediately.[34]

While Villa was establishing his personal government and remaining quiet otherwise, conditions in the capital were deteriorating. The Carranzistas had not succeeded in completely clearing the suburbs of Zapatistas, and in the outskirts of the city there were daily skirmishes, with numerous casualties. The Zapatistas cut off the city's water supply; with transportation entirely inadequate, food rapidly became scarce. Merchants were forced to accept Carranza fiat currency, while Villa currency was outlawed. These factors combined to cause more misery than had been known in the capital since the Revolution started. As early as February 3, 1915, when the Carranzistas had been in the city only two weeks, Cardoso de Oliveira reported to Washington that "the situation grows worse every day." [35] Other reports received in the United States said that all banks and most stores were closed. Carranza ordered the distribution of some thirteen thousand dollars among the poor, and General Alvaro Obregón, threatening to confiscate Church property, demanded a contribution of two hundred and fifty thousand dollars from the Roman Catholic clergy.[36]

To add to the confusion, Carranza suddenly expelled the Spanish minister on the grounds that he had given asylum to an associate of Villa. The minister went to Veracruz and was given refuge aboard the *U.S.S. Delaware*. To cap the climax of confusion, Villa invited him to come freely to any part of Mexico under Villista control.

As the situation in the unhappy capital continued to become worse, the foreign colony organized an "International Committee of Relief." Their well-meant efforts to help alleviate the misery were sharply rebuffed by Obregón, who demanded that the businessmen of the city contribute twenty million pesos, ostensibly for relief. The shortage of food, the International Committee charged, was brought about by Carranzista generals in order to force men to enlist. The day after the refusal of the committee's offer, Obregón made a public statement:

[34] National Archives, State Department File no. 812.00/13622, Oct. 28, 1914. Cf. Guzmán, *Memorias*, IV, 230–235.
[35] *Foreign Relations, 1915,* p. 650.
[36] *Independent*, LXXXI (Feb. 22, 1915), 271.

"At the first attempt at riot I will leave the city at the head of my troops in order that they may not fire a single shot against the hungry multitude, as the merchants did not accept the invitation which was made to them to assist the people and prevent violence." Next day he repeated: "I will not fire a single shot into any mob who may attempt to get what hunger has driven them to seize." [37] On March 3 some three hundred merchants and other businessmen were assembled, by Obregón's order, in one of the theaters. He made a violent harangue, after which he marched them all to prison, having surrounded the building with troops.[38] They were not detained long, but severe penalties were promised for any merchant who failed to open his shop or refused to accept Carranza currency.

Added to these incidents was a renewal of the attempt to transfer the capital to Veracruz on the grounds that Mexico City would be evacuated very soon.[39] And next Washington learned that the Carranzista authorities refused railway transportation to bring in food and other necessities which the International Committee had obtained.[40]

President Wilson was extremely indignant. He directed Secretary Bryan to prepare a strong personal note for Carranza, protesting against Obregón's extraordinary and unpardonable acts. To emphasize the gravity of the matter, Bryan was also told: "Ask Daniels if he has any ships with long range guns . . . which he could order to Vera Cruz at once." [41]

The correspondence which developed with the Carranza government during the next few days was more than slightly acrimonious. In accordance with the President's instructions, Bryan said: "When a factional leader preys on a starving city to compel obedience to his decrees by inciting outlawry and at the same time uses means to prevent the city from being supplied with food, a situation is created which it is impossible for the United States to contemplate longer with patience." He added that the United States would hold Carranza and Obregón personally responsible for the safety of Americans in Mexico City and would take any necessary measures to bring to account anybody

[37] *Foreign Relations, 1915*, p. 654.   [38] *Ibid.*, pp. 656–657.
[39] *Ibid.*, pp. 657–658.   [40] *Ibid.*, p. 658.
[41] National Archives, State Department File no. 812.00/14504 1/2, March 6, 1915. This note, initialed "W.W.," was written by the President personally on his own typewriter.

responsible for outrages. This strong warning was delivered to both Carranza and Obregón.[42]

Obregón pleaded that a subordinate of the First Chief could not receive an official communication from a foreign government. Carranza flatly denied the allegations in the notes and was highly incensed at the suggestion as to his personal responsibility. His indignation was particularly hot against the author of the note, and he threatened that, sooner or later, Bryan would have to answer for it.[43]

Carranza's formal reply, addressed to President Wilson personally, placed the responsibility for the deplorable conditions in the capital upon Villa, whom he again linked with the reactionaries. Carranza promised that upon the evacuation of Mexico City all foreigners would receive the protection which the Constitutionalist army always extended to them.[44]

The value of Carranzista protection was demonstrated the day before the evacuation. In the confusion of the withdrawal a number of outrages were perpetrated against Americans, and several other foreigners were murdered. The evidence was conclusive, but that did not keep the Carranzista authorities from denying flatly the truth of Cardoso de Oliveira's reports.[45]

Early in 1915 another problem arose to plague Washington. The touchy and delicate question of relations between the Constitutionalists and the Church threw the Mexican problem into the domestic political field in the United States. Ever since the outbreak of the Revolution there had been numerous—almost innumerable—reports that the Constitutionalists were deeply hostile to the Church. Careful investigation failed to substantiate most of the stories of the violation of nuns, murder of priests, and arbitrary confiscation of Church property, but people still believed them. Roman Catholic organizations in the United States stirred themselves from the first on behalf of their coreligionists in Mexico, and Roman Catholic voters formed an appreciable part of President Wilson's party. Although he was the son of a Presbyterian clergyman and Secretary Bryan was a rock-ribbed Protestant funda-

---

[42] *Foreign Relations, 1915*, pp. 659–661.

[43] *Ibid.*, p. 661. Cf. National Archives, State Department File no. 812.00/14547, March 11, 1915.

[44] *Foreign Relations, 1915*, pp. 666–668.   [45] *Ibid.*, pp. 671, 673.

mentalist, the administration could not turn a deaf ear to the appeals of American Catholics, even had it been totally unsympathetic. But the administration was not unsympathetic, and there seemed to be just enough substance to the unpleasant tales from Mexico to justify diplomatic action.

During the early part of the Revolution nearly all outrages against the Church were charged against the Constitutionalists, without distinguishing between the various Constitutionalist forces. After the break between Villa and Carranza it became apparent that most of the incidents that could be proved had been committed by Carranzistas. The number of such incidents which were verified by consular reports or by other impartial information seemed to increase sharply during the first few months of 1915.[46]

Villa was known to be not particularly friendly toward the Church, but few outrages against the Church were reported in areas under his control. In Sonora, the consuls reported that nothing of the kind had ever occurred.[47] In Chihuahua, Letcher cited several cases of the confiscation of Church property, the closing of Catholic schools, and the departure of priests from their parishes in fear of danger. He concluded his report with a lurid rumor that Fierro had kidnaped a beautiful young nun from a convent in Zacatecas and was holding her in Chihuahua. "There is no possible means of substantiating the story," Letcher said, "but similar acts affecting persons other than nuns have recently occurred, according to what should be regarded as fair evidence, and under present conditions the story does not appear particularly remarkable or extraordinary." [48]

Taken all in all, Villa and the Villistas seemed far less vindictive toward the Church and far less brutal in their treatment of the religious than the Carranzistas. On February 23, 1915, Father Francis C. Kelley, of the Catholic Church Extension Society, who had been corresponding with the State Department, wrote to the Secretary of State: "I think Villa now realizes the mistakes that were made. . . . I am well aware that nothing is to be expected of Carranza. . . . But I do believe that Villa can be reached, and I know positively that Mexican leaders in the United States are favorable." [49]

On the night of March 10 the Carranzistas left the capital, and the

[46] *Ibid.*, pp. 1004–1030.   [47] *Ibid.*, p. 1010.   [48] *Ibid.*, pp. 1014–1015.
[49] *Ibid.*, pp. 1019–1020.

Zapatistas re-entered the next morning, "in perfect order and amid popular enthusiasm representing all classes." The Zapatista commander immediately promised his full co-operation in obtaining transportation for food purchased by the International Committee of Relief and expressed his gratitude to the Diplomatic Corps for their efforts on behalf of the destitute people of the city.[50]

In contrast to the previous entry by the Zapatistas, a number of outrages against foreigners were reported, and in a few days it became known that an American, John B. McManus, had been killed in his own dooryard. Since Villa and Zapata were still allies, they were held jointly responsible by the United States government, as well as in American public opinion. Zapata promised a full investigation, and Villa gave a signed statement to the press, saying: "I will insist that the man or men responsible be brought before me and punished as such traitors deserve." [51] However good Villa's intentions may have been, actually he was powerless. He was in the north, and none of the troops in Mexico City were under his authority. Still, his indignation was in refreshing contrast to Carranza's habitual surly antagonism.

Reports about conditions in Mexico City received in the United States were vague and contradictory: "Conventionist Troops Maintain Order —Zapatistas Loot the City—Strict Enforcement of Law and Order— Murders and Outrages of Daily Occurrence." The difficulty of obtaining reliable news was accentuated by the fact that dispatches from Mexico City passed through Veracruz, where they were were read and censored by the Carranzistas.[52] The truth seems to be that, in spite of isolated outrages, the conduct of Zapata's troops was not too bad. None of Cardoso de Oliveira's reports after the reoccupation by Zapata reflect conditions as bad as those under the Carranza occupation. The British minister, who was not particularly favorable toward the Villa-Zapata faction, referred, in a message to his colleague in Washington, to the "improvement in [the] situation." [53]

The foregoing account of the events of early 1915 has little direct bearing upon relations between the United States and the *de facto* dictator of the north. The connection is nonetheless real in spite of

[50] *Ibid.,* p. 669.
[51] *Independent,* LXXXI (March 22, 1915), 416, and *Literary Digest,* L (March 27, 1915), 674–675.
[52] *Foreign Relations, 1915,* p. 654.
[53] *Ibid.,* p. 672.

being indirect. There was a striking contrast between Carranza's truculent reaction to every suggestion and Villa's amenability, between conditions in Mexico City under Carranza and under Villa and Zapata. Every act of the Carranza regime seemed to be calculated to cause Villa to rise in favor with the United States. It is hardly an exaggeration to say that Carranza was Villa's most effective propagandist in Washington at this time. An American commentator noted that, unlike Obregón's direct invitation to riot, "one is struck with the frequent mention of the fact that order is maintained wherever Villa and his generals are in control." [54] The United States was groping for a government in Mexico that would bring law and order with social and economic justice. Villa denied all personal ambitions and seemed to be sincere in his aspirations toward a strictly constitutional regime.

[54] McGregor, "Villa—Victor—Dictator," *Harper's Weekly*, LX (March 20, 1915), 280.

❧ XII ❧

Wilson's Dilemma: Villa or Carranza?

AS the early part of 1915 passed, the situation in Mexico daily became more obscure. Anxiously trying to decide which of the Mexican leaders the United States should support, President Wilson once again felt the need of information from somebody whose judgment he could trust. The personal representative whom he selected this time was DuVal West, a prominent lawyer and former Federal district attorney of San Antonio, Texas.

West's instructions were written and signed by the President himself. West was to visit the Mexican faction leaders and estimate their characters and capabilities. He was to ascertain their purposes and objectives and evaluate their relative chances of success. The President was "very anxious to know just what the moral situation" was in Mexico and whether any prospective settlement would be for the benefit of the common people or merely for the selfish ambition of the leaders.[1]

President Wilson's instructions for West expressed clearly and tersely the underlying basis for his Mexican policy—the welfare of the common people of the country. There was not a word, not even a hint, of pro-

---

[1] Woodrow Wilson Papers. West's instructions were in two letters, dated Feb. 8 and 10, 1915. They appear to have been written by the President himself, on his personal typewriter.

moting the material interests of the United States or of foreigners in
Mexico. The President's dilemma was to determine which of the
Mexican leaders was most likely to put the welfare of the people above
his own ambitions.

In spite of the fact that the President's instructions to West were almost altruistic, a strange belief has gained wide acceptance that there
was something underhanded or sinister about West's mission. A recent
American writer on Mexico has said: "Accepted generally as a fact,
although documentary evidence is lacking, is the story that on April
21, 1915, Duval West, United States special agent, proposed to give
Francisco Villa support and recognition . . . in return for cession of
Lower California."[2] Just why such a tale should be "accepted generally
as a fact" when, admittedly, there is no evidence has never been explained. But its acceptance in certain quarters has served to bespatter
the favor the United States showed Villa in the early part of 1915 and
has given a Machiavellian twist to the ultimate recognition of his
enemy, Carranza.

It so happened that in early 1915 there was considerable interest in
the United States in events occurring in Lower California. Some
American newspapers, from time to time, had proposed acquiring the
magnificent anchorage of Magdalena Bay, in the Mexican territory.
Then, following a series of war scares resulting from growing tension
between Japan and the United States, a Japanese cruiser, the *Asama*,
went aground on December 31, 1914, at Turtle Bay, not far from
Magdalena Bay. Several weeks passed before the *Asama* was refloated.
During that time fantastic rumors circulated widely in the more sensational newspapers that the Japanese were using the *Asama* as a blind
behind which they were constructing a naval base.[3]

These rumors were quickly exploded, but they continued to circulate
for a considerable time. Coinciding with DuVal West's mission, they
undoubtedly encouraged the idea that President Wilson might be following a tortuous course with a view to obtaining concessions in
Lower California through Villa. That President Wilson was even re-

[2] J. H. Plenn, *Mexico Marches* (Indianapolis, Ind., 1939). The present writer has
also heard this same statement from other students of Mexican history.

[3] "The Yarn of Turtle Bay," *World's Work*, CIX (April 28, 1915), 951. Similar
reports were repeated in numerous newspapers.

motely capable of such a thing is belied by his known character and beliefs, as well as by the instructions he personally wrote for West, his supposed tool in the nefarious scheme.

West's appointment was announced simultaneously with the publication of Carranza's decree forbidding his officials to have anything to do with foreign special agents. Newspapers in the United States remarked that this latest of Carranza's decrees would be extremely inconvenient for the special agent just appointed. The week following, on March 1, the press noted briefly that West had left El Paso to visit Villa and Carranza in turn.[4]

Reporting to the President several weeks later, West neither praised Villa as highly nor disapproved of Carranza as strongly as Paul Fuller had done. On arriving at Veracruz, late in March, West had to wait several days before seeing Carranza, who was ill at the time. As soon as his health permitted, Carranza received West with great cordiality. West explained that his mission was to obtain complete information for President Wilson. Carranza replied that he and all of his ministers were at West's disposal.[5]

This was the only interview West had with Carranza personally, but he had lengthy conversations with Luis Cabrera, Rafael Zubáran Capmany, and other high officials of the Constitutionalist government. He had no opportunity to see either General Obregón or General González, as they were both at the front.

West drew a strong contrast between the atmosphere in Villa's provisional government and that which he found at Veracruz. Villa's government was military, with civilian elements and civilian considerations pushed into the background. All thought and effort were concentrated on the war. At Veracruz, far distant from the fighting, all energy was devoted to planning the laws and reforms promised in the Plan of Guadalupe. The entire administration, as West observed it, was civilian rather than military.

West found further contrast between the two governments. Villa's officials were confident, but the Constitutionalists were not sanguine as

[4] *Independent*, LXXXI (Feb. 22, 1915), 271, and (March 1, 1915), 315.

[5] DuVal West, "Partial Report and Impressions Received at Vera Cruz," National Archives, State Department File no. 812.00/20721, April 5, 1915. Neither West's report on his visit to Villa's headquarters nor his final report could be located. The tenor of his report on Villa can be inferred from the report cited above.

to their prospects of final success; rather, he felt, they were somewhat doubtful. Remarks were prefaced with "If we are successful," instead of "When we win."

West's general estimate of the Constitutionalist leaders (except Carranza himself, upon whom he did not comment) was not uncomplimentary, but not wholly favorable. As a whole, they were men of higher type than Villa's officials, but some of them were not purely patriotic in their motives. They were capable of developing the ability to carry on a civil government if given the opportunity. But, West concluded, there was small chance that the generals would continue to obey Carranza; consequently, the Constitutionalists could not bring peace to Mexico.

West's report would appear, at first glance, to favor the Carranzistas over the Villistas. Carranza's officials were men of higher type than the men surrounding Villa. Carranza's government was a civil government, composed of civilians; Villa's government was purely military. In the United States, anything resembling militarism was traditionally regarded with deep suspicion. On the other hand, Villa and his officials seemed to be realistically aware that no reforms were possible without winning the war and establishing control over the country.

If President Wilson hoped that he would be able to make an immediate decision based on the information obtained by DuVal West, he was disappointed. West's report gave no hope that either Villa or Carranza would be able to bring peace or establish a constitutional government in Mexico in the predictable future. No settlement that would be for the benefit of the common people was even remotely in sight. The policy of "watchful waiting," consequently, had to be continued indefinitely, unless some sudden change in the situation indicated clearly what action the United States should take.

Through the spring of 1915 the mutual regard between Villa and General Scott continued and seemed to become stronger. There was a steady correspondence between them, with Scott, from time to time, making suggestions and dropping hints for Villa's consideration. In February, for example, Scott wrote a letter of introduction for a group of newspapermen who wanted an interview with Villa. A month later Villa replied, thanking Scott for giving him the opportunity to meet such an interesting group of men. On March 7 Villa wrote again to Scott, apologizing for his delay in replying to an earlier letter and saying that he had issued orders to Governor Maytorena to give guarantees, which Scott had suggested, to the Cananea Consolidated Copper Company. On April 2 Scott thanked Villa for his action in the Cananea matter and for a handsome Mexican blanket which Villa had sent him. Somewhat earlier Villa sent word to Scott through Carothers that he had been asked by a Japanese naval officer as to his attitude in case of war between Japan and the United States. He had replied, he said, that all of his resources would be at the disposal of the United States.[6]

The Chief of Staff of the Army (or any other military official) normally has no voice in the formulation of the foreign policy of the United States. This was especially true under President Wilson. Still, Scott's open friendliness with Villa must have had some effect upon the opinion of the Secretary of War. As a member of the cabinet, the Secretary of War had a definite voice in the administration's policies.

If the President had been inclined to shift his favor from Villa to Carranza after studying West's report, he was probably deterred by the fact that Carranza seemed suddenly to have acquired all of Villa's former phobia against Spaniards. Carranza's expulsion of the Spanish minister has been mentioned. Exercising its good offices during the next few months, the United States made several representations to Carranza's government about outrages and violence against Spaniards in places under Carranzista control. Every effort by the United States was either rebuffed with almost studied rudeness or evaded with legalistic pettifoggery. The correspondence led the editor of the *Independent* to remark that "Carranza is in disfavor in Washington."[7]

Attempted protection of Spaniards was only one of the diplomatic problems growing out of the Mexican situation in the spring of 1915. The Benton tragedy came to the fore again with unsuccessful efforts by Letcher to help Benton's widow recover her husband's ranch. In this matter the local Villista officials, with whom Letcher had to deal, were as evasive as the Carranzistas.[8] At the same time a considerable number of Turkish subjects (mostly Syrians) residing in Mexico furnished a new problem. Since Turkey was unrepresented in Mexico, the Turkish

[6] Hugh Lenox Scott Papers. The group of newspapermen referred to was accompanied by Gunther Lessing, who was attorney in the United States for the Division of the North.

[7] *Independent*, LXXXI (March 1, 1915), 312; *Foreign Relations, 1915*, pp. 1033–1034.

[8] *Foreign Relations, 1915*, pp. 1030–1031.

government asked the United States to use its good offices in their behalf. The United States was unable to accomplish much, but the Syrians added to the volume of correspondence between Washington and both the Villista and Carranzista governments.[9]

Another difficult problem was presented by the numerous Chinese in territory controlled by Villista partisans. The Chinese in Mexico were mostly tradesmen and small shopkeepers and were regarded as fair game in any brawl. In Sonora, Maytorena's Yaquis looted the Chinese colony at Nacozari, and the unfortunate people were in deathly fear of a massacre, such as had occurred at Torreón four years earlier. Consul Frederick Simpich reported that representations to Governor Maytorena were useless. Maytorena's undisciplined officers and men looted and tormented the helpless Orientals. At Carothers' request, Villa ordered Maytorena to protect the Chinese, but on this occasion Villa's commands seem to have been ignored. The Chinese in Sonora continued to suffer for months to come. The situation became so bad that one American consular officer, unable to obtain protection from Maytorena for the Chinese under his care, finally appealed to the nearest Carranzista commander, General Plutarco Calles.[10] The results of this appeal are unknown, but the necessity of making it seemed to indicate that Villa's control over Maytorena was far from absolute.

The protection of foreigners in Mexico was not the only problem faced by the State Department in the early part of 1915. A large part, probably the major part, of American capital in Mexico was invested in mines and related industries. Most of the mines and smelters were in territory controlled by Villa. Although the Tampico oil fields were currently held by the Carranzistas, Villa was expected shortly to invade (and probably conquer) that area. It was important to know, as soon as possible, just what policies he would follow on mineral and mining concessions of all sorts.

The answer to this question was given on March 19, when Decree no. 5 was issued at Villa's headquarters and temporary capital at Monterrey. The decree provided, in general terms, for the confiscation of all mining properties which had been abandoned, which had not been worked for sixty days or more, or upon which taxes had not been paid according to law. Owners of abandoned or suspended mines were given four months from the date of the decree to resume operations.

[9] *Ibid.*, pp. 1072–1076, 1086–1087.   [10] *Ibid.*, pp. 1088–1091.

Owners of concessions upon which work had never been undertaken were also given four months in which to start. Owners of property upon which taxes were in arrears were allowed ninety days to pay in full.[11]

On its face, Decree no. 5 does not appear to be drastic, but to Americans, with their tradition of the sacredness of private property, the word confiscation had an evil sound. Letcher, reporting on the decree, believed that it was the most radical measure ever proposed by any faction in Mexico. Since full compliance with the decree by any owner was practically impossible, the measure would lead to the confiscation of mining properties throughout Villista territory.[12]

The State Department shared Letcher's alarm over the way the decree might affect American owners of Mexican mining properties. Carothers was directed by telegraph to protest at once against the application of Decree no. 5 to property belonging to Americans or any other foreigners. Carothers was told to remind Villa that the United States had been forced to advise Americans to leave Mexico because of the dangers of the Revolution and could not yet advise them to return. Americans who remained in Mexico had found operations impossible because of the destruction of the railroads and the scarcity of labor. The requirement of the decree, that work must start immediately upon properties that had not been worked previously, was particularly unjust. Great expenditures would be necessary without knowing whether or not there was enough ore to make mining worth while.[13]

Carothers found Villa's officials willing to listen to reason. On April 16 he telegraphed from Irapuato that Decree no. 5 was not intended to interfere with or injure any legitimate mining operation. Its intention was to prevent speculation in dormant mining properties. Four days later Carothers discussed the matter with Villa personally. Villa assured him that he did not intend to enforce the decree strictly until he could give guarantees and furnish transportation. Immediately after the next battle with Obregón, he added, he would consider modifying the decree. He asked Carothers to assure the State Department that, meanwhile, Decree no. 5 would cause no international trouble.[14]

This welcome information was amplified, on April 19, by a memorandum from Villa's agent in Washington, Enrique C. Llorente, to the Secretary of State. The purpose of the decree, Llorente said, was to

[11] *Ibid.*, pp. 894–895.　　[12] *Ibid.*, p. 893.　　[13] *Ibid.*, pp. 895–896.
[14] *Ibid.*, pp. 899, 901.

prevent speculation and to guarantee that owners of abandoned or un-
worked property would bear their just share of taxation. The Villa
government had no intention of being unreasonable or arbitrary. The
application of the decree would not be confiscatory, nor would a nar-
row construction be placed upon it.[15]

A short time before the issuance of Decree no. 5, the Mine and
Smelter Operators Association, alarmed by reports that taxes were to
be increased sharply, had sent two representatives to Mexico to negoti-
ate with Villa's government. One of the two, A. J. McQuatters, was a
close friend of General Scott, a fact which may have contributed to the
relatively easy settlement of the anticipated difficulty.[16] On March 19
an agreement was signed under which the tax rates on metals and ores
exported from Villa's territory were fixed at a figure much lower than
had been feared. The agreement was embodied in an additional decree
issued on the same day as Decree no. 5. But in spite of Villa's reassur-
ances, the mineowners were still apprehensive. The two representatives
hurried from Villa's headquarters to Washington to urge the State Department to insist upon the unconditional repeal of Decree no. 5.[17]

Whether by coincidence or by design, almost simultaneously with
Villa's decree Carranza's government issued a decree dealing with the
taxation of mines and mining properties. Villa's tax decree was issued
after consultation with representatives of the mining industry; presumably the rates agreed upon were the maximum that could be extorted
without killing the goose that laid the golden eggs. Carranza's decree,
issued without any reference to the industry, laid extortionate export
taxes upon gold, silver, zinc, copper, lead, and their ores. Naturally, the
owners of mining property located in Carranza territory protested to
the State Department, which was again faced with the hopeless task
of persuading Carranza to be reasonable. The situation became even
more complicated when Carranzista officials attempted to collect taxes
from an American mining company whose properties lay in Villa's
stronghold of Chihuahua.[18]

Those early months of 1915 found President Wilson perplexed.
Which of the Mexican leaders would give Mexico the kind of govern-

[15] *Ibid.*, pp. 901–902.
[16] *Ibid.*, pp. 903–906. There is a possibility that General Scott may have used his
"good offices" in this matter.
[17] *Ibid.*   [18] *Ibid.*, pp. 899–900, 910–911.

ment that he hoped to see established? Which of the two principal leaders would unselfishly promote the welfare of the people and at the same time protect the lawful rights of foreigners in Mexico? DuVal West's report seemed to indicate that Carranza's government was less militaristic than Villa's. On the other hand, Carranza frankly intended to maintain a dictatorship until after the war, while Villa, from the very first, had advocated an immediate return to constitutional practices. Villa had originally been callous about the rights, even the lives, of foreigners. Recently Carranza had been the major offender, while Villa at least made a gesture toward protecting them. A commentator in *Harper's Weekly* remarked that General Obregón's recent acts in Mexico City, imprisoning ecclesiastics and forcing millions of dollars from property owners, made Villa's more liberal policies stand out in strong relief.[19]

Villa had repeatedly shown himself to be co-operative, while Carranza was almost contemptuous in his attitude toward the United States. Up to this time Villa's control over his subordinates had seemed to be firmer than Carranza's, but Governor Maytorena's disregard of Villa's orders for protecting the Chinese seemed to indicate that possibly Villa's authority was not as absolute as had been supposed. Thus, although the weight of evidence seemed to favor Villa as the leader who could achieve a just peace in Mexico, the evidence was far from conclusive. Short of active intervention, the only thing President Wilson could do was to continue to watch and wait.

[19] McGregor, "Villa—Victor—Dictator," *Harper's Weekly,* LX (March 20, 1915), 280.

❧ XIII ❧

Wilson's Appeal
to the Mexican People

PRESIDENT WILSON, in a phrase attributed to President Grover Cleveland, was confronted with a condition, not a theory. Mexico was hopelessly divided into two separate, independent, and bitterly hostile sovereignties, each claiming to be the supreme power in the country. President Wilson was not yet ready, in the summer of 1915, to abandon his announced policy of "watchful waiting" by a formal recognition of either Villa or Carranza; at the same time it was necessary to maintain diplomatic relations of a sort with each of them. Otherwise there could be no possibility of influencing them. The distinction between *de facto* recognition in a legal or diplomatic sense and the kind of recognition that was dictated by the situation as it actually existed is so fine that it is intelligible, probably, only to a trained specialist in international law. The legal representative of the Division of the North in the United States considered that the administration's policies in detailing a consular officer permanently to accompany Villa and certain "other circumstances were tantamount to *de facto* recognition." [1]

Many Americans predicted that Villa's next major move would be against Tampico, to gain possession of the oil fields and the port. From

---

[1] This information was given to the writer by Mr. Gunther R. Lessing, in a personal letter dated Sept. 27, 1957. Cited by Mr. Lessing's permission.

a purely military point of view his next effort should logically be directed against Obregón. Obregón's forces constituted Carranza's main strength. With them threatening his rear, Villa's possession of Tampico would be precarious. On the other hand, if Obregón were defeated, the oil fields would fall into Villa's hands with little effort on his part. Villa, self-taught though he was, was too good a soldier to overlook these considerations.

After the issue with Carranza became clear-cut, Villa's first concern was to prepare and equip his army for the test of strength that everybody knew must come. There was sporadic fighting between Villistas and Carranzistas from the first of the year on, but the two main armies did not meet. In Villa's territory, recruits were being added to the veterans, and a stream of munitions and equipment poured across the border or was landed at night on the beaches of the Gulf Coast.[2] The American attorney representing Villa's organization signed contracts, in his own name, for ammunition; a wholesale dealer in El Paso sold huge quantities of surplus United States Army clothing and equipment; lesser agents busied themselves in other places, purchasing and forwarding items needed to prepare for the showdown.[3]

All of this required money or unlimited credit. It was in the hope of putting the economy of his territory on a basis to furnish funds that Villa issued his Decree no. 5 and agreed to the contract on taxation with the mineowners. "The . . . Army needs abundant pecuniary elements . . . in order to carry to a satisfactory termination its patriotic duties . . . [and] to insure tranquillity."[4] There may have been, and probably was, justification for the fears of the mineowners, but it cannot be denied that Villa made an effort to encourage the reopening and operation of the smelters. A certain degree of success was attained, and the smelters, under protection of guards from the Villista army, went into partial production.[5] Threatened labor troubles, fomented by delegates of the Industrial Workers of the World, were discouraged by sharp warnings to the delegates, who decided that discretion was

[2] National Archives, Department of Justice File no. 90755-C-68, Nov. 24, 1915. The case of the schooner *Lucy H.* proved that picaresque adventures still occurred in the Gulf of Mexico.

[3] Mr. Gunther R. Lessing to the writer. See note 1, *supra*.

[4] *Foreign Relations, 1915*, pp. 894, 905.

[5] Isaac F. Marcosson, *Metal Magic: The Story of the American Smelting and Refining Company* (New York, 1949), pp. 232–233.

preferable to martyrdom.[6] Americans whose sympathies were inclined to the left considered that this branded Villa as an enemy of "labor," but more likely it was simply his direct method of ensuring that the revenue-producing smelters would not be interrupted during a time of crisis.

At the end of the first week of April, Villa's forces began moving south from Irapuato, while at the same time Obregón's army was moving north. A major battle was evidently near.[7] The next day, jubilant dispatches from Veracruz told of a great defeat for Villa, but Carothers telegraphed from Irapuato that Villa had announced that he was defeating the enemy.[8] Reports were so vague and contradictory that it was impossible to tell what was really occuring south of the border. The only thing certain was that Villa and Obregón were engaging in a major battle, the results of which might determine the future of Mexico. Claims and counterclaims appeared in the American press, to the bewilderment of the readers. On Monday, April 12, reports from Villa's headquarters said that the Carranza forces were beaten and completely demoralized. They were almost completely surrounded in the city of Celaya, according to the reports, and Villa was demanding that they move outside the city to fight so that the civilian populace would not be harmed by the bombardment.[9] The next day, however, the reports were reversed, and the newspapers carried news of a crushing defeat for Villa.[10]

Within a few days it became known that Villa's army, if not as completely defeated as the Carranzista communiqués indicated, had at least suffered a reverse. Obregón's first report was misleading, but the Villistas, after successfully penetrating into Celaya, had been driven out with severe losses. Again, the reports from the two sides were contradictory. Obregón claimed that he had captured 8,000 prisoners, 5,000 rifles, and 30 field guns, with a loss of only 200 casualties for himself—a claim that was probably absurd. Villa, for his part, telegraphed that he still held all his positions and was making preparations for the decisive fight.[11]

[6] O'Connor, *The Guggenheims: The Making of an American Dynasty*, p. 335.
[7] New York *Times,* Wednesday, April 7, 1915, 5:2.
[8] *Ibid.,* Thursday, April 8, 1915, 5:3.
[9] *Ibid.,* Monday, April 12, 1915, 5:1.
[10] *Ibid.,* Tuesday, April 13, 1915, 3:6.
[11] *Independent,* LXXXII (April–June, 1915), 140. Most American newspaper

Although the prolonged battle of Celaya proved, in the long run, to be the really decisive battle in the Villa-Carranza phase of the Mexican Revolution, the results were not immediately apparent. Although Villa no longer advanced southward, there was otherwise no discernible change in the military situation. He continued to rule the north as a dictator, his government continued to issue decrees with the force of law, and his relations with the United States remained on a friendly, not to say benevolent, basis. The battle of Celaya was a defeat, but not an immediate disaster. Its effects on Villa's political fortunes, and hence on relations between him and the United States, lay in the future.

Concurrent with the campaign of Celaya, a "side show" was developing in the extreme northeast of Mexico, which was of direct concern to the United States government and large numbers of American citizens. The important border city of Matamoros, across the Rio Grande from Brownsville, Texas, was held by a Carranzista garrison. The capture of Matamoros was important, for both political and military reasons. Before the battle of Celaya and while it was still widely believed that Villa's next major operation would be against Tampico, a large Villista force invested Matamoros on three sides. The situation threatened to become another Naco, with the bystanders on the United States side of the river suffering.[12]

The United States warned Villa that his troops must not fire across the border, a warning that Villa's Foreign Minister protested was unfair, since the Carranzistas in Matamoros had been permitted free access to the United States. It is quite likely that Villa himself knew nothing about this protest, made in his name, for he was in Monterrey at the time. In fact, only a few hours before the protest was forwarded from Chihuahua, Villa and several members of his staff, including General Felipe Angeles and Raúl Madero (brother of the murdered President and provisional governor of Tamaulipas), were dinner guests of the United States consul general, Philip Hanna. Hanna reported that Villa's conversation with the foreigners present (chiefly Americans) was "most friendly."[13]

---

readers, after months of exaggerated claims by the warring powers of Europe, had become thoroughly cynical about reports of victory by either side.

[12] *Independent*, LXXXII (April–June, 1915), 10. Cf. National Archives, State Department File no. 312.112 W 892/30, March 27, 1915.

[13] National Archives, State Department File no. 812.00/14719, March 27, 1915.

Villa was reported to be at Monterrey to direct operations against Matamoros and Tampico. While at Monterrey he imposed a special tax upon the merchants of the city which, naturally, they resented. Supposing that American residents of the city were included in the impost, Washington made an immediate protest.[14] Villa's reply was that Americans were not subject to the tax, which was to raise funds for the relief of the poor of Monterrey. The press noted that hundreds were said to be suffering from hunger in that city and that Villa had given aid to several thousands of people.[15]

Villa's presence in Monterrey may have been really for the purpose of supervising local operations in that area, or it may have been to mislead his enemies farther south. He did not delay at Monterrey. On March 29, two days after Consul General Hanna's dinner party, Carothers notified the State Department that Villa had just arrived unexpectedly at Torreón, on his way south. "I will accompany him." [16] Villa's southward journey did not end until he reached Celaya.

The Villista attack upon Matamoros was a failure. After several days it became apparent that the Carranzistas were too firmly entrenched, and were too strong, for the Villistas to be able to carry the city by assault. To attempt to starve out the garrison would have been folly; limitless supplies were available across the Rio Grande. The Villistas continued to blockade the city, and on April 10, several weeks after the unsuccessful assault, newspapers said that "a Villa army is pressing Matamoros." [17]

In the United States, photographs of General Alvaro Obregón now appeared, proclaiming him as "Mexico's New Strong Man." His defeat of the hitherto invincible Villa, it was said, made him Mexico's outstanding soldier and stronger than his chief, Carranza.[18] With these ideas about Obregón, a new crop of rumors arose. Villa was said to have executed several of his generals, in an insane rage after the defeat at Celaya; he had placed Felipe Angeles in arrest for insubordination, after a violent quarrel. Because of his senseless brutality, whispered the rumors, fear and distrust were growing in his army; Villista gar-

[14] *Independent*, LXXXI (March 29, 1915), 452.
[15] *Ibid.*, LXXXII (April–June, 1915), 10, 104.
[16] National Archives, State Department file no. 812.00/14371, March 29, 1915.
[17] New York *Times*, Saturday, April 10, 1915, 4:2.
[18] *Independent*, LXXXII (April–June, 1915), 65, 235–236.

risons were changing sides, and the Villista movement on the West Coast was losing force.[19]

By the end of April it was apparent that at least one more major battle must be fought before the campaign would be decided. Villa concentrated his forces in the vicinity of Aguascalientes, reinforcing the army with detachments withdrawn from other areas. Operations against Tampico were suspended, and the besieging force taken from Matamoros.[20]

Villa himself appeared to be as confident as ever. "I have the greatest hope that my army will not only whip Obregón, but will utterly annihilate his troops," he told newspaper correspondents.[21] Villista forces continued to gain local successes in various places. General Manuel Chao captured the town of Chico; Villistas occupied Victoria and the Gulf Coast port of Tuxpam.[22] Villa's headquarters claimed that he had captured Silao and routed the Federals there. Villa's troops admittedly evacuated Monterrey, but Villa denied Obregón's claim of a great victory with heavy Villista casualties.[23]

The battle of Celaya did not alter the attitude of the United States toward either of the antagonists. It was too early to predict that Carranza would win or that Villa would be unable to regain all that he had lost. Neither of the opponents changed his attitude toward the United States. Shortly before the battle, attempts to gain satisfaction for the murder of two American cattlemen by Carranzistas were fruitless. An American arrested at Puebla on unrevealed charges was taken to Veracruz and held there incommunicado, in spite of efforts by Consul Canada to obtain his release. In contrast, when an American was arrested at Chihuahua charged with passing counterfeit currency, Villa announced that he would receive an absolutely fair and impartial trial.[24] Apprehension excited by Decree no. 5 or by a new law for the confiscation of untilled agricultural land was not too deep because of Villa's previous reasonableness.[25]

Reinforcing favorable opinion of Villa in the United States was the

[19] *Ibid.*   [20] *Ibid.*

[21] "Turbulent Mexico," *World's Work*, CIX (April 14, 1915), 850.

[22] *Independent*, LXXXII (April–June, 1915), 65, 235–236.   [23] *Ibid.*

[24] New York *Times*, Friday, April 2, 1915, 9:4; Saturday, April 3, 1915, 7:3; Wednesday, April 7, 1915, 5:2.

[25] *Ibid.*, Thursday, April 15, 1915, 1:3.

experience of John W. Roberts, a correspondent for William Randolph Hearst's International News Service. Roberts wrote, he claimed, while actually under fire:

General Villa wants me to write everything I see in the fighting which is to take place tonight. . . .

When it became apparent that a heavy Constitutionalist attack was coming, he [Villa] turned to me, but there was no smile on his face. "I am sorry I got you into this, but since you are here, lie low in the trench. There is no chance for you to go to the rear now. God help you!"

According to his own story, Roberts was slightly wounded and knocked out. He was rescued from his uncomfortable predicament by an American soldier of fortune who was one of Villa's machine gunners.[26]

There was nothing in the news dispatches upon which the United States could base an opinion as to the real victor in the contest. DuVal West returned to Washington from Mexico in the first week of June and reported to the President at once. His report was not made public, but after conferring with him, President Wilson announced that there would be no change in policy. Despite the fact that West's report was not released to the press, rumors from apparently authentic sources said that it was dismal and pessimistic, with nothing to indicate any cause for confidence in the leaders of either faction. At the same time, it was said that West had given the President a more complete and accurate picture of conditions in Mexico than any of the previous personal representatives.[27]

Early in June reports of another major battle between Obregón and Villa began to circulate, with both sides, as usual, claiming victory. By June 14 it was definitely known that Obregón's army had defeated Villa near the city of León. Carranzista reports asserted that Obregón had taken the city, captured Villa's cavalry commander and his artillery, and driven Angeles in headlong rout to the mountains. The first reports received also said that Obregón had been killed at the moment of victory and that the new Constitutionalist commander would be General Benjamin Hill, the defender of Naco in the autumn of 1914.[28] The rumor of Obregón's death was, of course, an error. He was dangerously

[26] John W. Roberts, "Personal Glimpses: Entrenched with Villa," *Literary Digest*, L (June 18, 1915), 1485–1488.

[27] *Independent*, LXXXII (April–June, 1915), 383. Cf. *Outlook*, CX (June 9, 1915), 288.

[28] *Independent*, LXXXII (April–June, 1915), pp. 451, 492.

wounded, and the amputation of an arm was necessary to save his life, but he survived to resume command within a few weeks and ultimately to become both President of Mexico and the victim of an assassin's bullet.

President Wilson had evidently been meditating for some time on yet another attempt to bring the warring factions together and persuade them to agree upon a provisional president whom they would recognize pending the election of a constitutional executive. This time he determined to try a new approach—a new technique in international matters. On June 2, 1915, he made a public statement to the people of the United States, at the same time taking care that his statement was transmitted to the leaders of both parties in Mexico.

After summarizing the harrowing conditions existing in Mexico, the President informed the world that the United States was about to essay what it had not done before. The United States would lend its active "moral support to some man or group of men, if such may be found, who can rally the suffering people of Mexico to their support in an effort to ignore, if they cannot unite, the warring factions of the country." The President urged the leaders of the factions to act together, warning them, as a final provision of his statement, that the United States would otherwise be compelled to decide upon means to help Mexico save itself.[29]

This statement was not only transmitted through the usual diplomatic and consular channels to the recognized chiefs of the factions; it was practically broadcast throughout Mexico. All consuls and consular agents received it; it was sent to all leaders whose locations were known; and every effort was made to give it the widest possible publicity in Mexico. President Wilson did not address his statement to Carranza, Villa, and Zapata. He addressed it to all Mexicans and especially to all leaders. He was appealing over the heads of the several governments, directly to the Mexican people.

The first to acknowledge the statement was Provisional President Roque González Garza, who requested the good offices of the Brazilian minister and the United States government in conveying a message to Carranza and to Villa. González Garza offered to deliver up his office within twelve hours to any provisional president selected by the united revolutionists and appealed to Carranza to consider the matter care-

[29] *Foreign Relations, 1915*, pp. 694–695.

fully. His message to Villa, still nominally his subordinate, although they had been out of communication for weeks, was a request for Villa's opinion, "in order that I may know what to expect, as the inhabitants of the territory dominated by us, the City of Mexico and the Convention are inclined to favor the unification of the revolution. I wish to know your idea in this question." [30]

The Secretary of State forwarded González Garza's message to Villa, through Carothers, as soon as it was received in Washington. The President's statement, meanwhile, was being distributed through Mexico by American consular and other representatives, with varying results. Consul Gaston Schmutz, at Aguascalientes, informed the State Department that the local newspapers published the text of the statement without any comment at all, either pro or con. Consul William E. Alger, at Mazatlán, a city held by the Carranzistas, reported that the local military commander remarked, on reading it: "What a witty man Mr. Wilson is." The American Society of Mexico, interpreting the statement as presaging active intervention, was enthusiastic and hoped that the short time which the President said he would allow for the voluntary settlement of differences would be the minimum possible. [31]

Several days passed before responses from the leaders were received in Washington. Carranza's reply, if it can be called such, was the first: "Foreign Office to-day expresses General Carranza's thanks and states there is no reply." Villa's answer, given to Carothers for transmittal on June 11, 1915, was lengthy. It was an indictment of Carranza for seeking to establish a dictatorship and a justification of Villa's position in seeking to re-establish constitutional government and to hold elections. As for President Wilson's statement of prevailing conditions in Mexico, Villa took exception to certain details. The President charged that no sooner was a government established in Mexico City than irresponsible military leaders commenced to undermine it. This, Villa asserted, was not entirely correct. Carranza was the one who, after convoking the convention, refused to recognize the government it established. Villa refuted President Wilson's statement that there was no safety or protection for foreigners in Mexico by quoting a telegram DuVal West sent to the President on March 10, 1915: "I am glad to say that I have received an excellent impression of the prevailing quiet and order wherever I have been, and of the facilities and guaranties given to

[30] *Ibid.*, p. 697.   [31] *Ibid.*, pp. 698–700, 707, 708.

natives and foreigners in their work." Finally, Villa denied that the misery in Mexico was as terrible as had been depicted, and he declared also that Mexico had not yet reached such a degree of misery as to require foreign aid. The "conventionists" were willing again to invite all the people of Mexico to unite, but there could be no conference with those who ignored the constitution and "used their power in contempt of the rights of the people." [32]

President Wilson's statement did not produce the reaction for which he had hoped. Carranza had obviously rejected it, with a curtness that was unusual in diplomatic practice. Villa's reply, while more courteous, was as definitely a rejection. An effect which the President may not have foreseen was the fear aroused by what seemed to be a thinly veiled threat of active military intervention in his concluding phrases. Carothers, forwarding Villa's reply, at the same time sent another message at Villa's request, to be transmitted to Carranza. Villa urged upon the First Chief consideration of the dangerous possibility that the Científicos might easily return to power with American backing and that if the Mexican people refused to follow this group armed intervention might ensue. As a patriotic Mexican, he did not want to see American armed forces invading the territory of Mexico. Villa proposed an immediate conference and suggested that, if Carranza agreed, the preliminaries should be discussed at once.[33]

Villa and other Mexicans were not the only ones who believed that the President's statement might be an omen of trouble to come. On June 4, 1915, General Pershing wrote to Major General Frederick Funston, his immediate superior, saying that he was going on a short leave of absence but would return to El Paso immediately if it should be necessary.

Since the President's declaration on the Mexican situation, there has been more or less uneasiness among the people here. They say that Villa is likely to take offense, and they pretend to think that, in desperation, he might go so far as to threaten El Paso. I do not think that this is at all probable. The reports, however, indicate that Villa is not holding his own in prestige, and the consensus of opinion is that he will be compelled to give way to some stronger man. From the papers yesterday and today, Villa is more successful against Obregon than reports of the past week would lead one to believe.[34]

[32] *Ibid.*, pp. 701–704. [33] *Ibid.*
[34] John J. Pershing Papers, personal letter to Funston, June 4, 1915.

Pershing concluded by requesting Funston to transfer a battery of field artillery from Douglas, Arizona, to El Paso, to give the local populace a greater feeling of security.

Carranza did not bother to give Villa even as curt a reply as that he had given to President Wilson. Instead, he took a leaf from Wilson's book and issued a manifesto to the Mexican people. It was not a reply to Villa, since it was issued at Veracruz before his message could have been acted upon. It was definitely a reply to the President's statement, in similar form, but much lengthier. Justifying himself and his policies and government, he took a sharp slap at the United States by telling his compatriots that the labors of the Constitutionalist government had been greatly handicapped by the lack of understanding with the United States. The powerful American "Científico press" had consistently slandered his government with the object of presenting a false idea of the Revolution to the world. Making neither direct nor indirect mention of President Wilson's declaration, Carranza asserted that the Constitutionalist government controlled over seven-eighths of the national territory and nine-tenths of the population. Without specifically demanding recognition as the real government of Mexico, Carranza's manifesto was an argument for it.[35]

While all of this diplomatic correspondence was passing over the telegraph wires and while Carranza's manifesto was being prepared and issued, some of the most savage fighting of the Revolution was taking place. As related earlier, the series of battles at León resulted in a victory for the Carranzistas, even though Villa's army was not destroyed and was able to retire northward in fairly good order. But two major defeats in close succession destroyed totally the legend of Villa's invincibility. Distasteful though it might be to the United States, Carranza was looming more and more as the man who must be considered and with whom it would be necessary to deal.

[35] *Foreign Relations, 1915*, pp. 704–707.

❧ XIV ❧

Villa on the Defensive

ALL the world loves to be on the side of a winner, but as soon as he begins to lose, all the fainthearted, the timid, and the lukewarm sheer away. One of Villa's Mexican admirers has remarked: "Immediately after these events [the battles of Celaya and León], many of the revolutionaries lost faith in Villa, since such is the history of man." [1] Not only did Villa's Mexican support begin to drop away, but the reports of some of the American observers began to reflect lack of confidence in him and referred again to his bandit origin. On June 15, Consul Gaston Schmutz, at Aguascalientes, forwarded a report beginning: "Notwithstanding the boasted protection given to foreigners . . . which General Villa speaks of in his reply to President Wilson's note, he continues to issue confiscatory decrees against the merchants of this town." [2] Schmutz added that the merchants were compelled to accept worthless Villa currency, freight had been seized at the railway freight office, and work and dairy animals were confiscated from the farms and haciendas. He concluded his report with a passage that was almost a philippic:

It is positively disgusting to read the expression of high moral ideals in General Villa's reply to President Wilson's note and to see the contemptible and hypocritical defrauding of the ignorant peon for his personal gain and

[1] Campobello, *Apuntes sobre la vida militar de Francisco Villa*, p. 115.
[2] *Foreign Relations, 1915*, pp. 709–710.

175

the tyrannical brutal oppression with which he treats all who are not willing to bow down servilely and obey his infamous and senseless decrees.

The United States will never be able to assist this unhappy country until it puts aside all ideas of cooperation with such bandits as the man who calls himself the First Chief of the Conventionalist Party of Mexico.

Schmutz's report was in direct contradiction to the vast majority of previous dispatches that had stressed Villa's willingness and sincerity in protecting foreigners and foreign-owned property. There had been numerous messages charging Villa's subordinates with oppressing and abusing foreigners, but this was almost the first which alleged that Villa was personally responsible or which referred to his old calling of bandit.

In the United States there had just been a change in the important office of Secretary of State. William Jennings Bryan, unable to agree with the President's policies toward Germany and German submarine warfare, resigned on June 18, 1915, and was replaced by Robert Lansing. Lansing had been counselor of the State Department and was familiar with the problems which the department faced. The change in secretaries did not signify any change in policy; rather it indicated a continuation, since President Wilson was, in actual fact, his own Secretary of State. The new Secretary of State took office, by coincidence, at the critical moment when the relative stature of the two contenders in Mexico was changing rapidly. Thus, the administration could, without embarrassment, take a slightly different line in its relations with Villa and Carranza.

The increasing feeling in Washington that Villa, despite all the favor shown for him in the past, was already practically beaten in the Mexican contest was reflected in a telegram which Lansing sent to Silliman on June 18, 1915. In the nature of a follow-up of the President's statement, the message directed Silliman to intimate cautiously to Carranza that the United States might consider recognizing him, "in view of the way things appear to be shaping themselves." A condition was attached —Carranza must go all the way in conciliating and conferring with the principal factions. Otherwise, there was no hope that the United States would ever recognize his government.[3]

Secretary Lansing found it necessary, or at least desirable, to remind Carranza that the United States did not approve wholly of his conduct

[3] *Ibid.,* pp. 715–716.

of affairs. Silliman was directed to mention to Carranza that while the United States Army transport *Buford* was loading a cargo of corn and beans for the starving in Mexico the Ward Line steamship *Mexico* was loading, at Veracruz, an even larger cargo of beans for export from Mexico. Such an occurrence, which was presumably with the approval of Carranza's officials, did not make a good impression among the people of the United States.

The significance of Lansing's message lay in the fact that it was the first hint of recognition given to either Carranza or Villa. Carranza's earlier overtures for recognition had been ignored. Villa had never specifically requested recognition, so far as available records show, nor had any offer, even tentative, been made to him. Two months earlier it would have been inconceivable that any such hint could have been made to Carranza without a similar offer to Villa, but after the battles of May and June, the situation had changed.

Carranza's reply, on June 21, was an unequivocal refusal to consider treating with Villa and Zapata. He repeated that Villa represented the forces of reaction, whereas the Constitutionalists alone stood for the full realization of the hopes and aspirations of the Mexican people. For the United States to adopt any other course than the unconditional recognition of the Constitutionalist government would be both an injustice and a great calamity.[4]

Following the battles of León and extending into the month of July, the political and military situation became more and more confusing, to the point where it was almost impossible to tell what was really happening. Roque González Garza resigned (or was forced to resign) as Provisional President, and the rump convention elected Francisco Lagos Cházaro in his stead. González Garza was a Villista, but his successor was a protégé of Zapata—a further indication that Villa's name was no longer magic in conventionist circles. Almost unexpectedly the Carranzista forces from the Gulf Coast, under command of General Pablo González, entered and occupied Mexico City on July 11, but a week later had to evacuate again. A force of Villistas under Rodolfo Fierro was at Pachuca, threatening to join forces with the Zapatistas and effectively cutting the Carranzistas off from Veracruz.[5] The Zapatistas at once re-entered the city, but this time they did not conduct themselves with the discipline and restraint that had earned them good will earlier in the year. Among other acts, they imprisoned the manager and all the employees of the American-owned *Mexican Herald* and used the presses and facilities of the paper to publish their own newspaper. The Brazilian minister located Provisional President Lagos Cházaro with some difficulty and obtained an order for the release of the Americans and the return of the property, but nobody bothered to obey the order.[6]

Among the Zapatistas at this time there was a definite impression that the United States had become wholly favorable toward Carranza.[7] This feeling undoubtedly caused their change in attitude toward Americans, as shown by their abuse of Americans and the seizure of American property. To just what extent, if at all, the conventionists at Mexico City were in communication with the Villistas in the north is uncertain, but the same feeling may easily have been the basis for Villa's actions at Aguascalientes, which so aroused Consul Schmutz's indignation.

Fierro's spectacular raid was as barren of permanent military results as most great cavalry raids have been. He was compelled to retire northward, and after a period of completely anarchic confusion, General Pablo González again reoccupied Mexico City on August 3. This time the tenure of the Carranzistas in the capital was to be permanent —a fact that strengthened Carranza's position and thus, relatively, weakened Villa still further as a factor in the political situation.

With the situation as thoroughly confused as it was and with Villa suffering a succession of defeats, considerable wonder was aroused when General Felipe Angeles chose the latter part of June and early July to visit the United States. One rumor was that he had to leave Mexico because of the quarrel with Villa that was supposed to have taken place after the battle of Celaya. Another opinion was that he came to the United States as Villa's personal representative to attempt to bring before President Wilson Villa's own views on a possible compromise with Carranza. It was suggested also that his real reason was to plot a new revolution in Mexico and that his supposed mission for Villa was merely a blind to hide his actual purpose.[8]

The rumor that Angeles had broken with Villa was so persistent that

---

1915, pp. 726–727. This is one of the few examples in modern military history of a long-range cavalry raid.

[6] *Foreign Relations, 1915*, pp. 727–729.   [7] *Ibid.*, p. 721.

[8] *Outlook*, CX (May–Aug., 1915), 536–537.

he found it necessary to issue an emphatic denial within a few days after his arrival. The fact that he had not broken with his chief is amply proved by certain facts that were unknown to the public at the time. On June 16, almost before the dust had settled on the lost battlefields of León, Villa wrote to General Scott, asking him to arrange an interview for Angeles with President Wilson. This letter was followed by a note from Felix Sommerfeld to Scott on June 24, saying that Angeles was coming to Washington and was anxious to see both the President and the Secretary of War, if possible. There is no means of knowing whether or not Scott made any attempt to arrange for the desired interviews. As Chief of Staff of the Army, Scott could, with perfect propriety, receive a distinguished soldier from another country, but to go beyond that would be a breach of both neutrality and protocol. Angeles called at the War Department on June 29 and was received with the courtesy and geniality for which Scott was well known. But Scott maintained his reserve and was entirely noncommittal. His impressions of his visitor were highly favorable, and a few days later he wrote a note thanking Villa for the opportunity of becoming acquainted with Angeles and adding: "I have forwarded his business as much as I was able." [9]

The supposition that Angeles was in the United States to strengthen the weakening Villa cause is supported by his overt desire to see President Wilson. Additional evidence lies in a letter which he addressed to President Wilson on June 15, immediately after the defeat at León and before he left Mexico:

His Excellency, Woodrow Wilson, President of the United States of America.
When Victoriano Huerta had done all possible to bring about armed intervention by the United States and Señor Carranza had sent to the Government of that Nation an intemperate note whose text declared it to be an ultimatum, I relied upon the nobility of Your Excellency and on the good sense of the American people to prevent war and my hopes were not disappointed. Now that you have in the name of humanity and through sympathy for the Mexican people proposed to effect within a short time the pacification of my beloved country, I feel certain that your acts will be inspired by the strictest justice towards the contending factions the members of each one of which are so numerous and with the desire to secure for my country the greatest possible good.[10]

[9] Hugh Lenox Scott Papers.
[10] Woodrow Wilson Papers. (Translation made in the State Department for the President.)

Although Angeles was unable to gain any material aid for Villa or any promises of diplomatic support, he did succeed in conveying such a favorable impression of himself that the cause he represented gained a degree of sympathy. An interviewer, after an hour's conversation, said that his dominant characteristic was loyalty and predicted that he was a future president of Mexico. A considerable part of the interview was devoted to discussing an idea that had already gained favor in Washington, that one of the surviving members of Madero's cabinet should be selected as provisional president. This would be in accordance with the Mexican Constitution and would thus bring the Constitution back into operation. "I favor constitutional continuity," said Angeles. "Also such is the view of General Villa." To a nation accustomed to regard itself as being governed by law strictly in accordance with the Constitution, such a thought was bound to be attractive.[11]

Even though General Scott was unable to do much to further Angeles' mission, relations between Scott and Villa remained cordial throughout the summer of 1915. Villa sent Scott several telegrams about an automobile that was stolen from him and was believed to have been taken into the United States. On August 14 Scott informed him that the stolen vehicle had been recovered at Deming, New Mexico, and would be returned to him at once.[12] Telegrams and correspondence passed back and forth between the two men regarding the involved affairs of the Jabonera Company, in Torreón, a soap manufacturing company in which several Americans held interest. On August 17 Villa sent Scott a lengthy telegram, saying in part: "I arrived [this morning] in this city and am occupying myself that the Jabonera Company be closed immediately in conformity with what we agreed. I salute you affectionately." [13]

Among the complications produced by the continuing loss of Villa's military strength was the change in the situation in Sonora. Under the agreement made through Scott's diplomacy in January, the border town of Naco was to be neutral, Agua Prieta was to be held by the Carranzistas, and Nogales was to be held by Villa's supporter, Gov-

[11] McGregor, "Villa's Right-Hand Man," *Harper's Weekly*, LXI (July 24, 1915), 89–90. The Angeles portrayed by McGregor is vastly different from the conscienceless, scheming villain depicted by Gen. Bernardino Mena Brito in *El lugarteniente gris de Pancho Villa*. But Mena Brito was an enthusiastic Carranzista.
[12] Hugh Lenox Scott Papers.   [13] *Ibid.*

ernor Maytorena. Each side agreed not to attack the town allotted to the other, and the garrison of each town was to be limited to an agreed number of men. On July 19, 1915, Villa sent an indignant telegram to Scott, saying that the Carranzistas were flouting the agreement; they had converted Agua Prieta into a fortress and increased the garrison from the stipulated eight hundred men to more than twenty-five hundred. Villa respectfully asked Scott to interpose his influence to cause the Carranzistas to reduce the garrison to the figure previously agreed upon. If they refused to do so, Villa would consider himself released from his promise not to attack, and he would not be responsible for the consequences.[14]

Immediately after this telegram arrived in Washington there was further proof, if any were needed, that the Carranzistas regarded the previous winter's pact as being no longer binding. There was a small group of Maytorena's civil officials at Naco, who had been stationed there by the governor on February 1, shortly after the agreement neutralizing the place. The Carranzistas had protested the presence of these officials, claiming that Maytorena, in placing them there, had broken the agreement. Technically he may have done so, but no other action had been taken in the intervening months. On July 19 a Carranzista force, under General Plutarco Calles, suddenly appeared at Naco, killed some of the Villista officials, and drove the others across the boundary into the United States.

Enraged, Villa proposed to drive out the Carranzistas at once. On July 20, General Scott wrote to General James Parker that the Naco situation had almost got out of hand again. The Villistas were about to attack the place, "but I headed them off in time, and I hope that they will do as advised." [15]

After seizing Naco, Calles moved westward and began an attack upon Nogales, which was held by Governor Maytorena. This was a clear violation of the January pact, and the United States protested vigorously against such an open disregard of an agreement in which it was actively interested. Calles, thereupon, decided to content himself with an investment, without making an assault. Governor Maytorena professed to be not the least bit alarmed, as Calles would not venture within range of the defending artillery. Consequently, no projectiles could hit in United States territory. Maytorena also main-

---

[14] *Ibid.*   [15] *Ibid.* Cf. *Foreign Relations, 1915,* p. 798.

tained that he could easily have defended Naco but for the fact that a considerable portion of his available troops had been sent to the Yaqui River Valley, in order to protect American settlers there. A short time later Villa asked Scott if he was still bound by the January agreement, in view of Calles' clear violation of it. Scott's reply was that Calles' breach of his word did not justify Francisco Villa's similar action.[16]

During this confused and eventful summer of 1915, the situation in which the United States found itself was practically without precedent in diplomatic annals and practice. In spite of his military reverses and the continuing losses of territory and influence, Villa was still an important factor in Mexican affairs. In a large part of Mexico his word and his decrees carried all the force of law. Without according him recognition, or even the prospect of recognition, the United States was forced to acknowledge tacitly, if not formally, that he was the actual head of a real and operative government. Since his territory abutted upon the United States and a large proportion of American interests in Mexico were located there, the United States had to deal with him and through him, as though his regime were a recognized, legal government.

Few of the problems arising in the relations of the United States with the two rival governments in Mexico were solved as easily or as quickly as that posed by the sudden appearance of General Victoriano Huerta on the border in the midsummer, in company with General Pascual Orozco. Suspected, probably with justice, of plotting a new revolution, the two were promptly taken into custody, but were released on bail. Orozco jumped bail and disappeared. To make sure that Huerta would not do the same, he was placed in confinement at Fort Bliss, near El Paso.

Both the Villa and Carranza governments demanded Huerta's extradition to Mexico. Both, incidentally, had protested against Huerta's being allowed to land in the United States on his return from Europe. The Villista governor of Chihuahua, General Fidel Avila, telegraphed

[16] *Foreign Relations, 1915,* pp. 798–802. Cf. *Independent,* LXXXIII (July–Sept., 1915), 146, and the Hugh Lenox Scott Papers. A series of Indian raids in the Yaqui Valley in the spring had so endangered settlers, including several Americans, that the United States prepared to land a small Marine Corps expedition for their protection. To prevent this "invasion" of Mexican soil, Maytorena sent a considerable force to that area.

to the governor of Texas, stating that proper warrants had been issued
and requesting Huerta's surrender to the Chihuahua authorities. In
Washington, Villa's confidential agent, Enrique C. Llorente, wrote to
the Secretary of State, hoping that the governor of Texas would honor
the request from Chihuahua and pointing out that in 1013 the United
States had permitted the extradition of an accused criminal at the
request of the Huerta government, even though that government was
not recognized. From Austin, Texas, the attorney representing the conventionists in the United States telegraphed that the extradition of
Huerta was the only way to stop revolutionary plots in the United
States. "Our desire is to prevent attack [on] Juarez, so bullets will not
strike El Paso." [17]

If Huerta were tried by his Mexican enemies, there would be no
doubt as to the outcome. The State Department refused to be a party
to a judicial murder. To all applications for Huerta's extradition, one
answer was returned: "In reply you are informed that, owing to the
absence of a recognized Federal Government in Mexico and the well-
known conditions existing throughout the Republic, the Department
must decline to comply with the request for the extradition of General
Huerta." [18]

More difficult to solve, and containing seeds of much more trouble,
was the problem growing out of Villa's attempts to bolster his shrink-
ing treasury at the expense of the mineowners of his territory. As
mentioned before, American mine and smelter owners had been greatly
disturbed, earlier in the year, at the announcement of Villa's decree
on mines. They saw in Decree no. 5 an entering wedge for the ex-
propriation, if not the outright confiscation, of their properties. Villa
was persuaded to suspend his decree until later, but by the end of
July it was imperative for him to raise funds by any means possible—
and the mining industry seemed to be the most feasible source to tap.

On July 26, 1915, Carothers telegraphed that he had been told by
a member of the committee which represented the mineowners that
Villa demanded a loan of three hundred thousand dollars in gold. The
operators refused to grant the loan, and they were afraid that their
refusal might be used as an excuse for putting Decree no. 5 into immediate effect.[19]

[17] *Foreign Relations, 1915*, pp. 827–833.   [18] *Ibid.*, p. 835.
[19] *Ibid.*, p. 926.

It was probably coincidental that Villa's demand for a loan came upon the heels of a new Carranza decree, raising the tax on mining property from six pesos a hectare to twelve dollars in gold, with progressive increases for larger holdings. Such a tax was confiscatory, especially in view of the current conditions. The Secretary of State lost no time in directing Silliman to ask for a modification of the decree, and Carranza gained no favor in the eyes of the State Department.[20] Carranza could collect only in territory under his control, but theoretically the decree applied to all of Mexico.

On the last day of July, Edwards forwarded from Chihuahua more complete information about Villa's demands. On July 12, Francisco Escudero, Villa's Minister of Finance, had summoned the executive committee of the Mine and Smelter Operators Association and requested, in Villa's name, that they advance three hundred thousand dollars. They would be credited with that amount in future taxes and freight charges. The mineowners feared that their refusal might cause punitive enforcement of the mining decree; they were also afraid that if they complied Carranza would accuse them of aiding Villa. With Carranza's ultimate victory looming more and more as a probability, such a prospect was serious.[21]

On August 2 Villa ordered that all mining men meet at Chihuahua on August 9 "to receive a proposition of grave import." To ensure that the owners or fully authorized representatives were present, the order added that the properties of companies not attending would be closed and that negotiations with those attending would be binding upon all.[22] Villa, or his spokesman, refused flatly to indicate in advance anything about the propositions to be discussed. Naturally, the mineowners were reluctant to be bound in advance to something they did not know—to give Villa, in effect, a signed blank check. Since they had refused to advance him the loan of three hundred thousand dollars, they feared that his next demand would be for a forced loan. "It is our unanimous opinion that Villa's purpose is to obtain money unjustly and coercively," they said in a telegram to the Secretary of State on August 6.[23]

The State Department had an additional fear. Probably remembering Obregón's imprisonment of the Mexico City merchants who did not respond to his demands with sufficient enthusiasm, the department

[20] *Ibid.*, pp. 926–927.   [21] *Ibid.*, pp. 930–931.   [22] *Ibid.*, p. 931.
[23] *Ibid.*, p. 933.

feared for the personal safety of the representatives who might be without authority to bind their companies. Carothers received an urgent message on August 6, directing him to keep in touch with the mining men. He replied from El Paso the same day, saying that he expected to see Villa personally later in the day and would renew his efforts.[24]

The situation was so threatening, especially with the tension developing from the Carranzistas' seizure of Naco, the fortification of Agua Prieta, and the attack upon Nogales, that the United States government became seriously alarmed. It was well known that General Scott had great influence over Villa. On August 3 Carothers requested that Scott come to the border, because he might be able to control Villa, who would probably submit to his advice.[25]

Before Scott could leave Washington, Carothers wired again. Recognizing that Villa's demands upon the mineowners were prompted by his desperate need of funds, Carothers suggested that if arrangements could be made to open the Juárez packing houses Villa would have a legitimate source of revenue. Carothers would then have a point to use when trying to argue Villa out of forced loans and taxes upon foreign businesses.[26]

En route to the border, General Scott was interviewed by newspaper reporters in Chicago.

"Are you going to read the riot act to Villa?" the reporter asked. "No; I would not say that," was Scott's reply. "I will say, however, that Villa and I have always got along fine together. He once told me that whatever he and I set out to do along the Mexican border we would accomplish." [27]

The interview further quoted (quite possibly misquoted) General Scott as saying that he was confident that he would be able to bring the warring factions in Mexico together. "When I start out on something I usually do not quit until I have done what I started out to do."

It is unlikely that Scott had any instructions about attempting to bring the factions together, nor did he make any effort to do so. In his mission of bringing Villa to reason about the mines, he was eminently

[24] *Ibid.*, p. 932.   [25] Hugh Lenox Scott Papers.   [26] *Ibid.*

[27] San Antonio (Texas) *Daily Express*, Aug. 8, 1915, quoted by the Hon. James L. Slayden, M.C., in a speech on March 9, 1916, *Cong. Record*, 64 Cong., 1 sess., pp. 4846–4848.

successful. Carothers reported on August 10 that at a conference that morning Villa agreed to suspend the meeting of the mining companies' representatives and to return the confiscated property of foreign merchants in Chihuahua; the merchants would be prosecuted in the civil courts for infractions of the law, instead of being penalized arbitrarily. Scott reported the same. Significantly, Scott's report was directed to the Secretary of State, rather than to the Secretary of War, indicating that his mission was diplomatic and not military.[28] In a second conference, Scott, Carothers, and a committee representing the mineowners finally convinced Villa that his intended decrees regarding the mines were impracticable. Villa discussed with the mineowners the important problem of keeping the railroads in operation and agreed not only to permit them to import freely whatever they needed for working the mines but also to furnish military protection. The mineowners, in return, voluntarily agreed to present Villa with one thousand tons of coal, which he needed badly for military operations.[29]

The Mine and Smelter Operators Association, grateful for the assistance they had received, wrote to the Secretary of State: "We are particularly impressed by the peculiar ability of General Scott to make friends with and gain the confidence of such men as now dominate the political affairs of Mexico." [30] Carothers also wrote a personal letter to the Secretary of State, in which he said in part:

The real accomplishment by General Scott consists of changing Villa's line of thought. His agreeing to suspend all action against mining men destroys his entire plan of solving the financial situation. I do not believe General Scott should make further representations of individual cases but should be held in reserve for future difficulties. Last night Villa agreed on the Jabonera case [to which reference has already been made] to store and seal all stocks of raw material and other property leaving the factory closed down but everything fully protected until the solution of the peace problem is arrived at so that the case may be settled in civil courts under a constitutional government.[31]

Concurrently with the conferences between Scott and Villa, the administration was making still another attempt to effect some sort of a compromise in Mexico. Before the end of July rumors appeared in the press that the President would shortly make a final appeal to the

[28] *Foreign Relations, 1915,* pp. 934–935.
[29] *Ibid.* Cf. also the Hugh Lenox Scott Papers.
[30] *Foreign Relations, 1915,* p. 939.   [31] Hugh Lenox Scott Papers.

Mexican military leaders, in the hope of bringing peace to the country. At the same time it was positively stated that some officials in Washington were in favor of having Villa and other northern leaders select a provisional president who could be supported by the United States.[32]

Secretary Lansing invited the ambassadors and ministers of Argentina, Brazil, Chile, Bolivia, Uruguay, and Guatemala to meet with him on August 5. Upon conferring, they agreed to repeat, in effect, the procedure employed earlier and sent a direct appeal to a large number of influential people in Mexico. No public announcement was made about this decision, but rumors crept into the papers and, of course, became known to the Washington agents of the Mexican parties. On August 10, several days before anything was officially disclosed, Carranza's representative delivered a stiff memorandum to the Secretary of State, protesting against anything but unconditional recognition of the Carranza regime:

Mr. Carranza . . . is not aware of the exact nature of these conferences, [but] he has heard that Mexican affairs are discussed therein with the idea of settling them. . . .

The Constitutionalist Government . . . deems it its duty to make expressly known . . . the displeasure with which the Mexican Government and people would look upon any act which might have the effect or tend to frustrate the triumph, already practically attained, over the hostile reactionary factions by the Constitutionalist Army, which represents the ideals and hopes of the Mexican people.[33]

As for Villa, his attitude was already known. During his conferences with General Scott he indicated that he was willing to take part in such a conference, and even before that, he let it be known that he was not opposed to the idea.[34] In proof of his sincere willingness to make any sacrifice or effort to bring peace to Mexico, he pointed out on August 5, the day on which Secretary Lansing issued his invitation to the Latin American diplomats, that he had agreed unhesitatingly to President Wilson's earlier suggestions to the faction leaders.

The message sent out by the assembled diplomats was, in substance, an appeal to all the Mexican leaders, both military and political, to meet at some place in Mexico outside the combat zone, in order to exchange ideas and take steps toward the re-establishment of con-

[33] New York *Times*, Wednesday, July 28, 1915, 7:3.
[33] *Foreign Relations, 1915*, pp. 734–735.   [34] *Ibid.*, pp. 733, 736.

stitutional government. The signatories—the Secretary of State and the Latin American ambassadors and ministers—suggested that a suitable place for the conference could be neutralized and that the first essential step would be the issuance of a call for immediate general elections. As a final injunction, the message stated that an answer was expected within ten days.[35]

The first reply received in Washington was from Villa. It was dated at Torreón on August 16 and was sent to the State Department by Llorente on August 19. He felt, Villa said, that he had the power and resources to continue the struggle until the high ideals of the Revolution were realized. Nevertheless, he cordially accepted the good offices of the several diplomats for promoting a conference to bring Mexico a peace consistent with national honor.[36]

Villa's reply was dispatched within twenty-four hours after he received the message, but Carranza did not reply for nine days. On August 24 Silliman received a memorandum from Jesús Acuña, Carranza's acting Minister of Foreign Affairs. The First Chief, the memorandum said, had received and read the circular sent to him. He wished to know if the several signatories were acting under authority of their respective governments or if they had sent the communication in their private capacity and without official character.[37] The snub was obvious, and the diplomats were equally curt in replying, through the State Department: "My signature to the communication of August 11 was in my official capacity."

Carranza did not reply formally until September 10, and then his reply was a categorical refusal. His control over Mexico, he said, was now so complete and the reactionaries led by Francisco Villa, who had been bribed to rebel against the government, were so nearly annihilated that his government would not compromise upon a single point.[38] Carranza repeated the early history of the Revolution, as he did in practically all diplomatic communications, and he renewed his demand that the governments represented by the signatories should recognize his regime.

Villa's Washington agent, meanwhile, again wrote to the Secretary of State, thanking him and the Latin American diplomats for their friendly interest and assistance. Charles B. Parker, who now represented the United States in Mexico City, forwarded favorable replies

---

[35] *Ibid.*, pp. 735–736.   [36] *Ibid.*, pp. 737–738.   [37] *Ibid.*, p. 738.
[38] *Ibid.*, pp. 746–748.

from Zapata and several other revolutionary chiefs of southern Mexico.[39]

On September 18 the Secretary of State and the diplomats met again to consider the replies that had been received. On the Carranza side, twelve generals, eight state governors, and two city mayors had responded. Their replies unanimously stated that the matter was one for the decision of the First Chief alone. As subordinates, the matter was entirely outside their province. A somewhat larger number of Villistas had sent replies, a fact from which an important inference was drawn. Although most of the answers referred the matter to Villa, several made no reference at all to any higher authority. This indicated that on the Carranzista side there was a central authority, recognized by all subordinates, but the Villistas were a loose federation of independent *caudillos,* each with his own personal following.[40]

The conference between the Secretary of State and the Latin American diplomats on September 18 lasted for several hours. All the participants desired earnestly that their governments present a completely united front on the Mexican question. Consequently, all aspects and angles of the problem were discussed. Since the diplomats' hope that their good offices would eventually produce a working and workable compromise in Mexico was clearly impossible because of Carranza's attitude, an alternative was necessary. Such an alternative had been considered in an earlier meeting; if the Mexicans could not, or would not, compromise, recognition must be accorded to that faction or leader who showed the greatest promise of being able to guarantee protection to natives and foreigners. The conferees could not, of course, take any action by their own authority. All that they could do was to submit identical recommendations to their respective governments. As to what recommendations they would make, they were not yet prepared to say. The situation in Mexico was still too confused, too fluid. Further information was vitally necessary. After a long discussion, it was decided to invite both factions to submit additional information and arguments.[41]

Both sides sent briefs for consideration, the Carranzistas on October

[39] *Ibid.,* p. 739. The Brazilian minister, Cardoso de Oliveira, who had represented the United States for so long, left Mexico early in August. Charles B. Parker was thereupon designated as "representing United States interests in Mexico," apparently without diplomatic or consular status.

[40] *Ibid.,* pp. 752–762. Cf. *Senate Documents,* 64 Cong., 2 sess., no. 324, p. 10.

[41] *Foreign Relations, 1915,* p. 762.

7 and the Villistas the following day. Both briefs were largely repetitions of what had been said many times before. Arredondo, the Carranzista agent in Washington, again traced the history of the Revolution from the original uprising under Madero. He attributed the inception of the revolt against Huerta entirely to Carranza's initiative, determination, and courage and blamed the rupture between Villa and Carranza entirely upon Villa. Arredondo maintained that the Constitutionalist government now controlled all but unimportant parts of Mexico and predicted that these would be brought under the First Chief's authority within a very short time. He pointed out in conclusion that the Constitutionalist leaders who had received the conference's communication had all referred the matter to Carranza. In contrast, the Villistas and Zapatistas had replied as individuals. This proved clearly that the Constitutionalists were a coherent and disciplined group—"a real government from the point of view of international law." [42]

The memorandum presenting the Villista side of the case, submitted by Llorente, was signed by Díaz Lombardo, General Felipe Angeles, and General Roque González Garza, the former Provisional President, and by Llorente himself. They did not repeat the history of the Revolution but maintained that their side was still capable of achieving victory. Military operations, they said, had been practically suspended since the receipt of the note of August 14, which had given hope that the Revolution would be ended peaceably. The latest act of the conference, promising to recognize the faction that seemed to be able to dominate the situation, was again plunging all Mexico into bloodshed. The apparent superiority of the Carranzistas was transitory, but it would take more than three weeks for either faction to establish any real control. Villa was more than willing to eliminate himself, providing that Carranza was also eliminated. Finally, it was utterly impossible for Carranza to demonstrate that he really controlled as much territory as he claimed. Actually, he controlled far less than Díaz did in 1877 and 1878, and yet the United States had refused to recognize Díaz for nearly eighteen months. [43]

There is a deep difference between this message and previous messages that had been received from Villa and his government. Psychologically, as well as on the battlefield, Villa was now on the defensive.

[42] *Ibid.*, pp. 764–765.   [43] *Ibid.*, pp. 765–766.

This fact could not have escaped the notice of the keen observers in the diplomatic conference, straining for every detail of significance. The arguments submitted were not arguments showing Villa's strength —they were arguments against the recognition of Carranza. It is doubtful that Villa himself realized this, but Felipe Angeles, as a student of the history of warfare, must have known that although the defensive can win occasional battles it seldom wins wars.

❧ XV ❦

Wilson's Recognition of Carranza

IN spite of the tragedy in Europe, friction with Germany over the *Lusitania,* and pressing domestic issues, Mexico could still attract the attention of the American public. By this time newspapers, almost daily, reported skirmishes between American troops and raiders who dashed across the Rio Grande, looted, murdered, and burned and then fled back to the safety of Mexico. Secretary Lansing's conferences with the Latin American diplomats were not secret, even though no conclusions were revealed, and when an announcement was made that a final meeting would be held on October 9, editorial speculation decided that this probably meant Carranza's recognition.[1] Newspaper columns for the last part of September and the opening week of October carried arguments pro and con, with the weight of editorial opinion strongly opposed to recognition of the Constitutionalist government. General Roque González Garza, the former Provisional President, who was in Washington as a special representative of Villa, issued a statement that regardless of recent reverses Villa's military strength was still fully equal to Carranza's and that anarchy would follow Carranza's recognition.[2]

As a result of the extensive newspaper discussion, the reading public was not altogether surprised when the State Department announced

[1] *Independent,* LXXXIII (Sept. 27, 1915), 419.
[2] *Ibid.,* LXXXIV (Oct. 4, 1915), 11.

on October 11 that "the Conferees, after careful consideration of the facts, have found that the Carrancista [*sic*] party is the only party possessing the essentials for recognition as the de facto government of Mexico, and they have so reported to their respective governments." [3] This statement did not constitute formal recognition, but it was an obvious prelude.

Although the events of the preceding few weeks prepared the way for Carranza's recognition, the shift in the administration's attitude was somewhat of a shock to those who believed in Villa's abilities and sincerity. On the day of the announcement General Scott wrote to James R. Garfield, a prominent lawyer who was interested in Mexico, that the change in the administration was completely inexplicable. Three days later, still puzzled and shocked, Scott wrote again to Garfield, saying, among other things: "Mr. Lansing told me [just before Scott's last mission to the border] to say to Villa that under no circumstances would we recognize Carranza." Scott, incidentally, did not deliver this message. [4]

Formal recognition of the Carranza regime as the *de facto* government of Mexico was accorded on October 19, 1915, with the concurrence of the Latin American countries represented in the conference. The long period of doubt, of "watchful waiting," was at its end. The United States was still neutral, but its future neutrality would be distinctly more benevolent toward Carranza than it had ever been toward Villa. This was shown on the very day of the formal recognition, when President Wilson reimposed the embargo upon arms and munitions for Villa while allowing the export of munitions consigned to the *de facto* government. [5]

In all probability the decision to recognize Carranza was not made as suddenly as the circumstances of the moment seemed to indicate. It was the announcement, rather than the decision, that was so suddenly made as to evoke surprise even from those who might be presumed to know in advance what was brewing. As is well known, President Wilson was, to a great extent, his own Secretary of State; that

---

[3] *Foreign Relations, 1915*, p. 767.

[4] Hugh Lenox Scott Papers. James R. Garfield, a son of President James A. Garfield and Secretary of the Interior in President Theodore Roosevelt's cabinet, had been in Mexico earlier in the year. General Scott gave him a letter of introduction to Villa, whom he visited.

[5] *Foreign Relations, 1915*, pp. 780–782.

is, he made the major decisions personally. Secretary Lansing did not know, only two months before, that there was any probability of recognizing Carranza. This is amply attested by his instructions to General Scott, already mentioned. General Scott, in his memoirs, records:

I went to call upon the President upon my return from the border to make my report, and told him that there were rumors that he intended to recognize Carranza and urged him not to do it. He did not reveal his intentions then but he recognized Carranza in a few months, in October, 1915. I never knew why. I asked the officers of the State Department, junior to the Secretary, why such a thing had been done, for they had all advised against it, a month previous to the recognition.[6]

Since President Wilson took nobody into his confidence, his reasons are conjectural, but a large number of complex factors undoubtedly contributed to his final decision. First and most obvious was the recommendation of the diplomats, based upon the visible increase in Carranza's political and military strength after the battles of Celaya and León. With the friction developing between the United States and the belligerents in Europe, particularly Germany, it was more and more important for the administration to be free to devote all of its attention and effort to that quarter. On this basis alone, the definite prospect of a Carranza victory was enough to justify logically the recognition of the Constitutionalist regime.

The prospect of a complete Carranza victory was not in itself enough to account for the loss of the apparent favor which Villa had so long enjoyed. Villa had consistently been co-operative and willing to fall in line with the ideas and policies of the United States, while Carranza, with equal consistency, had been unco-operative and truculent almost to the point of insolence. Since the Mexican faction that received the active support of the United States would probably be the ultimate victor, the mere fact that Carranza was winning over his most formidable enemy does not account for his sudden rise in the administration's estimation. There were other and deeper-lying reasons.

[6] Hugh Lenox Scott, *Some Memories of a Soldier* (New York, 1928), pp. 516–517. The inferences to be drawn from General Scott's statement are quite different from the conclusions reached by Dr. Louis G. Kahle, that Secretary Lansing had long foreseen the recognition of Carranza. Cf. Louis G. Kahle, "The Recognition of Venustiano Carranza," *Hispanic American Historical Review*, XXXVII (Aug., 1958), 353–372.

From the beginning of the break between Villa and Carranza the pro-Carranza propaganda in the United States was voluminous and was conducted with a skill and attention to the current prejudices of the American people that indicated that the managers knew exactly what they were doing. More than that, the Carranza propagandists seem to have had ample funds. At some time in the fall of 1914, early in the dispute between Villa and Carranza, the "Mexican Bureau of Information" was established in New York City, with offices in the Whitehall Building. A stream of pamphlets, press releases, and interviews poured out from that source. Although the war in Europe was but a few weeks old, the American public was already becoming suspicious of overt official propaganda. For that reason, probably, the "Mexican Bureau of Information" found it expedient to include a notice in its earlier publications that "the Mexican Bureau of Information has no official connection with the Mexican General Consulate in this city nor the Mexican Embassy in Washington, D.C." At first no attempt was made to show Francisco Villa as a deep-dyed villain but rather as a well-meaning though badly mistaken, simple, and misled person. The main emphasis was on the justice and reasonableness of Carranza's program and policies. The groundwork was laid in these initial papers for the form that future Carranzista propaganda was to follow consistently. Villa was presented as the unwitting, and possibly unconscious, tool of the reactionaries. One of the earliest pamphlets from the Bureau bore the title, *"Red Papers" of Mexico: An Exposé of the Great Científico Conspiracy to Eliminate Don Venustiano Carranza.*[7] The material published by the "Mexican Bureau of Information" was well written and attractively designed and printed. In this it was far more subtle than the propaganda directed by some of the warring European powers trying to influence American public opinion in their own favor. In short, the Carranzista propaganda bears evidence of having been actually written by highly skilled Americans, rather than Mexicans.

With open warfare between Villa and Carranza, no further effort was made to show Villa as mistaken or misled. Unfortunately for Villa,

[7] As far as the writer has been able to ascertain, there is no complete catalogue of the material published by the "Mexican Bureau of Information." Most of the papers bear no identification beyond the Bureau's name and address, but a few are shown as having been printed by the firm of Edgar Printing and Stationery Company, 68 West 39th Street, New York City.

his career as a famous (or notorious) bandit lent itself perfectly to the new propaganda line. He now became a desperado of the most villainous kind. An example was a small pamphlet bearing the bitterly ironic title, *Gen. Francisco Villa, Candidate for the Nobel Peace Prize*, which depicted Villa as a scarcely human monster, whose ruthless greed, overwhelming ambition, and sadistic cruelty were the causes of all of Mexico's sorrows.[8]

The Carranzista writers and pamphleteers did not confine themselves to such efforts as the one just described. Appealing to American intellectuals whose interests went further than newspapers and short articles, lengthy books were published extolling Carranza and belittling Villa and the Villista side. Typical was *Carranza and Mexico*, by Carlo de Fornaro, with chapters by a Colonel I. C. Enriquez, Charles Ferguson, and M. C. Rollandi. Published in 1915 and hence written before the issue in Mexico was decided in favor of Carranza, the book was outwardly an impartial study of the situation and the leaders—with conclusions 100 per cent in favor of Carranza. Here again Villa appears as a tool of rich and utterly unscrupulous men, the Científicos. Fornaro insinuated that the same elements that backed Huerta were supporting Villa, almost that Huerta himself was back of Villa.

The Huerta agents . . . put their heads together to devise a means of breaking up the successful revolution. The reactionary junta watched the events with keen interest. As soon as Villa proved his ability as a general, he was chosen as the easiest and most convenient tool to break up the harmony between the revolutionists.[9]

As suggested by Carranza himself, said Fornaro, Villa's ignorance made him a natural pawn in the game. Evil reactionaries supplied him with money and advisers. "The Villa press agents began to fill the magazines and Sunday papers with romantic stories about the bandit general, the Washington, the Lincoln of Mexico. . . . Villa became a marionette in the hands of politicians who pulled the strings." [10] Fornaro claimed that in the summer of 1913 as much as two hundred dol-

[8] Included in the John J. Pershing Papers, in the Library of Congress. Written by one Victor Poncelot, this pamphlet bears no date, no place of publication or identification of the publisher. The context indicates that it was written some time in 1915.
[9] Carlo de Fornaro, *Carranza and Mexico* (New York, 1915), p. 177.
[10] *Ibid.*, pp. 178–179.

lars were paid to a single writer for an article on Villa for a New York newspaper.[11] Overlooked entirely was the inconsistence of accusing Villa and his supporters of spending vast sums for propaganda when such works as Fornaro's own book and the publications of the "Mexican Bureau of Information" were proof that the Carranzistas were likewise spending money without restraint. A cynic might say, without expressing sympathy for Villa, that this was a case in which the Carranzistas were diverting attention from their own mysterious financial sources. It is unhappily true in propaganda that if enough mud is thrown some of it is sure to stick.

Even before the Revolution made Villa more than locally famous, stories about him were in common circulation in the cities and countryside of Durango and Chihuahua. His early career as a bandit made him a natural target for what would later be called a "whispering campaign." As mentioned before, Dr. Carlos Rusk, forwarding an account of Villa's early life to General Pershing in September, 1914, remarked that it was impossible for one man to have committed all the crimes credited to Villa and that for years every crime in Durango and Chihuahua was blamed on him.[12] Passed by word of mouth from one horrified, or fascinated, narrator to another, such stories lost nothing in successive repetitions. The tales "snowballed," and by the time Villa became a serious opponent of Carranza his reputation in certain quarters might be likened to a combination of Caligula, Nero, Robin Hood, Jesse James, Al Capone, and Murder, Incorporated. Typical was a report, "Data Relative to a Part of the Criminal Life of Francisco Villa," prepared for General Scott in April, 1914, by the Provost Marshal at El Paso. Necessarily based upon hearsay, the report includes scores of crimes, ranging from murder and robberies in which the loot was a million dollars down to the theft of bedding and women's clothes.[13] The Provost Marshal said that his information was reliable, but it is quite evident that General Scott took the report with a grain of salt.

In addition to the old stories, innumerable new stories speedily became current soon after the rupture with Carranza. That they were deliberately concocted and circulated by Villa's enemies cannot be proved, but the continual stream of them after the autumn of 1914

[11] *Ibid.* The writer has been unable to find any unusual number of laudatory articles on Villa published in the summer of 1913.
[12] John J. Pershing Papers.   [13] Hugh Lenox Scott Papers.

cannot be purely coincidental. Soon after the occupation of Mexico City by Villa and Zapata, hostile propagandists, with an eye on both American sympathies and Mexican, discovered (or originated) tales that might almost be classed as works of art. Villa's casualness about human life, as shown by the killing of Benton, added credibility and served in lieu of proof. An authority on the Villa legend has said: "A large part of the derogatory legends . . . were spread as political propaganda . . . by Carranzistas." [14] Atrocity stories affected the attitude of some observers whose reports went to the State Department and may possibly have influenced President Wilson when he made his final decision.

But by the summer of 1915 the war in Europe had made atrocity stories stale. The determining factor in the decision to recognize Carranza may have been not Villa's supposed brutality but the carefully nurtured idea that Carranza stood for the welfare of the common people whereas Villa was a tool of "the interests." President Wilson's election in 1912 was the climax of the "Progressive Movement," and his greatest political interest was in the passage of measures designed to break the control which "Wall Street" was popularly believed to exercise over the nation. Whatever came out of "Wall Street" was, *ipso facto*, evil, and the most damning thing that could be said of a public man was that he favored, or was favored by, that source of all iniquity. Long before Villa and Carranza split, there had been insinuations that Villa was merely a front behind which the bankers of New York and London, with their Científico vassals, were plotting to restore the halcyon days of Porfirio Díaz.[15]

From the first, anti-Villa propagandists stressed that Villa was a "reactionary." During the Aguascalientes convention Carranza's personal representative, Roberto Pesqueira, asserted that Villa was assisted at the convention by Huertistas and Científicos and was supported by the "special interests that have played such an important part in American politics and sustained the corrupt Administrations of the past." [16] From that time, the Carranzistas seldom referred to Villa and his following in terms other than as the "reactionaries." The

[14] Haldeen Braddy, "Doroteo Arango, *alias* Pancho Villa," *New Mexico Folklore Record,* V, no. 5 (1950–1951), 4–8.

[15] Similar charges had been made earlier. Cf. The New York *Times,* Monday, May 4, 1914, 2:5.

[16] *Independent,* LXXX (Nov. 9, 1914), 195.

expression "counterrevolutionaries" was not then in use, but had it been, it would have been used, since that was exactly the impression that the Carranza faction was trying to convey. No opportunity was ever lost to couple Villa's name and party with the rich who stood to lose by the Revolution and with the predatory capitalists who were vaguely, but genuinely, feared in both the United States and Mexico. Erosion will eventually wear away the hardest stone.

President Wilson's decision to recognize Carranza may have been influenced when it became known that certain extreme conservatives had expressed opinions favoring Villa. For example, General Harrison Gray Otis, owner of the Los Angeles *Times,* noted for his hidebound conservatism and bitter antilabor beliefs, wrote to General Scott on August 21: "Gen. Villa's utterances are very strong and apparently sincere. . . . It was a sorry day for Mexico when Gen. Diaz was expelled from the country." [17] Nor could the President's confidence in Villa as the friend of the common man of Mexico have been strengthened if it came to his attention (as it probably did) that Harry Chandler, Otis' son-in-law and business partner, was indicted in May, 1915, for conspiring to foment an insurrection against the Carranzista governor of Lower California. [18]

Other rumors and items of information undoubtedly reached the President's ears. Before the outbreak of the Revolution there was a vague report that the Standard Oil Company (the epitome of "big business" and anathema to all "Progressives") was engaged in questionable efforts to obtain drilling concessions in Mexico. The highest officials of the company positively and emphatically denied it, and until June, 1914, nothing further was heard about the matter. Late in that month Special Agent R. L. Barnes, of the Department of Justice, received information that "representatives of the Standard Oil Company have been endeavoring to secure, and probably have secured, valuable concessions in Mexico, through Villa." [19]

One of the curious phenomena of American liberalism is the way in which some American ultraliberals have been obsessed at times with

---

[17] Hugh Lenox Scott Papers. Otis' reasons for writing this (and several other letters to Scott) are obscure. There is no indication that he and Scott were personally acquainted, let alone intimate enough for confidential correspondence.

[18] *Independent,* LXXXI (March 8, 1915), 352.

[19] National Archives, Department of Justice File nos. 90755–833, 861, 863, 882, 890, E-1 and E-2. Agent Barnes reported this as a rumor, not as an ascertained fact.

almost worshipful admiration for certain of the Mexican political leaders. In support of that statement one needs only to cite the lyrical praises of President Lázaro Cárdenas written in the 1930's and such works as Emile Joseph Dillon's book on General Alvaro Obregón in the early 1920's.[20] Probably the first idol to inspire the admiring reverence of the extreme liberals of the United States during his own lifetime was the dour *hacendado,* Venustiano Carranza. Thus, not only was Villa under the carefully nurtured suspicion of being a tool of "Wall Street," but Carranza was assured of being depicted by liberal writers as the very incarnation of the ideals and aspirations of true liberalism.

Foremost among those singing the praises of the First Chief was a man in whom President Wilson placed great confidence, Lincoln Steffens. One of the earliest and most famous of the "muckrakers," he was probably more responsible than any other individual in awakening the people of the United States to the supposed dangers of "big business" and to the frequent connections between business and political corruption. Steffens arrived in Mexico late in 1914 or early in 1915, after Carranza had transferred his capital to Veracruz. Before going to Mexico, however, Steffens took care to satisfy himself as to which side was worthy of his support.

The reds in New York who were watching Mexico were on Villa's side, but the only reason they gave was that he was at least a bandit, a Barabbas, whereas Carranza was a respectable, land-owning bourgeois. Jack Reed talked that way, and he later went in on Villa's side. I thought of a trick I used to practice in making a quick decision in politics at home. . . . If I could find out which side Wall Street was on, I could go to the other with the certainty of being right. So I inquired down there for the big business men with Mexican interests, called on and invited several of them to luncheon. They came eager to "start me off right." And they agreed that Villa was the man. Their reason?

"Well, you see, we have tried out both of them and Carranza, the ——, we can't do a thing with him. He won't listen to reason. Obstinate, narrow-minded, proud as hell, he has thrown us out again and again. Whereas Villa . . . You mustn't get the idea that just because he's a bandit he's no good. We have had him seen and—he's all right, Villa is." [21]

[20] Emile Joseph Dillon, *President Obregón, a World Reformer* (Boston, 1923).

[21] Lincoln Steffens, *The Autobiography of Lincoln Steffens* (New York, 1931), p. 715.

Knowing in advance that anyone whom Wall Street opposed must be right, Steffens found no difficulty in confirming his opinion on arriving in Mexico. Although Steffens spoke no Spanish, he had little difficulty in gaining the First Chief's confidence, even to the point of asking Carranza point-blank just what was back of Villa's break.

"We know exactly," the First Chief said, and because he is so slow, so unwilling to talk, one of his impetuous staff officers spoke up and explained:

"We know who got to Villa and what the price was exactly because the same man and the same interests that we see near Villa now came to us first and told us what they wanted and what they'd pay."

"And," added another, "the people see those same men around Villa. They hear the rumors of the price and they see the signs of his turnover to the foreigners. . . ." [22]

Steffens became one of the most enthusiastic of the pro-Carranza and anti-Villa propagandists. In fact, to all intents and purposes he became a Carranzista public relations officer. His personal acquaintance with President Wilson and with Colonel Edward M. House, the President's closest adviser, made Steffens doubly effective as an agent to create an atmosphere unfavorable to Villa. He had at least one personal interview with President Wilson and was sure of getting his ideas to the President through Colonel House, to whom he addressed a whole series of letters in the summer and early autumn of 1915.[23]

Steffens, as shown in his published works, was not unsympathetic toward radicals and the idea of revolution. No such charges could be made against that staunch progressive, John Lind, who had been the President's personal envoy to Mexico during the days of Huerta. Originally, during the first stages of the revolt against Huerta, Lind was favorably disposed toward Villa, but in the course of time his views changed markedly. He finally believed that the interests that backed Huerta were behind and supporting Villa, and since Lind had grown up politically in the atmosphere of the Progressive Movement, he was deeply suspicious of anyone charged with being under the influence of "the interests." He gained, moreover, a sincere respect for Carranza. Lind's record, in both domestic affairs and his management of

[22] Steffens, "Making Friends with Mexico," *Collier's Magazine*, LVIII (Nov. 25, 1916), 4.

[23] Steffens, *The Letters of Lincoln Steffens*, ed. by Ella Winter and Granville Hicks, I [1889–1919] (New York, 1938), 356–359.

his difficult mission to Mexico, inspired confidence in his judgment, and when he joined those urging the recognition of Carranza, his recommendation carried great weight.[24]

With the constant insinuations that Villa was really a front for capitalistic wealth trying to revive the palmy days of Porfirio Díaz came reports from some American consular officials that Villa was not the basically humane character that favorable reports had depicted him as being. Early in July, 1915, Vice-Consul Homer C. Coen reported from Durango the case of a certain "Mr. Chanel," a French citizen, accused of taking charge of the property of Mexicans who had fled from the Villista army. General Calixto Contreras publicly threatened to cut off Mr. Chanel's head. Villa was not personally involved, but General Contreras was supposedly one of his subordinates, and he was therefore responsible. The affair caused a considerable volume of correspondence between the State Department, the French Embassy in Washington, and Coen.[25] Late in August, Coen sent in another report that Villa had taken eleven prominent Mexican citizens of Durango to Torreón as prisoners, maltreating them terribly on the way.[26] Coen evidently submitted additional reports, for on September 10 James R. Garfield wrote to General Scott that Coen's reports from Durango seemed to be deeply colored against Villa.[27]

The most damaging reports came to Washington not from representatives of the State Department but from Collector of Customs Zach E. Cobb, at El Paso. Although an official of the Treasury Department, Cobb seems to have spent more time acting as a volunteer agent of the State Department than he did in the performance of his regular duties. In May, 1915, he reported that Villa's increasing abuses were driving foreigners against him and that his worthless currency was heightening the discontent of his own people.[28] Two months previously, Cobb had urged the necessity of making Villa and his followers live up to their agreements and assurances. Large quantities of stolen property, frequently stolen from Americans, were being passed over the border by the Villistas.[29] The attitude implied in these two dispatches was distinctly different from that displayed by Cobb a year

[24] Stephenson, *John Lind of Minnesota,* pp. 279–310.
[25] *Foreign Relations, 1915,* pp. 1065–1067.   [26] Hugh Lenox Scott Papers.
[27] *Ibid.*
[28] *National Archives,* State Department File no. 812.00/14999, May 11, 1915.
[29] *Ibid.,* File no. 812.00/14473, March 2, 1915.

before. In June, 1914, Cobb remarked in a personal letter to General Scott that Villa, barring unforeseen developments, would continue to grow as the most forceful personality of the revolution.[30] At about the same time, in a letter to Boaz W. Long, the chief of the Latin American Division of the State Department, Cobb wrote that, so far, Villa "has apparently been free from the influence of the big special interests. It seems exceedingly important that he should be kept free from such entanglements." Cobb requested authority from the department to warn Villa's representatives not to become entangled with Sherburne Hopkins.[31] By August 1 following this correspondence, Cobb had become convinced that "through concessions to associates Villa is surrounded by corruption, and through men like Summerfelt [*sic*] and Hopkins is in imminent danger of being drawn into alliance with big special interests." [32]

Cobb's reports thereafter were uniformly unfavorable to Villa. In fact, he seemed to develop a phobia, a personal hatred of Villa. In August of the following year Carothers recommended measures to reopen the Juárez packing houses to enable Villa to raise funds without imposing taxes or forced loans upon foreigners. Cobb opposed the scheme bitterly, on the grounds that the cattle slaughtered would be stolen animals. On August 17, 1915, General Scott wrote a strong personal letter to the Secretary of State, warning him that Cobb had changed (probably, he felt, because of worry over personal losses) and was trying to undermine the work that Scott and Carothers had accomplished. Cobb, Scott said, was saying that no trust could be placed in Villa, but this was emphatically not true, as Villa, to Scott's knowledge, had kept his word in all cases.[33]

Reports such as Coen's and Cobb's were not as numerous as the favorable reports submitted by Carothers over a period of many months, nor were they quite as authoritative as Paul Fuller's report to the President. The anti-Villa propaganda necessarily then had to impeach the impartiality or integrity of such important witnesses. With Paul Fuller the problem was relatively easy. He was a devoted Roman Catholic, *ergo*, he must be committed to the re-establishment of the Church and the clericals to their favored position in Mexico. On

[30] Hugh Lenox Scott Papers.
[31] National Archives, State Department File no. 812.00/12741, July 3, 1914.
[32] *Ibid.*, File no. 812.00/12706, Aug. 1, 1914.   [33] Hugh Lenox Scott Papers.

August 7, 1915, Lincoln Steffens wrote to Colonel House: "The Church and the other privileged interests here and abroad are desperately bent upon robbing Carranza and the revolution of the fruits of their victory. . . . I have learned since I have been down here that Mr. Paul Fuller . . . is the chief counsel of the Catholic Church in the United States." [34]

Carothers, being a Protestant, was not vulnerable in his religious associations, nor was he ever connected, so far as anybody charged, with the "big special interests" that aroused such horror in Collector Cobb. Carothers had lived in Mexico for over thirty years. For several years of that time he was connected with the State Department as a consular agent, and during all the period he had been in business for himself, in mining and real estate. Therein lay his Achilles heel. Since he had been in the mining and real-estate businesses, he must, therefore, be sympathetic toward the old order. There was innuendo that he was a strong supporter of Huerta until it became apparent that Huerta's regime was doomed, and then he switched to Villa. In just what way Carothers supported Huerta was never specified. But his infamy, according to rumor, reached depths far beyond that. In June, 1914, Congressman William Kent, of California, sent several letters to the President which he had received from one René Leon, of El Paso, Texas. Leon asserted that Carothers and Villa were business partners. He did not say what kind of business they were engaged in, but since Villa had been a bandit and had been accused of basing his butcher business in Chihuahua upon stolen cattle, the inference was fairly obvious. Kent was careful to inform the President that he could not vouch for Leon's veracity or accuracy.[35]

Continuous repetition of the allegation that Villa was a tool of unscrupulous capitalists and other heartless reactionaries was bound to leave a deep impression upon many persons. Continual stress upon his supposed viciousness and brutality, ignoring the undoubted fact that all factions in Mexico were just as cruel and ruthless by American standards, inevitably produced an emotional image of a monster with whom the United States, in all decency, could not be associated. Never was any concrete proof brought forth in support of Villa's subservience to "Wall Street," but with sufficient repetition, specific evi-

---

[34] Steffens, *The Letters of Lincoln Steffens,* I, 357.
[35] Woodrow Wilson Papers.

dence was not necessary—an unhappy principle of wartime propaganda with which the world, at that time, was not as familiar as it has
since become.

The crowning touch in swinging opinion, the opinion that counted
in making decisions and policies, came when the leadership of organized labor came out flatly in favor of Carranza. Initially American labor, insofar as it held any common opinion on the Mexican
quarrel, seemed to favor Villa. In May, 1915, the commanding general
at Fort Bliss, Texas, reported that the ammunition and weapons flowing to the Villistas of Sonora were coming mainly from mining and
labor centers in the United States.[36] A little earlier in the year, however, the Carranza government made an agreement with the labor
unions of Mexico whereby, in return for Carranza's support, they
undertook to furnish municipal guards and to form a brigade for the
Constitutionalist army.[37] In other ways Carranza courted the favor of
organized labor, an attitude that paid dividends when Samuel Gompers, president of the American Federation of Labor, on September
22, 1915, wrote a lengthy and strongly worded letter to President
Wilson endorsing Carranza and his government.[38]

Whatever the reasons may have been that motivated President
Wilson's decision to recognize Carranza, they were certainly not the
reasons charged by some of the more fervid of the ultraliberals, who
asserted that "overwhelming" evidence proved that Villa reached
an understanding with Wilson during the Veracruz occupation and
at the same time made up his differences with the Científicos. In
furtherance of this plot, Carothers became Villa's chief adviser, and
Cardoso de Oliveira, accused of being "a pronounced clerical, a friend
of Villa, and a violent enemy of Carranza," was named as United States
representative in Mexico City. Thus, the State Department, with William Jennings Bryan directing its activities, became openly an anti-
Carranza and pro-Villa agency, while American consular officers in
Mexico were active Villista spies, using United States codes for the
transmission of military information.[39]

[36] National Archives, War Department Files, an unnumbered report dated May 8,
1915.
[37] *Independent*, LXXXI (March 1, 1915), 312.
[38] Woodrow Wilson Papers.
[39] John Kenneth Turner, *Hands Off Mexico* (New York, 1920), pp. 45–51. Turner
was also the author of *Barbarous Mexico*, giving a lurid account of the horrors of the

According to the school of thought that reached these conclusions the recognition of Carranza was actuated by pique and a spirit of revenge, because of Villa's patriotic refusal to grant territorial concessions to the United States. Comment is unnecessary, except to point out that despite positive assertions of "overwhelming" evidence, not a single item of proof has ever been exhumed. The tale, which appears to be merely a variation of the story of DuVal West's "secret" mission, has unfortunately been widely circulated and believed.[40]

One additional fact must be considered in evaluating the various factors that may have influenced President Wilson's decision. In the mid-summer of 1915, because of the volume of correspondence and business relating to Mexico, a special Division of Mexican Affairs was added to the State Department. There is no record of the advice and information that the new division transmitted to the Secretary of State and the President, but one can reasonably conjecture that it was not especially favorable toward Villa. The chief of the new division was Leon J. Canova, and the division was anti-Villa from the start.[41]

President Wilson was a statesman who kept his own counsel and made his own decisions, with the courage to take full responsibility for them. Whether for good or ill, by his decision on October 9, 1915, Venustiano Carranza's government was recognized as the *de facto* government of Mexico. On that date Francisco Villa reverted to his original status of bandit and outlaw as far as the United States was concerned. The cycle seemed to be complete, but Villa was still a factor in the affairs of the two nations.

Díaz regime. He was prosecuted for libel by the Mexican Embassy in Washington for this. At the time of writing *Hands Off Mexico* he was connected with the Rand School of Social Science, a well-known center of extremist thought. The obvious misstatements and inaccuracies in the above statement make any analysis unnecessary.

[40] Cf. Plenn, *Mexico Marches*, p. 58. Gen. Bernardino Mena Brito, in *El lugarteniente gris de Pancho Villa*, accepts this idea without question.

[41] It will be recalled that Canova had aroused Villa's enmity by escorting Gen. Eduardo Iturbide out of Mexico during the series of executions in Mexico City, while Villa and Zapata occupied Mexico City.

❧ XVI ❧

Villa's Defeat at Agua Prieta

OCTOBER, 1915, found Villa in Chihuahua, busily reorganizing and regrouping his forces. In spite of heavy casualties and large-scale desertions, he still commanded a formidable army. Frank Rhoades, an American who had recently seen and talked to Villa, wrote to General Scott that although Villa's forces were badly disorganized they were not, in any sense, destroyed. Nearly all of Villa's subordinate commanders were still loyal, even if the absoluteness of his control over them, under the new circumstances, was problematical.[1] Nobody doubted his complete control over the troops under his direct command and observation.

Villa was informed promptly that the Secretary of State and the Latin American diplomats had found the Carranza regime the only one qualified for recognition as a *de facto* government. First reports indicated that he took the news quietly, remarking that the war had just begun. He had suffered losses, and his financial condition was bad, but "a dozen nations could not keep Carranza from failure."[2] Rhoades told General Scott further that Villa did not, outwardly, seem to hold any resentment against the United States, although, Rhoades added, "I am sure he feels that his confidence has been violated, and I am not sure but that I fully agree with him."[3]

[1] Hugh Lenox Scott Papers, Oct. 13, 1915.
[2] *Independent*, LXXXIV (Oct. 18, 1915), 91.
[3] Cf. note 1, *supra.* These statements of Villa's reception of what must have been

Villa's next operation was an open secret. He had lost all of his sea-ports and all the main border ports except Juárez. Agua Prieta, opposite the American city of Douglas, Arizona, had been held continuously by the Carranzistas since the preceding year. The garrison of Agua Prieta was a standing threat to Villa's rear. The capture of the place would simultaneously eliminate that danger, make an additional port of entry available, and destroy the only vestige of Carranza's authority in north-ern Sonora. An extended base, from which new operations could be launched, would thus be consolidated. Villa must capture Agua Prieta at all costs.

The Carranzistas were well aware of the danger. The garrison at Agua Prieta was completely isolated from all other Carranza forces. The force which Villa could bring against Agua Prieta was overwhelm-ing. His main force, estimated variously from ten thousand to fifteen thousand men, suddenly vanished from Chihuahua in mid-October, moving to the northwest.

During the period of preparation for the campaign in Sonora, a con-siderable part of Villa's forces was grouped in the vicinity of Casas Grandes and Colonia Dublán, prosperous colonies of Mormons who had been there for many years, turning the desert into productive farms and ranches. Villa maintained rigid discipline, and no violence was offered to any of the Mormons, but he requisitioned their wagons, horses, and other properties. He offered to allow the owners of requisi-tioned horses to accompany the army to care for their animals and bring them back after the campaign. Three men availed themselves of this offer, escaping to the United States when it became apparent that Villa would be defeated.[4]

Toiling through the deserts and the fastnesses of the Sierra Madre, for days Villa's army was lost to public view. The beleagured Ca-rranzistas at Agua Prieta, meanwhile, had a stroke of good fortune. It was no part of the policy of the United States, after recognizing

---

most unwelcome news disagree diametrically with more picturesque accounts that he broke into such a rage that no one dared come near him. Cf. Harris, *Pancho Villa and the Columbus Raid*, pp. 80–81, and Francisco Bulnes, *The Whole Truth about Mexico* (New York, 1916), pp. 378–379.

[4] Raymond J. Reed, "The Mormons in Chihuahua: Their Relations with Villa and the Pershing Punitive Expedition, 1916–1917" (master's thesis, University of New Mexico, 1938), pp. 14–16. The above information was given to the writer of the thesis by one of the three men mentioned.

Carranza, to allow Villa to regain his strength by establishing himself firmly along the border in Sonora and Chihuahua. President Wilson approved a request from the *de facto* government to be allowed to reinforce Agua Prieta through the United States, and trainloads of soldiers, artillery, munitions, and equipment poured through Douglas, Arizona, into Mexico. General Plutarco Calles, in command, surrounded the town on three sides with deep entrenchments, aprons of barbed wire, and machine guns emplaced to sweep all approaches. By intensive labor and free use of the privilege of shipping munitions and material through the United States, the defenders were able to make Agua Prieta almost impregnable before the first Villistas appeared in the mountain passes to the east.[5]

Before this, from the outbreak of the Revolution, the United States had been careful not to give any sort of material aid to either side. Armed Mexican forces were never permitted on American soil, even during the period when the United States was openly hostile to Huerta and favorable toward the Constitutionalists. The change proved that the administration, once having recognized Carranza as the leader most likely to be able to bring peace, order, and justice to Mexico, was determined to back him to the limit.

The first signs of increasing military activity on the Arizona-Sonora border occurred on October 21, when General Urbalejo's Yaqui Indians suddenly occupied Naco.[6] Anticipating serious trouble, the garrison at Douglas was strengthened until it included three regiments of infantry, a regiment of field artillery, and several troops of cavalry—a force strong enough to cope with any situation likely to arise.

Definite information of Villa was received late in the afternoon of October 30, when Carothers telegraphed to the State Department that Villista troops were immediately south of Slaughter's Ranch, eighteen miles east of Douglas. An American patrol had talked to members of Villa's staff, who said that they were locating the international boundary and that Villa himself was about ten miles to the east. He expected to camp that night opposite Slaughter's.[7]

Although Villa had been informed previously that it was probable

[5] *Independent*, LXXXIV (Nov. 15, 1915), 259. Cf. The New York *Times*, Wednesday, Oct. 27, 1915, 19:1.

[6] National Archives, War Department Files, Weekly Report no. 135, Commanding General, Southern Department, Oct. 27, 1915.

[7] National Archives, State Department File no. 812.00/16649, Oct. 30, 1915.

that the United States would recognize Carranza, the first news that recognition had been actually accorded did not reach him until he was approaching Agua Prieta. Carothers and Colonel Herbert Slocum, 13th Cavalry, while disagreeing as to the time when Villa received this unwelcome news, both reported that Villa became very angry and declared that he would have no further dealings with the United States. He vowed that he would take Agua Prieta in spite of President Wilson and was willing to fight both the United States and the Carranzistas together, if necessary.[8]

On the United States side of the border the troops had been busy for several days, digging trenches from Douglas to the first range of hills to the east. This was not a continuous line of trenches, but rather a series of mutually supporting strong points which would have exacted a heavy toll of any Mexican forces attempting to cross into the United States.[9]

The scene was set for a battle that is almost unique in military history, in that observers were able to watch it from the side lines, like a football game, with relatively little danger to themselves. The Villa forces approached, the American trenches were manned, and the American artillery went into previously selected positions, shortly before daybreak on November 1. The Villista advance across the open plain was clearly visible from the American positions and evoked favorable comment from the watching American officers. Shortly after noon the Carranzista artillery in Agua Prieta opened fire, and for the rest of the afternoon and the evening there was a heavy exchange of fire between the defenders and the attackers. At one-thirty in the morning Villa launched his assault, his men pushing home their attack with desperate courage. It was all to no avail, for the Villistas learned, as both sides on the Western Front in Europe had already learned, that an assault against a position covered with barbed wire, defended by cross-firing machine guns, supported by artillery firing high explosive, is doomed to failure.[10]

[8] *Ibid.*, File nos. 812.00/16653, Oct. 31, 1915, and 16679, Nov. 1, 1915. Slocum's dispatch was addressed to General Funston, the department commander, who was en route to Douglas at the time.

[9] The remains of most of these field fortifications were visible several years later, when the writer saw them.

[10] Col. Abner Pickering, 11th Infantry, "The Battle of Agua Prieta," *United States Infantry Journal*, XII (Jan., 1916), 707–710. This is an eyewitness account by the commanding officer of one of the United States regiments at Douglas.

Nor were the weapons and the Carranzista entrenchments the only tactical feature of the battlefield that contributed to Villa's defeat. For the first time, probably, in Mexican military history, the battlefield was illuminated. Villa's previous successes in night attacks caused him to have great faith in them, but at Agua Prieta the night was turned into day by powerful searchlights, the beams of which not only revealed the oncoming attack but blinded the attackers.[11] These searchlights caused much bitterness among the Villistas and were quickly added to the grudge they were building up against the United States. As it became apparent during the next few days that their defeat was helped, if not entirely caused, by the new policies of the United States, rumors began to circulate among the Villistas that the searchlights were furnished by the United States Army and manned by United States soldiers and, finally, that the lights were located on the United States side of the boundary.[12]

At first, nobody on the American side of the international line realized how completely crushing Villa's defeat had been. The afternoon following the attack Carothers informed the State Department that Villa had been repulsed with small losses but was preparing to renew his attack. Later in the same day he sent another dispatch saying that General Funston had held a short conference with Villa that morning.[13]

Throughout the battle the United States forces in Douglas were mere observers, prepared for instant action. Knowing this may have had something to do with the fact that the commanders on both sides were anxious to avoid any trouble with the United States. Carothers reported on the first day of the fighting that "so far both sides appear fully aware of [the] danger of firing on [the] American side." [14] Inevitably, however, shots fell into Douglas, and several people were killed and wounded in the American city. General Funston reported by telegraph to The Adjutant General immediately after the night attack that most of the shots falling into American territory came from the south and southeast (i.e., from the Villista side). He believed that both sides were

[11] *Ibid.* Cf. also Campobello, *Apuntes sobre la vida militar de Francisco Villa,* p. 117. It is interesting to note that during the Korean War the use of searchlights to illuminate the battlefield was hailed as something new in warfare.

[12] Cf. Löhndorff, *Bestie ich in Mexiko,* pp. 301–304, and Pinchon, *Viva Villa!* p. 334. The power for these searchlights undoubtedly came from the United States, and the crews may have been American adventurers.

[13] National Archives, State Department File nos. 812.00/16672 and 16673, Nov. 2, 1915.

[14] *Ibid.,* File no. 812.00/16656, Nov. 1, 1915.

doing their best to avoid firing into the United States and was positive that he could not prevent occasional danger to Americans unless he were given authority to cross the border and drive the Villa forces away. Like Carothers, Funston believed that Villa would renew the attack at once, but, differing from the information Carothers had received, Funston reported that Villa's losses were heavy.[15]

The conference between Villa and General Funston took place at the international boundary, about a mile east of Douglas. The conference was at Villa's request; Funston was somewhat doubtful as to its propriety but consented because Villa might have something important to discuss. Just what Villa may have had in mind is unknown. The interview lasted only some ten minutes, and Funston's only comment was that "[Villa's] attitude was quite satisfactory." [16]

Villa did not resume the attack, although Carothers could not believe that he had really given up so soon. Funston watched the Villista withdrawal and felt a degree of professional admiration at the skillful way in which Villa screened the town while he passed his forces westward around it; in addition, like the other American observers, he noticed that the conduct of Villa's men under fire was excellent. By the afternoon of November 3, the Villista army had disappeared, and its whereabouts was unknown.[17] The immediate danger of complications from the fighting at Douglas was over.

General Funston's orders from the War Department authorized him to open fire upon the combatants in Mexico if necessary to put a stop to firing into the United States. Funston had a reputation as a "fire-eater," and when reports were received of Americans being hit in Douglas by shots fired in Mexico, his failure to retaliate immediately probably caused some comment in Washington. He evidently felt that his action, or rather inaction, might be misconstrued, for in his brief telegraphic report he justified himself:

It may not be understood at War Department why in view of existing orders I have not fired upon the contending parties considering the fact that some bullets and shell struck on the American side and three men of seventh infantry wounded. This was not done because of evident fact that both com-

---

[15] *Ibid.*, File no. 812.00/16689, Nov. 1, 1915.
[16] *Ibid.*, File no. 812.00/16727, Nov. 3, 1915. This was General Funston's official report to The Adjutant General.
[17] *Ibid.*

manders were doing all they could to prevent injury to Americans. The principal faults were committed by Calles men and I could not in fairness have opened on Villa without treating Calles the same.[18]

General Funston's brief interview with Villa on November 3 was probably the last occasion on which an American official saw and talked to him face to face. His resentment against the United States and his bitterness at American ingratitude must have been increasing hourly, as the magnitude of his disaster sank deeper into his consciousness. Regardless of his bitterness, he was scrupulously fair with the Americans who remained with him. He advised Dr. Harle, whom he had rescued from prison, to leave at once because of the feeling in the army and presented him with a fine horse.[19] Another American physician, Dr. J. W. Ward, who had served with Villa for fourteen months, remained until the forces reached Naco.[20] The three Mormons who came along to look out for their requisitioned horses suffered no violence, and after the news of Carranza's recognition they escaped with such ease that apparently no obstacle was placed in their way.[21] The only offense against Americans that could be charged to Villa's responsibility at this time was the arrest of two Red Cross doctors who were working on the battlefield. The first reports were that they had been murdered by Carranzistas, but it later developed that they were seized by Villistas, robbed, and condemned to death. They were immediately released. It is possible that the Red Cross emblem saved their lives— it is also possible that the matter came to Villa's personal attention.[22]

From Agua Prieta the defeated Villistas moved westward to Naco and rested there a few days. Their increasing hostility toward the United States was becoming apparent. As for Villa himself, it was learned that before entering Sonora he had ordered the confiscation of the properties of the American Smelting and Refining Company. Carothers notified the State Department on November 5 that Villa had demanded a forced loan of twenty-five thousand dollars from each of four American companies in his territory and was threatening to con-

---

[18] *Ibid.* [19] Bush, *Gringo Doctor*, pp. 234, 241.

[20] Reported to the Secretary of State by Collector of Customs Zach Cobb, who hated Villa thoroughly (National Archives, State Department File no. 812.00/16771, Nov. 11, 1915).

[21] Reed, *The Mormons in Chihuahua*, pp. 14–16.

[22] *Independent*, LXXXIV (Nov. 15, 1915), 259.

fiscate all the cattle of the Cananea Cattle Company.[23] Villa announced openly that he intended to seize all horses and saddle equipment, no matter to whom they belonged.[24] This was an attitude vastly different from what he had expressed before.

Leaving Naco, Villa moved his forces southward for a final, desperate attempt to redeem the Villista cause. Nogales was still in the possession of Villa's Sonoran sympathizers, but Hermosillo, the capital of the state, was occupied by Carranzistas. The capture of that city and the destruction of the garrison would give Villa a new lease on life and would provide a base from which he might yet conquer all of Mexico. In spite of the defeat at Agua Prieta, he kept his army under firm control. Desertions had reduced its strength, but it was still formidable and now consisted of a hard core of determined, disciplined fighters. Villa claimed, according to the International News Service, to have seventeen thousand men, but more modest estimates placed his strength at approximately ten thousand. Regardless of the actual number, he still had a force strong enough to cause anxiety among his enemies.[25]

A slashing, determined attack, in the old Villa style, was beaten back from Hermosillo with losses that destroyed completely the army's morale. Met by withering cross fires from carefully emplaced machine guns, shot down in swathes by riflemen lying behind the invulnerable adobe walls of the houses, the attack was foredoomed to failure. The attack on Agua Prieta resulted in defeat—the attack on Hermosillo was a disaster. In a panicky withdrawal, the Villistas were harassed by long-range artillery, and the hard Villista army began to disintegrate.[26] By the end of November, Villa was finished as a major factor in Mexican politics. The fortune which had attended him for so long had abandoned him at the battle of Celaya, and he had never been able to regain its favor.

[23] *Ibid.*, LXXXIV (Nov. 8, 1915), 220. Cf. the New York *Times*, Saturday, Oct. 30, 1915, 6:6.

[24] National Archives, State Department File no. 812.00/16717, Nov. 5, 1915.

[25] Bisbee (Arizona) *Daily Review*, Nov. 15, 1915, quoted in Samuel S. Fain, "The Pershing Punitive Expedition and Its Diplomatic Background" (master's thesis, University of Arizona, 1951), p. 47. Cf. Carothers' dispatch to the Secretary of State, National Archives, State Department File no. 812.00/16761, Nov. 10, 1915.

[26] *Literary Digest*, LI (Dec. 11, 1915), 1395. Cf. the *Independent*, LXXXIV (Dec. 6, 1915), 381, and (Dec. 20, 1915), 463. A fictional, but vivid and not improbable, description of this battle, most likely based on eyewitness accounts, is given by Löhndorff, *Bestie ich in Mexiko*, pp. 314–318.

Since they could not go southward, the shattered remnants of Villa's army drifted northward toward Nogales, which was still held by friendly forces. En route they committed all the atrocities which seem to be inseparable from a breakdown in the discipline of an army. Villa was supposed to have promised his men freedom to loot Hermosillo, in lieu of the pay he could not give them. Unable to redeem even this promise, he was accused of leading the way and furnishing an example in ravaging and plundering as his disorganized bands straggled toward the border.[27]

While these events were taking place, the Carranzistas were not the only ones conducting a campaign against Pancho Villa. At El Paso, Collector Zach Cobb constituted himself a one-man diplomatic and consular force whose sole objective appeared to be to bring about Villa's complete and final downfall. Cobb made it his immediate mission to cut off supplies for Villa passing through El Paso, to prevent Villa's gaining any revenue by exports through Juárez, and by these means to render Juárez untenable for the Villista garrison. If he could accomplish this, Cobb would succeed in closing Villa's last gateway to the outer world.

To achieve his ends, Cobb was determined, first, that no coal which was destined for Villa or which might fall into Villa's hands would cross from El Paso into Villa territory. On October 29 he sent a telegram addressed to the Secretary of State personally, informing him of the situation. Cobb recommended that the State Department obtain an injunction to prevent rolling stock of the Mexican National Railways from returning to Mexico. This would be a guarantee that Villa could not obtain any coal. The Alvarado Mining Company, said Cobb, would not co-operate with him and had continued to operate in Mexico after other American firms had shut down, thereby helping Villa by paying taxes. If the Alvarado Mining Company should protest in Washington, as Cobb expected them to do, he asked that the complaint be disregarded until the situation at El Paso was cleared up. "The one prevailing talk among our Americans in Mexico has been the demand for a strong hand. A strong hand here, provided most discreetly exercised, can do nothing but good." [28]

---

[27] Reported to the Secretary of State by Consul Louis Hostetter, National Archives, State Department File no. 812.00/17053, Dec. 27, 1915.
[28] *Ibid.*, File no. 812.00/16636, Oct. 29, 1915.

Three days later, just as the Villista forces were reeling back from their defeat at Agua Prieta, Cobb informed the State Department that he had ordered all cattle shipments to be held on the Mexican side of the border until they were found satisfactory for entry. Thus, no Villa export .tax would be paid. Recommending that an embargo be placed on importations of cattle from Mexico, Cobb added: "If I may be permitted to suspend Villa revenue . . . you may expect Juarez to be abandoned or to turn over soon. There are already encouraging indications." [29]

With obvious satisfaction, Cobb reported to the Secretary of State two days later that Villa's American lawyer (whom he did not name) demanded coal, because the Villistas had none to run their trains. "They did not get it." To make sure that none of the American coaldealers lost by these measures, the Carranza consul in El Paso had quietly arranged to buy all the coal accumulated, as soon as the Carranza forces occupied Juárez. Villa's American lawyer made chilling threats about what the Villistas would do if they could not get coal, but Cobb was obdurate.[30]

There the matter rested for several days. On November 8 Cobb sent an anxious telegram to the Secretary of State, requesting that Secretary of the Treasury McAdoo be informed that the change-over in Juárez was due that night and would be imperiled if the Villistas obtained any coal. "Ask him please permit me delay passage today. Please rush answer." The Secretary of State rushed the request to the Treasury Department, resulting in authority for Cobb to hold up shipments for forty-eight hours.[31]

Carothers, who was still at Douglas, reported that Villa was now irresponsible and dangerous. He was subject to violent fits of temper and was capable of any extreme. To prevent his gaining a new foothold on the border, Carothers urged that the measures recommended by Cobb be applied at other places. Coal and everything else that might be of use to Villa should be embargoed.[32]

Cobb received information from the general manager of the El Paso and Southwestern Railroad that there was a plan to transfer Villa's

[29] *Ibid.*, File no. 812.00/16674, Nov. 2, 1915.
[30] *Ibid.*, File no. 812.00/16705, Nov. 4, 1915.
[31] *Ibid.*, File nos. 812.00/16735 and 16737, Nov. 8, 1915.
[32] *Ibid.*, File no. 812.00/16739, Nov. 8, 1915.

wounded to Juárez through the United States. Believing that this might serve as an encouragement to Villa's garrison at Juárez, Cobb recommended that the immigration authorities refuse the necessary permission. He pointed out that there were hospitals nearer Naco, in both Mexico and Arizona.[33]

Cobb did not wage his lone-handed war against Villa without encountering opposition. He anticipated that complaints would be made in Washington against his somewhat arbitrary measures, and he was right. Referring to a complaint which had been submitted, the Treasury Department told him curtly: "There is absolutely no legal authority for Customs to interfere with any shipments to Mexico in usual course of commerce and other than munitions of war. The Department insists on your being governed accordingly and giving no more cause for complaints of this character." [34]

Unabashed by this reprimand, Cobb appealed to the Secretary of State, who was in no position to encourage insubordination by an official of another government department, even had he desired to do so. Secretary Lansing's reply to Cobb was the good advice that "it is feared that your anxiety to eliminate Villa element may cause friction between you and Treasury Department. You should comply with that Department's instructions. This Department cannot ask Treasury to countermand them." [35] Cobb, nevertheless, was persistent. Enlisting the assistance of one Johnson, of "Phelps Dodge, Southwestern Railroad," he found a purchaser for all the coal presumably destined for Villa, and once again prevented the shipment.[36]

Straining every effort to eliminate Villa from the scene, Cobb was deeply incensed at General Funston's report that the Carranzistas were more guilty than the Villistas of firing into the United States during the battle of Agua Prieta. An indignant telegram to the Secretary of State, addressed for his personal attention, said:

Published report of General Funston, favoring Villa in disparagement of Carrancistas, was untimely and unfortunate in its effect here of encouraging Villa and the commercial pirates who sustain him. While this is temporary, there is a more serious and permanent interference with your work. Mexicans cannot understand how high American Generals can thus boost Villa without

---

[33] *Ibid.*, File no. 812.00/16705, Nov. 4, 1915.
[34] *Ibid.*, File no. 812.00/16759, Nov. 10, 1915.
[35] *Ibid.*   [36] *Ibid.*, File no. 812.00/16770, Nov. 11, 1915.

representing the views of the President. The inconsistency between this and the authoritative utterances of the Government is available to those fighting your efforts to give Mexicans the impression that a communication being transmitted for Villa to General Scott has given the unfortunate intimation that Villa can thus go over your head [sic]. As you know, during the time that General Scott made serious mistakes here, I sought to avoid any criticism that might be personal. If his attitude is the same now as it was then, and if he is still intimately counselling with Garfield, since developed to be employed by the Maderos, and Smith, I respectfully submit the necessity of putting the lid on him.[37]

Cobb's hopes that the Carranzistas were going to move into Juárez were not to be fulfilled for almost two months. On December 23, 1915, General Obregón finally informed him that the troops of the *de facto* government were at last in possession of Juárez.[38]

Coincidental with Villa's campaign against Agua Prieta and the beginning of Cobb's campaign against Villa's finances and transportation were troubles encountered by Villa's trusted agent, Felix Sommerfeld. One may safely assume that Sommerfeld was being kept under surveillance by the Federal authorities, but his woes arose from nothing as spectacular as violation of the neutrality laws or the President's embargo on the shipment of munitions to Villa. On October 28, 1915, Sommerfeld was arrested at his suite at Hotel Astor, in New York, charged with common theft. The indictment was seventeen years old. The complainant claimed that he recognized Sommerfeld, while the latter was testifying as a witness in court, as the person who had stolen a large sum of money from him in 1898. Sommerfeld was able to furnish bail, and apparently the case never came to trial. The arrest and the attendant publicity undoubtedly handicapped his activities, especially as he was suspected of being connected, in some way, with the secret German agents who—popular imagination was beginning to believe—were numerous in the United States.[39]

The disaster to Villa's army at Hermosillo, coming upon the heels of the defeat at Agua Prieta, was the final step in changing the Villista

[37] *Ibid.,* File no. 812.00/16715, Nov. 5, 1915. This somewhat extraordinary communication is unsigned, but there seems little doubt as to the authorship.

[38] *Ibid.,* File no. 812.00/17004, Dec. 23, 1915.

[39] New York *Times,* Thursday, Oct. 28, 1915, 4:5. The trial at which Sommerfeld was testifying when supposedly recognized involved fraudulent passports and alleged German secret agents.

attitude toward the United States to bitter hostility. The Villistas were certain that they would have been victorious at Agua Prieta if the garrison had not been reinforced through the United States and that the crushing blow at Hermosillo would not have occurred. The United States was seemingly responsible for all their ills. As the retreating Villistas reached the international line at Nogales, their hatred culminated in open violence. On November 25 two Villista colonels, seeing Consul Frederick Simpich and the collector of customs near the Nogales Customhouse, shouted insults and vile names. The uproar attracted twenty or thirty mounted Villista soldiers, who immediately joined in, adding their own insults and threatening the two Americans with their weapons. Excitedly, several of them rode across the boundary, still shouting and waving their pistols. General Funston, reporting this incident to The Adjutant General, was unable to explain why the American guards present failed to open fire, except for the fact that there was no officer present.[40] Randall, the Villista governor of Sonora (who had replaced Maytorena), sent an immediate apology but excused the disorder on the grounds that it was caused by the prohibition on exporting food from the United States for the Villista troops.

Fearing more serious trouble, Funston at once reinforced the garrison at Nogales as soon as he received word of the incident. His fears were justified, and the reinforcement was timely, for in the next few days the Villistas made no secret of their complete enmity. They did not cross the border again, but at three different times they opened fire from the Mexican side. Their truculence did not last long, for by this time all American troops at Nogales had definite orders. Mexican fire was returned promptly, and the Villistas learned, for the first time, the deadly accuracy of American rifle fire. It was so discouraging that their combativeness cooled appreciably.[41]

On this note the eventful year 1915 ended. The opening of the year saw the United States watching Francisco Villa with favor as a possible —even probable—savior of Mexico. His bitter enemy seemed fated to do and say the wrong thing at the wrong time always. Villa was cooperative, while Carranza was continually in opposition. Villa's reputation as the outstanding soldier of the Mexican Revolution was at its

[40] National Archives, State Department File no. 812.00/16855, Nov. 24, 1915.
[41] *Ibid.*, File nos. 812.00/16856 and 16858, Nov. 24 and 26, 1915, respectively. Cf. the *Literary Digest*, LI (Dec. 11, 1915), 1395.

highest. But suddenly his good fortune vanished. The defeats at Celaya and León started him on the long downgrade to final defeat, and the virtual destruction of his forces at Hermosillo sealed his fate. His opponent had risen in favor as his fortunes declined, and the end of the year found Villa again a hunted fugitive in the mountains of Sonora and Chihuahua.

❧ XVII ❧

Massacre at Santa Ysabel

THE situation at Nogales, still held by Villistas, continued to be tense. Late in the afternoon of November 26 a telegram, undated, arrived in Washington from Consul Frederick Simpich, saying that earlier in the day Villista troops had fired on American soldiers. At the time of writing the message the Americans were vigorously returning the Mexican fire. The firing was evidently the Villistas' final gesture of hatred and defiance, for almost simultaneously with this telegram another arrived from Simpich stating that the Carranzistas now occupied Nogales and that order was restored.[1]

The United States did not hold Villa personally responsible for the open violence of his soldiers. Through Carothers, the Secretary of State offered Villa safety and refuge in the United States and promised to obtain amnesty for his followers.[2] It seemed so certain that Villa would seek asylum in the United States that on December 18 the commanding general of the Southern Department (Funston) was ordered to give Villa full protection as a political refugee, provided that he guaranteed protection to Americans in the territory he still controlled.[3] Just how Villa might be able to control his followers in Mexico while he was a refugee in the United States was not explained.

[1] *Foreign Relations, 1915,* p. 820.
[2] *Ibid.,* p. 778. Cf. the *Independent,* LXXXIV (Oct.–Dec., 1915), 220.
[3] Hugh Lenox Scott Papers.

For some time after the Carranzistas occupied Nogales, Villa's where-abouts was unknown. Three days before the Carranza forces moved into Juárez, Cobb heard a third-hand report, which he considered reliable, that Villa was on his way there. Other rumors reached Cobb's ears at the same time that Villa would probably try to reach Juárez from Sonora by passing through the United States in disguise. Cobb was also somewhat disturbed because the Villistas in El Paso seemed to be getting bolder in their attitude, an omen which he did not like at all.[4]

The rumors and Cobb's fears were without foundation, for Villa did not attempt to pass through United States territory. Instead, with a small band of his more devoted and determined (or desperate) follow-ers, he disappeared into the almost unknown wilds of the Sierra Madre, suddenly turning up at the city of Chihuahua around the middle of December. He arrived to find that some of his generals were no longer in agreement with him and that there was a "third party" movement. Governor Avila, of Chihuahua, after several conferences, probably rather stormy, telegraphed to President Wilson that "having done all that lay in our power and . . . bent our efforts toward having Don Francisco Villa relinquish the supreme command of the Conventionist Army, we have at last prevailed on . . . [him] to agree to leave the country on the understanding that Your Excellency will extend full guaranties to him." This statement, according to Avila, was with Villa's full knowledge and consent.[5]

The order to General Funston just mentioned shows that President Wilson was willing to extend the requested guarantees. Further indica-tion of Villa's apparent intention to abandon the struggle in Mexico came to light a few days after Avila's telegram to President Wilson, when the Carranzista consul at El Paso gave Cobb a copy of a telegram from Avila to Obregón, saying that he firmly believed that Villa was about to retire. Obregón answered that he would accept unconditional surrender, and nothing else, from Villa's officers but that Villa himself was outlawed. The consul told Cobb that he believed that Villa was on the point of coming to the United States.[6] This was on December 18, 1915. The next day Carothers notified the State Department that Villa

[4] National Archives, State Department File nos. 812.00/16846, Nov. 23, 1915, and 812.00/16862, Nov. 26, 1915.

[5] *Foreign Relations, 1915*, p. 777.   [6] *Ibid.*, p. 778.

was holding conferences regarding the surrender of the State of Chihuahua and would probably come to the United States to take advantage of the offer of sanctuary. This was confirmed by information forwarded by Cobb the same day.[7]

All this information seemed to be so official and authoritative that border officials who were cognizant probably expected to see Villa at almost any moment. It is apparent that despite appearances the information was incorrect or unduly hopeful. While Carothers and Cobb were predicting the probability of Villa's early appearance north of the border, Sommerfeld telegraphed to General Scott that rumors of Villa's resignation and flight from Mexico were "fakes" and an interview that Villa was supposed to have given to the correspondent of the New York *American* was fraudulent.[8]

Whether or not Villa ever had any serious intention of leaving the fragments of his army and giving up the fight in Mexico no one can say. One thing is certain—he did not go into exile as a political refugee. Villa continued to pose a problem, for as long as he held together a group of followers capable of fighting and as long as he was obeyed over a large stretch of territory, he was still a factor in Mexican and international politics.

At Juárez as at Nogales, the Villistas heralded their imminent departure by a gesture of enmity toward the United States. On December 21, shortly before Obregón moved his troops into the city, General Pershing reported that a squad of Mexicans had opened fire on Americans from a point half a mile east of the international bridge. This was a deliberate attack and had killed an American railway car inspector (a civilian) while going about his duties. Pershing immediately covered the whole front of the city with troops, giving them orders to return vigorously any Mexican fire directed toward the United States.[9]

Shortly after, Juárez was turned over to the *de facto* government. The Villista soldiers were disarmed and mustered out, and in the happy belief that peace and law and order were about to settle once again over northern Mexico, the border country began to breathe easily.[10] An occasional rumor or report ruffled the new tranquillity

[7] *Ibid.*, pp. 778–779.
[8] Hugh Lenox Scott Papers. Cf. "Villa's 'First Aid' to Washington," *Literary Digest*, LII (Jan. 1, 1916), 5.
[9] *Foreign Relations, 1915*, pp. 820–821.   [10] *Ibid.*, pp. 779–780.

somewhat, but such things were only to be expected in a country that had been racked by civil war for five years. Along with the defiant firing by Villista soldiers at Juárez came a report that Villa was holding thirty employees of the Madera Lumber Company—all of them American citizens. He was said to be holding them as hostages for the payment of an assessment he had levied against the company, and he threatened the complete destruction of the company's property if the assessment were not paid at once.[11]

In spite of such reports (the truth of the one just mentioned has never been established), many Americans who had left interests or businesses in Mexico began to make preparations to return. As early as November 23, only a few days after the battles at Hermosillo, Obregón urged American mining companies in Sonora to resume operations, assuring them that the *de facto* government would guarantee the safety of their employees and properties.[12]

Outside of those directly concerned, the interest of the American public in Mexico had died down. News items from and about Mexico were again relegated to the back pages of the newspapers or omitted altogether. Public, and to a great degree governmental, attention was directed toward the vast struggle in Europe, to the recurring crises over the submarine problem, and to exciting anticipation of the coming presidential campaign of 1916. Senator Albert Fall, of New Mexico, with the obvious purpose of embarrassing the administration and possibly of gaining ammunition for use in the campaign, introduced a lengthy resolution demanding that the President furnish various items of information regarding relations with Mexico.[13]

Outwardly, Mexico might show appearances of resuming the ways of peace, but Villa was still free in the mountains of Chihuahua. On Tuesday, January 11, 1916, a short paragraph in the newspapers told that one P. Keane, a bookkeeper on the Hearst ranch at Babicora, Chihuahua, had been taken from the ranch by a band of Villistas and shot. There was no marked reaction on the part of the American people, nor does any official notice seem to have been taken of the murder.[14]

---

[11] Bisbee (Arizona) *Daily Review,* Dec. 18, 1915, p. 1, quoted in Fain, "The Pershing Punitive Expedition and Its Diplomatic Background," p. 48. Cf. *Current Opinion,* LX (Feb., 1916), 72–75. Some accounts say that Villa threatened to burn the Americans alive, but that is doubtful.
[12] *Foreign Relations, 1915,* p. 954.   [13] *Ibid., 1916,* pp. 463–464.
[14] New York *Times,* Tuesday, Jan. 11, 1916, 9:3.

A week later, the news was suddenly horrifying. Black headlines told that seventeen Americans had been taken from a railway train and shot down in cold blood. Brief information, including the names of the victims, as far as they were then known, had come to the British consul at El Paso from his colleague at Chihuahua. Immediately afterward the Carranza officials had clamped a strict censorship on telegrams, and further details were unknown.[15]

The massacre had occurred on January 10. For some reason the news did not reach the United States for two days. When details were published, the facts were as grim as the bare first reports had indicated. La Cusi Mining Company, American owned and operating mines in Chihuahua, had closed down when the State Department had advised all Americans to leave Mexico. After recognition of the Carranza government after assurances were given that it was safe to resume operations and that the *de facto* government guaranteed full protection, the company decided to reopen its mines, which were located at Cusihuiriáchic, Chihuahua. The general manager, Charles R. Watson, received his instructions from the owners, in Chicago, and proceeded to El Paso, where his staff were already assembled. Leaving El Paso, the party went to Chihuahua, there changing trains. A few hours after leaving Chihuahua, near the cattle station of Santa Ysabel, the train was stopped by a gang of armed men, led by Pablo López, a Villista colonel.[16]

An eyewitness gave a vivid account of the terrible scene that followed. José María Sánchez a Mexican employee of the company, was on the same train. A newspaper reporter quoted him as saying:

We were in two coaches, one occupied by Americans, the other by twenty of us Mexican employees.

No sooner had the train been brought to a standstill by the wreck the bandits had caused ahead than they began to board the coaches. . . . They rifled our pockets, took our blankets and even our lunches. Then Col. Pablo Lopez, in charge of the looting of our car, said:

"If you want to see some fun, watch us kill these gringos. Come on, boys," he shouted to his followers. They ran from the coach, crying, "Viva Villa!"

[15] *Ibid.*, Wednesday, Jan. 12, 1916, 1:1.
[16] Ernest Otto Schuster, *Pancho Villa's Shadow* (New York, 1947), pp. 199–201. Cf. Mexico–United States Special Claims Commission, *Report*, "The Santa Ysabel Case" (Washington, 1926), pp. 7–8.

and "Death to the gringos!" I heard a volley of rifle shots, and looked out the window.

Manager Watson was running toward the Santa Ysabel River, a short distance away. Four other Americans were running in other directions, the Villistas shooting at them. Some of the soldiers dropt to their knees for better aim. Watson fell after running about a hundred yards. He got up, limping, but went on a short distance further, when he threw up his arms and fell forward, his body rolling down the bank into the river. . . .

While this was going on, other Villistas crowded into the Americans' coach. I could not see what happened in there, as a frightful panic broke out in our car. Later I learned that the Americans were unarmed.

Pearce was shot as he sat in the coach. I saw Wallace's body on the ground at the carstep. He had been shot through the back. Another body was on top of Wallace's. The other Americans were herded to the side of the coach and lined up.

Colonel Lopez selected two of his soldiers as executioners, and this nearly precipitated a fight among the bandits over who should have the privilege of shooting the Americans. . . .

Colonel Lopez ordered the "mercy shot" given to those who were still alive, and the soldiers placed the ends of their rifles at the victims' heads and fired. . . .

All bodies were completely stript of clothing and shoes.[17]

It may be doubted that the language and expression of the account are Sánchez' own, but the general accuracy of his statement is beyond question. Unknown to the Villistas one member of the party, Thomas B. Holmes, made his escape, by one of those chances that can be considered almost miraculous. Running at the same time as Watson, Holmes fell into some bushes and lay still. Evidently thinking him dead or overlooking him altogether, the bandits paid him no further attention, and he crawled into some thicker brush near the river, where he remained until the murderers had gone away.[18] Holmes was unable to see as much of the tragedy as Sánchez, but his account of what he was able to see agrees substantially with what Sánchez related.

Although the bandits who committed the atrocity were Villistas, the degree to which Francisco Villa was personally involved has never been definitely determined. Pablo López was captured by the Carranzistas in April and promptly executed. After his death the Carranzista gov-

[17] *Literary Digest,* LII (Jan. 22, 1916), 157–158.
[18] *Foreign Relations, 1916,* p. 652.

ernor of Chihuahua, Don Ignacio Enriquez, quoted López as having said: "Villa ordered me to commit the Santa Ysabel massacre. Villa was behind a hill near the scene." [19]

It is only fair to say that Villa denied this vehemently. He is said to have admitted ordering the seizure of the payroll, but he did not, he asserted, give any orders to molest the Americans.[20] In any case, the act was perpetrated by men who, nominally at least, acknowledged his authority. They shouted, "Viva Villa!" while the murders were being committed. Villa's ultimate, and legal, responsibility is beyond question. At a later date, and within our own times, American and Allied military commissions have condemned and executed as war criminals men whose responsibility for atrocities committed by subordinates was far less clear than Villa's on this occasion.

In spite of Villa's clear responsibility, to this day there are Americans who are convinced of his innocence. One ascribes a large part of Villa's hatred of Americans to the Santa Ysabel affair—hatred resulting in his murderous raid into the United States a few weeks later. According to this apologist, Villa, already angered by the recognition of Carranza and help given to the Carranzistas, became enraged and deeply embittered at the unfairness of being accused of responsibility for the horror at Santa Ysabel.[21]

Coming closely after recognition of the Carranza government and growing directly out of that government's assurances that Americans could return to Mexico safely, the Santa Ysabel affair threatened to provoke a major crisis. The Secretary of State telegraphed to Zach Cobb to request that the Chihuahua authorities dispatch troops immediately to capture and punish the murderers.[22] To Silliman, who was at Carranza's headquarters, instructions were sent to bring the matter to Carranza's personal attention at once. The Americans were murdered in accordance with what was reported to be Villa's announced policy and in territory which the Carranza forces were supposed to control. Carranza, the State Department said, must be urgently requested to send adequate forces to pursue and capture the bandits and also to garrison adequately the various mining camps in Chi-

[19] El Paso *Herald,* April 29, 1916, quoted in Robert J. Casey, *The Texas Border and Some Borderliners: A Chronicle and a Guide* (New York, 1950), p. 378.

[20] Schuster, *Pancho Villa's Shadow,* pp. 202–203. Schuster escaped being a member of the ill-starred party only because of illness.

[21] Pinchon, *Viva Villa!* pp. 335–336.   [22] *Foreign Relations, 1916,* p. 651.

huahua.[23] Telegraphic instructions were sent to Edwards, at Chihuahua, to request the local military authorities to send forces to safeguard the employees and property of the Madera Lumber Company.[24]

The immediate reaction of Americans within possible reach of Villa was to get out of Mexico at once. Even such concerns as the Alvarado Mining Company and the Hearst ranch took measures to evacuate their American employees. Zach Cobb urged the State Department to require that all Americans leave Chihuahua, as he was convinced that the Carranza authorities were incapable of protecting them. The Mexican officials at Juárez, whom he saw almost daily, were anxious to please but were not properly organized and, he hinted, were somewhat concerned about their own safety. Large numbers of demobilized Villa soldiers in Juárez and the city of Chihuahua, without employment, constituted a very real danger.[25]

A telegram of similar tenor from Consul General Hanna, at Monterrey, urged that steps be taken to get all Americans out of danger zones at once. Hanna believed that the Carranza government was in earnest in its desire to "improve conditions," but he was clearly doubtful as to that government's ability to carry out its good intentions.[26]

Lack of confidence in the ability of the Carranza government to capture and punish the murderers was accentuated by rumors that the Carranzistas were not really trying. As an example, Representative Julius Kahn, of California, forwarded to the State Department a telegram he had received from a C. A. Pringle, of San Francisco, charging that "the most casual investigation . . . will show that Carranza is not doing anything to apprehend . . . those guilty of the massacre of our citizens." [27] This allegation was stated somewhat more strongly than most of those received but was fairly typical. More restrained and based on cooler judgment was a report from General Pershing to General Funston, in which he said: "There is little confidence in Carranza among Americans coming out of Mexico and many Mexicans are of the same mind." [28]

As a consequence, the Villista atrocity at Santa Ysabel threatened to destroy entirely the new harmony between the United States and the *de facto* government. Spurred on by such reports as those just cited

[23] *Ibid.*, p. 653.   [24] *Ibid.*, p. 654.   [25] *Ibid.*, p. 655.   [26] *Ibid.*, p. 659.
[27] *Ibid.*, p. 662.   [28] *Ibid.*, pp. 662–663.

and by such reports as one submitted by Edwards that not a single member of the Villa gang had been captured after several days and that the matter was obviously secondary with the Carranza authorities, the State Department began sending a series of "needling" notes.[29]

The Carranza government, fearing intervention as a result of the massacre, very promptly took what action was feasible. From the perspective of half a century after the events, it seems that their failure to capture and punish the murderers was due not to lack of willingness but, instead, to their scanty resources and widespread military commitments throughout the rest of Mexico. In short, the Carranza government simply did not have enough troops to do what was expected. Zapata was still in the field, and a large-scale campaign against the Yaquis was under way. Together with the garrisons which were absolutely necessary in the centers of population, these forces used up a large portion of the Constitutionalist army.

Carranza immediately gave orders for pursuing the bandits and issued a formal decree placing Francisco Villa, Rafael Castro, and Pablo López outside the protection of the law. Any citizen might seize and kill them, the only requirement being identification.[30] Contradicting the allegation that not a single member of the murder gang had been punished, the Carranzistas claimed that eleven were killed within two days after the massacre.[31] A reward payable in gold was offered for the criminals, and two Villista generals, captured on January 14, were executed the same evening, although their complicity in the affair was highly doubtful.[32] Because of the possibility that the gang might break up and its members disappear into the anonymity of the Mexican colonies in the United States, Carranza requested the State Department to take measures to ensure that they did not cross the border.[33] At first thought such a possibility may seem farfetched, but stranger things have happened, and the State Department took the suggestion seriously.

Because of the obvious willingness of the Carranza government to take such action as it could, the threatened diplomatic crisis did not materialize. Carranza believed that the massacre was committed for the

[29] *Ibid.*, pp. 469, 662–663, 665.   [30] *Ibid.*, pp. 465, 659–660.
[31] *Arizona Daily Star* (Bisbee), Jan. 18–19, 1916, quoted in Fain, "The Pershing Punitive Expedition and Its Diplomatic Background," p. 50.
[32] *Foreign Relations, 1916*, p. 657.   [33] *Ibid.*, pp. 466–467, 661.

deliberate purpose of provoking an international crisis, and the thought of American intervention was a nightmare to him always.[34] General Pershing, at El Paso, heard rumors that "the object of all this is . . . to provoke intervention." [35]

While Carranza feared intervention because of the Villistas and as cool and impartial an observer as General Pershing thought it worth while to note rumors that intervention was the motive, the ultraliberals who saw Villa as the cat's-paw for the evil interests of Wall Street were sure of it. Lincoln Steffens was in Mexico City at the time of the massacre:

I remember going late one afternoon into the American Club in Mexico City and finding the place crowded with my drinking, hilarious countrymen who grabbed me and shot me up to the bar to drink. "Drink, man, drink. It is coming."

"What? What's the matter?" I asked.

"Haven't you heard the news?"

I had not, and they told me that seventeen Americans had been shot down by Mexicans in northern Mexico.

"Seventeen of 'em!" they shouted. "Seventeen of 'em slaughtered in cold blood!"

"But why," I staggered mentally, "why do you celebrate the killing of Americans?"

"Don't you see?" They explained: "It means intervention. You don't suppose that those blankety-blank pacifists in the Wilson administration can refuse now to send the army, do you?" [36]

The popular reaction in the United States was horror and indignation, but there was no widespread excitement or demand for intervention. In El Paso, General Pershing reported, there was some disorder the evening of the funeral of the victims. Crowds gathered, and several Mexicans were beaten, but there were no really serious incidents.[37] The administration faced nothing to compare with the public pressure that forced the McKinley administration into war with Spain. Public opinion, as reflected in the press, favored moderation, was against military action except as a last resort, and recognized that the Carranza

[34] Ibid., p. 659.   [35] *Ibid.,* p. 663.
[36] Steffens, *The Autobiography of Lincoln Steffens,* p. 735.
[37] *Foreign Relations, 1916,* p. 663.

government had not been in power long enough to have had a fair trial of its abilities.[38]

If the general public was moderate in its attitude, the same could not be said of the bitter political enemies of President Wilson and the administration. From the first, they seized upon every opportunity to use Mexico as a club with which to belabor the harried man in the White House, and the Santa Ysabel massacre was too good an opportunity to be missed. If Villa had been searching for some means of embarrassing President Wilson (which he may have been doing), he must have been pleased at the results. Former President Theodore Roosevelt issued a statement in which he said, in part:

This dreadful outrage is merely an inevitable outcome of the policies which have been followed in Mexico for the last five years, and, above all, the last three years. The policy of watchful waiting, the policy of not interfering with "blood spilling," the policy of asking the South- and Central American republics to take from us the responsibility that we were too timid to take has borne its legitimate results. . . .

When the great war ceases we shall have earned the contemptuous dislike of every combatant, and if we don't do our duty in Mexico one or all of them will surely seize Mexico themselves.[39]

One may note that Theodore Roosevelt ascribed at least a part of the blame to his party rival, Taft, and indirectly hinted at the desirability of seizing Mexico for ourselves. But Roosevelt's statement was a model of restraint compared to some of the utterances in Congress. As might be reasonably expected, the most vehement denunciations came from the "Old Guard," but even a few Democrats and "Progressives" joined in the hue and cry. Representative Frank Mondell, of Wyoming, made a savage attack upon the President and his policies, charging the administration with actual bad faith and with turning Villa against the United States by the sudden and inexplicable favor accorded to Carranza. Commenting sarcastically upon the supposed inconsistency of the President's policies and actions, Mondell delivered a forensic gem worthy of preservation:

The Spanish mind is untrained in the diplomatic gymnastics of this administration and unable to follow the limitless and labyrinthian allocutions

[38] "The Mexican Murders," *Literary Digest*, LII (Jan. 22, 1916), 157–159.
[39] *Ibid.*

through which the administration demonstrates that what it detested, ab-
horred, and abjured last summer or last week is law and gospel today. They
are unaccustomed to accept a phrase as a substitute for a fact, and do not
move quickly to a realization that you may properly, logically, or honestly do
today that which on yesterday you called on high heaven to witness that you
would never do.[40]

In the Senate, the Western progressive, Senator William Borah, was
almost as vindictive as the "Old Guard." Borah later became known
as an uncompromising isolationist and a staunch defender of the idea,
popular in the 1930's, that the United States could maintain its neutrality by keeping its citizens at home; but on this earlier occasion his
views were far different. He described the President's Mexican policy
as "that compromising and side-stepping, procrastinating, apologizing,
un-American policy of leaving the American citizen to struggle for himself against bandits and outlaws, against assassins and murderers." [41]

Quite naturally, there were demands for immediate armed intervention. Senator Works, of California, introduced Senate Joint Resolution
no. 78, calling for intervention, and Senator Sherman, of Illinois, introduced a resolution calling for joint intervention with the six Latin
American countries that had joined the United States in recommending
Carranza's recognition.[42] These, and similar resolutions in the House of
Representatives, were lengthily and acrimoniously debated but stood
no chance of adoption by either house. There was no real enthusiasm
on the part of the American people for any military adventures in
Mexico.

In spite of the horror aroused by the senseless murder of the seventeen defenseless Americans at Santa Ysabel, public interest quickly
faded. The war in Europe and numerous domestic problems were what
really engaged public opinion. The submarine problem and battles on
the Western Front quickly crowded Mexico from the front pages, and
the quick death of public interest in Mexico must have disappointed
those politicians who hoped that they had at last found a major issue
for the coming presidential campaign.

Santa Ysabel and its repercussions marked an abrupt change in the
course of the relations of the United States and the American people
with the ex-bandit who had risen to power and esteem and then re-

[40] *Cong. Record*, 64 Cong., 1 sess., p. 1320.   [41] *Ibid.*, p. 943.
[42] *Ibid.*, pp. 937–938, 1060.

verted to banditry. For two long years there had been "a double sovereignty claimed even on our border in northern Mexico." [43] Thinly disguised as a special representative, George C. Carothers had remained with the ruler of northern Mexico as a diplomatic representative of the United States. Relations between the United States and Pancho Villa had been substantially those between two recognized powers. This condition had continued to exist to a considerable degree even after the recognition of the Carranza regime as the *de facto* government of Mexico. After the debacle of Hermosillo, it was fully anticipated that Villa would take refuge in the friendly safety of the United States. The murders at Santa Ysabel marked the end of any pretense of friendliness. Villa was now as bitter and vengeful an enemy as the United States had in the world. All future relationships would be those of undisguised hostility—at the muzzles of the guns.

After Santa Ysabel, Francisco Villa was no longer a positive factor in the relations of the United States and Mexico, but he did not thereby cease to be a factor. Not only with the *de facto* government of Venustiano Carranza but with other countries as well, Villa continued to be a complicating and disruptive factor—and important on that account. The United States was fated to have trouble not only with Villa but because of Villa.

[43] Secretary of the Interior Franklin K. Lane, in an authorized interview, July 18, 1916, quoted in James Brown Scott, *President Wilson's Foreign Policy: Messages, Addresses, Papers* (New York, 1918), pp. 399–400.

⨎ XVIII ⨎

Villa's Raid on Columbus

FOLLOWING the Santa Ysabel massacre, the people of the border country remained tense with fear. For months past there had been a constant series of incursions into the United States by small bands of Mexicans. This was particularly true in the lower Rio Grande Valley, the scene of Cortina's raids three-quarters of a century before. Nearly every raid took its toll of life and property. The thin lines of United States troops guarding the border could not possibly close all avenues of approach from Mexico, nor was it possible to organize any means by which raids could be anticipated and forestalled. The troops were handicapped in pursuit of raiders by stringent orders forbidding them to cross the international line under any circumstances or for any reason. In addition to the raids from Mexico, there were almost innumerable instances of Mexicans firing from concealment, on their own side of the border, at Americans on United States soil.[1]

Uneasiness among the residents of the border areas was intensified during the summer of 1915 by vague rumors of a wild scheme among the Mexicans to invade the United States and regain their lost territories of Texas, New Mexico, Arizona, and California. Most of the

[1] The writer has been told by officers who were on the border at this time that orders required troops fired upon from Mexico to retire immediately without returning the fire. The writer has been unable to verify this but has little doubt that such was the policy.

people of the United States had never heard of the "Plan of San Diego," and of those who did, outside the border states, probably the majority dismissed it as merely an unusually sensational product of "yellow journalism" at its worst. To the people on the isolated ranches and in the small settlements of the Rio Grande Valley and the borders of New Mexico and Arizona, it was far from being a ludicrous myth. It was a real peril, and nonetheless real because of the fantastic impossibility of its aims.[2]

In addition to the apprehension caused by newspaper accounts of the Mexican plot, there was the fear of what Villa might do in retaliation for the recognition of his bitter enemy and for the undeniable aid extended by the United States to that enemy. The people of El Paso fully expected to see Villistas pouring across the river and were highly doubtful of General Pershing's ability to repel invaders with the few hundred troops under his command.[3] A certain Frank S. Thomas, of Topeka, Kansas, who claimed to be one of Villa's representatives in the United States, wrote to Senator Charles Curtis, on December 15:

By private code my advices from Mexico for two days by wire from sources I consider absolutely reliable is to the effect that the continued permission of our State Department for Carranza to transport his troops over American territory and American rails to where he needed them most to fight Gen. Villa has so infuriated the Mexican people of the interior, a large majority of whom are opposed to Carranza, that there is very great danger. I think it probable that there will be a massacre of Americans, not in the north alone, but in all Mexico.[4]

---

[2] The "Plan of San Diego" is still a mystery, but there can be no doubt that it existed and had a great appeal for the illiterate part of the population of the northern tier of Mexican states. The plan, in general terms, called for uniting Mexico in a war against the United States to regain the lost territories and for the systematic extermination of male Americans in those territories. Cf. Cumberland, "Border Raids on the Lower Rio Grande, 1915," *Southwestern Historical Quarterly*, LVI (1954), 286–290, and the *Cong. Record*, 64 Cong., 1 sess., pp. 4846–4848. General Funston attributed many of the raids to this plan. See also *Annual Report, Commanding General, Southern Department, F/Y 1916*, pp. 3–15, and *Foreign Relations, 1916*, pp. 570–572.

[3] John J. Pershing Papers. Vol. III of General Pershing's personal scrapbooks is full of newspaper clippings of the month of Aug., 1915, dealing with the anticipated Villa attack. On Sept. 20, 1915, Pershing received information that Villa planned an immediate attack on El Paso if the United States recognized Carranza.

[4] *Congressional Record*, 64 Cong., 1 sess., pp. 1193–1194. Senator Curtis for some reason did not produce this letter before the Senate until Jan. 18, 1916. He informed

In spite of such dire forebodings, February, 1916, passed quietly. Villa dropped from sight and almost completely disappeared from the headlines of the newspapers. Early in the month there was brief mention of him when Carranza officials claimed to have captured documents proving that Villa had agreed to allow the Japanese to establish a base somewhere on the Pacific coast of Mexico, in return for a million dollars in gold and a supply of ammunition.[5] The alleged documents were never produced for examination, and since the report seemed so obviously designed to influence American opinion, nobody took it very seriously.

At some time during February, there was a revival of the rumors that Villa intended to come to the United States. This time he was coming not as a political refugee but to clear himself of the accusation that he was responsible for the Santa Ysabel massacre. According to accounts widely accepted at the time, George L. Seese, a representative of the Associated Press, was approached by an agent of Villa, asking his cooperation. After several conferences, Seese agreed to escort Villa secretly to Washington to seek an interview with President Wilson. Villa approved the arrangements, but at the last minute the head of the Associated Press vetoed the whole scheme.[6]

If this story is true, it probably added to the already heavy burden of Villa's hatred for the United States and his belief that the gringos were faithless toward him. Another consideration worthy of thought is the possibility that the story is essentially true as related but that Villa never had any real intention of coming to the United States and was merely lulling his enemies while he matured his plans and preparations for his next step. This possibility is purely conjectural, and the real truth can never be known.

The details of the plan for Villa to come to the United States were not publicized, of course, but responsible American officials on the border were undoubtedly apprised of it. Consequently, there was no particular surprise when, in late February, it became known that Villa

---

the Senate that he had known Thomas all the latter's life. Senator Stone, of Missouri, also stated that he was acquainted with Thomas.

[5] New York *Times*, Saturday, Feb. 4, 1916, 6:6.

[6] Col. Frank Tompkins, *Chasing Villa: The Story behind the Story of Pershing's Mexican Expedition* (Harrisburg, Pa., 1934), p. 41. General Scott gave full credence to this story. Cf. *Some Memories of a Soldier*, pp. 517–518.

and his band (no longer a real army) were slowly moving northward toward the border. For American officials to keep in touch with Villa's movements reliably was impossible. Neither the State nor the War Department had any sort of secret intelligence service; there were no funds for the hire of trustworthy agents. For information about Villa's movements Americans were dependent upon voluntary informers and such information as the Carranzistas might pass on. At the best, most of such reports were vague and unsatisfactory. Not until March 3 was there any information that seemed to be authentic. On that day the indefatigable Zach Cobb telegraphed to the State Department that Villa, with three hundred men, had left a place near Madera, Chihuahua, on March 1 and was moving toward Columbus, New Mexico. At the time Cobb posted the message, Villa was supposed to be west of Casas Grandes. "There is reason to believe," Cobb said, "he intends to cross to the United States and hopes to proceed to Washington." [7]

On March 6 the Carranzista commander in Juárez, General Gavira, informed reporters that Villa was en route to the border, and Gavira told George L. Seese privately that Villa was not coming to vindicate himself—he intended to cause some incident that would force the United States to intervene in Mexico.[8] This interesting bit of information, or conjecture, was promptly given to General Pershing, who replied that he had heard so many such rumors that he was inclined to take them all with a grain of salt. The cry of "Wolf!" had sounded many times on the border, and no wolves had yet appeared.

On Tuesday, March 9, there were brief items in the newspapers, dated at El Paso the day before, saying that Villa was believed to be at Las Palomas, Chihuahua, only a few miles from Columbus, and that he had killed two Americans, Edward J. Wright and Frank Hayden, between Casas Grandes and Janos. The papers added that there was no word as to Wright's wife and infant son. Villa's presence at Las Palomas was confirmed in later reports to the State Department, but there was no further information about the two Americans.[9]

Other sources reported that Villa was close to the border, but the reports differed so much that it was impossible to determine the truth by any means except actual reconnaissance—and this was out of the

[7] *Foreign Relations, 1916*, p. 478.
[8] *Ibid.*, p. 479. Cf. Tompkins, *Chasing Villa*, p. 42.
[9] New York *Times*, Thursday, March 9, 1916, 1:4.

question. A Bruno (Gunther?) Lessing is said to have informed General Pershing that Villa was near the border, a fact which Pershing undoubtedly knew already.[10] The El Paso *Times,* on March 8, 1916, announced that Villa was expected to attack Palomas, where there was a small Carranzista garrison.[11]

All this information, and more too, went to Colonel Herbert J. Slocum, commanding officer of the 13th Cavalry, at Columbus, the American garrison nearest to where Villa was supposed to be. The information coming in was so vague, so contradictory, that it was virtually impossible for Slocum to form a true picture of the situation. For example, on March 8, Seese, the Associated Press representative, who had his own sources of information, received reports placing Villa simultaneously at three widely separated localities.[12]

Slocum received definite and authentic information on March 7. That morning three Americans and a Mexican, employees of the Palomas Land and Cattle Company, encountered Villa and about five hundred men making camp on the Casas Grandes River. Two of the Americans, named McKinney and Corbett, rode directly into the camp and were seized. The other American, Marcus M. Marshall, a son of the president of the company, and the Mexican employee successfully made their escape. What they had seen was promptly reported to Colonel Slocum.[13]

Slocum's immediate concern was to determine Villa's movements, as far as possible. He could not send patrols south of the border to make contact and observe, and patrols north of the border could accomplish exactly nothing. His only recourse was to send someone who could lawfully cross the border without exciting comment. After some persuasion, the Mexican employee agreed to undertake the dangerous mission. His report, a day later, indicated that Villa was actually moving

[10] Stevens, *Here Comes Pancho Villa,* p. 287. Stevens gives no authority for this statement.

[11] El Paso *Times,* March 8, 1916, in Harris, *Pancho Villa and the Columbus Raid,* p. 84.

[12] Tompkins, *Chasing Villa,* p. 43.

[13] There is some doubt as to who actually made this report. Marcus Marshall, in a letter to his father (quoted in the *Cong. Record,* 64 Cong., 1 sess., Appendix, p. 626), said that he, himself, submitted the report. Major Elmer Lindsley, who acted as interpreter for Colonel Slocum, said that the report was made by the Mexican employee, known only as "Antonio." Cf. Tompkins, *Chasing Villa,* pp. 43–44.

southward, away from the border.[14] This was reassuring, but not conclusive. Slocum, with one or two members of his staff, rode to the border gate and talked to the commanding officer of a small Carranzista detachment stationed there. The Carranzista denied any knowledge of Villa's whereabouts or movements, and it was noted that as Slocum and his party approached the Mexicans hastily manned a position already prepared and located so as to resist an attack from the United States.[15]

Not only did the Carranzistas in the vicinity of Columbus disclaim any knowledge of Villa and display no enthusiasm toward finding out anything, but their superiors in Juárez were apathetic. There was a large Carranzista garrison at Juárez, but Cobb reported to the State Department on March 8 that no effort was being made either to pursue or to attack the Villa band known to be south of Columbus. The authorities in Juárez claimed that they did not have troops to spare and that pursuing forces from Chihuahua had failed utterly to make contact.[16]

Such was the situation on the night of March 8–9, 1916, as Slocum knew it. The fog of war was thick, and there was no means of penetrating it. An additional complication lay in a telegram from the department commander two days before. Funston informed Slocum that there was reliable information that Villa intended to surrender to United States authorities; there was a rumor, which Funston believed unreliable, that Villa planned a raid into the United States.[17] Slocum ordered additional patrols and reinforced his outposts; he could do no more. The zone for which he was responsible was some sixty-five miles long, and his total force consisted of less than three hundred officers and men.[18] The vague and shadowy information available did not justify depriving the command of rest by a continuous alert, and any dispersion of the small force would have been criminal.

The early part of the night was quiet. The little town and the camp

[14] Young Marshall said that Slocum asked him to return to Mexico and observe the Villista movements and then completely ignored his report. Major Lindsley stated positively that Slocum sent Antonio. It is entirely possible that Slocum sent both.

[15] Tompkins, *Chasing Villa*, p. 45. Tompkins was convinced that the Carranzistas knew all about Villa and that some of them joined in the subsequent attack.

[16] *Foreign Relations, 1916,* p. 479.   [17] Tompkins, *Chasing Villa,* p. 46.

[18] *Ibid.,* p. 47. Cf. "The Columbus Raid," *United States Cavalry Journal,* XXVII (April, 1917), 490.

were dark, relieved only by the stars and an occasional kerosene lamp.[19] Several hours after midnight the Officer of the Day, Lieutenant James P. Castleman, sat reading in the adobe shack where he was required to remain during his tour of duty. He was completely clothed, with his pistol and belt lying on the bunk. At four o'clock he closed his book, rose, and buckled on his belt—there was a cry, a shot, and the glass of the window shattered as a bullet cracked past his head. He threw open the door and faced a Mexican, who leveled a rifle at him. Castleman's reactions were fast—he fired first, killing the intruder instantly.[20]

At the same time, in a nearby adobe house, Lieutenant John P. Lucas, commander of the Machine Gun Troop, who had arrived in camp on the midnight train from a polo trip to El Paso, was awakened by the sound of someone riding past. Looking out the window, he saw the silhouettes of men with Mexican-style sombreros. Just then the firing started, and Lucas, unable to find his boots, ran barefooted to his troop, fortunately escaping the notice of the invaders.[21]

Within a few minutes the crackle of rifle and pistol fire, wild shouts of "Viva Villa!" and the glow from burning buildings in the town turned the scene into a miniature inferno. To get his machine guns into action took Lucas several minutes. For very cogent reasons they were kept under lock and key at the guard tent. Likewise, rifles, pistols, and ammunition were normally kept locked.

The Mexicans followed a definite plan. They made simultaneous attacks on the camp and into the town, using as a covered approach a deep ditch that ran through the camp and town. Their patent familiarity with the terrain argues that the plan was based on accurate information and had been made well in advance. It is said that some of the Mexican dead were later identified as men who had been seen in the town several days preceding the raid, and this is not improbable.

The story of Villa's raid upon Columbus has been related many times,

[19] George Marvin, "Invasion or Intervention," *World's Work*, XXXII (May, 1916), 53.

[20] James Hopper, "What Happened at Columbus," *Collier's Magazine*, LVII (April 15, 1916), 11. Cf. Tompkins, *Chasing Villa*, p. 49, and "The Columbus Raid," *United States Cavalry Journal*, XXVII (April, 1917), 490–496.

[21] Lucas' personal account, as given in Tompkins, *Chasing Villa*, pp. 50–53. Lucas was the commander of the American forces at Anzio, in World War II, and commanding general of the Fourth Army and of the last American Military Mission to China.

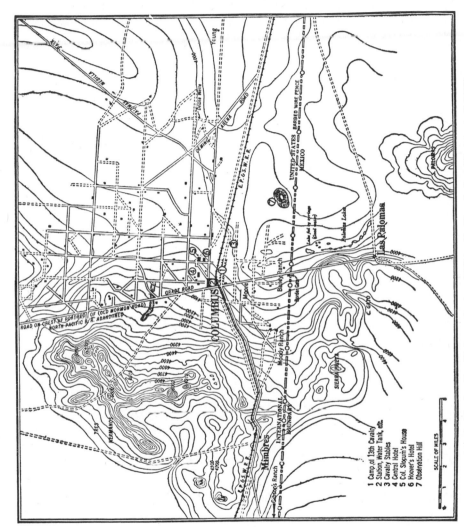

Map 2. Columbus, New Mexico, at the time of Villa's raid. (From *Review of Reviews*, April, 1916.)

1 Camp of 13th Cavalry
2 Station, Water Tank, etc.
3 Cavalry Stables
4 Central Hotel
5 Col. Slocum's House
6 Hoover's Hotel
7 Observation Hill

SCALE OF MILES

both by Americans who were present and by Mexicans who were either there or who obtained information from participants. There is one point that has not been sufficiently stressed—the speed with which the discipline and training of the Americans enabled them to overcome the initial surprise and inflict punishing losses on the raiders. When the first rush of Mexicans poured into the camp, almost the only soldiers awake were the guard and the kitchen police, who were preparing breakfast. These, fighting with kettles of scalding water, potato mashers, kitchen knives, butcher's cleavers, and bare fists, threw the initial attack into confusion. In brief time, as such things go, organized resistance and counterattack cleared the town and camp, and about daybreak the Mexican bugles began sounding "Recall." A little more than an hour had elapsed from the time the first shots were fired.[22]

The Villistas rode rapidly southward, apparently ignoring the detachment of Carranzistas at the border gate. Twenty minutes after they left, Major Frank Tompkins mounted one small troop of thirty-two men and pursued. Three hundred yards south of the border the Villistas had left a covering detachment on a hill. Cutting the border fence, Tompkins' little command charged the hill boldly, unharmed by the wild fire from the Mexicans, who broke and ran for their horses as the Americans reached the foot. At the summit the Americans dismounted and opened fire, killing over thirty before the enemy galloped out of range.[23]

Realizing suddenly that he had crossed the border and invaded Mexico without any authority whatever, Tompkins sent a hasty message to Colonel Slocum, whose reply authorized him to continue the pursuit. While waiting for Slocum's reply, Tompkins was joined by Lieutenant Castleman with a detachment, bringing the pursuing force to a strength of fifty-six enlisted men and four officers. A total of sixty men was a small force with which to pursue an enemy whose strength was variously estimated at from three hundred to five hundred men.

Tompkins decided to continue. In the next three hours the Americans engaged Villa's rear guard three times more, each time the Villistas

[22] Robert S. Thomas and Inez V. Allen, *The Mexican Punitive Expedition under Brigadier General John J. Pershing, United States Army, 1916–1917,* Office of the Chief of Military History, Department of the Army (Washington, 1954), p. 15. Hereafter referred to as Thomas and Allen, *Official Monograph.*

[23] Tompkins, *Chasing Villa,* pp. 55–57.

making a hasty departure as soon as American rifle fire took its toll. Shortly before noon, with men and horses showing signs of exhaustion and with ammunition almost expended, Tompkins broke off and returned slowly to Columbus. On the march back, a distance of about fifteen miles, almost a hundred dead Villistas were counted, along with two abandoned machine guns and quantities of other material and loot from the town.[24] With the loss of the sixty-seven additional dead who were picked up in and about Columbus, Villa's men paid dearly for his adventure.

The smoke had scarcely died down from the burning buildings before rumors began to spread—rumors of something very mysterious about Pancho Villa's raid into the United States. To most Americans the act of a Mexican bandit invading and defying the power of the United States was either the act of a madman or something more sinister. What could be his motive? To the considerable, and very vocal, body of American ultraliberals, the answer was simple and obvious. The evil force impelling Pancho Villa to invade the United States and kill peaceful American citizens in their own homes lay in predatory American "interests." Representative Meyer London, a Socialist congressman from New York, voiced this idea with a dogmatic finality that admitted of no argument to the contrary:

It is scarcely believable that this satanic performance of Villa was a mere accident. The truth will be known some day, and the world will learn that the bandit, Villa, was the mere tool of interests which sought to embroil the United States in a war with Mexico.

That there are powerful interests whom nothing would suit better than the annexation of Mexican territory can not be successfully contradicted.[25]

Even the staid and usually unsensational *Christian Science Monitor* arrived quickly at a similar conclusion. On March 11, in its editorial columns, was the statement:

Villa is but a tool operated by an unseen hand. . . . He serves the purpose of keeping Mexico in a turmoil, of preventing the accomplishment of Carranza's task of pacification, or at least he helps materially in postponing this accomplishment, and in keeping the way open for some such favorite of the clericals and aristocrats as Felix Diaz.

Manifestly the purpose of the raid in New Mexico was to provoke intervention by the United States, that all Mexico might rally to the Villa standard.

[24] *Ibid.*   [25] *Cong. Record*, 64 Cong., 1 sess., pp. 5020–5021.

There are people of great influence on the northern side of the border who would, all unwittingly, play into the hands of those who are behind the bandit and who are spurring him on.[26]

The belief in some quarters that the raid on Columbus was the result of a dastardly plot by callous and unscrupulous American capitalists was so vehement that rumor eventually went to the length of saying Pancho Villa had nothing at all to do with the raid. Edgcumb Pinchon, who subscribed to this theory, voiced the belief in a series of dramatic, rhetorical questions:

Why to this wretched desert hamlet forty miles from the nearest city . . . should come brisk gentlemen in smart New York clothes but a week before the raid? What was their business? How did it happen that the raid was made immediately after a part of the garrison had been withdrawn, and while but one officer, a lieutenant, remained on duty in the camp southeast of the town? Why did the attackers, apparently some four hundred strong, and easily in force to perpetrate a massacre, persistently fire their rifles in the air, and, in the course of a three-hour occupation of the hamlet, confine their attention chiefly to looting, inflicting only such casualties as . . . would seem inevitable *even if their instructions had been merely to make a gesture?* Why, when it is the invariable custom of Mexican troops to charge with a battle-cry, and then save their breath for the business in hand, did the attackers monotonously chant for three hours, "Viva Villa! Viva Villa!"

Pancho Villa, busily absorbed on March 9, 1916,—the day of the raid—in his cat-and-mouse game, at Casas Grandes, two hundred miles to the south hears the first word of mouth rumor of the raid only some hours after the American breakfast table has absorbed the last morning extras.[27]

This remarkable passage is unsupported by a single shred of evidence.

Few proponents of Villa would go as far as the writer just quoted, but many of Villa's old friends found it difficult to believe that he would be so insane as deliberately to make an attack on an American town, knowing what the consequences must be. His friend of many years, Dr. Ira Jefferson Bush, said: "Did Villa lead that attack in person? That question has been asked many times. I feel sure he did not. Several of his followers have told me that he was opposed to the raid and was overruled by his officers and men."[28]

[26] *Christian Science Monitor,* vol. VIII, no. 90 (March 11, 1916), by permission of the Christian Science Publishing Society. An editorial of similar tone appeared in the issue for March 14.

[27] Pinchon, *Viva Villa!* pp. 338–339.   [28] Bush, *Gringo Doctor,* pp. 243–244.

General Scott, whose belief in Villa had not failed as yet, said in his memoirs:

I have always believed that Villa came to the border for the purpose of going to Washington, and found the plan quashed, that his men there, hungry and naked, got out of hand and started to loot the town against Villa's will. I am further guided in this belief by a surgeon of Albuquerque, N.M., who said that a Mexican boy, whom he took into the hospital and kept until he was well, told him that he held Villa's horse while the raid was on, and that neither of them went into the town.[29]

It is strange that General Scott, a professional soldier, should fail to recognize the fact that Villa, an experienced combat commander, would be much more likely to remain at his "command post" than to be leading the attack in the sense of actually heading the onslaught. And against the charitable opinions of General Scott and Dr. Bush stands the incontestable fact that the raid, as mentioned before, showed careful and detailed reconnaissance and planning of a kind that cannot be done in a few hours.

The idea that the raid was forced on an unwilling Villa by half-mutinous followers is amply refuted by positive evidence. Papers lost in the hurried retreat and recovered by the Americans showed that the attack was planned as early as January 6, two months before.[30] There was an eyewitness, moreover, whose firsthand testimony has been strangely overlooked by Villa's apologists. Mrs. Maude Wright, the widow of one of the men murdered by the Villistas several days before, was forced to accompany the raiders to Columbus.[31] Released by Villa personally as the Mexicans began to fall back from the attack, she made her way into the burning town, witnessing horrors while on her way. In her account of her terrible ordeal, a few hours after her release, she said: "From the first I knew that Villa intended to attack Columbus. It was freely discusst [sic] by the men and officers. Some of the latter

[29] Gen. Hugh Lenox Scott, *Some Memories of a Soldier*, pp. 517–518. Cf. Testimony of Jesús Paiz, *Fall Committee Report*, pp. 1616–1621. Paiz was evidently the Mexican boy referred to by Scott.
[30] Thomas and Allen, *Official Monograph*, ch. i, p. 14. The writer has seen several references to these lost papers but has been unable to locate them. They are referred to in a personal letter from Carothers to General Scott, written on March 13, 1916, which is included in the Hugh Lenox Scott Papers. Carothers stated in the letter that he had examined the papers himself.
[31] New York *Times*, Thursday, March 9, 1916, 1:4.

told me that Villa intended to kill every American he could find, but they pointed to me as an example of their decision not to harm women." [32]

This evidence disposes of the idea either that Villa was not present at Columbus or that he was not really responsible for the raid. It is worthy of note that Mexican writers who consider Villa a national hero do not suggest that he was elsewhere or that he was not fully responsible for what happened on that eventful March morning. This is true both of serious historians and of the writers who treat Villa's career and personality in a romantic vein, true both of Villa's admirers and of those whose sympathies lay on the other side in the Mexican struggle. [33]

There remain, however, other facets of the Columbus raid that are still not clear. Villa's motives probably will remain forever in the realm of speculation. Perhaps Villa hoped, as suggested by the *Christian Science Monitor,* to cause Mexico to rally to his standard in a burst of patriotic enthusiasm stimulated by the common hatred of the gringo. [34] Perhaps, also, knowing Carranza as he did, he foresaw Carranza's stubborn refusal to co-operate with the United States and hoped thereby to involve Carranza in a war with the northern neighbor. A well-known Mexican publicist who knew Villa personally says that "revenge was a constant in his personal make-up"; moreover, there were good horses and quantities of equipment and supplies north of the border, to be had for the taking. "Also, perhaps, Villa wanted to show the world that he was *'muy hombre,'* in order to counteract the defeats Carranza had inflicted on him recently." [35]

Aside from the insoluble mystery of why Villa did it, there are certain details that whet the interest and curiosity. One can only ask questions, but unlike the rhetorical questions quoted earlier, the answers are not implicit in the questions themselves. Why, in the midst of looting, did

[32] *Ibid.,* Friday, March 10, 1916, 1:5. Cf. Raymond J. Reed, "The Mormons in Chihuahua," Appendix. Reed sent Mrs. Wright a questionnaire, in the answers to which she confirmed her earlier published statements. So far as the writer knows, Mrs. Wright's testimony has never been questioned.

[33] E.g., Campobello, *Apuntes sobre la vida militar de Francisco Villa,* pp. 124–125; Torres, *Vida y hazañas de Pancho Villa,* pp. 43–53; Rafael F. Muñoz, *Pancho Villa, rayo y azote* (Mexico City, 1955), pp. 112–114; Gen. Alberto Salinas Carranza, *La Expedición Punitiva* (Mexico City, 1936), pp. 99–111.

[34] *Christian Science Monitor,* vol. VIII, no. 90 (March 11, 1916).

[35] Dr. Alberto Rembao, in a personal letter to the writer, Feb. 18, 1958.

the Villistas make a special effort to locate Sam Revel, a Jewish merchant of Columbus?[36] Even more titillating to the curiosity is why George L. Seese, the ubiquitous Associated Press representative, arrived in Columbus several days before the raid and made an effort to obtain the services of a special telegraph operator at Columbus only a few hours before the raid.[37] These questions, and others similar, are not likely to be answered.

Villa's raid on Columbus was not a turning point in relations between him and the United States. The turn had been made already. But it was the beginning of new complexities and harassments in relations between the United States and Mexico, and because of the raid Villa was responsible for developments of far deeper importance than he could have foreseen.

---

[36] Roy E. Stivison, M.D., "When Villa Raided Columbus," *New Mexico Magazine*, XXVII (Dec., 1950), 41. Cf. Testimony of Mrs. Laura Ritchie, *Fall Committee Report*, p. 1601.

[37] Testimony of W. S. Murphy, *Fall Committee Report*, pp. 1579–1580.

≫ XIX ≪

Start of the Punitive Expedition

IMMEDIATE popular reaction was rage and a demand for the punishment of the criminals who had murdered peaceful American citizens in their homes. The doubts as to Villa's personal responsibility, which plagued some of his admirers and friends, never affected the American public, especially after the publication of a message from Slocum to General Pershing—that Villa himself led the attack and that prisoners said that Villa vowed death to all Americans.[1] "Watchful waiting" was over; the time for drastic action had at last arrived. Even the normally cautious and conservative *Independent* said:

The murderer Villa and his fellow bandits must be punished. . . . The United States Government must perform the task itself. The armed forces must seek out the murderers of Columbus and put them to death. They must follow the trail wherever it leads; they must use whatever means are necessary to bring the guilty to book. We are not waging war; we are administering justice. We shall not assail the rights of any other people; we shall merely defend our own. To do less would be national dishonor.[2]

On the day following the raid, while the American public was indignantly demanding quick action, in Congress there appeared, outwardly, to be little or no interest. On the morning of March 10 the

[1] National Archives, State Department File no. 812.00/17450, March 9, 1916. This report, from Pershing to Funston, was given to the press.
[2] *Independent*, LXXXV (March 20, 1916), 404.

Senate sedately pursued its routine, debating the Kennebec River Bridge, rural post roads, and pensions. No notice was taken of the events of the day before until the morning was well advanced. Senator Porter J. McCumber asked for unanimous consent to read a resolution he had introduced, authorizing the President to employ the armed forces in Mexico. The resolution was duly read, but Senator William J. Stone objected to consideration of it, and under the Senate's rules it could not be debated until the following day. Only by a parliamentary subterfuge did Senator Henry F. Ashurst, of Arizona, manage to get in a few oblique remarks on the subject of conditions on the border.[3]

In the House of Representatives the scene was almost identical. Near the end of the morning Representative William R. Smith, of Texas, who represented a border constituency, obtained unanimous consent to speak for ten minutes on border conditions. A brief discussion followed, without any particular reference to the Columbus raid, at the end of which the House resumed the question of pensions.[4]

One cannot suppose that the Senators and Representatives were callously lacking in interest in what had happened or were not as anxious as any other citizens to avenge the murders at Columbus. The usual congressional procedure had to be followed, and in such cases the initiative customarily comes from the executive. The cabinet was known to be in session during the morning, and Senator Stone, in offering his objection to immediate consideration of the McCumber resolution, said that Congress should wait until receiving the President's recommendations. Even the President's most vociferous opponents were reluctant to lay themselves open to accusations of playing politics at such a moment.

The first official information about the raid to reach Washington seems to have been forwarded by the tireless Zach Cobb. At nine o'clock in the morning of March 9 he telegraphed, quoting a message he had just received from the deputy collector of customs at Columbus: "Columbus attacked this morning, 4:30 o'clock. Town partly burned. They have retreated to west. Unable to say how many were killed."[5] Cobb added such meager details as he knew at the time. Later in the day Cobb's information was confirmed by telegrams from Carothers, who was at El Paso, and from Letcher, at Chihuahua, who received the

[3] *Cong. Record,* 64 Cong. 1 sess., pp. 3883–3884.   [4] *Ibid.,* pp. 3905–3907.
[5] *Foreign Relations, 1916,* p. 480.

news from the Carranzista General Gutiérrez. In the War Department the news of the raid came from General Pershing, to whom Colonel Slocum had telephoned as soon as possible after the Mexicans disappeared into the hills to the south.[6]

Carranza received the news at about the same time, presumably, as the officials in Washington. The Carranzista consul at El Paso, Andrés G. García, sent a prompt telegram to the First Chief, informing him that Villa, with four hundred men, had attacked Columbus. General Pershing had informed García that the Americans had repulsed the attack and pursued the bandits. "General Pershing asked me if the government would accept the cooperation of the American forces, permitting them to cross the line if necessary. I replied to him that I was not qualified to answer, but that I would communicate the request to you."[7] García later sent a second telegram to Carranza, confirming his first and adding that the Americans had crossed into Mexico in their pursuit of the bandits.

Carranza's reaction was prompt. He telegraphed to his commander in Chihuahua, General Luis Gutiérrez (who had confirmed García's information), directing him to move troops at once to impede Villa's retreat to the Sierra and to rescue an American and thirteen Mexican employees of the Palomas Land and Cattle Company who had been taken prisoner. But the closing sentence of Carranza's instructions to Gutiérrez did not bode well for future co-operation: "At the proper time I will communicate to you the attitude you should take if it is confirmed that American forces are going to cross the border."[8] Carranza's message to General Agustín Millán, his commander in Veracruz, was even less promising: "Relations with the United States are very delicate because of Villa's act, about which I presume you know. Proceed at once to [the city of] Vera Cruz and take all precautions against a landing of American marines, which you will resist."[9]

In Washington the Secretary of State, knowing nothing of Carranza's attitude but hopeful of the best, sent a message to Silliman and Belt, late in the afternoon of March 9. They were directed to call Carranza's attention to the raid and to the fact that Villa's forces were known to be in the vicinity of Casas Grandes several days before, with the local

---

[6] *Ibid.*, pp. 480–481.

[7] Salinas Carranza, *La Expedición Punitiva* (Mexico City, 1936), p. 115. General Salinas Carranza had access to the Mexican archives of the period.

[8] *Ibid.*, p. 121. [9] *Ibid.*

Carranza forces too weak to take action. The United States was suspending judgment until further information became available, but the situation was the most serious that had occurred since the beginning of the Revolution. The United States fully expected Carranza to do all within his power to exterminate the outlaws who had committed the outrage.[10]

Carranza's reply was given to Silliman at Guadalajara late the following night, March 10. To save time, instead of translating the message before sending it, Silliman telegraphed the Spanish text, relying upon the State Department to make its own translation. In the rather lengthy dispatch Carranza expressed deep regret to hear of the "lamentable occurrence" at Columbus. Doubtless, Villa had been so relentlessly pursued by General Luis Gutiérrez that crossing the border was the only recourse open to him. This unhappy incident, Carranza continued, bore a close resemblance to events of the century before, when Apache Indians from the United States raided into Sonora and Chihuahua, committing all sorts of atrocities. At that time there was an agreement between the two governments, providing reciprocally for crossing the border in pursuit of hostiles. Carranza recommended strongly that such an agreement be effected again. Mexican government troops should be accorded the privilege of pursuing outlaws into the United States, while the same right would be given United States forces *"if the raid effected at Columbus should unfortunately be repeated."* [11]

Unknown to the United States, Carranza took further steps the following morning, March 11, 1916, looking to a possible, even probable, complete rupture with the United States because of Villa's raid. Orders were telegraphed to the commanders in Sonora, Generals Diéguez and Calles, to dispose their troops so as to resist an invasion from the United States, to prepare for the destruction of the railroads leading south from Nogales, Naco, and Agua Prieta, and to assemble a supply of dynamite hand grenades.[12]

The administration in Washington had actually decided upon its course of action hours before Carranza's reply and suggestion were received. At six o'clock in the evening, March 10, a brief statement was given to the press by the State Department: "An adequate force will

[10] *Foreign Relations, 1916*, p. 481.
[11] *Ibid.*, p. 485. The present writer's italics.
[12] Salinas Carranza, *La Expedición Punitiva*, p. 122.

be sent at once in pursuit of Villa with the single object of capturing him and putting a stop to his forays. This can be done in entirely friendly aid of the constituted authorities in Mexico and with scrupulous respect for the sovereignty of that Republic." [13]

At about the same time a warning order was sent from the War Department to General Funston: "President has directed that an armed force be sent into Mexico with the sole object of capturing Villa and preventing further raids by his band, and with scrupulous regard to sovereignty of Mexico." [14]

Although the announcement from the State Department actually meant that the projected expedition had no other mission than the pursuit and capture of Villa, it was seized upon by the press as meaning that Villa was to be taken "dead or alive," a picturesque phrase that appealed to the American public. The legend that Pershing had orders to get Villa, "dead or alive," has persisted with such vitality as to be practically an integral part of the Villa myth, and it has given rise to the frequently expressed idea that the Punitive Expedition was a humiliating failure.

The actual orders for the expedition into Mexico were quite different. Following the warning order, a detailed telegram of instructions, on the same day, directed Funston to organize from the troops in the Southern Department an adequate force to cross into Mexico "in pursuit of the Mexican band which attacked the town of Columbus, New Mexico." The force, to be under Brigadier General John J. Pershing, would have completed its mission when Villa's band, or bands, were known to be broken up. Nothing whatever was said about the capture of Villa himself.[15]

These instructions were drawn up by General Scott, who purposely omitted any reference to the personal capture of Villa. The new Secretary of War, Newton D. Baker, came into the War Department from the cabinet meeting of March 10 and went to the office of the Chief of Staff. It was Baker's first day in office—a rather rough "breaking in." Seating himself before General Scott's desk, he said, according to the general's memory of the conversation:

"I want you to start an expedition into Mexico to catch Villa."
This seemed strange to me, and I asked:

[13] *Foreign Relations, 1916*, p. 484.   [14] *Ibid.*, p. 483.
[15] Hugh Lenox Scott, *Some Memories of a Soldier*, pp. 520–521.

"Mr. Secretary, do you want the United States to make war on one man? Suppose he should get onto a train and go to Guatemala, Yucatan, or South America; are you going to go after him?"

He said, "Well, no, I am not."

"That is not what you want then. You want his *band* captured or destroyed," I suggested.

"Yes," he said, "that is what I really want." [16]

Accordingly, Scott drew up instructions which Secretary Baker approved then and there and which were telegraphed to General Funston at once.

The news of the State Department's press release was probably forwarded to Carranza immediately after it was published. On the next day, March 11, Carranza's Washington representative, Eliseo Arredondo, received a lengthy dispatch, which he read to the Secretary of State late in the afternoon of March 12. Carranza spoke ominously, hoping that the two countries would not be drawn into war because of the Columbus incident.

If the government of the United States does not take into consideration the mutual permission for American and Mexican forces to cross into the territory of one another in pursuit of bandits and insists on sending an . . . army into Mexican soil, my Government shall consider this act an invasion of national territory.

Carranza continued that there could be no justification for the invasion of Mexico; such an act would play directly into the hands of Villa and the reactionaries who wanted to force intervention.[17]

Carranza, like most Mexicans, distrusted the United States. Mexican suspicion was deepened by articles such as one by Lincoln Steffens, published in Mexico City, telling at length of the total corruption of the United States government and its complete domination by "the interests." [18] Although the State Department could not know the orders Carranza had already issued to his military commanders, it received early information that he did not take a friendly view of the possibility of American troops entering Mexico. At midnight of March 12, Belt telegraphed from Querétaro, where Carranza had temporarily located his capital, the full text of a proclamation published in an 11 P.M. edition

[16] *Ibid.*, p. 519.   [17] *Foreign Relations, 1916*, p. 486.
[18] *Acción Mundial* (Mexico City), vol. I, no. 1, Feb. 5, 1916.

of the local newspaper, the *Opinión*. In this proclamation Carranza called on the Mexican people to be prepared for any emergency. The First Chief had not yet received a reply from the United States, but he knew that troops were massing on the northern frontier to enter Mexico. The Constitutionalist government could not permit such an outrage against the dignity of the nation, regardless of American excuses and promises to respect Mexican sovereignty. If war should result, the United States alone would be responsible. The proclamation closed with an appeal for all Mexicans to afford full protection to Americans residing among them.[19]

Carranza's previous communications and his Querétaro proclamation, plus additional information from Cobb, showed unmistakably that he was bitterly unfavorable toward American pursuit of Villa into Mexico.[20] Nevertheless, the Mexican reply of March 10 was taken by the State Department as authorizing United States forces to enter Mexico if reciprocal permission were granted to Mexican forces. Probably this conclusion was strengthened by a part of Carranza's note of March 11, which Arredondo read to the Secretary of State on March 12: "If the Government of the United States does not take into consideration . . . mutual permission for American and Mexican forces to cross into the territory of one another. . . ."[21] The State Department completely overlooked the final provision of the Mexican note of March 10, that United States forces might cross into Mexico in case of *future* raids. It is possible that this oversight was deliberate and intentional, as the Mexicans firmly believed, but more likely it was completely unintentional. The note was translated in the State Department, and it is a safe assumption that the translation was made hurriedly. It is not beyond possibility that the Secretary of State (or whatever official was responsible for reading it) may not have read to the very end, where the Mexican proviso was appended, almost as if it were an afterthought.

On March 13, believing that Carranza had agreed to the expedition, Secretary Lansing sent a friendly and cordial note, freely granting the *de facto* government the right to send its troops into the United States

---

[19] *Foreign Relations, 1916*, p. 487.
[20] *Ibid.*, p. 484. Cobb telegraphed on March 10: "Indications are Carranza authorities will resent American troops entering Mexico."
[21] *Ibid.*, p. 486.

in pursuit of outlaws, on a reciprocal basis. The United States was sincerely gratified, he said, at the spirit of co-operation shown by the *de facto* government and understood that the proposed arrangement "is now complete and in force and the reciprocal privileges thereunder may accordingly be exercised by either Government without further interchange of views." [22] With this, all diplomatic arrangements for pursuing Villa into his native fastnesses seemed to be complete and satisfactory. This belief was reinforced when Belt informed the State Department that the United States note had created an extremely favorable impression and that Foreign Minister Acuña had said: "It [the note] will relieve the very delicate situation that has developed owing to the Columbus affair." [23]

President Wilson was anxious that no one, American, Mexican, or other, might misunderstand the motives of the United States and the mission of the expeditionary force, that no one could charge that the United States was using Villa's raid as an excuse for imperialistic designs upon Mexico. To allay any lingering suspicion, on March 13 a statement was handed to Arredondo for his government, saying that "the military operations now in contemplation by this Government will be scrupulously confined to the object already announced, and that in no circumstances will they be suffered to trench in any degree upon the sovereignty of Mexico or develop into intervention." [24]

On the same day additional instructions were sent to Funston, to be passed on to Pershing. The War Department stressed that the expedition was limited to the pursuit and destruction of Villa's band. Although the force must be strong enough to accomplish its mission, it should not be so large as to arouse suspicion that it might have other objectives.[25] In addition to all the official messages, General Scott sent Funston a personal letter on March 17, repeating what had been already said and adding: "It is most important that operations in Mexico be entirely free from possibility of criticism resulting from arbitrary or violent conduct. . . . Our withdrawal from Mexico must leave the Mexican people convinced, from the conduct of our troops, of our justice and humanity." [26] Not if President Wilson or any other official in Washington could help it, would Villa be the cause of trouble with the newly recognized *de facto* government of Mexico.

[22] *Ibid.*, pp. 487–488. [23] *Ibid.* [24] *Ibid.*, p. 489. [25] *Ibid.*
[26] Scott to Funston, March 17, 1916, included in the John J. Pershing Papers.

Assured, as they thought, of Carranza's acquiescence, the War and State Departments were encouraged further by a proclamation issued on March 13 by the newly appointed Minister of War and Marine, General Alvaro Obregón, to the governors of the border states:

Our Government having entered into an agreement with that of the United States to the North providing that the troops of either government may cross the border in pursuit of bandits who are committing depredations along our frontier, I advise you of same in order that you may in turn advise all commanders along the border in order that they may make judicious use of these powers, taking care in each case to act in accord with the military authorities of the American army in order that the pursuit of these bandits may give the best results.[27]

A detailed narrative of the activities, trials, and tribulations of the Punitive Expedition is beyond the intended scope of this investigation, which is not meant to be a military study. A certain number of purely military events and considerations must be interjected, however, to clarify the situation as it evolved—a situation growing out of the change in attitude of the United States and Pancho Villa toward each other.

Within a few hours after the raiders had disappeared, telegraph instruments began clicking in garrisons and military stations all over the United States. Troop trains began rolling toward the border, and marching columns converged toward Columbus. General Pershing established his headquarters at Columbus, and on March 14 he issued his General Orders, no. 1, organizing the Punitive Expedition and specifying the policies which must be followed. The force was organized as a provisional division, consisting of two cavalry brigades and an infantry brigade. Everyone in the command was strictly enjoined to exercise the utmost care not to mistake and fire upon Carranzista troops. Officers and soldiers were directed to "endeavor to convince all Mexicans that the only purpose of this expedition is to assist in apprehending and capturing Villa and his band." [28]

The hastily prepared plans for the expedition called for crossing the border on March 14, but a snag appeared immediately. The commander of the small Carranzista detachment at Las Palomas said that he would resist unless he received other orders. A rush telegram directed Belt to

---

[27] Thomas and Allen, *Official Monograph,* ch. ii, pp. 7–8. The passage quoted is from General Pershing's official report on the expedition.

[28] Tompkins, *Chasing Villa,* pp. 72–73.

ascertain if any special instructions had been issued to Carranza's military commanders and if the officer at Las Palomas had asked for instructions. "Also tactfully and unofficially find out probable attitude of General Carranza if our troops crossed the border in face of protest of local commander." [29]

In the meantime, before the message to Belt could arrive at Querétaro, Silliman had an informal and very friendly conference with the Ministers of Foreign Relations and War. They both assured him that the *de facto* government would acquiesce in and approve sending American troops into Mexico in pursuit of Villa. For some unknown reason, the message to Belt did not reach him until March 18. The reply which he received at the Ministry of War and Marine was reassuring: "There is now complete understanding between Mexican and American forces." [30]

The Punitive Expedition did not wait for a reply to the message sent to Belt. The plan was to enter Mexico in two columns, one from Columbus and one from Culberson's Ranch, near the southwestern corner of New Mexico. The Culberson column was to move unhampered by wheeled transportation, cutting Villa's probable line of retreat near Colonia Dublán and Casas Grandes, with the additional mission of arriving in time to save the Mormon colonists from Villa's vengeance. Two regiments of cavalry and a battery of artillery, comprising the Culberson column, crossed the border in the early hours of the morning of March 15, 1916. The start was delayed for several hours by an automobile accident in which General Pershing was involved but from which he emerged unhurt. The column from Columbus crossed the international line some hours later, with the 13th Cavalry in the lead. The advance guard, commanded by Major Frank Tompkins, found Las Palomas completely deserted, except for one old couple. The Carranzista commander who had said that he would resist the passage of American troops had decided that resistance would be futile or had received orders from higher up. The further march of the column was uneventful, except for finding the body of an unknown American, blindfolded, hands tied behind, and shot through the back of the head.[31]

By a grueling march, the column from Culberson's arrived at Colonia Dublán on March 17, at about 8 P.M. Men and horses were fagged,

[29] *Foreign Relations, 1916*, p. 490.   [30] *Ibid.*, pp. 491–492.
[31] Tompkins, *Chasing Villa*, pp. 74–75.

and it is difficult to say who felt the greater relief, the troopers on seeing the trim Mormon colony or the Mormons, who had been exposed helplessly to the danger of Villa's violence. The colonists, a few nights before, had actually seen Villa's campfires in the distance, but through the interposition of Divine Providence, as they devoutly believed, he had passed by. It was feared that he would return, but as one of the Elders recorded: "What a relief when a long line of United States troops toward evening filed down the western slopes and established camp near the colony. So rapidly had they come that Mormons and Mexicans were not aware of their approach. Knees bent in gratitude." [32]

The Columbus column, with a somewhat greater distance to cover and moving more slowly, did not arrive at Colonia Dublán until March 20. With the junction of the two columns the Punitive Expedition was concentrated. Villa had not been caught between the hammer and the anvil, as Pershing had hoped, but there had been no real expectation that he would be. The Mormons had been saved from a possible massacre, and the expedition was ready to start its hunt in earnest.

[32] Thomas Cottam Romney, *The Mormon Colonies in Mexico* (Salt Lake City, 1938), pp. 240–241.

≈ XX ≈

Friction between
Carranza and Washington

FOR several days there was no news from the Punitive Expedition except that it had crossed the border. Higher military headquarters could not communicate with Pershing, as he was far from the nearest telegraph and beyond operating range of the field radio sets of the time. A message from him finally arrived on March 20, saying that the natives seemed to be friendly and the local Carranza forces were friendly but passive.[1]

In Washington this news was probably received with relief, for on March 18 Carranza had tossed a bomb into the diplomatic calm that had followed the assurances that his government was not unfavorable to the expedition. Arredondo called at the State Department on that day and informed the Secretary of State that the Mexican government had just received reliable information that a force of American troops had crossed the border into Mexico. The consent for crossing the border mentioned in the note of March 10 was intended to apply, on a strictly reciprocal basis, only to possible *future* occurrences such as the unfortunate raid on Columbus. The *de facto* government could not possibly agree to American forces entering Mexico before the exact terms of a definite reciprocal agreement were decided.[2]

This was startling, especially as the United States, relying upon the

[1] *Foreign Relations, 1916,* p. 498.   [2] *Ibid.,* p. 493.

258

supposed acquiescence of the Carranza government, had just telegraphed to Special Representative James L. Rodgers, directing him to
make an important request of Carranza. The War Department was
painfully aware that the supply of Pershing's forces in Mexico would
be a problem difficult to solve. Several thousand men and horses con-
sume vast quantities of food and forage, and it was well known that
local procurement in northern Mexico was impossible. All supplies for
the expedition had to be hauled by wagon from the nearest railhead in
the United States, which was Columbus. The standard army "escort
wagon" was pulled by four mules and had a capacity of three thousand
pounds. A considerable part of the cargo space on each wagon was
taken up by forage for the mules, reducing appreciably the amount of
"pay load." The roads, moreover, were so rudimentary that the wagons
could not be loaded to full capacity. If Carranza could be persuaded
to permit shipping supplies by rail from El Paso, the supply problem
would be greatly eased. On March 18, therefore, Rodgers was directed
to request that Carranza issue orders to allow the shipment of supplies
for the Punitive Expedition from Juárez via the Northwestern Railway
to Casas Grandes.[3]

Carranza's reply, the next day, was an echo of his previous note. The
American request "has caused great surprise to the Mexican Government, for it had not until now received any official notice that American
troops had crossed into Mexican territory." The Mexican government,
the note continued, was still more surprised that such a crossing had
taken place while negotiations were under way for an agreement on the
terms and conditions that would govern crossing the frontier by troops
of both countries. No mention at all was made of the request to use the
railroad, but Carranza demanded full information as to the number of
troops, the exact composition of the force, the identity of the commander, and "the causes which occasioned their crossing." [4]

The question of the Northwestern Railway was tossed back and forth
for several weeks, while Pershing found his supply problem more and
more difficult. Carranza himself suggested eventually that, instead of
formally granting the United States government the use of the railroad,
supplies for the expedition could be shipped as ordinary freight con-

[3] *Ibid.*, p. 492. Rodgers had been designated to represent the United States with
the *de facto* government, pending the appointment of an ambassador.
[4] *Ibid.*, pp. 497–498.

signed to civilians in the area. The United States was more than agreeable to this suggestion, and The Adjutant General was directed to arrange to have the newspaper correspondents with the expedition designated as consignees. Still, the necessary instructions to the Mexican civil and military authorities were not forthcoming from the *de facto* government. One excuse after another was found for delay, culminating in a demand for the names of the consignees. Rodgers curtly refused to give this information, since the United States was fully observing its part of the agreement.[5] Finally and grudgingly, Carranza permitted limited quantities of supplies to move over the railway, disguised as private shipments to individuals.

Simultaneously with the correspondence over the railroad, the two governments were negotiating for the definite agreement that Carranza demanded. At the end of March the *de facto* government submitted a draft protocol for consideration by the United States. In substance, the suggested agreement was the same as in the previous century for the pursuit of hostile Indians. Crossings could be made only in uninhabited areas, no force could remain in the territory of the other nation for more than fifteen days, any pursuit was to be undertaken within three days after the flight of the outlaws, and a pursuing force must return to its own country immediately after making contact with the outlaws.[6]

Replying on April 3, Secretary Lansing expressed gratification at the friendly spirit of the Mexican government, but he excepted the Punitive Expedition from the terms of the proposal, since a strict interpretation of the protocol would force immediate withdrawal. It would, Lansing said, be both unwise and impracticable to withdraw Pershing's force just at the moment when the destruction of the Villistas seemed imminent. Carranza returned a curt and unqualified refusal to except the Punitive Expedition and suspended further discussion, "considering that the expedition sent by the Government of the United States to pursue Villa is without warrant." The expedition, Carranza insisted, could not fulfill its object because Villa's band had been already dispersed and there were ample Mexican troops to exterminate the remainder. It was high time, therefore, to discuss the immediate withdrawal of the United States forces from Mexico.[7]

General Pershing, meanwhile, although harassed by increasingly dif-

[5] *Ibid.*, pp. 503, 504, 508, 509–512.   [6] *Ibid.*, pp. 501–502.
[7] *Ibid.*, pp. 501–502, 515–517.

Map 3 (see following pages). (From Colonel H. A. Toulmin, Jr., *With Pershing in Mexico*.)

The operations of the Punitive Expedition. (From Colonel H. A. Toulmin, Jr., *With Pershing in Mexico*.)

(A) Main route of advance and line of communication (main motor-truck route). Interrupted arrow-headed line. Solid lines, arrow headed. Cavalry operations, units indicated by conventional signs.

(1) Columbus, N.M. The expedition's principal base; scene of the Villa attack the night of March 8–9 which precipitated the Punitive Expedition.

(2) Colonia Dublán and Casas Grandes. From March 17. The first advanced base and the site of the southern terminal of the field telegraph line and the radio station; later Pershing's headquarters after the withdrawal following the Parral incident.

(3) El Valle; an advanced supply depot. Pershing arrived here by motor on March 28 en route to Namaquipa (Namiquipa), where he arrived March 29. Villa had defeated the Federals at Namiquipa on March 28.

(4) Rancho San Gerónimo. Pershing's headquarters from March 29 to April 8, when he followed the advance cavalry southward and established headquarters at Satevó.

(5) Major Dodd's movement across the Continental Divide with one squadron of the 7th Cavalry. He attacked Villa at Guerrero driving the Mexicans northeast in the direction of Providencia and Santa Ana. (March 29.)

(6) March 30. A squadron of the 10th Cavalry (Negro) marches west from Bachíniva to intercept Villa's retreat from Major Dodd's force. Major Tompkins with two troops of the 7th Cavalry moves from Namiquipa via Santa Ana and Providencia to encircle Villa. A squadron of the 11th Cavalry moves south up the Río Santa María to block that valley against any movements by Villa to the north.

(7) April 6. Major Dodd's squadron of the 7th beats the country west of the Continental Divide to cut off Villa's retreat to the west.

(8) April 6–12. Major Tompkins with two troops ("K" and "M") of the 13th Cavalry pursues Villa south to Parral followed by a detachment of the 10th and a squadron of the 11th. Major Dodd moves east across the Divide on Parral.

(9) April 12. Foulois flies from Satevó to Chihuahua where he learns of the attack by Mexican Federals on Major Tompkins' two troops of the 13th Cavalry at Parral.

(10) June 21. Troops "C" and "K," 10th Cavalry, are attacked by Mexican Federals at Carrizal.

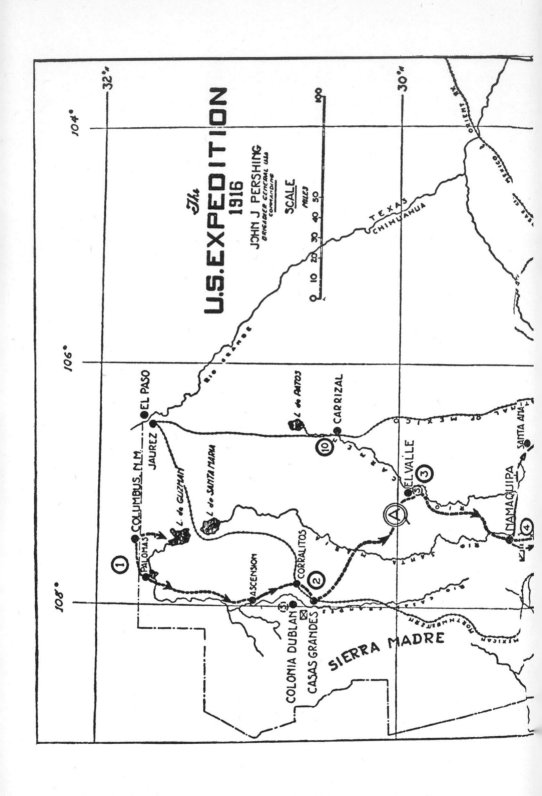

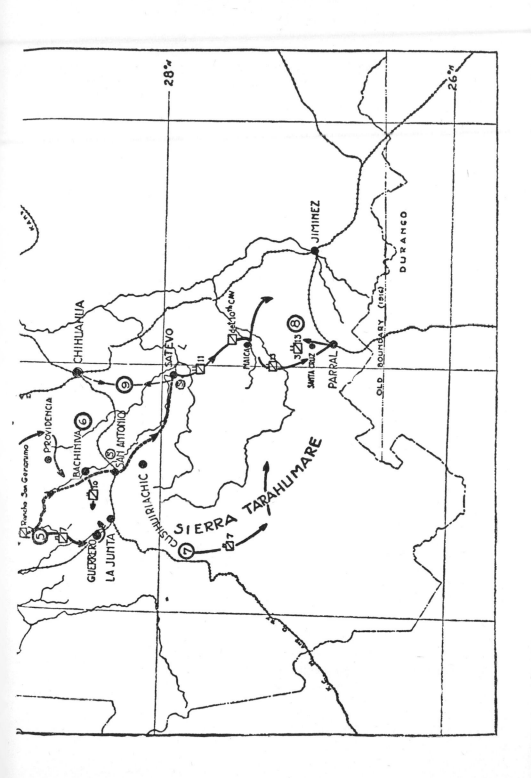

ficult supply problems, was making strenuous efforts to locate and fight the Villistas. The troops of the expedition were suffering actual hardship, but Pershing pushed them on relentlessly.[8] Small, rapidly moving columns penetrated deep into Chihuahua, probing, questioning, and ready to fight at an instant's notice. The Apache Indian Scouts, employed on active service for the first time in many years, had to be restrained with a firm hand, for to them a Mexican was a Mexican, and they drew no distinction between Carranzistas and Villistas.[9] Colonel George F. Dodd, sixty-three years of age, commanding the 7th Cavalry, led his column in an exhausting night march across broken, unknown country, striking a large force of Villistas near Guerrero at daybreak on March 29, 1916, dispersing the band, killing at least thirty, and wounding many more. Two machine guns, a large number of small arms, and a herd of horses and mules remained in the hands of the Americans when the fight was over. Several Carranzista prisoners, slated for execution, were rescued. Villa himself was not present, having been wounded two days before, but the commander of the band, General Hernandez, was identified among the dead.[10]

Increasing indications appeared which showed that the Carranza government and forces were deeply suspicious. On March 19, before Washington had received any direct news from Pershing, Carranza protested against the rumored occupation of Casas Grandes by the expedition. (The rumor was unfounded.) Turning the other cheek, the War Department sent explicit orders forbidding Pershing to occupy any town.[11] Reports began seeping in of suspicious troop movements in Sonora and the other border states. The State Department directed the consuls along the border to ascertain quietly the strength and disposition of Carranza forces in their respective consular districts and to report immediately any changes that occurred. The department wanted particularly to know if any increase had taken place since March 10.

[8] The late Col. Thomas L. Sherburne, who was a captain in the 5th Cavalry in the Punitive Expedition, once told the writer: "I have been in three wars, and for unmitigated hardship, the Punitive Expedition was the worst of all."

[9] James A. Shannon, "With the Apache Scouts in Mexico," *United States Cavalry Journal*, XXVII (April, 1917), 539–557. Shannon was in command of the Indian Scouts throughout the Punitive Expedition. He was killed in the Battle of the Argonne, in World War I.

[10] Tompkins, *Chasing Villa*, pp. 80–88. Cf. *Cong. Record*, 64 Cong., 1 sess., p. 5220.

[11] *Foreign Relations, 1916*, pp. 497, 500.

Rodgers was instructed to call the *de facto* government's attention to these rumors and to express the hope that they were not true, since all available troops should be in pursuit of Villa.[12] General Funston received reports from reliable "special agents" that orders had been sent to Mexican border commanders to move all locomotives, except those necessary for local use, to the interior immediately. In case the United States intervened, the railroads must be destroyed. From El Paso, Brigadier General J. F. Bell, who had succeeded Pershing in command there, reported: "There were 27 locomotives at Juarez two weeks ago, but today there is only one." [13] Vice-Consul Blocker telegraphed from Eagle Pass, Texas, that the Mexican consul at that place had advised an American friend to stay out of Mexico, since there was going to be trouble between the two governments.[14]

The fact was that Mexican resentment against the United States was almost strong enough to overcome the antipathy of the Mexican factions for each other. Villa's raid made him something of a popular hero, and even many educated Mexicans regarded the attack on Columbus as more than a mere act of banditry—it was a magnificent gesture of daring and defiance.

For a force of two or three hundred men to attack a town defended by six hundred and fifty American soldiers, well equipped, well officered and well armed, can hardly be called brigandage. If a pirate in a frail canoe were to attack an English armored cruiser in mid-ocean it could not be classed as piracy, but as the act of a reckless fighter.[15]

In short, Mexicans were patriotically proud of Villa's courage and audacity. Only by taking a strong stand could Carranza overcome the popularity Villa had gained by his attack upon the United States. Commenting on Carranza's initial orders to Diéguez and Calles to prepare to resist an American invasion, Alfonso Taracena remarked dryly: "It is said that all this is a maneuver by Carranza to appear before the Mexican people as a great patriot." [16]

The obviously increasing tension between the two governments in

---

[12] *Ibid.*, pp. 500–501.   [13] *Ibid.*, p. 513.   [14] *Ibid.*, p. 512.
[15] Francisco Bulnes, *The Whole Truth about Mexico: President Wilson's Responsibility* (New York, 1916), p. 378. Bulnes was a well-known Mexican mining engineer, a member of various learned societies, and a former deputy and senator. His background indicates the probability that he was a conservative sympathizer.
[16] Taracena, *Mi vida en el vértigo de la Revolución Mexicana*, p. 377.

the weeks following the entry of the Punitive Expedition into Mexico was immediately reflected in the United States in the usual crop of suspicions that, somehow, the sinister influence of "Wall Street" was involved. Representative Meyer London, the Socialist congressman from New York, in a speech before the House charged that "there are powerful interests whom nothing would suit more than the annexation of Mexican territory. . . . The administration is unwittingly playing into the hands of the annexationists . . . [and] strengthening the hand of Villa." [17] Senator Henry F. Hollis, of New Hampshire, in a speech before the Westchester Democratic Club accused "capitalistic jackals" of deliberately planning the Mexican crisis.[18]

Whether brought about by the callous selfishness of capitalists or by Carranza's stubborn concept of his public duty, the Punitive Expedition was in a perilous situation within a short time after entering Mexico. By the end of the first week of April the situation was so ominous that General Funston, whom nobody ever accused of being timid, wrote to his friend, Lieutenant Colonel Joseph T. Dickman: "I do not know how long this Pershing thing is going to continue. It seems to me that Pershing has accomplished about all he was sent for. . . . It does not seem dignified for all the United States to be hunting for one man in a foreign country." [19]

In the atmosphere of growing distrust and suspicion, of Mexican doubts of the real motives of the Americans and deepening resentment at American soldiers on Mexican soil, during the afternoon of April 12 a small column from the 13th Cavalry approached the town of Parral, in the southernmost part of the State of Chihuahua. The force, commanded by Major Frank Tompkins, who had led the pursuit after the raid on Columbus, consisted of two troops, totaling less than one hundred men. The day previous a Carranzista officer had invited Tompkins to come to Parral, assuring him that arrangements would be made for a campsite and for food and forage. But when the force arrived at Parral, nobody would admit knowing anything about an invitation for the Americans to enter, and within a few minutes a howling mob was shouting, "Viva Villa!" Accompanied by General Lozano, the local

---

[17] *Cong. Record*, 64 Cong., 1 sess., p. 5021.

[18] *Christian Science Monitor*, vol. VIII, no. 103 (March 27, 1916), p. 7.

[19] Hugh Lenox Scott Papers. There had been several fights with Villista bands, not mentioned in this discussion. Cf. *Literary Digest*, LII (April 15, 1916), 1082–1085.

Carranzista commander, Tompkins commenced to withdraw. The mob, now joined by many Carranzista soldiers and egged on by an agitator whom Tompkins took, from his appearance, to be a German, in a short time was completely out of hand. Shots were fired. In self-defense the Americans returned the fire, and a full-dress battle was under way. Tompkins' men inflicted severe losses on the pursuing crowd, materially lessening its enthusiasm but losing two Americans killed and having several wounded (including Tompkins himself).[20]

As was almost customary, the first information to reach Washington seems to have come from Zach Cobb, who received it from Letcher, at Chihuahua. Letcher, in turn, had been informed of the incident by General Gutiérrez, who feared that the situation thus created was serious.[21] Cobb's information was confirmed on the morning of April 13 by an indignant note presented at the State Department by Arredondo. The Americans were accused of having fired first and of having provoked the trouble by being in Parral in the first place. According to the Mexican note, the townspeople were prevented from following the retreating Americans by the Constitutionalist troops—a statement that did not accord with Tompkins' personal observation. Arredondo again appeared at the State Department later with a personal message from the First Chief himself, demanding the immediate withdrawal of the American forces from Mexico before incidents even more serious could arise. The main issue was at last in the clear.[22]

Lansing's reply to this demand was a flat refusal, until Villa was either captured or rendered harmless. The Secretary of State suggested ironically that "the best way to hasten the withdrawal of the American troops would be for the *de facto* Government to throw enough of their military forces into the region where Villa must be in hiding to insure his speedy capture." Withdrawal of the expedition would result in encouraging Villa and his followers, a result which Lansing was "unable to believe was desired by the *de facto* Government." [23]

Carranza and his officials were willing to take their chances on enhancing Villa's cause by forcing an American retirement. Rodgers reported from Mexico City that all high government officials were determined upon it, saying that the presence of American troops, par-

[20] Tompkins, *Chasing Villa*, pp. 137–144.
[21] *Foreign Relations, 1916*, pp. 514–515.　　[22] *Ibid.*, pp. 513–514.
[23] *Ibid.*, pp. 518–519.

ticularly infantry and artillery, implied distrust of Mexico.[24] Pershing
reported that the farther south the expedition penetrated the more open
and marked was the hostility displayed by the people. There had been
a few instances of genuine co-operation by Carranza forces and civil
officials, but the general attitude was obstructive. Pershing could not,
he informed the War Department, accomplish his mission unless he
were given authority to seize the railroads and take possession of Chihuahua, both city and state.[25]

While tension increased, the interchange of communications between
the two governments reflected no real desire for war by either party.
A slightly more conciliatory note was interjected, and a new suggestion
brought out, when Arredondo transmitted to the State Department a
memorandum which Obregón had received from General Luis Gutiérrez, in Chihuahua. Gutiérrez suggested that the Parral incident, "which
we all deplore," resulted from the lack of communication between
Pershing and himself. By inference, Gutiérrez blamed Pershing for not
having kept him completely informed, so that the troops of both governments could be so disposed as to eliminate any chances of conflict.[26]
To demonstrate the good will and good faith of the United States,
Rodgers was directed to assure Carranza personally that rumors that
the United States was friendly to certain enemies of the *de facto* government were entirely false. Carranza received Rodgers, when he delivered the message, with marked cordiality. Asked about the delay in
supply arrangements for the American forces, Carranza made no promises, but Rodgers optimistically felt sure that Carranza would look into
the matter. In summarizing, Rodgers stated that Carranza's attitude was
"exceedingly satisfactory to-day," and yet only twenty-four hours earlier
Rodgers had advised that the American consuls in certain districts use
their own judgment as to whether or not they should stay at their posts,
because of the personal danger involved.[27]

At this juncture, with Americans and Carranzistas eyeing each other
askance, with the two countries in the proverbial position of sitting on
a keg of powder, Secretary Lansing suggested a personal conference
between General Scott and General Obregón, or some Mexican officer
of high enough rank to be able to speak authoritatively. Such a conference might clarify the situation and make real co-operation possible

[24] *Ibid.*, p. 519.   [25] *Ibid.*, pp. 521–522.   [26] *Ibid.*, p. 523.
[27] *Ibid.*, pp. 525, 527.

between American and Mexican forces. No doubt, the Secretary of State remembered General Scott's demonstrated ability to unravel complicated politico-military situations and his combination of tact and firmness in previous dealing with Mexicans.[28] Sending the senior officer of the entire United States Army to treat with the Mexican Minister of War would be, moreover, a silent demonstration of the gravity with which the United States regarded the situation and at the same time an unspoken compliment to the *de facto* government of Mexico.

Carranza adopted the suggestion without delay, and on April 24 Obregón left Mexico City secretly, en route for the border.[29] Secrecy was considered necessary, both for Obregón's safety and to avoid undue excitement and unfounded rumors. In the past few years General Scott had conferred with Villa several times. He was now about to confer with one of Villa's bitterest and most determined enemies on grave issues which Villa himself had caused.

[28] *Ibid.*, pp. 527–529.   [29] *Ibid.*, pp. 528, 533.

∝ XXI ⊱

The Scott-Obregón Conferences
and the Fight at Carrizal

AT first thought it might seem that the conferences between Scott and Obregón, as well as other events of the spring and summer of 1916, are outside the restricted field of the relationships between the United States and Francisco Villa. At the end of April, Villa's whereabouts was completely unknown, and his name was scarcely mentioned during the conferences. Formal diplomatic contact between the United States and Mexico was entirely with Carranza's *de facto* government, and there were times when Carranza, rather than Villa, seemed to be the real enemy. Nevertheless, the tension and acrimony had its ultimate source in Villa's raid on Columbus. Thus, in a broad sense, the Scott-Obregón conferences, the tragic little fight at Carrizal, the series of conferences at New London in the autumn of the year, all had their roots in the relations between the United States and the superbandit of Chihuahua.

As Obregón left Mexico City for the border, the situation between the United States and the *de facto* government seemed to be deteriorating, if such a thing were possible. Rodgers reported that Mexico City was full of talk of impending trouble and that the officially controlled *Pueblo* carried an editorial hinting at the possibility of war.[1] General Pershing reported that the inhabitants of San José del Sitio refused to sell supplies to Major Robert L. Howze's command and had attacked

[1] *Foreign Relations, 1916,* p. 528.

the camp at night. Near San Borja, Chihuahua, Howze was threatened by a force of Carranzista cavalry, which made an overt attempt to provoke a fight. In the next few days Howze was twice attacked by parties of unidentified Mexicans, who found, to their chagrin, that such action was highly dangerous.[2] Funston received a report from the State Department that some five thousand Carranzista troops on the Chihuahua-Sonora border were ready to move. The situation was critical and delicate. To forestall criticism and prevent as much trouble as possible, Funston wired orders to Pershing to suspend the search and hold his troops in place until after the conference.[3]

The information that Carranza had approved the suggestion for a conference between the two military chiefs and that Obregón had already left the capital produced a mild flurry. Unlike most previous interchanges with Carranza, this time the First Chief had made his decision so quickly that there was no time to arrange the usual preliminaries. General Scott was absent from Washington, and Obregón's exact destination and time of arrival were unknown. Rodgers was directed hurriedly to find out just where Obregón expected to meet Scott and to explain to Carranza that if Obregón were not met on his arrival at the border it was because no one knew his plans. Consul Edwards was telegraphed to meet Obregón if and when he arrived at Juárez and to make all arrangements for an interview if Obregón arrived before Generals Scott and Funston.[4]

A lengthy telegram from the War Department gave full and explicit instructions to Scott and Funston. They were to meet Obregón and discuss with him "the future military operations of our forces." They were given full authority to discuss and settle all purely military questions and were specially directed to urge upon Obregón the advantages of full co-operation with the Punitive Expedition, for "the Government of the United States has no pride involved in who makes the capture [of Villa] and its only interest is that it should be done expeditiously." The two American generals were ordered to refuse to discuss the withdrawal of the Punitive Expedition and were to inform Obregón, if he should bring up the matter, that it was a diplomatic question to be decided only by higher authority. Recognizing that Obregón probably had definite instructions from his government as to what he could and could

[2] *Ibid.*, p. 530. [3] Hugh Lenox Scott Papers.
[4] *Foreign Relations, 1916,* p. 529.

not discuss, the Americans were directed to inform the Secretaries of War and State at once what bases Obregón presented for negotiations.[5]

The first meeting was held in Juárez on the last day of April. The Mexicans were anxious to have the conferences held on Mexican soil, a point over which the Americans did not think it worth while to argue. As had·been feared, Obregón insisted upon the immediate withdrawal of American forces from Mexico. Since Scott and Funston were instructed to obtain the use of the railroad for supplying the Punitive Expedition and to arrange for closer co-operation of the Carranza forces, an impasse existed from the start. After two hours of amicable, but futile, conversation, Scott adjourned the meeting on the grounds that he had to inform his government of the Mexican position. He telegraphed to the Secretary of War that Obregón declined "to discuss anything but withdrawal." [6]

A quick reply from the War Department authorized Scott to say that the United States would consider moving the expedition to a point closer to the border than it was at the time and that complete withdrawal would take place as soon as there was full assurance of safety from further attacks. The United States was willing to concede that Villa himself was probably eliminated as a serious factor in the situation, but there was still the possibility of raids by bands of Villistas. Indeed, such raids were continuing. A second message from the Secretary of War to Scott, the same evening, suggested that if there were further deadlock he adjourn the conference on pretext of asking for additional instructions. This would gain time in which to concentrate outlying detachments of Pershing's force, which must take "every precaution . . . against sudden or general attack." [7]

The following day, May 1, 1916, Scott and Funston sent a joint telegram to Washington. They said that practically everything mentioned in the previous day's message from Washington had been discussed before the conference adjourned. Under the circumstances, they both felt that nothing could be accomplished from a meeting in which the same proposals would be presented again. They were both, consequently, in agreement that no further sessions should be held until the War Department sent additional instructions.

Alarming reports were coming in. Scott heard from reliable sources that secret orders had been issued in Mexico to crush or annihilate the

[5] *Ibid.*, pp. 530–532.   [6] *Ibid.*, pp. 533–534.   [7] *Ibid.*, pp. 534–535.

American forces unless immediate withdrawal were agreed upon. All sources of information indicated that the Mexican generals believed that the United States was unprepared to resist, and they were fully confident of their ability to destroy the Punitive Expedition. Funston had already sent orders to Pershing to draw in all of his scattered detachments and had warned all border commanders to take full precautions. Both Scott and Funston urgently recommended that forces on the border be strengthened at once to prevent attacks and permit the concentration of the Regular Army to meet eventualities.[8]

Further information confirmed the seriousness of the situation. It was noted that Generals Gutiérrez and Calles, who had been in Juárez during the first session of the conference, had left suddenly for their commands. From Douglas, Arizona, Colonel Walter S. Scott forwarded a copy of the orders which General Arnulfo Gómez had received from Carranza: "Dispose your troops that they shall be in a position to cut off American expeditionary forces now in Chihuahua. The action must be sudden and will take place after the Scott-Obregón conference." [9]

The conference held on April 30 was open, although reporters were not permitted to be actually in the conference room. Obregón, nevertheless, was in front of a Mexican audience which he had to satisfy. He dared not make the slightest concession for fear of shaking the none too firm hold the *de facto* government had on the loyalty of the Mexican people. Hence he was willing to listen when mutual friends suggested that it would be advisable for him and General Scott to get together privately, so that they could discuss matters freely, unhampered by spectators or by the presence of aides, staff officers, and other outsiders. On the evening of May 2 Obregón asked A. J. McQuatters, who was one of the mutual friends, to ascertain if he could meet General Scott secretly in McQuatters' room, at the Paso del Norte Hotel in El Paso, to discuss the situation alone.[10]

In the best "cloak and dagger" tradition Scott and Obregón made their way to McQuatters' room, attempting to elude newspaper report-

<hr />

[8] *Ibid.*, pp. 535–536.   [9] *Ibid.*, pp. 536–537.

[10] *Ibid.*, pp. 537–538. General Scott's account of the secret conference given in his memoirs (*Some Memories of a Soldier*, pp. 527–528) differs in some details from the account given in his official report. The memoirs were written years after the event, so that it is likely that the official report is more accurate. The McQuatters mentioned is the same person who represented the mine and smelter operators in conferences with Villa the previous summer.

ers and other inquisitive individuals who were watching them closely. The group which assembled was small, consisting only of the two generals, an interpreter, McQuatters (who drafted papers and also assisted in interpretation), and, in the last stages, a stenographer. Hours were spent discussing and arguing every point, with Obregón insisting upon immediate withdrawal of the Punitive Expedition. For twelve hours Scott kept Obregón engaged in conversation, so that he would not walk out of the room and "fall under hostile influence waiting in the hallway." (Undesired observers had successfully trailed the quarry.)

Finally, at noon the next day, a tentative agreement was reached, after a continuous struggle of wills which, Scott said in his report, "was not equalled by any similar struggle with the wildest and most exasperated Indian hitherto encountered." [11] In his memoirs, Scott recalls:

I told him that if he wanted to lose his country, the surest way for him to do it would be to attack Pershing. I mentioned General Nafárete over in the Province [sic] of Tamaulipas, who was encouraging the building of a bandit force for an attack on Brownsville with the support of Carranza. I said:

"No doubt you want Pershing to leave Mexico, but if you don't change all that and stop those preparations in Tamaulipas, instead of getting rid of Pershing here, you will have another Pershing over there in addition, and who knows then if either will ever come out of Mexico? . . .

How I kept Obregón from leaving I have never known. He was the secretary of war of a friendly power, and he could not be struck on the head with a sandbag and kept locked in a closet until he signed. At any time he could have thanked me . . . and asked to have his car called; why he did not I do not know to this day. My effort was to make it so pleasant he would not want to leave and there may have been present in his mind the consequences of a rupture. [12]

The agreement, with which Scott was not altogether satisfied but which he believed was the best he could obtain, provided for the gradual withdrawal of the Punitive Expedition. The *de facto* government promised, in return, that it would intensify its efforts to capture Villa and destroy his following. [13]

Obregón suggested, and Scott agreed at once, that both of them

[11] *Foreign Relations, 1916,* p. 538.
[12] Hugh Lenox Scott, *Some Memories of a Soldier,* pp. 527–528.
[13] *Foreign Relations, 1916,* pp. 538–539.

remain until the governments had examined the agreement. Thus, any differences could be adjusted without loss of time. The United States accepted the agreement immediately, but for several days nothing was heard from Mexico City. One rumor said that Carranza approved, but another, equally authoritative, said that he strongly disapproved. On May 6 the First Chief authorized a press release saying that the conference had reached an amicable agreement, but he informed Rodgers that certain changes in detail would be necessary.[14]

The final result was a disappointment to everyone who hoped that a workable solution to the difficulties between the two countries had been achieved. The simple "changes in detail" that Carranza demanded negated the entire spirit of the agreement; he insisted that the United States must fix an early date for withdrawing the expeditionary force. Obregón returned to Mexico City, and again reports came in telling of northward troop movements in Mexico. A joint telegram from Scott and Funston to the Secretary of War urged at least 150,000 additional troops for the border and calling out the National Guard of Texas, New Mexico, and Arizona without delay.[15] (The entire United States Army included less than 100,000 men.)

General Pershing had, meanwhile, continued the search for Villa, except for the period when movements were "frozen" by Funston's orders. Sixty-three-year-old Colonel George Dodd, again pushing himself and his men and horses remorselessly through the hills, struck a large Villista band near Tomochic, late in the afternoon of April 22. In a running fight that lasted until dark, at least thirty Villistas were killed and wounded. The remainder disappeared in the darkness, completely demoralized.[16]

On May 5, 1916, Major Robert L. Howze, in response to an appeal for protection from the inhabitants of Cusihuiriáchic, after an all-night march struck a completely unprepared and totally surprised band of Villistas. This time darkness could not interrupt the pursuit, which continued until horses began dropping from exhaustion. The survivors of the Villista band, barely half the original number, broke into a disorderly flight, every man for himself.[17]

[14] *Ibid.*, pp. 540–541.   [15] *Ibid.*, pp. 543–544, 547–550.
[16] *Ibid.*, p. 530. Cf. Tompkins, *Chasing Villa*, pp. 177–180.
[17] S. M. Williams, "The Cavalry Fight at Ojos Azules," *United States Cavalry Journal*, XXVII (Jan., 1917), 405–408. Williams, who was an officer of Major Howze's squadron, was in the fight.

Early in the Punitive Expedition there was a report that Villa had been badly wounded in a fight near Guerrero, but since then there had been no reliable information about him. Indeed, to this day, his movements and whereabouts during April, 1916, are somewhat of a mystery. There is evidence that on one occasion he may have hidden in a cave with a few faithful followers while American troops passed nearby. This is not impossible and is the probable basis for the improbable legend that he made it a practice to observe and view the American forces from mountain caves whenever he felt the urge to do so.[18]

As for the negotiations with Carranza's government, on May 22 Arredondo handed the State Department a note of impressive length which he had just received from Mexico City. In this note the diplomatic politeness and tone of conciliation of previous notes was lacking. The *de facto* government complained that another American force had entered Mexico without permission or justification and demanded that the Punitive Expedition be withdrawn immediately.[19] There was an unmistakable threat of war if the United States did not comply and a plain inference that the motives of the United States in Mexico were imperialistic. Finally, as a climax, the note included a bitter complaint that a shipment of machinery for the manufacture of munitions, consigned to the *de facto* government, had been embargoed.[20] The note was so aggressive and recriminatory that the Secretary of State did not release it to the press, for fear it would arouse public antagonism. Carranza's government felt no such qualms, for it was given to the press in Mexico City, and Carranza's officials appeared to be well pleased with it.[21]

[18] Tompkins, *Chasing Villa*, p. 166. Cf. Torres, *Vida y hazañas de Pancho Villa*, pp. 87–90, and Rafael F. Muñoz, *¡Vámonos con Pancho Villa!* (Madrid, 1931), pp. 277–278. Muñoz states that he received his information from a member of Villa's personal escort. Gen. Bernardino Mena Brito, a bitter anti-Villista, advances the startling theory that Villa, whom he considered a "stooge" of American imperialists, was secretly in Washington, conferring with President Wilson during the period of his disappearance (*El lugarteniente gris de Pancho Villa*, p. 288).

[19] A small American force entered Mexico on May 7, 1916, in pursuit of a bandit gang, alleged to be Villistas, that raided Glen Springs, Texas, on May 6. Cf. *Foreign Relations, 1916*, pp. 540, 542, 544–546.

[20] *Ibid.*, pp. 552–563. The Spanish text of this extraordinary diplomatic communication is in *Labor internacional de la Revolución Constitucionalista de México*, pp. 252–269.

[21] *Foreign Relations, 1916*, p. 566.

The acute tension continued through May into June, with numerous petty raids, many of which took a toll of life, particularly along the lower Rio Grande. In some instances the local Carranza commanders tried to apprehend the raiders, but in others there was convincing evidence that the raiders were Carranzistas.[22] On June 1 President Wilson let it be known that he had no intention of yielding to the Mexican demand for the withdrawal of Pershing's force from the country. But fortunately, and in spite of what each country regarded as deep provocation, the uneasy peace remained unbroken.[23]

The situation remained unchanged until mid-June. The *de facto* government received no reply to its embittered note of May 22, which the President had, so far, ignored. Failing to persuade the United States to order the withdrawal of the expedition, by either arguments, threats, or promises, Carranza decided to resort to direct pressure upon the expedition itself—to place a limit on its movements, the overstepping of which would place the United States in the position of an aggressor. On June 16 General Pershing received a note from General Jacinto B. Treviño saying that any further movement of American troops in any direction except toward the border would be resisted by the *de facto* government's troops. "I communicate this to you for your knowledge for the reason that your forces will be attacked by the Mexican forces if these instructions are not heeded." [24]

Pershing's reply was brief. He had received no such instructions from his own government, he said, and would, therefore, use his own judgment as to the direction in which his troops would move in pursuit of bandits or seeking information. If anything happened, the responsibility for the consequences would rest upon the Mexican government.[25]

For several weeks past, Pershing and his staff had devoted much thought to measures to prevent antagonizing the Carranza forces and to action that would be taken in case of an open rupture. From late in May, Pershing's standing orders were that all patrols and detachments sent out by the Punitive Expedition must avoid camps and stations occupied by the troops of the *de facto* government. Patrol commanders were instructed: "Make every effort to avoid collision, but if attacked, inflict as much damage as possible, having regard for the safety of your own command." Combat missions were tentatively assigned to the

[22] *Ibid.*, pp. 573–576.   [23] *Literary Digest*, LII (Jan.–June, 1916), 1819.
[24] *Foreign Relations, 1916*, p. 577.   [25] *Ibid.*

units of the expedition, and if war occurred, the Punitive Expedition would take the offensive immediately.[26] Happily, it was never necessary to implement the plans which were carefully prepared in detail.

On June 20 the administration finally answered the Mexican note of a month before. The reply was unique in the long correspondence which had been carried on with the various governments and factions in Mexico. Never before had the United States government spoken as strongly or as directly. Mincing no words, the reply cited instances proving the hostility of the Carranza government for the United States. The failure to reach any sort of working agreement was the direct responsibility of Carranza himself, who was much more concerned with the form of the agreement than with capturing the outlaws who had raided and murdered in the United States. The American note made no categorical assertion that Carranza had lied, but the inference was clear. For reasons stated in detail throughout the communication, the "request of the *de facto* Government [for immediate withdrawal of the expedition] can not now be entertained." If the Mexican government resorted to arms, as was so broadly hinted, "the Government of the United States would surely be lacking in sincerity and friendship if it did not frankly impress upon the *de facto* Government that the execution of this threat will lead to the gravest consequences." [27]

In this explosive atmosphere, a dispatch from Rodgers, late on June 21, seemed to indicate that a spark had fallen. A bulletin from the Ministry of War and Marine announced that Americans and Carranzistas had clashed in Chihuahua that morning. The Mexican commander, General Felix U. Gómez, had been killed, and several American soldiers were taken prisoner.[28] The report was confirmed the next day, with additional information that Mexican losses were heavy and that the American prisoners had been taken to the city of Chihuahua.[29] Up to this point Washington had no information except that from Mexican sources. The administration would not take action without full knowledge. Orders were rushed to Pershing to make no move until authorized by the War Department.[30]

The grim little fight at Carrizal, Chihuahua, on June 21, 1916—

---

[26] John J. Pershing Papers. Notes covering the items mentioned above are in General Pershing's pocket notebook, which he carried throughout the campaign.
[27] *Foreign Relations, 1916*, pp. 581–582.   [28] *Ibid.*, p. 592.
[29] *Ibid.*   [30] *Ibid.*, p. 593.

a forgotten battle in a forgotten war—was the last and most serious of the incidents that threatened to bring an open clash between the United States and Mexico. It grew out of Pershing's determination not to be surprised by Carranzista troops moving unobserved upon his forces. By active patrolling he endeavored to keep watch over all areas from which the Punitive Expedition might be threatened.

On June 17, Captain Charles T. Boyd, commanding Troop C, 10th Cavalry, was directed to report to the commanding general for orders. Pershing told him:

A large concentration of Carrancista [*sic*] troops is reported in the vicinity of Ahumada, on the Mexican Central Railroad. Information has been received that this force is being assembled in conjunction with other de facto forces from Pearson and Nueva Casas Grandes [*sic*]. Take your troop and reconnoiter in the direction of Ahumada and obtain as much information as you can regarding the forces there. This is a reconnaissance only, and you will not be expected to fight. In fact, I want you to avoid a fight if possible. Do not allow yourself to be surprised by superior numbers. But if wantonly attacked, use your own judgment as to what you shall do, having due regard for the safety of your command. I then went on to tell Captain Boyd of General Treviño's order to attack our troops if we should send them west, east, or south. And further told him that it would not be wise to go into any place garrisoned by Carrancista troops.[31]

Troop C moved out on its mission—two officers, twelve noncommissioned officers and twenty-nine privates. Moving eastward, on the evening of June 20 they encountered Troop K, of their own regiment, at Santo Domingo Ranch. Troop K, commanded by Captain Lewis Morey, was on a mission similar to that of Troop C. The two troops joined, and Captain Boyd, as senior officer, assumed command of the whole force. Together, the two troops had a total strength of eighty-

---

[31] National Archives, Punitive Expedition Records, Box 70, "Memorandum from General Pershing for the Inspector General, Headquarters, Punitive Expedition, Camp Dublan, Mexico, June 30, 1916." Pershing and Boyd had known each other for years. Numerous entries in the Pershing Papers show that Pershing held Boyd in the highest regard, personally and professionally. There is evidence that Boyd's regimental commander specially selected him for the mission upon which he met his death because of his diplomacy and tact. Cf. George Brydges Rodney, *As a Cavalryman Remembers* (Caldwell, Idaho, 1944), pp. 274–278. The 10th Cavalry was one of the four Negro regiments added to the Regular Army after the Civil War. It had an impressive battle record.

four, of all ranks and including two civilian guides, one of whom was a Mexican and the other an American Mormon.[32]

Next morning the little force, still moving toward Ahumada, approached the pueblo of Carrizal, which was occupied by a Carranzista garrison. This fact must have been known to Boyd, because a Mexican patrol from Carrizal had been at Santo Domingo for a few minutes the previous evening. The Mexican patrol had, of course, informed its own commander, General Felix U. Gómez, who prepared at once to attack the Americans at Santo Domingo but before doing so telegraphed to his superiors at Juárez for instructions. He was ordered to remain at Carrizal but to resist any attempt by the Americans to pass through.[33] Next morning, as the Americans approached, General Gómez rode forward to meet them.

What followed was so confused that it is impossible to separate the wheat from the chaff in the various accounts. Boyd sent a brief message, addressed to the "Jefe Político, Ahumada," stating that he was on a peaceful mission and requesting that the chief Mexican military officer be informed of his movements. The note was delivered to General Gómez, who sent a message to Boyd suggesting that he bring his force forward for a conference. Fearing a trap, Boyd rode forward, accompanied only by an interpreter and an orderly and leaving the command some distance behind. The two officers talked together for several minutes. Just what passed between them is a mystery, but it is clear that Boyd insisted that he must pass *through* the town, while Gómez warned him against the attempt.[34] In obvious irritation both returned to their commands. Boyd gave his orders quickly, the Americans dismounted and deployed and moved forward, and the Mexicans opened fire.

Returning the fire, the dismounted troopers advanced steadily, killing General Gómez with their first volley. The Mexicans were

[32] National Archives, Punitive Expedition Records, Box 70.

[33] 1st Capt. Daniel González, "The Fight at Carrizal." This article, which was published in one of the Mexican military journals, was translated by the present writer upon its appearance, in 1933. Unfortunately, at some time in the years following and in the course of several major moves, the writer has lost the reference and cannot now identify the publication in which it appeared.

[34] *Ibid.* Boyd's message, addressed to the "Jefe Político" and General Gómez' reply, the latter partially illegible from bloodstains, are in the National Archives, Punitive Expedition Records, Box 70. Cf. *Independent*, LXXXVII (July 3, 1916), 8–9, for Captain Morey's statement of what happened.

thrown into some confusion by the unexpected accuracy and deadliness of the American rifle fire, but they did not break. Boyd was killed within a few yards of the machine gun that was the core of the Mexican resistance, and a few minutes later his lieutenant, Henry Rodney Adair, was shot through the heart. A few hundred yards away, in Troop K, Captain Morey was wounded, and in both troops the number of dead and wounded was increasing. Somewhat disorganized by their advance and left without an officer to give orders and co-ordinate efforts, the Negro soldiers began to drift to the rear in small groups. A few were taken prisoner, but more refused to surrender and quickly proved to the Mexicans that, even leaderless, they were still dangerous, inflicting punishing losses on their pursuers.[35] The battle of Carrizal was an American defeat but a Pyrrhic victory for the Mexicans, who later admitted losing seventy-four men.

Further details of the fight itself would be of small interest. The first anxiety of the government in Washington and of Pershing's military superiors was to obtain complete and accurate information as to what had happened. On June 22 Funston sent Pershing a peremptory and almost frantic telegram:

Why in the name of God do I hear nothing from you. The whole country has known for ten hours through Mexican sources that a considerable force of your command was apparently defeated yesterday with heavy losses at Carrizal. Under existing orders why were they there so far from your line. Being at such a distance I assume that now nearly twenty-four hours after affair news has not reached you who was responsible for what on its face seems to have been a terrible blunder.[36]

The administration acted promptly and decisively. A sharp note to the *de facto* government was actually an ultimatum, although no threat was expressed. Ignoring an accusation that the Americans were re-

---

[35] The foregoing summary of the Carrizal fight is taken from several sources, in addition to 1st Captain González' narrative. Cf. Capt. O. C. Troxel, "The Tenth Cavalry in Mexico," *United States Cavalry Journal*, XXVIII (Oct., 1917), 199–208; Capt. Lewis S. Morey, "The Cavalry Fight at Carrizal," *ibid.*, XXVII (Jan., 1917), 449–456; Testimony of George Turner, *Fall Committee Report*, pp. 1561–1568; numerous papers in National Archives, Punitive Expedition Records, Box 70. In addition, the writer, as a lieutenant in the 10th Cavalry when veterans of the Punitive Expedition were still on active duty has conversed with many men who were in the fight.

[36] National Archives, Punitive Expedition Records, Box 70.

sponsible because they disregarded Treviño's orders, the State Department demanded the immediate release of the prisoners and the return of all United States property and equipment. In the future, Secretary Lansing added, the United States expected all announcements of policy by the *de facto* government to be communicated through regular diplomatic channels, rather than through subordinate military commanders.[37]

Mexican popular opinion, at this time, did not credit the United States with power or Americans with any courage. This opinion was expressed in a cartoon published in a Mexico City newspaper on July 6, showing a bold-looking Mexican with a rifle in one hand and with the other pointing a knife at a timid and cowering Uncle Sam.[38] But Carranza and his advisers probably realized that Mexico would stand no chance whatever in a war with the United States. In spite of his undeniably truculent and aggressive attitude, it is safe to say that the last thing Carranza really wanted was such a war. To avoid provoking the United States to the point of retaliation, steps toward conciliation were necessary.

Hence, on June 28 the Foreign Minister informed Rodgers that orders had been issued for the immediate release of the Carrizal prisoners. When asked what the *de facto* government intended to do about the other demands, he first attempted to evade the issue but finally said that he would consult the First Chief. Asked further if the orders to Treviño had been revoked, he replied that the Minister of War might have changed the orders. Rodgers believed that the Carranzista officials were trying to gain time and would delay as long as possible.[39]

Faced with the unhappy fact that troops of the Punitive Expedition had been fired upon and taken prisoner, that a group of raiders into the United States had been positively identified as Carranzistas, and that the incidents mentioned in the United States note of June 20 were incontrovertible, the *de facto* government resorted to the strongest propaganda defense possible—a sudden offensive. A surgeon at Chihuahua who treated the Mexican wounded after Carrizal asserted that the wounds he examined could have been inflicted only by ex-

[37] *Foreign Relations, 1916*, p. 595.
[38] *Acción Mundial* (Mexico City), July 6, 1916.
[39] *Foreign Relations, 1916*, p. 597.

plosive bullets.[40] On the same day on which Rodgers was pressing the Foreign Office for answers to his questions, Arredondo submitted a complaint to the State Department about atrocities alleged to have been committed by the troops of the Punitive Expedition. General Pershing, it was claimed, had arrested some three hundred peaceful inhabitants of La Cruz and subjected them to maltreatment before releasing them. Arredondo claimed further that a column of American troops, three thousand strong, moving toward Valle de San Buenaventura, was committing all sorts of outrages. The Apache Indian Scouts were distinguishing themselves particularly by the fiendish atrocities they were committing.[41] General Pershing, his attention called to the allegations, replied that he had been aware of such rumors for some time, that they were entirely false, and that they were deliberately circulated by Carranzista officers for the purpose of inflaming the population against the Americans.[42]

Feeling against the United States and hostility to individual Americans continued to run high in Mexico for a considerable time, punctuated by a number of disagreeable incidents. Carranzista soldiers at Tampico fired upon a launch that had been ferrying refugees to the *U.S.S. Marietta.* The launch was finally returned to its normal anchorage escorted by the *Marietta,* whose commander notified the authorities that a single shot would be followed by the "gravest consequences." At Mazatlán, on the West Coast, the governor proclaimed that war was about to be declared against the United States. A party sent ashore from the *U.S.S. Annapolis* to escort the American consul aboard was arrested, and the sailors remaining in the ship's boat were fired upon. They returned the fire, wounding several of the assailants.[43]

This latter incident was in the middle of July. Before it occurred the *de facto* government, evidently alarmed by the Frankensteinish monster they had conjured up, had adopted a much more conciliatory

[40] Salinas Carranza, *La Expedición Punitiva,* p. 306. This was a favorite allegation to make against an enemy at that time. One is reminded of the "positive" evidence that American forces in Korea employed bacteriological weapons.

[41] *Foreign Relations, 1916,* p. 597. The Apache Indian Scouts were probably capable of doing this if they were allowed, but they were actually kept under tight discipline and close surveillance by Lieut. James Shannon, an officer who was noted for his strictness and fairness.

[42] *Ibid.,* p. 607. Accusing the enemy of atrocities is, of course, a propaganda device as old as war itself.

[43] *Ibid.,* pp. 598–599, 602–603.

tone. On July 4, 1916, a note from the Mexican Ministry of Foreign Affairs, after a brief and genuinely objective summary of the differences between the two countries, pointed out that certain Latin American countries had offered their friendly services in mediation of the difficulties. The Mexican government inquired whether the United States would be willing to accept such mediation, or was it possible that direct negotiations between the two governments might still be successful? [44]

The reply of the United States was prompt and cordial. The United States was ready at any time to exchange views as to a practical plan to solve the difficulties between the two countries. Thereupon, the Mexican Foreign Minister, speaking for Carranza, suggested that each government name three commissioners, to meet at a place to be decided upon. Again the United States accepted promptly, President Wilson proposing that the instructions for the commissioners be made broad enough to enable them to consider all questions pending between the two countries. At this, Carranza's deep-rooted suspicion of the United States manifested itself, and he hesitated, fearing that "pending questions" might include such matters as possible cession of Mexican territory or claims against Mexico.[45] His doubts finally satisfied, Carranza announced the appointment of Luis Cabrera, Ignacio Bonillas, and Alberto Pani to represent Mexico. President Wilson was delayed for several days in naming the American commissioners, but late in August he announced the appointment of the Honorable Franklin K. Lane, Secretary of the Interior, George Gray, and John R. Mott.[46]

A detailed recounting of the long-drawn series of conferences, lasting six months, is unnecessary. The pattern was similar to that of the conferences between Scott and Obregón. The Mexicans insisted upon immediate and unconditional withdrawal of the Punitive Expedition as the *sine qua non* before other problems could be considered. The Americans insisted upon security for the border. The Mexicans maintained that the *de facto* government was well able to guarantee security. The Americans doubted this and were skeptical of the Mexican contention that Villa was now powerless to harm. The American doubts and position were strengthened in the early autumn by the sudden resurrection of Pancho Villa at the head of an "army,"

[44] *Ibid.,* p. 599.   [45] *Ibid.,* pp. 600–605.   [46] *Ibid.,* pp. 606–607.

scattering the Carranzistas before him in Chihuahua. Even this did not cause the Mexicans to change their stand. At length the conference was adjourned, as much a failure as all previous conferences in solving basically the disputes between the two nations. The results, however, were not completely negative. The conference provided a lengthy period in which passions could cool and a sane appraisal of all factors could be taken by responsible officials. In averting what appeared in the early summer to be an inevitable war, the conference was a success. Possibly the hope or expectation of this was the underlying reason that Carranza suggested it and President Wilson accepted.[47]

[47] *Ibid.*, *1917*, pp. 916–938.

☙ XXII ☙

The Last of the Punitive Expedition

DURING the months following the Columbus raid and during the long period of tension with Carranza's *de facto* government, the border people were understandably nervous, and none more so than those who lived adjacent to the territory where Villa had operated for so long. As in the Spanish-American War, when seaboard communities demanded that a battleship, or at least an armored cruiser, be anchored nearby, the border communities with one voice demanded military protection. They had greater reason for apprehension than the people of the Atlantic coast in 1898, but unfortunately the small Regular Army of 1916 could not be stretched beyond a certain point.[1]

Shortly after the raid Senator Fall received a letter from D. A. Richardson, of Douglas, Arizona, saying that the Mexican general in Agua Prieta, ten city blocks distant from the very center of Douglas, had forty pieces of artillery. There were seven thousand Mexican cavalry stationed six miles to the south, while the total garrison at Douglas was only eighteen hundred infantry and three hundred cavalry, two full miles out of the town.[2] Evidently lacking faith in the ability of the United States Army to protect them, citizens of Douglas

---

[1] The writer has had occasion to note several similar instances, such as a demand, early in 1942, by the mayor of a small Kansas city for a balloon barrage over his city immediately, for protection against Japanese and German air raids.

[2] *Cong. Record*, 64 Cong., 1 sess., p. 4741.

and Bisbee (about twenty miles distant) organized themselves into a semimilitary local defense company, prepared to resist a bandit raid on either town.[3]

The inhabitants of southeastern Arizona seemed unusually sensitive to any suggestion of bandits. Villistas were seen lurking behind every mesquite bush. Early in July, 1916, rumor located a band of fifty Mexican bandits hiding in the Chiricahua Mountains, preparing to raid the ranches of the San Simon Valley. Rumor even specified that the first raid would take place on July 9, when the store at Chiricahua Siding was to be looted. At Douglas, 1st Lieutenant Jonathan M. Wainwright, commanding Troop C, 1st Cavalry, recieved orders late in the afternoon of July 8 to march at once to the threatened place. Marching all night through a driving Arizona summer rainstorm, Wainwright reached Chiricahua Siding at daybreak, having covered forty miles. There was no visible sign of bandits, but inquiry placed them in Teck's Cañon. Pushing his weary men and horses into the mountains, Wainwright found the Mexicans—a peaceful party of local woodcutters gathering firewood.[4]

Three days before the clash at Carrizal and as soon as the government knew of Treviño's communication to Pershing, President Wilson took the unprecedented step, on June 18, of ordering the entire National Guard into Federal service for duty on the border. The Guard of the border states, except California, had been mobilized earlier, on the recommendation of Scott and Funston, when it became apparent that the conference with Obregón was going to accomplish nothing. Through the last ten days of June and the first week of July troop trains from all parts of the Union rolled toward the border.[5] In varying degrees of preparation for field service, with considerable disorder and disorganization, with miscellaneous equipment, but with wholehearted enthusiasm, the National Guard settled itself in camps and stations from Brownsville to the Pacific Ocean. Most of

[3] Robert Glass Cleland, *A History of Phelps Dodge, 1834–1950* (New York, 1952), p. 174.

[4] Jonathan M. Wainwright, "A Forced March," *United States Cavalry Journal,* XXVII (April, 1917), 186–188. Wainwright was the defender of Corregidor in World War II. The normal day's march for cavalry was about twenty-five miles.

[5] New York *Times,* Monday, June 19, 1916, 1:7–9; Thursday, June 22, 1916, 1:4; Saturday, June 24, 1916, 1:3. Cf. *Literary Digest,* LIII (July–Dec., 1916), 54–56.

the units were below strength, and the staff and the railroads were so unaccustomed to large-scale troop movements that the amateur soldiers were not too comfortable while en route. From Cleveland, Ohio, came the story that guardsmen raided a commission house because they had not eaten for thirty-six hours. Units arrived at El Paso without uniforms. At San Antonio, when a troop train was delayed by a broken rail, the train commander at once formed his men for defense against the anticipated Mexican attack.[6]

Under the law of the time the National Guard could not be required to serve outside the United States, and its combat value was questionable without a lengthy period of training. Still, its presence on the border gave the people a feeling of security and made the slender Regular Army forces available for whatever the future might bring forth. The Guard was consequently received with unconcealed pleasure by both civilians and military.

If the local population received them joyfully, the guardsmen themselves were not so happy when they saw the country in which they were to spend the next several months. Men accustomed only to the summer green of the Mississippi Valley and Atlantic seaboard or to the great cities of the country were horrified at the desolation of the border desert.

During the interminable dispute with Carranza, little or nothing had been heard of Villa himself. He was known to have been wounded, and there were persistent rumors that he was dead, but otherwise he dropped from the news in the summer of 1916.[7] But Villa was tough, and he still had thousands of admirers and devoted followers among the people of Durango and Chihuahua. Then suddenly came a message from Zach Cobb on September 1, saying that a battle between Carranzistas and bandits near Satevo, which had previously been reported as a government victory, was a stunning victory for Villa, who was very much alive. He had killed an estimated two hundred Carranzistas and driven the remainder north in disorder. There were unconfirmed reports that he had whipped the government forces again near Santa Ysabel and then disappeared into the mountains.[8]

---

[6] Earle E. Perrenot, "The National Guard Fiasco," *Out West Magazine*, XLIV (1916), 76–77. Cf. the *Independent*, LXI (July–Dec., 1916), 75–77, and *World's Work*, XXXII (May–Oct., 1916), 485–486.

[7] Tompkins, *Chasing Villa*, pp. 80–88.   [8] *Foreign Relations, 1916*, p. 608.

Three weeks later the news was still more startling. Pancho Villa, who, the Carranzistas had claimed, was either dead or so completely beaten as to be innocuous, suddenly descended upon the city of Chihuahua. The Mexican Embassy in Washington made haste to assure the State Department that this was merely a flash in the pan. General Treviño's forces in the city had successfully driven the raider away with heavy losses, and reports that a large part of the Chihuahua garrison had joined Villa were utterly without truth.[9] The embassy's information, nevertheless, was at variance with that which came to the American military authorities from several different sources. General Funston was informed that Villa's raid upon Chihuahua was a huge success. Villa liberated the prisoners from the penitentiary, secured some sixteen automobile loads of small arms and ammunition, and left the city with fifteen hundred men more than he had when he entered. The volunteers joining him included Treviño's personal bodyguard and most of the artillerymen of the garrison.[10] Villa was again a factor in the Mexican situation, and a factor that could not be ignored. Within a few days his influence and his authority were again paramount over a large part of his old territory.[11]

In spite of Villa's sudden revival, the press reported early in September that both Funston and Pershing believed that the time had come to withdraw the Punitive Expedition from Mexico. Pershing was quoted as having said that Villa's prestige was so shaken that he could not be a serious factor in affairs.[12] If Pershing ever made such a statement and recommendation, by September 25 he had revised his opinion. On that date he wrote to General Scott, saying, among other things: "The Mexican people were very proud of Villa's raid [upon Columbus]." Pershing believed that the Punitive Expedition had punctured the Mexican popular idea that Villa could drive the Americans out of Mexico whenever he might choose to do so. Pershing regarded the actual capture or killing of Villa himself as not important. "[It] would accomplish little, as far as Mexico is concerned. Other bandits would take his place."[13] By the opening of November, with Villa's power increasing daily in spite of halfhearted efforts by the Carranzistas to

[9] *Ibid.*, pp. 610–611.   [10] *Ibid.*   [11] *Ibid.*, p. 612.
[12] *Independent*, LXXXVII (Sept. 24, 1916), 328. The writer has been unable to verify this statement from any authoritative source and is inclined to doubt that Pershing made it. Pershing never spoke on political topics.
[13] John J. Pershing Papers, personal letter from Pershing to Scott, Sept. 25, 1916.

scotch it, Pershing was constrained to report that Villa's prestige was growing and the numbers of his forces increasing, although there was reason to believe that the increase in strength was largely due to whole-sale impressments.[14]

An immediate and striking effect of the sudden recrudescence of Villa's power was the instant end of the possibility that President Wilson would withdraw the Punitive Expedition at once. On October 9 Scott notified Pershing: "The President prefers to keep you where you are for the present."[15] The President wanted the expedition to remain as a threat until the disputes with Carranza were finally re-solved, but Villa added to the reasons for keeping it in Mexico.

Villa's revival was almost a guarantee that the commissioners meet-ing at New London (later at Atlantic City) would be unable to devise a formula by which the disagreements between the United States and Carranza's government could be settled. The Mexican commissioners, as has been mentioned, insisted upon the immediate and unconditional withdrawal of the Punitive Expedition before any other matters could be considered or discussed. The American commissioners could not seriously entertain any assurances from a government "whose ability to fulfill any obligations that might be incurred . . . had been placed in serious doubt."[16]

Villa's sudden raid into the city of Chihuahua in September as-tonished everybody who believed that his cause was dead or dying, but a second descent upon the city, on November 23, was even more unbelievable. There were three days of confused and bitter fighting in the suburbs and city, and the Carranzistas fled. The occupation of the city by the Villistas was brief and was marked by excesses that Villa had carefully avoided at the height of his power. The unfor-tunate Chinese of the city were the chief sufferers; scores of them were massacred in cold blood.[17]

Spectacular though Villa's sudden success was, it lacked substance. Government forces, by December 7, had regained possession of Chihuahua after some hard fighting. Yet it is possible that Villa was fighting primarily to gain artillery and munitions and had no idea of attempting to retain his conquest. All intelligence reports agreed that each time Villa left Chihuahua he had more men and a greater supply

[14] *Foreign Relations, 1916,* pp. 612–613.   [15] John J. Pershing Papers.
[16] *Foreign Relations, 1917,* p. 917.   [17] *Ibid., 1916,* pp. 617–619.

of munitions than when he entered. From his post in the vicinity of Casas Grandes, General Pershing was watching the situation with concern. Telegraphing to the department commander, he urged that he be authorized to move at once "against this pretender," whose growth should be nipped in the bud.[18]

Whatever may have been Villa's real hopes and motives in the fall of 1916, there was one small group of Americans who had no doubts at all as to what lay back of his revival. The ultraliberals, whose spokesman was Lincoln Steffens, were sure that Villa was moving in obedience to the dictates of sinister capitalistic interests. On October 6 Steffens wrote to Colonel E. M. House, hoping thereby to bring what he had to say to the President's personal attention: "Just before I left New York . . . I was told convincingly that 'Wall Street' had completed arrangements for one more raid of Mexican bandits into the United States; to be timed and so atrocious that it would 'settle the election;' beat Wilson and elect Hughes." [19] This "tip" was not intended for public circulation, but Steffens was anxious that his overall estimate of the Mexican situation, and the influences really back of the turmoil, should be given to the whole American people. He wrote:

While Carranza and his young, inexpert, but very earnest cabinet are struggling with the many, many problems of reconstruction and peace, the *émigrés* and the other old masters of Mexico are trying to find and finance in Havana, London, and El Paso a Napoleon: Pancho Villa; Felix Diaz— any strong enough to lead a new army into Mexico for another war to "save the distracted people from themselves," and yet weak and wicked enough to deliver them back to the old system.[20]

The presidential election of 1916 came during the most spectacular phase of Villa's reascent to power and while the commissioners of the two nations were futilely attempting to settle grievances and differences. In April, a few days after the Parral incident, "Colonel" George Harvey, originally a Wilson supporter but latterly one of the President's most bitter and vociferous opponents, predicted that Pancho Villa and Wilson's former support of him would be a major campaign issue.[21] For months past the President's political enemies had never lost

[18] *Ibid.*, p. 623.   [19] Steffens, *The Letters of Lincoln Steffens*, I, 386.
[20] Steffens, "Making Friends with Mexico," *Collier's Magazine*, LVIII (Nov. 25, 1916), 5.
[21] *Collier's Magazine*, LVII (April 22, 1916), 18.

an opportunity to bring up some phase of his Mexican policy, and particularly the favor he once showed Villa, in an effort to discredit him and raise an issue that would defeat him at the polls. For example, Senator Henry Cabot Lodge, with cutting irony, once spoke of a rumor that the administration "felt that he [Villa] must be a good man because he neither drank nor smoked." [22]

The opposition tried bravely to make a major issue of Mexico in the 1916 presidential campaign. The Republican platform was conveniently vague as to what that party would do if it attained office but left no doubt that the President's Mexican policy was 100 per cent mistaken. The Republican candidate, in his speech of acceptance on July 31, excoriated the policies and methods that had been followed. In somewhat less dignified and more forceful terms, ex-President Theodore Roosevelt blamed Wilson for Santa Ysabel, for Columbus, and for "The Humiliation of the Army." [23]

The Democrats contended that their opponents wanted active intervention in Mexico—a desire inspired by the reactionary monopolists of the Republican Party who wanted the old regime restored in Mexico. This was a point which the President's supporters belabored at considerable length. They made little mention of Villa but stressed the promise of peace for Mexico which would result from the Carranza regime.[24]

However vehement the Republicans were in denouncing President Wilson's Mexican policies or however enthusiastic the Democrats may have been in endorsing them, it is highly doubtful that the Mexican issue played any noteworthy part in determining the outcome of the election. Other issues of greater importance and more direct interest engaged the attention of the voters. The important fact was that President Wilson's re-election meant the continuation of his Mexican policy.

The year 1916 ended with Mexico still rumbling with dangers for the United States. The Punitive Expedition still occupied Mexican soil without the benefit of Carranza's blessing. Petty bandits raided across the line and were pursued into Mexico by United States soldiers, and Pancho Villa was again on the loose, gaining power and prestige,

[22] *Cong. Record*, 63 Cong., 3 sess., p. 1018.

[23] *Republican Campaign Text Book, 1916*, pp. 4–8, 48–49, 171–183.

[24] *Democratic Text Book, 1916*, pp. 13–14, 55–78. The parts of the Democratic platform referring to Mexico were written by Lincoln Steffens.

as well as arms, recruits, and munitions. On Christmas Eve he drove the Carranza forces from his old stronghold of Torreón, recouped his treasury by a forced loan, and made a rabble-rousing speech, telling how he would soon drive Pershing from Mexico. He offered no violence to foreigners of the city, except the unhappy Chinese, who seemed to have replaced the Spaniards as the objects of his particular aversion.[25]

In spite of Villa's reappearance, he did not seem now to menace the border or vital American interests. His zone of operations was deep in Chihuahua, and the mobilization of the National Guard gave local protection to all areas likely to be profitable targets for raids. The Punitive Expedition was merely marking time at Casas Grandes, and meanwhile the war clouds over the Atlantic were deepening and becoming darker day by day. Early in January, 1917, Consul General Philip Hanna advised the State Department that in his "candid opinion . . . the withdrawal of the American troops from Chihuahua would produce satisfactory results and would place the responsibility for restoring order in Mexico on the *de facto* government where it belongs." [26]

On January 30, 1917, General Funston reported to the War Department that the withdrawal from Mexico had commenced and would be completed on February 5. On that date Pershing telegraphed from Columbus: "Expeditionary forces returning from Mexico crossed line to-day, last troops leaving Mexico at 3 P.M." [27]

Some minor diplomatic problems attended the retirement of the expedition. First, what should be done with the prisoners captured in Mexico? All of them, twenty-one in number, were tentatively identified as having been in the Columbus raid and hence were criminals wanted in New Mexico to answer charges of murder. After consideration, Pershing was ordered to bring them to the United States, where he confined them in the post stockade at Columbus, to be held until the civil authorities decided what to do with them.[28] The second problem was more difficult. Scores of terrified and helpless Chinese had fled to the safety of the Punitive Expedition's lines when Villa started his pogrom against them. In common decency and humanity they could not be left to Villa's mercy, but the entry of Chinese into the United States was forbidden by law. General Funston courageously took

[25] *Foreign Relations, 1916*, p. 624. Cf. *Foreign Relations, 1917*, p. 905.
[26] *Foreign Relations, 1917*, p. 904.   [27] *Ibid.*, pp. 907–908.   [28] *Ibid.*

the responsibility of authorizing Pershing to bring them across the border with the expedition. A series of conferences between high officials in Washington finally resulted in authorization of food and other necessities for them and their eventual formal admission into the United States to work for the army.[29]

The Punitive Expedition did not capture Villa, and for that reason many have considered it a humiliating failure. There were no tangible trophies except a few machine guns, some small arms, and twenty-one prisoners. Because of the expedition, the United States and Mexico had stood on the brink of war for months. But the results were not all negative; it cannot be considered the total failure that many critics have made of it. In spite of the renaissance of his power and his fulminations against the United States, Villa never again posed a serious threat. Too little attention has been paid to the fact that the warlike ardor of the *de facto* government cooled appreciably after word got about of the losses their forces suffered at Carrizal. Indeed, the Mexican losses in that tragic and unnecessary little fight were so severe that many Mexicans are convinced that American strength was several times what it actually was.[30] The Punitive Expedition was not the spectacular success it would have been if it had brought Pancho Villa, in handcuffs, back to Columbus. But the profit, while not tangible, was nonetheless real.

Nor was the profit resulting from the expedition entirely in the fields of politics and diplomacy. The United States Army was customarily spread over the country in widely scattered small posts and stations. Since 1911 the bulk of the mobile forces had been deployed along the border from the Gulf of Mexico to the Pacific Ocean. Under such circumstances there was no possibility at all of training under centralized direction, of accustoming the staff to handling and providing for large masses of troops in the field. There was little or no opportunity for any senior officer to observe and evaluate subordinates under war conditions. The Punitive Expedition, by the mere fact of its existence over

[29] *Ibid.*, pp. 1088–1092.

[30] 1st Capt. Daniel González, whose account of the fight has been cited, estimated the American strength at two hundred. Col. Genevevo Rivas Guillén, who succeeded in command of the Mexicans upon General Gómez' death, believed that the Americans numbered at least one hundred and fifty, while other Mexican writers have placed the figure as high as four hundred. Cf. Salinas Carranza, *La Expedición Punitiva,* pp. 294–295.

a period of several months, did much to correct these deficiencies. As soon as active operations ceased, General Pershing instituted a program of intensive training and of experiment with equipment and methods, the like of which had never before been essayed in the army.[31] The troops grumbled, as soldiers always will; some of the officers would not have felt flattered at what the general said about them in his reports to the department commander, but they trained with an intensity that was previously unknown. Not least, General Pershing came to the fore as a determined and skillful troop leader, practical in his methods and ruthless in driving his subordinates to the objective. For both himself and his officers and men, the Punitive Expedition was a first-class school for a greater expedition that was to follow within a few months.

[31] John J. Pershing Papers. Cf. National Archives, Punitive Expedition Records, Box 70, and 1st Lieut. George S. Patton, "Cavalry Work of the Punitive Expedition," *United States Cavalry Journal,* XXVII (1917), 426–433. The latter is the Patton who became famous in World War II.

≫ XXIII ≪

Villa, the United States, and Germany

THUS far, in considering the impact of the United States and Pancho Villa upon each other, it has been possible to say with reasonable assurance that certain events occurred because of certain preceding events. For example, the bitter dispute with Carranza would not have occurred if Villa had not raided into the United States and murdered American citizens in their own homes. In addition to such direct results, there are indications that Villa's raid into New Mexico may have had indirect repercussions, the ultimate effects of which were far-reaching beyond the wildest imagination of the moment. Villa's action probably influenced the policies of Imperial Germany, and thus affected the entire warring world of 1917. Admittedly, such an outcome of Villa's rage at the United States cannot be proved beyond doubt, but the possibility and the evidence are worth considering.

During all the time the Punitive Expedition was in Mexico, the war in Europe continued unabated. From the start, the United States had tried to maintain a strict neutrality, but the actual conditions of the war, including a tight blockade of Germany through the over-whelming power of the British fleet, made the position of the United States one of nonbelligerency rather than of real neutrality. Notwith-standing the large number of Americans of German descent who were sentimentally sympathetic toward the Fatherland, the unconcealed sympathies of the vast majority of the American people were in favor of France and Great Britain. This feeling was strengthened by the German invasion of Belgium, the severity of the subsequent military government in that unhappy country, and such stupidities as the sinking of the *Lusitania* and the execution of Edith Cavell. Germany's submarine warfare, in a desperate attempt to overcome British naval superiority, shocked public sentiment in the United States. The result was an acrimonious interchange, concluding eventually with a German pledge to observe the recognized rules of warfare at sea.[1]

With Great Britain controlling the sea, the Allies were able to supplement their own resources by huge purchases in the United States. Beginning early in the war, an increasing volume of munitions and supplies of all sorts poured from the United States into Great Britain and France. The Allies' burden was greatly eased by their ability to avail themselves of the markets and factories of the United States, while Germany and Austria-Hungary were correspondingly handicapped. Any action by Germany which would divert part of the stream of war materials into other channels would be clear gain for itself. If the United States were to become deeply involved in Mexico, the greater part of the weapons and munitions being produced in American plants would be needed in America and would never reach the Western Front.

To just what extent the continued turmoil in Mexico, Villa's raid, Carranza's intransigence, and the rabid hatred of the United States shown by Mexicans of all classes may have been due to subtle German efforts is impossible to say with any certainty. Nearly fifty years have passed since those events, and normally all documentary records of such activities are carefully and quickly destroyed. That President Wilson suspected strongly that the situation in Mexico was not altogether spontaneous was shown by remarks he made to his trusted private secretary, Joseph Patrick Tumulty. Speaking privately, the President predicted that some day the American people would understand why he hesitated to intervene in Mexico. The reason was that Germany was anxious to have American attention and effort directed away from the war in Europe. A war between the United States and Mexico would accomplish that purpose. "It begins to look as if war with Germany is inevitable," the President concluded. "If it should

[1] *Foreign Relations, 1915, Supplement,* p. 526.

come—I pray God it may not—I do not wish America's energies and forces divided, for we shall need every ounce of reserve we have to lick Germany."[2]

In different terms, but in much the same sense, Secretary of State Robert Lansing recorded in his private diary a few days before the recognition of Carranza: "Germany desires to keep up the turmoil in Mexico until the United States is forced to intervene. . . . When we recognize a faction as the Government, Germany will undoubtedly seek to cause a quarrel between that government and ours."[3]

The evidence upon which President Wilson and Secretary Lansing based their opinions has never been revealed, but they were not men who would form such opinions without ample reason. Numerous circumstantial items indicate that there was real substance behind their views.

It was reported that a grand-jury investigation in New York City brought out that German financial support had been extended to both Carranza and Villa. The statement was made that in eighteen months over three hundred Americans were killed in Mexico, while during the same period not a single German lost his life, by either accident or design. Newspaper reports told of new German faces being seen in Mexico, and it was asserted that orders had been found directing a German reserve officer living in New York City to proceed to Mexico for duty.[4] Mexicans were not lacking who suspected that Germany was, in some way, involved in the troubles of their country. Manuel Palacios Roji, a Carranzista sympathizer, asserted that huge sums of German money were expended in the promotion of Villa's fortunes, a belief in which many American officials were inclined to concur.[5] So widespread and accepted was the belief that German in-

[2] Joseph Patrick Tumulty, *Woodrow Wilson as I Know Him* (Garden City, N.Y., 1921), p. 159.

[3] Robert Lansing, *Diary*, quoted in Arthur S. Link, *Woodrow Wilson and the Progressive Era, 1910–1917* (New York, 1954), p. 134, note.

[4] Randolph Wellford Smith, *Benighted Mexico* (New York, 1916), pp. 13, 165, 189–190.

[5] Manuel Palacios Roji, *La mano de Alemania en México* (Mexico City, 1919), pp. 119–120. Cf. John Price Jones, *America Entangled: The Secret Plotting of German Spies in the United States and the Inside Story of the Sinking of the Lusitania*, introd. by Roger B. Wood, former assistant U.S. attorney in New York (New York, 1917), pp. 144–146. This is a somewhat lurid "popular" account, but it purports to be based upon official documents. Cf. also Link, *Woodrow Wilson and the Progressive Era*, p. 200. note.

fluence was promoting the troubles between the United States and Mexico that a National Guardsman, bored with the monotony of border duty, surmised that the lull in activity was probably caused by a delay in the remittance of German gold.[6]

To cite other items of purely circumstantial evidence or other rumors that gained wide acceptance in 1916 and 1917 would be repetitious. The evidence that Germany was responsible for the anti-United States activities and attitude of Villa and Carranza is inconclusive and would not for one moment stand the scrutiny of a historian who demands documentation. In this case, however, the lack of tangible evidence does not logically lead to a historical verdict of not guilty. The successful espionage agent or *agent provocateur* seldom leaves records to satisfy the curiosity of future historians; if he were to do so, he would not last very long. To suppose for a moment that the lack of documentary evidence of German activities in Mexico is proof that such activities did not exist—that Germany was overlooking a golden opportunity to weaken its enemies and prevent a possible accession to their ranks—is somewhat naïve. The famous Zimmerman note did not spring spontaneously in a void but must have had a carefully prepared basis.

German interest in what was happening between Mexico and the United States in the spring of 1916 is amply demonstrated by the amount of attention the German press gave to the Columbus raid and subsequent events. German newspapers did not, of course, give as much space to the raid as American newspapers, but in view of the remoteness of the incident from Europe and the critical and gigantic battles the German Army was fighting at that time, the attention given to the situation in Mexico was extraordinary.[7] One Berlin newspaper was careful to inform its readers that a large number of American cavalrymen were killed by Mexicans in the raid and that the Punitive Expedition might result in a widespread war against Mexico.[8]

After the Carrizal fight the German newspapers blossomed out with

[6] Roger Batchelder, *Watching and Waiting on the Border* (Boston and New York, 1917), p. 207.

[7] The writer bases this statement upon a detailed examination of the extensive collection of German newspapers of World War I in the library of the Hoover Institution on War, Revolution, and Peace, Stanford University.

[8] Cf. the Berlin *Vossische Zeitung*, March 9 and 10, 1916, and the *Berliner lokal Anzeiger*, March 10, 11, 15, 1916.

large headlines: "Der amerikanische-mexikanische Konflikt," "Der Konflikt mit Mexiko," "Zuspitzung der Lage in Mexiko." [9] The Berlin *Continental Times,* an English-language propaganda newspaper, through the entire spring of 1916 freely predicted war between the United States and Mexico and did not seem to be the least disturbed at the prospect. Its report of the Carrizal fight stated that one hundred Americans were taken prisoner by the Mexicans—a figure somewhat in excess of all other estimates, including the Mexican.[10]

The hopeful belief that a full-scale war in Mexico would effectively prevent the United States from taking an active role in wider affairs was based on a conviction that the United States was, in a military sense, practically impotent. Accustomed to a carefully prepared organization ready for war at all times and convinced that they themselves were the most competent soldiers in the world, the German military heads were traditionally contemptuous of the American forces improvised for each war as it occurred. Both popular and professional military opinion of the United States Army was summarized in 1911, at the time of the Moroccan crisis, by a Colonel Gaedke, reputed to be a "famous military critic and specialist," in the *Berliner Tageblatt:*

The United States does not possess any army in the full sense of the term. All that the Government at Washington can put into the field is a collection of disjointed fragments of troops of the various arms without any unity or cohesion. . . . The American Army is wanting in reserves, in commissariat, in training. There are really no military railroads in the country, no proper means of transport, and practically no officers. The Army is deficient in training and in everything else that is necessary for the constitution of an armed force.[11]

Colonel Gaedke's supercilious opinion of the military capabilities of the United States was fully shared by the responsible higher officers of the German Army. On May 3, 1916, the Chief of the General Staff, General Erich von Falkenhayn, sent a memorandum to the Imperial Chancellor, referring to "the secret war in which [the United States] . . . has long been engaged against us" and offering the opinion that

[9] *Leipziger neueste Nachrichten,* June 23, 1916; *Berliner Börsen Zeitung,* morning edition, June 23, 1916; Berlin *Täglische Rundschau,* June 21, 1916.

[10] Berlin *Continental Times: A Journal for Americans in Europe,* June 26, 1916.

[11] "German Scorn for Our Army," *Literary Digest,* XLII (April 1, 1911), 617–618.

open American hostility would not make the slightest difference to Germany.[12] The Punitive Expedition and the subsequent mobilization of the National Guard confirmed German opinion of the military impotence of the United States. A noted military critic and writer, Colonel Friedrich Immanuel, estimated that not more than fifty thousand men of the Regular Army could be made available for a war in Mexico, while the highest number of National Guardsmen would not be over eighty thousand—and their combat value would be highly questionable. To expand these small forces into an army large enough for a war in Mexico would take a long time, and the effort would be greatly complicated by the low esteem in which the warlike spirit was held in the United States. Mexico, Immanuel believed, was much better organized for war and the Mexican people were innately much more warlike. Consequently, all advantages would rest with Mexico. He solemnly suggested that in the coming war it would be well for the United States to remain strictly on the defensive and protect the frontiers against Mexican invasion.[13]

Germany's hopeful belief that the Punitive Expedition proved that the United States could take no effective military action in world affairs was strengthened by a telegram, on July 25, 1916, from Count von Bernstorff, the German ambassador in Washington. By some unrevealed means the message fell into the hands of the ubiquitous British naval intelligence, presided over by Admiral Sir Reginald Hall: "It becomes clearer and clearer that the American Government has drawn back from a rupture because her military resources are not sufficient to face a war with Mexico. On every hand there was an absence of the first necessities of war. . . . The decision . . . rests with Carranza and Villa." [14]

In the full conviction that the United States was really helpless and could do no more than try to bluff, the chiefs of the German Empire met at General Headquarters at Pless Castle on August 31, 1916, to

[12] Carnegie Endowment for International Peace, *German Official Documents Relating to the World War* (New York, 1923), II, 1151–1152. Hereafter referred to as Carnegie Endowment, *German Documents.*

[13] Friedrich Immanuel, Colonel, Imperial German Army, Retired, "The Military Forces of Mexico and the United States," *Leipziger neueste Nachrichten,* June 24, 1916. Colonel Immanuel was the author of numerous works on military history and tactics, as well as several general works on German history.

[14] Admiral Sir William James, *The Eyes of the Navy: A Biographical Study of Admiral Sir Reginald Hall* (London, 1953), p. 124.

confer on ways and means of bringing the war to a victorious end. The Imperial Chancellor was present, along with Field Marshal von Hindenburg, General Erich Ludendorff, Admiral von Capelle, several cabinet ministers, and other officials of the highest rank. Unrestricted submarine warfare, which would probably bring the United States into war, was debated pro and con at great length. No decision was reached at that time, but there can be no doubt that most, if not all, of the officials present felt that Germany could safely ignore the United States. The reopening of submarine warfare was purely a matter of expediency for Germany to decide at its own convenience and without regard to anything that the United States might do.[15] Germans could not believe that there was any danger from a country that was unable to mobilize its reserve forces promptly for lack of sleeping cars, nor could they believe that an improvised army composed of "cowboys and roughriders" would constitute any military threat on the Western Front.[16] If anything, a declaration of war by the United States would benefit Germany by cutting down on the shipments of arms and munitions to the British and French.[17]

According to Count von Bernstorff, the final decision to unleash the submarines without regard to consequences was not taken until January 9, 1917, but meanwhile active preparations had gone on quietly.[18] In October, 1916, the German minister in Mexico City reported that Carranza was very friendly toward Germany and was willing to support German submarines in Mexican waters. Two weeks later the Foreign Ministry in Berlin directed the minister in Mexico City to sound out Carranza on the establishment of submarine bases in Mexican territory, hinting at substantial rewards if Mexico agreed.[19] It is worthy of note that President Wilson's trusted personal adviser, Colonel E. M. House, had warned him that a display of apparent powerlessness in Mexico would strongly influence Germany's attitude,

[15] Carnegie Endowment, *German Documents*, II, 1154–1163.
[16] James W. Gerard, *Face to Face with Kaiserism* (New York, 1918), p. 107. "The statement in the American papers that our National Guard could not mobilize for Mexico because of lack of sleeping cars caused much ridicule here, where they go to the front in cattle cars."
[17] *Ibid.*, p. 259.
[18] Count Johann von Bernstorff, *Memoirs* (New York, 1936), p. 152.
[19] James, *The Eyes of the Navy*, pp. 135–136.

by convincing the Germans that they could reach final victory before the United States could become a decisive factor in the war.[20]

Having made the irrevocable decision and being thoroughly convinced that the United States could not interfere, Foreign Minister Zimmermann and the Minister of Marine, Admiral von Capelle, appeared before a secret meeting of the Finance Committee of the Reichstag on January 31, 1917, to allay any fears and doubts that the Reichstag might have. Zimmermann belittled any menace from America. Admiral von Capelle was specific: "From a military point of view [America's entrance into the war] means nothing. I repeat: *From a military point of view America is as nothing.* I am convinced that almost no American will volunteer for war service. That is shown by the lack of volunteers for the conflict with Mexico." [21] At six o'clock that same evening, while Pershing's tired troopers were marching toward the border, Ambassador Gerard, in Berlin, was notified that at twelve midnight, only six hours away, unrestricted submarine warfare would begin.[22]

Whether or not the United States would have taken the decisive stand against Germany that it did in the winter of 1917 if the Punitive Expedition against Pancho Villa had developed into a full-scale war is a question the answer to which must remain for all time in the realm of pure speculation. One cannot doubt that the chiefs of the German Empire fervently and devoutly hoped that Villa's raid upon Columbus would result in drying up the stream of munitions and war material flowing from the ports of the United States to the armies of Germany's enemies. Likewise, anybody who could doubt for a moment that the Germans were more than willing to do anything within their ability and power to bring about such a result would be more than naïve— he would be guilty of self-deception. It was ironical that President Wilson's stiff determination that the United States must not become involved in a major and totally unnecessary war in Mexico was misinterpreted in Germany as a demonstration of military weakness. If

[20] Howard F. Cline, *The United States and Mexico* (Cambridge, Mass., 1953), p. 179.

[21] Hans Peter Hanssen, *Diary of a Dying Empire,* trans. by Oscar O. Winther (Bloomington, Ind., 1953), pp. 162, 170. Hanssen was a member of the Finance Committee and was present at the secret session mentioned. The italics are his.

[22] James W. Gerard, *My Four Years in Germany* (New York, 1917), p. xi.

Francisco Villa, primitively intent upon vengeance by killing Americans and damaging the United States to the best of his limited ability, had been deliberately deceiving Germany into the belief that the United States was completely negligible, he could not have been more success-ful. With visual proof that the United States could not mobilize a huge army at a moment's notice and that the entire available military strength of the United States was concentrated in the desert wastes of the border, Germany knew that its hour had come. The proof is cir-cumstantial and inferential, though nonetheless convincing. An indirect but very real line of descent connects Pancho Villa with the first Amer-ican Expeditionary Force in France.

⍦ XXIV ⍦

End of the Trail for Villa

ON April 6, 1917, the United States declared war against Imperial Germany. From that moment Pancho Villa and affairs in Mexico ceased to be of major importance to the United States except insofar as they affected the war effort against Germany. The border still remained turbulent, with little groups of bandits frequently trying their luck by raiding and looting in the United States. Small forces of United States troops repeatedly crossed the international line in pursuit of raiders, to the perpetual indignation of Carranza's government. There was, however, one important difference in the situation. The expansion of the United States Army from a mere handful to a force of several millions of men made larger forces available for patrolling and border protection. The vast army that the United States was shortly pouring across the Atlantic undoubtedly gave the truculent Mexican leaders food for thought. Carranza never again threatened the United States with war, nor did Pancho Villa make any attempt to carry out the bloodcurdling threats he was supposed to have made.

Although, with the declaration of war against Germany, Mexican affairs declined in relative importance to the United States, it did not mean that Mexico was ignored or that Mexican matters were neglected. From the start there was no doubt where Mexican sympathies lay in the world conflict. Mexicans had been too long accustomed to regard the Colossus of the North as their traditional enemy for them to realize just what a German victory would eventually mean. At the formal inauguration of Carranza as constitutional President of Mexico, the German minister was greeted with cheers and applause, while the newly appointed United States ambassador took his seat amid a chorus of hisses and catcalls.[1]

With such overt Mexican antipathy toward the United States, the Germans did not give up hope that the Mexican situation might be shaped to Germany's benefit. In late March, 1917, only a few days before the United States declared war, British naval intelligence learned that Zimmermann had directed the minister in Mexico City, Von Eckhardt, to find out just what kinds of munitions and arms Mexico wanted. A few days later it was reported that Germans in Mexico expected to receive three cargoes of munitions consigned to Villa, the cargoes to be landed on the West Coast somewhere between Mazatlán and Manzanillo.[2] In spite of such German efforts, there is no evidence that any appreciable supply of weapons and munitions ever reached Villa or any other Mexican leader from German sources. Allied control of shipping and command of the sea were too thorough and complete, and Allied information too all-pervasive, for more than a relatively minute quantity of war material to slip secretly across the beaches of Mexico.

As for Pancho Villa himself, his star continued to reascend over his old territory in Durango and Chihuahua. He even became confident enough to approach the border again, although he was careful not to step across. In April, 1917, an attack by Villistas forced a small Carranzista garrison to take refuge in the United States, at Ruidosa, Texas, surrendering their arms to United States troops there. On May 30 a sudden descent upon Ojinaga by Villa caused a repetition of the scenes that had taken place there on his arrival in 1914. The Carranzista garrison, like their Huertista predecessors, found safety under the protection of United States forces. Unlike the previous occasion, the United States did not intern the refugees but permitted their immediate return to Mexico to take part in the campaign against Villa.[3]

Villa made no attempt to hold Ojinaga, or even to remain close to the

[1] Maximino Valdes, *Impresiones de México: Prólogo del General Francisco J. Múgica* (Mexico City, 1918), p. 209. Cf. Vicente Blasco Ibañez, *Mexico in Revolution* (New York, 1920), pp. 68–69.

[2] Hendrick, *The Life and Letters of Walter Hines Page*, III, 353.

[3] *Foreign Relations, 1917*, pp. 940–942.

border, but disappeared three days later. One can only guess at his motives and objectives, but it is reasonable to surmise that he needed the arms and ammunition which could be captured at Ojinaga and wanted to prove to the world that Pancho Villa was still a force to be taken into account. There is also the possibility that he wanted temporary contact with the border to receive supplies smuggled to him from the United States.

There was to be no rest for the hapless Carranzista garrison of Ojinaga. On November 15 the Secretary of State was informed that a force of Villistas estimated at a thousand men was again attacking the place. Bullets were falling into the United States, and scores of Mexicans were streaming across the river to safety. Later in the day a message from Cobb said that the Villistas were completely victorious and that three hundred Carranzistas had crossed the Rio Grande and surrendered to the Americans.[4]

The year 1917 provided still other instances of Carranzista soldiers taking refuge in the United States from pursuers, presumably Villistas. The situation became so annoying that Secretary Lansing rather sharply suggested that the *de facto* government would do well to postpone a projected campaign in the oil-field region and devote its energies and resources to safeguarding the border until danger of bandit raids was finally eliminated.[5]

Throughout 1918 Villa kept himself at a safe distance from the border. He continued to build his strength in northern Mexico, particularly in the State of Chihuahua, and kept the Carranza forces off balance by a continual series of pinprick, hit-and-run raids against isolated garrisons and sensitive points. American military authorities watched his activities as closely as possible, and nearly every week intelligence reports included such items as "On July 19th Villista forces defeated a Carranza column near El Mulato, Chihuahua, scattering the Carranzistas, who retreated to Ojinaga." [6]

Villa and his followers did not feature prominently among the makers of direct trouble for the United States during 1918, but his enemies, the Carranzistas, took his place and stood in the front rank. Raid and counterraid kept a large part of the border in a continual turmoil. Each

[4] *Ibid.*, p. 944. [5] *Ibid.*
[6] National Archives, War Department Files, Weekly Report, Headquarters, Southern Department, July 27, 1918.

entry into Mexico by United States troops brought a vehement protest from the Carranza government, which still took no effective measures to prevent raids. Indeed, there was clear evidence in several instances that the raiders were Carranzista soldiers.[7] In spite of this fact, the angry protests by the Carranza government at the repeated violation of Mexican soil by American troops finally brought the Secretary of State to the point of suggesting that United States troops be forbidden to enter Mexico or fire into Mexican territory without specific instructions from the War Department—a suggestion which Secretary Baker refused to approve.[8]

It was clearly apparent through 1918 and well into 1919 that the Revolution and civil war in Mexico were far from settled. The operations necessary for the *de facto* government to maintain itself were much more than mere "mopping up" of scattered rebel bands. The habit of civil war was too deeply implanted in Mexican society by this time, the unsatisfied popular discontent too widespread, to be eliminated immediately. In the summer of 1918 President Wilson's former personal envoy, DuVal West, now the United States district judge at San Antonio, temporarily left his judicial bench at the suggestion of Postmaster General Burleson and made another trip into Mexico. He reported that he was able to persuade a group of revolutionaries who were starting a new movement to lay down their arms, but he was not at all optmistic as to the situation as a whole.[9]

The situation was encouraging for Villa, whose prestige had continued to grow until his followers again constituted a formidable army. His power and activities were handicapped by financial difficulties, but he hoped to be able to correct that. Assembling his forces in the autumn of 1918, after the harvest was in and food and forage were available over the country, he struck and looted Villa Ahumada, on the Juárez-Chihuahua railway. Three Americans, captured near the place, were, to the surprise of everyone, released without being harmed. On December 12 he suddenly raided and looted the mining camp at Cusihuiriáchic, seizing ten thousand dollars from the mining company and burning the company's woodpile. This, he explained, was not an act of vandalism but was to force the company to purchase more wood and

[7] *Foreign Relations, 1918*, pp. 569–570, 574–575.   [8] *Ibid.*, pp. 556–572.
[9] Woodrow Wilson Papers, July, 1918.

thus to provide work for the people.[10] On January 22, 1919, a surprise descent upon the mining camp at Santa Eulalia netted still more funds for the Villa exchequer and gained more prestige for Villa himself. As during his earlier career, in these later movements Villa was careful not to offer any personal harm to Americans and other foreigners. The American consul at Chihuahua explained this *volte-face*:

Americans recently taken and released by Villa feel that if not time, then policy, has somewhat softened his attitude toward them. Once again in command of a considerable force, Villa no doubt has renewed hopes of not only receiving steady contributions from the companies but also . . . recognition as a political factor to be reckoned with and not a mere bandit. Working along this line of thought it should be noted that Villa is now . . . addressing the mine and farm laborers telling them to claim their rights and demand more wages. . . . If . . . no Americans are killed and the companies continue operating it will be said that Villa has again established friendly relations with the Americans, and is not only receiving ammunition from the United States but is also obtaining money from Americans.[11]

In the same report the consul informed the State Department that Villa's greatest single need was ammunition. Nevertheless, there is no indication that lack of ammunition handicapped his operations noticeably. The National Association for the Protection of American Rights in Mexico, a frankly interventionist organization, charged that Villa obtained 60 per cent of his ammunition from the United States, while the remaining 40 per cent was furnished by the Carranzistas, either by capture from them or by downright purchase.[12]

By the spring of 1919 Villa was strong enough to undertake more serious operations than the petty raids of 1917 and 1918. On April 19, at the head of a force estimated at twelve hundred well-mounted, well-equipped men, with Felipe Angeles as his second in command, Villa appeared at Parral without warning. A short battle, a violent assault, and the Villistas were left in undisputed possession of the city, with the Carranzistas scattering in rout. Carefully sealing off the town from communication with the outer world, the Villistas proceeded methodically and systematically to loot. Foreign property and private houses

[10] *Foreign Relations, 1919,* II, 565–567. [11] *Ibid.,* pp. 565–568.
[12] *Fall Committee Report,* pp. 466–468.

were scrupulously respected, although the mining companies were required to make a heavy contribution. Mexican commercial houses were carefully and thoroughly sacked. The net profit for Villa's treasury was estimated at half a million dollars gold—sufficient to buy a considerable quantity of ammunition.[13]

Through the spring of 1919 disorder and revolutionary activity in northern Mexico continued to grow. New recruits joined Villa's ranks, and old supporters rejoined in increasing numbers. In March, Felipe (or Federico) Cervantes, his former chief of staff, was captured near Socorro, Texas, with eighteen men, trying to slip across the international line to join his old chief. The Mexican ambassador in Washington immediately demanded that these men be tried for violation of the United States neutrality laws. They were duly found guilty and were given stiff sentences, but for every one who was caught and tried, probably several dozen were undetected.[14]

Early in June, 1919, it became known that the Villa forces were moving northward toward the border. As a precaution General Peyton C. March, the Chief of Staff of the United States Army (successor to General Scott), telegraphed instructions to the commanding general of the Southern Department to prevent any threat to the United States and authorizing him to move troops into Mexico if necessary. At El Paso, the local commander, Brigadier General James B. Erwin, reported successively on June 11, 12, and 13 that everything was quiet and that he did not anticipate an attack on Juárez by Villa.[15] It was, consequently, something of a surprise when, a few minutes after midnight, June 14–15, Villistas suddenly launched a heavy attack upon Juárez from the east. It was not a surprise in the same sense as that which had occurred at Columbus, for this time the United States forces were on the alert, and Villa's men made no attempt to move out of their own country. Two hours after the initial attack the Villistas were in possession of the greater part of the city, with the Carranzistas taking refuge in the citadel, Fort Hidalgo. At four o'clock a Carranzista counterattack cleared the Villistas out of part of the city, but the battle was not by

---

[13] National Archives, War Department Files, Weekly Report, Headquarters, Southern Department, May 3, 1919. Cf. *Fall Committee Report,* pp. 443–444.

[14] *Foreign Relations, 1919,* II, 555–557.

[15] National Archives, War Department Files, AG 319.1 Mex. Border, 6–30–10, 7–1–18.

any means over. Meanwhile, scores of terrified Chinese took refuge at the United States Immigration Station.[16]

For several hours relative quiet prevailed, but late in the afternoon Villa resumed the attack. He was something of a specialist in night attacks and in the past was usually successful. The volume of fire increased steadily, with bullets frequently striking in United States territory. By nightfall there had been several casualties, with two soldiers and several civilians, including two women, among the wounded. United States forces were in position, in readiness for whatever might happen. Late at night General Erwin received reports that shots from Mexico were striking around the command post of the American artillery and that one soldier had been killed there and another wounded. A quick investigation by Colonel Francis W. Glover, General Erwin's chief of staff, proved beyond doubt that the shots were being fired by Villistas but also that the Carranzistas were not entirely guiltless. Glover risked his life to obtain this information.[17]

General Erwin decided that the situation required action without any further delay. American plans had been laid and preparations made well in advance. With a crash the American artillery opened fire on predetermined targets (according to tradition, the Juárez race track, where a large number of Villistas were known to be encamped). Down the Rio Grande, below Juárez, two cavalry regiments, standing in readiness for hours, crossed the river on a ponton bridge quickly thrown across by the engineers. The movement into Mexico by the cavalry was complete a few minutes before 11 P.M. With the cavalry in position to threaten the Villista retreat, American infantry began crossing directly from El Paso, after Colonel Glover had warned the Carranzistas to "get out of the way if you don't want to be hurt."[18]

The battle did not last long. It was Villa's second personal encounter with American troops, and it was disastrous—even more disastrous than the pursuit after the Columbus raid. Demoralized by the high explosive and shrapnel of the American artillery, fired with an accuracy and

---

[16] *Foreign Relations, 1919*, II, 557.

[17] *Fall Committee Report*, pp. 1573–1576.

[18] *Ibid*. The 7th U.S. Cavalry (Custer's regiment) was commanded by Colonel S. R. H. Tompkins, a fabulous and colorful character affectionately known as "Tommy" Tompkins. He was an elder brother of Major Frank Tompkins, who has been mentioned in several places in this narrative.

rapidity they had never seen before, Villa's men had no stomach to face the cold bayonets of the Negro infantrymen who moved upon them in a steady, relentless line. The Villistas ran to the rear, and shortly after daybreak their retirement was changed into a panic-stricken flight by a galloping pistol attack by the American cavalry. In a few minutes the flight became a wild race for safety—every man for himself. Before the sun was high, the army which Villa had so carefully nurtured for months and which, the evening before, seemed to be on the point of capturing Juárez ceased to exist as a military force. With a few followers Villa himself vanished into the hills, and "Villismo" as a factor in Mexican politics and the international situation vanished, never to be resurrected.

The battle lost, Felipe Angeles attempted to convince General Erwin that the shots which had precipitated American intervention came all from the Carranzistas and were fired with the deliberate intention of forcing intervention. General Villa, he said, had given strict orders against any firing in the direction of the United States. In spite of the high regard which the American officers held for Angeles personally, Erwin and his staff were unconvinced, and in any case, it was too late.[19]

The Carranzistas whom the Americans encountered as they moved into Mexico were unfeignedly glad to see them, and all American troops were back in the United States before noon of June 17. Nevertheless, the local Carranzista commander, General Francisco González, felt it his duty to protest against the violation of Mexican soil, even though the opportune arrival of the Americans had probably saved him from a Villista firing squad. Several days later and long after the last American soldier had recrossed the river, the Carranza government voiced its usual protest and promoted González to the rank of general of division (major general) in recognition of his firmness in maintaining the national dignity.[20] In reply, the United States offered no apologies or explanations beyond the statement that the intervention was a necessary protective measure.

Francisco Villa was nearing the end of his long trail. For several months he wandered, a hunted fugitive, through the mountains of Chihuahua. His faithful coadjutor, Felipe Angeles, was captured and shot. Minor difficulties arose from time to time for which Villa received the blame, as when a band of "Villistas" captured and held for ransom two American aviators who had made a forced landing in Mexican territory.

[19] *Ibid.*   [20] *Foreign Relations, 1919,* II, 535.

A quick thrust by a small column of United States troops saved the aviators but brought grumbles from Carranza. Finally, after his bitter enemy, Venustiano Carranza, had been overthrown and murdered, Villa made his peace with the new regime established by his other old enemy, Alvaro Obregón, and was granted the enormous hacienda of Canutillo, near Parral, in the heart of his old hunting ground.

During his retirement, whatever his feelings may have been about the United States government, Villa seemed to harbor no resentment against individual Americans. On one occasion, making a chance acquaintance of an American while on a railway journey, he spent some time in very friendly conversation, even permitting the American to examine his ivory-gripped revolver and finally showing the scars on his leg, where he had been wounded.[21]

Villa was interviewed at Canutillo by an American journalist, who took his courage in hand and boldly went to the hacienda. A little subtle flattery paved the way, the visitor comparing Villa to Lenin, Sun Yat-sen, Gandhi, and other great revolutionists. Villa softened, showed the school he was preparing for the children of the hacienda, told of the six hundred acres he had planted to wheat, and detailed his plans for stocking the hills with cattle.

"Poor, ignorant Mexico," he said slowly. "Until she has education nothing much can be done for her. I know—I was twenty-five before I could sign my own name. . . . And I know what it is to try to help people who can't understand what you are trying to do for them. I fought ten years for them. I had a principle: I fought ten years so that poor men could live like human beings, have their own land, send their children to school, and have human freedom."

Villa hesitated, and then went on again. "But it wasn't much use. Most of them were too ignorant to understand the ideas. That's the reason why I quit fighting. I fought as long as the traitor Carranza was in power, but now that Obregón is at the head I'd be doing more harm than good, so I stopped. . . . Nothing much can be done at all until the common people are educated."[22]

What might have been the outcome of Villa's social efforts no one can know. Whether or not he remained quietly as a social-minded

[21] Personal letter, dated Oct. 10, 1958, to the writer from Mr. Eugene Weston, Jr., of Los Angeles, who was the American involved.
[22] Frazier Hunt, *One American and His Attempt at Education* (New York, 1938), pp. 232–233.

hacendado, he was a threat to any government in Mexico City by his mere existence. Too many thousands of peons and humble people in the north would be ready to rally to a shout of "Viva Villa!" in case of trouble. On June 21, 1923, leaving Parral in his open car and accompanied by two or three of his faithful "Dorados" as bodyguards, he slowed down at a street intersection. A blast of gunfire from an adobe house at the corner killed him instantly. The threat was over, and Pancho Villa had reached the end of his trail.

≫ XXV ≪

Conclusions

HISTORIANS of the Wilson era have, understandably, concentrated largely on the war with Germany and the issues of domestic reform. As a result, relations with Mexico have been neglected. Nevertheless, between 1913 and 1919, Wilson was faced with serious problems growing out of the Mexican Revolution. The relationships with Francisco Villa were a part of the larger problems of general relations with, and because of, Mexico. For many months the future of Mexico, in which the United States was vitally interested, seemed to lie in his hands. Since the two nations interacted upon each other, Villa would thus influence the future of the United States as well.

The complex and violent situation which arose on the border during the Mexican Revolution was not new. Except for the last two decades of the Díaz regime, a condition of almost continual guerrilla warfare was the normal state of affairs. Raids and counterraids, forays and reprisals, were commonplace. General Pershing's Punitive Expedition was far from being the first American force to penetrate deep into Mexico in pursuit of raiders who had murdered, looted, and burned north of the border. It was the first expedition to pursue a band whose leader had enjoyed a long period of favor, or quasi-recognition, by the United States.

Myth and legend have distorted Pancho Villa until it is difficult to form a reasonable estimate of what the man was really like. To some, the fact that he was a bandit and killer before the Revolution is proof that he was guilty of all the subhuman crimes with which he has been charged, that his social ideals could be no higher than those of a gangster. To others, Villa was a Robin Hood, driven unwillingly into a life of violence and devoting that life unselfishly to robbing the idle rich for the benefit of the deserving poor.

There is no question that he was a man of keen intelligence. He was uneducated, but he was alert, determined, tenacious, and personable enough to captivate such men as General Scott and Paul Fuller. He could arouse almost worshipful adulation in thousands of followers. He was capable of stern self-discipline, but at the same time he was a man with a temper that often made him as dangerous as a wounded tiger.

To conclude, as some have suggested, that Villa joined Madero in 1910 only for increased opportunities for loot—to argue that he never developed beyond being a bandit—is to ignore two obvious facts. First, as an independent freebooter he would have enjoyed opportunities for loot that he could not possibly have had as an officer of Madero's forces. Second, in his later career as an independent commander the booty acquired was uniformly used to maintain his army.

Villa's original motives for joining Madero were probably simple. Because of his early experiences with Porfirian law and justice and his long training in violence, one may assume that revenge was a strong factor in his decision. A Mexican writer who knew him personally has remarked that revenge was always "a constant in his make-up." As a revolutionary with Madero he would be in a position for revenge against the wealthy who had expropriated the earth and against the Díaz officials who were their agents.

Revenge was undoubtedly a major factor, but it is not, by itself, a completely satisfying explanation. Villa's social and political ideas and ideals were probably primitive, but only an enemy could say that he had none or that they were merely the ideals of a robber. Just what was said in Villa's interviews with Madero and Don Abrán González remains unknown. But one may reasonably conclude that they persuaded him that in the Revolution they were planning lay hopes for the future happiness of the Mexican people.

Having joined the Revolution against the interests that were exploiting Mexico, Villa continued remorselessly, according to his own lights, to the end. Not a single item of evidence, beyond the bare assertion of avowed enemies, supports the accusation that he became the tool of reactionaries and foreign capitalists. He was unquestionably influenced by the intellectuals with whom he surrounded himself; he was, by no means, plastic in their hands, as claimed by enemies and paid propagandists.

Villa was consistently friendly toward Americans and co-operative with the United States up to the time when President Wilson recognized Carranza. He was, moreover, too primitive in his emotions, too strong in his passions, to be capable of complete dissimulation. His attitude was in marked contrast with that of other Mexican factional leaders, especially Carranza. That Villa was sincere is proved by too many instances to leave any reasonable doubt.

The recognition of Carranza changed Villa into an open enemy of the United States. Despite his enmity there are some writers who have maintained that he was not personally responsible for the Columbus raid. This contention is not supported by any convincing evidence. Villa was not a man who went halfway, and his hatred was as strong as his friendship. There is ample evidence not only that he was responsible for the Columbus raid but that he personally led it.

Most widespread of the misconceptions regarding Villa is the view that General Pershing's Punitive Expedition was a mortifying failure. This error grows out of the mistaken notion that Pershing's mission was to "take Villa dead or alive." No such orders were given. General Pershing was directed by the Secretary of War to break up and disperse the outlaw band that had raided Columbus. This mission was accomplished so thoroughly that Villa never again threatened the United States. Although the Punitive Expedition did not accomplish anything spectacular, it was far from a fiasco.

Part and parcel of the myth of the expedition's failure is the legend that Villa played "cat-and-mouse" with clumsy, heavily armed, slow-moving American soldiers, who blundered through the mountains and deserts in a hopeless effort to overtake him. The senior officers of the expedition, including Pershing himself, were men who had had a wide experience in just the sort of warfare they encountered in Mexico. General Funston, under whose over-all supervision the expedition operated, was an old guerrilla himself and was the captor of Aguinaldo.

Far from being a game of "cat-and-mouse" played by Villa, the campaign more closely resembled "hare-and-hounds," with Villa in the unhappy role of hare.

The acute friction between the United States and Carranza that developed in the summer of 1916 would probably not have arisen if the Punitive Expedition had not entered Mexico. Although the expedition was the immediate cause of the war scare, Pershing's presence in Mexico probably made Carranza more cautious about his threats. His utterances became noticeably less aggressive after the Carrizal fight. There two understrength troops of Negro soldiers, deprived of the leadership of their officers and suffering defeat, exacted such a toll of Mexican lives as to prove how dangerous an attack on the expedition would be.

It is probably not entirely coincidental that Imperial Germany's decision to embark upon unrestricted submarine warfare regardless of consequences came closely upon the heels of the Punitive Expedition and the troubles with Carranza's government. The German military authorities believed that the United States had committed all available forces to the Mexican venture. This conviction, together with the unpreparedness revealed by the movement of the National Guard to the border, undoubtedly contributed to German belief that the United States could be defied with impunity. Moreover, there was a general belief in the United States during the war that German influence lay back of Villa's invasion. No convincing substantiation of this belief has ever come to light, but there are strong indications that Villa, indirectly, played an important part in Germany's final decision.

Villa's final elimination as a military factor and political force in Mexico was directly due to the intervention of American forces in his last attempt to capture Ciudad Juárez. The legend of his invincibility had been destroyed by his defeats in the summer of 1915 and by the disastrous failure of his assaults at Agua Prieta and Hermosillo, in which the United States was involved. When the first salvos from American artillery blasted into Villa's forces at Juárez, the brittle military structure he had so carefully reconstructed during 1917 and 1918 was shattered instantly. At that moment Pancho Villa's political hopes were destroyed, once and for all.

The wisdom of President Wilson's recognition of Carranza was open to legitimate doubt at the time, but now no doubt remains. While the

United States owed Villa a debt of gratitude on a score of different counts, the real issue at the moment was which of the two leaders would be best for Mexico. Villa's ignorance, his violent passions, his complete ruthlessness, would have made him impossible as the head of a nation with problems as complex and serious as those of Mexico. Regardless of his sincerity, his aspirations and ideals, it is improbable that he could have been a constitutional ruler. Almost certainly he would have become a military dictator as heavy-handed and arbitrary as Porfirio Díaz.

During Villa's rise from an obscure bandit to a position of power, his relations with the United States and with numerous individual Americans were important in shaping his course. With American favor he seemed destined to be the future chief of Mexico. Under the guidance of General Hugh L. Scott and George Carothers he gave promise of overcoming the handicaps of his illiteracy and bandit background. Without American favor he was lost. At the same time his presence conditioned the attitude and policies of the United States toward Mexico and all of the Mexican leaders. The results of the relationships that developed between the United States and Pancho Villa were real, even though imponderable in many respects. For good or ill, Pancho Villa helped shape the history not only of his own country but of the United States as well.

Americans Not Widely Known

Who Are Mentioned in the Narrative

Belt, John W. American consular officer; assistant to John R. Silliman.

Canova, Leon J. State Department special agent at Villa's headquarters; assistant to George C. Carothers; later the first chief of the Division of Mexican Affairs in the State Department.

Carothers, George C. State Department special agent with Villa; a long-time resident of Mexico and former consular agent at Torreón.

Cobb, Zach. Collector of customs at El Paso, Texas.

Coen, Homer C. United States vice-consul at Durango.

Edwards, Thomas. United States consul at Ciudad Juárez.

Fuller, Paul. Prominent New York attorney; President Wilson's personal representative in Mexico, August–September, 1914.

Hamm, Theodore C. United States vice-consul at Durango.

Hanna, Philip C. United States consul general at Monterrey.

Hostetter, Louis. United States consul at Hermosillo.

Letcher, Marion. United States consul at Chihuahua.

McQuatters, A. J. American mining man in Mexico; member of a committee representing the mine and smelter operators in negotiations with Villa; assisted General Scott in conferences with Obregón.

O'Shaughnessy, Nelson. American diplomat; first secretary of the American Embassy in Mexico City; chargé d'affaires after the recall of Ambassador Henry Lane Wilson.

Parker, Charles B. American diplomat; in charge of United States interests in Mexico after the recognition of Carranza and before the appointment of an ambassador.

Rusk, Dr. Carlos (or Charles). Chief physician for the American Smelting and Refining Company; a friend of both General Scott and General Pershing.

Seese, George L. Associated Press representative on the border at the time of the Columbus raid.

Silliman, John R. American consular officer; State Department special agent with Carranza.

Simpich, Frederick. United States consul at Nogales, Sonora.

West, DuVal. Prominent attorney of San Antonio, Texas; President Wilson's personal representative in Mexico early in 1915; later became a Federal judge.

Bibliography

1. Manuscripts

John J. Pershing Papers. Library of Congress, Washington, D.C.
Hugh Lenox Scott Papers. Library of Congress, Washington, D.C.
Woodrow Wilson Papers. Library of Congress, Washington, D.C.

2. Archival Material

National Archives
  Department of Justice files, 1912–1916.
  State Department Files: Mexico, 1912–1916.
  War Department. Adjutant General Files, 1916–1919.
  ——. Old War Records, 1898.
  ——. Punitive Expedition Records.

3. Government Documents

UNITED STATES

Commerce and Labor, Department of. *Daily Consular and Trade Reports,*
    vol. III (July–Sept., 1912).
Congressional Record, 63d and 64th Congresses, 1914–1916.
House of Representatives Document no. 1237, 64 Cong., 1 sess., 1916.
House of Representatives Miscellaneous Document no. 64, 45 Cong., 2
    sess., 1878.
House of Representatives, Report and Accompanying Documents of the

Committee on Foreign Affairs on the Relations of the United States with Mexico, 45 Cong., 2 sess., 1878.

Labor, Department of. *Labor Conditions in Mexico,* Bulletin no. 38, 1902.

Official Records of the Union and Confederate Armies in the War of the Rebellion, 1st ser., vols. XV and XXXIV.

Papers Relating to the Foreign Relations of the United States, 1873, 1878, 1882, 1886, 1911, 1912, 1913, 1914, 1915, 1916, 1917, 1918, 1919, 1920.

Senate Documents, 64 Cong., 1 sess., no. 324, 1916; 64 Cong., 2 sess., nos. 491, 686, 1917; 66 Cong., 2 sess., no. 285, 1920.

Senate Subcommittee on Mexican Affairs. *Investigation of Mexican Affairs.* 4 vols. Washington, 1920. (The "Fall Committee" proceedings.)

Thomas, Robert S., and Inez V. Allen. *The Mexican Punitive Expedition under Brigadier General John J. Pershing, United States Army, 1916–1917.* Washington: War Histories Division, Office of the Chief of Military History, Department of the Army, 1954.

MEXICO

Archivo Histórico Diplomático Mexicano. *Un siglo de relaciones internacionales de México (á través de los mensajes presidenciales).* Mexico City: Secretaría de Relaciones Exteriores, 1935.

Carranza, Venustiano. *Reply of Don Venustiano Carranza to the Chief of the Northern Division; The First Chief of the Constitutionalist Army in Charge of the Executive Power to the Mexican People; Refutation of the Manifesto of General Francisco Villa.* Mexico City, 1914.

Contreras Arias, Alfonso. *Mapa de las provincias climatológicas de la República Mexicana.* Mexico City: Secretaría de Agricultura y Fomento, 1942.

Hacienda Pública de México á través de los informes presidenciales, a partir de la independencia hasta 1950, con notas aclaratorias. Mexico City: Secretaría de Hacienda y Crédito Público, 1950.

Labor internacional de la Revolución Constitucionalista de México. Mexico City: Secretaría de Gobernación, n.d.

Memoria que en cumplimento del precepto constitucional presentó al séptimo congrèso de la Unión en el primer periodo de sus sesiones. Mexico City: Ministro de Relaciones Exteriores, 1873.

Mexico's Oil: A Compilation of Official Documents in the Conflict of Economic Order in the Petroleum Industry, with an Introduction Summarizing Its Causes and Consequences. Mexico City: Government of Mexico, 1940.

Nota enviada por el Gobierno Constitucionalista al de la Casa Blanca: Con motivo de las incursiones de tropas americanas en territorio Mexicano. Mexico City: Secretaría de Relaciones Exteriores, 1916.

Report of the Committee of Investigation Sent in 1873 by the Mexican Government to the Frontier of Texas. Trans. from the official edition made in Mexico. New York, 1875.

Villa, Francisco. *Manifesto Addressed by General Francisco Villa to the Nation and Documents Justifying the Disavowal of Venustiano Carranza as First Chief of the Revolution.* Chihuahua, n.d. (1914?).

GREAT BRITAIN

Parliamentary Debates, 30 Parl. of the United Kingdom of Great Britain and Ireland, 4 sess., 5th ser., 4 George V. Vols. 58, 59, 60, 61, 63, 65.

4. Monographs, Autobiographies, Reminiscences, Biographies

Adler, Selig. *The Isolationist Impulse: Its Twentieth Century Reaction.* New York, 1957.

Altamirano, Ignacio M. *Historia y política de México (1821–1882).* Mexico City, 1947.

Arnold, Oren. *Thunder in the Southwest: Echoes from the Wild Frontier.* Norman, Okla., 1952.

Azuela, Mariano. *The Under Dogs.* Trans. by E. Manguía. New York, 1929.

Baerlin, Henry. *Mexico, the Land of Unrest, Being Chiefly an Account of What Produced the Outbreak in 1910, Together with the Story of the Revolution to This Day.* London, n.d.

Baker, Ray Stannard. *Woodrow Wilson: Life and Letters.* 4 vols. Garden City, N.Y., 1931.

Batchelder, Roger. *Watching and Waiting on the Border.* Boston and New York, 1917.

Beals, Carleton. *Brimstone and Chili: A Book of Personal Experiences in the Southwest and Mexico.* New York, 1927.

——. *Porfirio Diaz, Dictator of Mexico.* Philadelphia, 1932.

Bernstorff, Count Johann von. *Memoirs.* New York, 1936.

——. *My Three Years in America.* New York, 1920.

Bishop, William Henry. *Old Mexico and Her Lost Provinces: A Journey in Mexico, Southern California, and Arizona.* London, 1883.

Blasco Ibañez, Vicente. *Mexico in Revolution.* New York, 1920.

Bourke, Capt. John Gregory. *An Apache Campaign in the Sierra Madre: An Account of the Expedition in Pursuit of the Hostile Chiricahua Apaches in the Spring of 1883.* New York, 1886.

Braddy, Haldeen. *Cock of the Walk: Qui-qui-ri-quí! The Legend of Pancho Villa.* Albuquerque, N.M., 1955.

Brenner, Anita, and George R. Leighton. *The Wind That Swept Mexico: The History of the Mexican Revolution, 1910–1942.* New York, 1943.

Brimlow, George Francis. *Cavalryman Out of the West: Life of General William Carey Brown.* Caldwell, Idaho, 1944.

Bulnes, Francisco. *The Whole Truth about Mexico: President Wilson's Responsibility.* Trans. by Dors Scott. New York, 1916.

Bush, Dr. Ira Jefferson. *Gringo Doctor.* Caldwell, Idaho, 1939.

Calero, Manuel. *The Mexican Policy of President Wilson as It Appears to a Mexican.* New York, 1916.

Callahan, James Norton. *American Foreign Policy in Mexican Relations.* New York, 1952.

Callcott, Wilfred Hardy. *Liberalism in Mexico, 1857–1929.* Stanford, Calif., 1931.

Campobello, Nellie. *Apuntes sobre la vida militar de Francisco Villa.* Mexico City, 1940.

Carnegie Endowment for International Peace. *Diplomatic Correspondence of the United States: Inter-American Affairs, 1831–1860,* vol. IX. Washington, 1937.

———. *German Official Documents Relating to the World War.* New York, 1923.

Casey, Robert J. *The Texas Border and Some Borderliners: A Chronicle and a Guide.* Indianapolis, Ind., 1950.

Castillo, José R. *Historia de la Revolución Social de México: Primera etapa, la caída del General Díaz; Apuntes y observaciones para formar la historia de México de 1908 á 1915.* Mexico City, 1915.

Cerwin, Herbert. *These Are the Mexicans.* New York, 1947.

Cleland, Robert Glass. *A History of Phelps Dodge.* New York, 1952.

Cline, Howard F. *The United States and Mexico.* Cambridge, Mass., 1953.

Creel, George. *The People Next Door: An Interpretive History of Mexico and the Mexicans.* New York, 1926.

Creelman, James. *Diaz, Master of Mexico.* New York, 1911.

Cumberland, Charles Curtis. *Mexican Revolution: Genesis under Madero.* Austin, Texas, 1952.

Cusi Mining Company. *Evidence Submitted to the State Department in the Matter of the Killing of C. R. Watson, Manager of the Cusi Mining Company, and Others, near Santa Ysabel, in the State of Chihuahua, Mexico, January Tenth, Nineteen Hundred and Sixteen.* Winston, Payne, Strawn & Shaw, Attorneys. Chicago, n.d.

Daniels, Josephus. *Shirt-Sleeve Diplomat.* Chapel Hill, N.C., 1947.

——. *The Wilson Era: Years of Peace, 1910–1917.* Chapel Hill, N.C., 1944.

Davis, Britton. *The Truth about Geronimo.* New Haven, Conn., 1929.

De Bekker, L. J. *The Plot against Mexico.* New York, 1919.

Dillon, Emile Joseph. *Mexico on the Verge.* New York, 1921.

——. *President Obregon, a World Reformer.* Boston, 1923.

Dunn, Frederick Sherwood. *The Diplomatic Protection of Americans in Mexico.* New York, 1933.

Enciso, X. *El ataque á Ciudad Juárez y los acontecimientos del 14 al 18 de junio.* El Paso, Texas, 1919.

Fain, Samuel S. "The Pershing Punitive Expedition and Its Diplomatic Background." Master's thesis, University of Arizona, 1951.

Foix, Pere. *Pancho Villa.* Mexico City, 1950.

Foppa, Tito. *La tragedía mexicana.* Barcelona, Spain, n.d.

Fornaro, Carle de. *Carranza and Mexico.* New York, 1915.

Forwood, Sir William B. *Recollections of a Busy Life, Being the Reminiscences of a Liverpool Merchant, 1840–1910.* Liverpool, 1910.

Franke, Paul. *They Plowed Up Hell in Old Cochise.* Douglas, Ariz., 1950.

Garibaldi, Giuseppe. *A Toast to Rebellion.* Garden City, N.Y., 1937.

Gerard, James W. *Face to Face with Kaiserism.* New York, 1918.

——. *My Four Years in Germany.* New York, 1917.

Gibbon, Thomas Edward. *Mexico under Carranza: A Lawyer's Indictment of the Crowning Infamy of Four Hundred Years of Misrule.* New York, 1919.

Gilpatric, Guy. *Flying Stories.* New York, 1946.

González, Gen. Manuel W. *Con Carranza: Episodios de la Revolución Constitucionalista.* Monterrey, Mexico, 1933–1934.

——. *Contra Villa: Relatos de la campaña de 1914–1915.* Mexico City, 1935.

González-Blanco, Edmundo. *Carranza y la Revolución de México.* Madrid, 1916.

Gregg, Robert D. *The Influence of Border Troubles on Relations between the United States and Mexico, 1876–1910.* Baltimore, Md., 1937.

Grey, Viscount Edward. *Twenty-five Years, 1892–1916.* 2 vols. New York, 1925.

Griffin, Charles C. *Concerning Latin American Culture: Papers Read at Byrdcliffe, Woodstock, New York, August, 1939.* New York, 1940.

Gruening, Ernest. *Mexico and Its Heritage.* New York, 1928.

Gutierrez de Lara, L., and Edgcumb Pinchon. *The Mexican People: Their Struggle for Freedom.* Garden City, N.Y., 1914.

Guzmán, Martín Luis. *Memorias de Pancho Villa.* 4 vols. Mexico City, 1934.

——. *A orillas del Hudson.* Mexico City, n.d.

Guzmán, Martín Luis. *La querella de México.* Madrid, 1915.

Hanssen, Hans Peter. *The Diary of a Dying Empire.* Trans. by O. Winther. Bloomington, Ind., 1955.

Harris, Larry A. *Pancho Villa and the Columbus Raid.* El Paso, Texas, 1949.

Hendrick, Burton J. *The Life and Letters of Walter H. Page.* 3 vols. Garden City, N.Y., 1925.

Horgan, Paul. *Great River: The Rio Grande in North 'American History.* 2 vols. New York, 1954.

Houston, David F. *Eight Years with Wilson's Cabinet, 1913–1920, with a Personal Estimate of the President.* 2 vols. Garden City, N.Y., 1926.

Hunt, Frazier. *One American and His Attempt at Education.* New York, 1938.

James, Admiral Sir William. *The Eyes of the Navy: A Biographical Study of Admiral Sir Reginald Hall.* London, 1955.

Jones, John Price. *America Entangled: The Secret Plotting of German Spies in the United States and the Inside Story of the Sinking of the Lusitania.* Introd. by Roger B. Wood, former assistant United States attorney in New York. New York, 1917.

Lane, Anne Wintermute, and Louise Herrick Hall, eds. *The Letters of Franklin K. Lane.* Boston and New York, 1922.

Link, Arthur S. *Woodrow Wilson and the Progressive Era, 1910–1917.* New York, 1954.

Löhndorff, Ernst F. *Bestie ich in Mexiko: Wahre Erlebnisse.* Bremen, 1927.

Lutz, Ralph Haswell. *Documents of the German Revolution: Fall of the German Empire, 1914–1918.* Stanford, Calif., 1923.

McCaleb, Walter F. *The Public Finances of Mexico.* New York, n.d.

McCorkle, Stuart Alexander. *American Recognition Policy towards Mexico.* Baltimore, Md., 1933.

McCreery, Henry Forbes. "German Opinion of the United States during the 1916 Submarine Crisis." Ph.D. dissertation, Stanford University, 1947.

Marcosson, Isaac F. *Metal Magic: The Story of the American Smelting and Refining Company.* New York, 1949.

María y Campo, Armando de. *La navegación aerea en México.* Mexico City, 1944.

Martin, Percy F. *Mexico of the Twentieth Century.* 2 vols. London, 1907.

Mecham, J. Lloyd. *Church and State in Latin America: A History of Politico-ecclesiastical Relations.* Chapel Hill, N.C., 1934.

Mena Brito, Gen. Bernardino. *El lugarteniente gris de Pancho Villa (Felipe Angeles).* Mexico City, 1938.

Mexican Bureau of Information. *"Red Papers" of Mexico: An Exposé of the Great Científico Conspiracy to Eliminate Don Venustiano Carranza; Documents Relating to the Imbroglio between Carranza and Villa.* New York, 1914.

————. *Speech by Luis Cabrera before the Convention, Mexico, D.F., October 5, 1914.* New York, 1914.

Miles, Lieut. Gen. Nelson A. *Personal Recollections and Observations of General Nelson A. Miles, Embracing a Brief View of the Civil War; or, From New England to the Golden Gate, and the Story of His Indian Campaigns, with Comments on the Exploration, Development, and Progress of Our Great Western Empire, Copiously Illustrated with Graphic Pictures by Frederic Remington and Other Eminent Artists.* Chicago and New York, 1896.

Moats, Leone B. *Thunder in Their Veins: A Memoir of Mexico.* New York, 1932.

Morton, F. Rand. *Los novelistas de la Revolución Mexicana.* Mexico City, 1949.

Muñoz, Rafael F. *El hombre malo: Villa ataca Ciudad Juárez y la marcha nupcial.* Mexico City, 1930.

————. *Pancho Villa, rayo y azote.* Mexico City, 1955.

————. *¡Vámonos con Pancho Villa!* Madrid, 1931.

Notter, Harley. *The Origins of the Foreign Policy of Woodrow Wilson.* Baltimore, Md., 1937.

Obregón, Gen. Alvaro. *Ocho mil kilómetros en campaña: Relación de las acciones de armas efectuadas en más de veinte estados de la república durante un periodo de cuatro años.* Mexico City, 1917.

O'Connor, Harvey. *The Guggenheims: The Making of an American Dynasty.* New York, 1937.

O'Reilly, Maj. Edward S. *Roving and Fighting: Adventures under Four Flags.* London, 1918.

Ortigoza, Manuel. *Ciento catorce días de sitio: La defensa de Naco.* Mexico City, 1916.

O'Shaughnessy, Mrs. Edith. *A Diplomat's Wife in Mexico.* New York, 1916.

————. *Intimate Pages of Mexican History.* New York, 1920.

Palacios Roji, Manuel. *La mano de Alemania en México.* Mexico City, 1919.

Palmer, Frederick. *The Life and Letters of General Tasker Howard Bliss.* New York, 1934.

————. *Newton D. Baker: America at War.* 2 vols. New York, 1931.

Pani, Alberto J. *Mi contribución al nuevo régimen (1910–1933).* Mexico City, 1936.

Papen, Franz von. *Memoirs.* Trans. by Brian Connell. London, 1952.

Parker, Dr. George. *Guaracha Trail: Adventures of an American Doctor Battling for a "Lost" Silver Mine in the Bandit Country of Northern Mexico.* New York, 1951.

Pettus, Daisy C., ed. *The Rosalie Evans Letters from Mexico.* Indianapolis, Ind., 1926.

Pinchon, Edgcumb. *Viva Villa! A Recovery of the Real Pancho Villa, Peon, Bandit, Soldier, Patriot.* New York, 1933.

Puente, Ramón. *Hombres de la Revolución: Villa (Sus auténticas memorias).* Los Angeles, Calif., 1931.

———. *Vida de Franciso Villa, contada por él mismo.* Los Angeles, Calif., 1919.

———. *Villa en pié.* Mexico City, 1937.

Ramsaye, Terry. *A Million and One Nights: The History of the Motion Pictures.* 2 vols. New York, 1926.

Reed, John. *Insurgent Mexico.* New York, 1914.

Reed, Raymond J. "The Mormons in Chihuahua: Their Relations with Villa and the Pershing Punitive Expedition, 1916–1917." Master's thesis, University of New Mexico, 1938.

Rembao, Alberto. *Chihuahua de mis amores y otros despachos de mexicanidad neoyorquina.* Mexico City, 1949.

Rippy, J. Fred. *The United States and Mexico.* New York, 1926.

Robledo, Federico P. *El constitucionalismo y Francisco Villa á la luz de la verdad.* Matamoros, Mexico, 1915.

Robleto, Hernán. *La mascota de Pancho Villa: Episodios de la Revolución Mexicana.* Mexico City, 1934.

———. *Obregón, Toral, la Madre Conchita.* Mexico City, 1935.

Rodney, Col. George Brydges. *As a Cavalryman Remembers.* Caldwell, Idaho. 1944.

Romero Flores, Jesús. *Anales históricos de la Revolución.* Mexico City, 1939.

Romney, Thomas Cottam. *The Mormon Colonies in Mexico.* Salt Lake City, Utah, 1938.

Ross, Edward Alsworth. *Seventy Years of It: An Autobiography.* New York, 1936.

———. *The Social Revolution in Mexico.* New York, 1923.

Ross, Stanley R. *Francisco I. Madero, Apostle of Democracy.* New York, 1955.

Salinas Carranza, Gen. Alberto. *La expedición punitiva.* Mexico City, 1937.

Schuster, Ernest Otto. *Pancho Villa's Shadow.* New York, 1947.

Scott, Maj. Gen. Hugh Lenox. *Some Memories of a Soldier.* New York, 1928.

Scott, James Brown, ed. *President Wilson's Foreign Policy: Messages, Addresses, Papers.* New York, 1918.

Seymour, Charles. *The Intimate Papers of Colonel House, Arranged as a Narrative.* 4 vols. Boston and New York, 1926.

Shadley, Frank William. "The American Punitive Expedition into Mexico, 1916–1917." Master's thesis, College of the Pacific, 1952.

Shaw, Albert, ed. *President Wilson's State Papers and Addresses.* New York, 1918.

Smith, Launa M. *American Relations with Mexico.* Oklahoma City, Okla., 1924.

Smith, Randolph Wellford. *Benighted Mexico.* New York, 1916.

Steffens, Lincoln. *The Autobiography of Lincoln Steffens.* New York, 1931.

Stephenson, George M. *John Lind of Minnesota.* Minneapolis, Minn., 1935.

Stevens, Louis. *Here Comes Pancho Villa: The Anecdotal History of a Genial Killer.* New York, 1930.

Stirrat, May. "Francisco Villa's Raid on Columbus, New Mexico." Master's thesis, University of New Mexico, 1935.

Taracena, Alfonso. *Mi vida en el vértigo de la Revolución Mexicana (Anales sintéticos, 1900–1930).* Mexico City, 1930.

Thompson, Wallace. *The Mexican Mind: A Study of National Psychology.* Boston, 1922.

Tigner, James L. "The Relations of the United States and Mexico, 1909–1914." Master's thesis, Stanford University, 1949.

Tompkins, Col. Frank. *Chasing Villa.* Harrisburg, Pa., 1935.

Toor, Frances. *A Treasury of Mexican Folkways: The Customs, Myths, Folklore, Traditions, Beliefs, Fiestas, Dances, and Songs of the Mexican People.* New York, 1947.

Torres, Ing. Elias L. *La cabeza de Villa y 20 episodios más.* Mixcoac, D.F., Mexico, 1938.

——. *Como murió Pancho Villa.* Mexico City. n.d.

——. *Vida y hazañas de Pancho Villa.* Mexico City, n.d.

Toulmin, Col. H. A. *With Pershing in Mexico.* Harrisburg, Pa., 1935.

Travesí, Gonzalo G. *La Revolución de México y el imperialismo yanquí.* Barcelona, 1914.

Tumulty, Joseph P. *Woodrow Wilson as I Know Him.* Garden City, N.Y., 1921.

Turner, John Kenneth. *Barbarous Mexico.* Chicago, 1910.

——. *Hands Off Mexico: The Case against Intervention; The Intervention Conspiracy; Wilson and Intervention; A Solution for the Mexican "Problem."* New York, 1920.

Turner, Timothy G. *Bullets, Bottles, and Gardenias.* Dallas, Texas, 1935.

Tweedie, Ethel Brilliana. *The Maker of Modern Mexico, Porfirio Diaz*. New York, 1906.

Urquizo, Gen. Francisco L. *"Recuerdo que . . .": Visiones aisladas de la Revolución*. Mexico City, 1934.

Valades, José. *Las caballerías de la Revolución (Hazañas del General Buelna)*. Mexico City, 1937.

Valdes, Maximino. *Impresiones de México: Prólogo del General Francisco J. Múgica*. Mexico City, 1918.

Vasconcelos, José. *Breve historia de México*. 6th ed. Mexico City, 1950.

Vásquez-Santa Ana, Higinio. *Canciones, cantares y corridos mexicanos*. Mexico City, n.d.

Wells, William V. *Walker's Expedition to Nicaragua: A History of the Central American War and the Sonora and Kinney Expeditions, Including All the Recent Diplomatic Correspondence, Together with a New and Accurate Map of Central America and a Memoir of General William Walker*. New York, 1856.

Whetten, Nathan L. *Rural Mexico*. Chicago, 1948.

White, Owen P. *Out of the Desert: The Historical Romance of El Paso*. El Paso, Texas, 1923.

Wilson, Henry Lane. *Diplomatic Episodes in Mexico, Belgium, and Chile*. Garden City, N.Y., 1927.

Winter, Ella, and Granville Hicks, eds. *The Letters of Lincoln Steffens*. 2 vols. New York, 1938.

Winton, George B. *Mexico, Past and Present*. Nashville, Tenn., 1928.

5. Articles

Adams, Cyrus C. "Northern Mexico: The Scene of Our Army's Hunt for Villa," *Review of Reviews*, LIII (April, 1916), 421–423.

"Advance into Mexico, The," *Outlook*, CXII (March 22, 1916), 654–655.

"America in Mexico," *Living Age*, 7th ser., CCLXXXI (April, 1914), 56–58.

"American Intervention in Mexico: A Poll of the European Press," *Outlook*, CVII (May 2, 1914), 17–18.

American Resident, An (pseud.). "The Situation in Mexico," *Outlook*, CIV (Aug., 1913), 1003–1006.

"American Responsibility," *Outlook*, CVIII (Dec. 2, 1914), 752–753.

Barker, J. Ellis. "America's Foreign Policy and the Mexican Imbroglio," *Living Age*, 7th ser., CCLXXXI (June 6, 1914), 579–592.

"Benton Mystery in Mexico, The," *World's Work*, CVI (March 7, 1914), 508–509.

"Big Business behind the Mexican Muddle," *Literary Digest*, XLVII (Nov. 15, 1913), 935–936.

"Bloodletting in Mexico," *Harper's Weekly*, LVIII (Dec. 13, 1913), 4.

"Blundering into Mexico," *New Republic*, II (1915), 32–33.

Blythe, Samuel G. "Mexico: The Record of a Conversation with President Wilson," *Saturday Evening Post*, May 23, 1914.

Braddy, Haldeen. "Doroteo Arango, *alias* Pancho Villa," *New Mexico Folklore Record*, V (1950–1951), 4–8.

——. "Man of a Million Faces," *Texas Parade*, XII (1952), 26–27.

——. "Pancho Villa, Man and Hero," *Southwest Review*, XIII (July, 1937), 338–342.

——, with John H. McNeely. "Francisco Villa in Folksongs," *Arizona Quarterly*, X (1954), 5–16.

"British Press on Benton's Fate," *Literary Digest*, XLVIII (March 7, 1914), 481.

Browne, Porter Emerson. "On 'Keeping Out of War,' and 'Swapping Horses,' and Things," *Collier's Magazine*, LVIII (Oct. 7, 1916), 30–31.

Call, Tomme Clark. "Formation of Mexican Foreign Policy," *Mexican Life*, XXX (Oct. 1, 1954), 15.

"Calling Out the Guard," *World's Work*, XXXII (Aug., 1916), 437–452.

Carol, William. "The North and South War in Mexico," *World's Work*, XXVII (Jan., 1914), 298–306.

"Carranza Wants Us to Withdraw," *Independent*, LXXXVI (April 24, 1916), 127.

"Cavalry Equipment in Mexico," *United States Cavalry Journal*, XXVII (Nov., 1916), 230–232.

"Cavalry Fight at Columbus, The," *United States Cavalry Journal*, XXVII (Nov., 1916), 183–185.

"Cavalry Fight at Ojos Azules, The," *United States Cavalry Journal*, XXVII (Jan., 1917), 405–408.

"Cavalry Work of the Punitive Expedition," *United States Cavalry Journal*, XXVII (Jan., 1917), 427–433.

"Chances of Intervention," *Literary Digest*, L (June 26, 1915), 1522.

"Chase after the Elusive Villa," *Outlook*, CXII (April 12, 1916), 320.

"Columbus Raid, The," *United States Cavalry Journal*, XXVII (April, 1917), 409–416.

"Conferring over the Mexican Expedition," *Independent*, LXXXVI (May 8, 1916), 200.

Constantine, Arthur. "Carranza at Close Range," *North American Review*, CCV (April, 1917), 566–576.

"Constitutionalist Rule in Mexico," *Literary Digest*, XLIX (Aug. 29, 1914), 335–336.

Creelman, James. "President Diaz, Hero of the Americas," *Pearson's Magazine*, XIX (March, 1908), 231–277.

Cumberland, Charles Curtis. "Border Raids in the Lower Rio Grande Valley—1915," *Southwestern Historical Quarterly*, LVII (Jan., 1954), 284–311.

Curphey, Alfred. "Mexico from Within," *Living Age*, 7th ser., CCLXXXI (June 6, 1914), 657–669.

"Day's Work in Mexico, The," *Literary Digest*, XLVII (Dec. 20, 1913), 1213.

"Drifting toward Intervention in Mexico," *Literary Digest*, LII (May 27, 1916), 1515.

Dunn, Robert. "With Pershing's Cavalry," *Collier's Magazine*, LVIII (Sept. 23, 1916), 8.

Elser, Frank B. "Pershing's Lost Cause," *American Legion Monthly*, XII–XIII (July, 1932), 14.

Emerson, Edwin. "How Mexicans Fight," *Outlook*, CIV (May 24, 1913), 199–207.

"End of a Chapter, The," *Outlook*, CXV (Feb. 7, 1917), 218–219.

"End of the Chase after Villa," *Current Opinion*, LX (May, 1916), 304–305.

Estes, Capt. George H. "Internment of Mexican Troops," *United States Infantry Journal*, XII (1915), 38–57, 243–264.

"Experiences in Mexico," *United States Cavalry Journal*, XXVII (Nov., 1916), 232–235.

"Fall of Torreon, The," *World's Work*, CVI (April 11, 1914), 783.

"Field Notes from Mexico and the Border," *United States Cavalry Journal*, XXVII (Nov., 1916), 171–182.

"French Criticism of Our Mexican Methods," *Literary Digest*, XLVIII (March 14, 1914), 546.

Fuller, Paul. "The Case for President Wilson," *World's Work*, XXXII (Oct., 1916), 641–649.

Gates, William. "The Four Governments of Mexico," *World's Work*, XXXVII (April, 1919), 654–665.

"German Criticism of Our Mexican Policy," *Literary Digest*, XLVIII (May 23, 1914), 1243–1244.

González, 1st Capt. Daniel. "The Fight at Carrizal," trans. by Clarence C. Clendenen, 1933.

Gresham, William Lindsay. "The Swashbuckling Saga of Pancho Villa," *Saga Magazine*, XIV (Aug., 1957), 50.

Harriman, Mrs. Borden. "Matamoros—A War Film," *Harper's Weekly*, LX (1915), 494–496.

Hart, Albert Bushnell. "Mexico and the Mexicans," *World's Work*, XXVII (Jan., 1914), 272–289.

——. "The Postulates of the Mexican Situation," *Annals of the American Academy of Political Science*, LIV (July, 1914), 136–147.

Hopper, James. "What Happened at Columbus," *Collier's Magazine*, LVII (April 15, 1916), 11.

"How the Revolution Affects Business in Mexico," *Current Opinion*, LV (Dec., 1913), 450–452.

"Huerta as a Dictator," *Literary Digest*, XLVII (Oct. 23, 1913), 737–739.

Hughes, Rupert. "The Big Hike," *Collier's Magazine*, LVIII (Nov. 11, 1916), 5.

Hyde, George Edward. "A Plain Tale from Mexico," *New Republic*, II (Feb. 13, 1915), 38–39.

Kahle, Louis C. "The Recognition of Venustiano Carranza," *Hispanic American Historical Review*, XXXVIII (Aug., 1958), 353–372.

Kennedy, J. M. "The Real Trouble in Mexico," *Fortnightly Review*, XCV n.s. (1914), 1046–1054.

"Killing Foreigners in Mexico," *Literary Digest*, L (March 27, 1915), 674–675.

Kyne Peter B. "With the Border Guard," *Collier's Magazine*, LVIII (May 9, 1914), 9.

"Land Reform Prospects in Mexico," *Literary Digest*, XLVIII (March 28, 1914), 684.

Lea, Tom. "The Affair of the Fifteen Aprils," *Southwest Review*, XXXVI (1951), 8–12.

"Life on the Border—A Guardsman's Letter," *Outlook*, CXIII (Aug. 23, 1916), 946–947.

"Lifting the Lid from the Mexican Kettle," *Literary Digest*, XLVIII (March 21, 1914), 601–603.

London, Jack. "The Trouble Makers of Mexico," *Collier's Magazine*, LIII (June 13, 1914), 13–14.

Lowry, Edward G. "What the President Is Trying to Do for Mexico," *World's Work*, XXVII (Jan., 1914), 261–266.

McGregor. "Huerta and the Other Leaders," *Harper's Weekly*, LVIII (May 9, 1914), 12–14.

——. "The Mexican Revolution," *Harper's Weekly*, LVIII (Dec. 20, 1913), 24–26.

——. "Villa—Victor—Dictator," *Harper's Weekly*, LX (March 20, 1915), 280.

McWilliams, Carey. "The Mystery of Ambrose Bierce," *American Mercury*, XXII (1931), 330–337.

Martin, Percy F. "The Crisis in Mexico," *Fortnightly Review*, XCIV n.s. (1913), 676–687.

——. "Mexico," *Edinburgh Review*, CCI (April, 1915), 344–357.

Marvin, George. "The First Line of Defense in Mexico," *World's Work*, XXXII (Aug., 1916), 416–424.

——. "Invasion or Intervention," *World's Work*, XXXII (May, 1916), 40–62.

——. "Villa," *World's Work*, XXVII (July, 1914), 269–284.

Mason, Alfred Bishop. "The Cause of the Revolution in Mexico," *Unpopular Review*, III (1915), 379–387.

Mason, Gregory. "The Dough-Boy and the Truck," *Outlook*, CXIII (May 31, 1916), 277–283.

——. "Going South with Carranza," *Outlook*, CVII (May 2, 1914), 19–25.

——. "The Man Hunt in Mexico," *Outlook*, CXII (April 19, 1916), 892–911.

——. "Mexico—From the Inside Looking Out," *Outlook*, CXIII (May 10, 1916), 92–96.

"Massacre of Americans in Chihuahua, The," *Current Opinion*, LX (Feb., 1916), 73–75.

"Mexican Land Question, The," *Outlook*, CXIII (May 10, 1916), 228–229.

"Mexico," *Nation*, XCIX (Sept. 24, 1914), 365–366.

Middleton, James. "Mexico, the Land of Concessions," *World's Work*, XXVII (Jan., 1914), 289–298.

"More Mexican Complexities," *Literary Digest*, XLIX (July 11, 1914), 48.

Morey, Capt. Lewis S. "The Cavalry Fight at Carrizal," *United States Cavalry Journal*, XXVII (Jan., 1917), 449–456.

"Moving toward Peace in Mexico," *Literary Digest*, XLIX (July 4, 1914), 7–8.

"Newspapers' Attitude toward Villa in 1914," *Literary Digest*, XLVIII (May 16, 1914), 1166–1167.

"Northern Mexico Lost to Huerta," *Literary Digest*, XLVIII (Jan. 24, 1914), 144–145.

"Odor of Kerosene in the Mexican Upheaval, The," *Current Opinion*, LV (Oct., 1913), 231–232.

"Oil Influences in Mexico," *Outlook*, CVII (Aug. 1, 1914), 766–767.

"On the Trail of Villa," *Scientific American*, CXIV (March 25, 1916), 326–327.

"Our Debt to Villa," *Literary Digest*, XLVIII (May 16, 1914), 1166–1167.

"Our Punitive Expedition into Mexico and Its Possible Consequences," *Current Opinion*, LX (April, 1916), 229–231.

"Our Unprepared Militia," *Literary Digest,* LII (June 3, 1916), 1617.

Palmer, Frederick. "Mexico: Watchful Perspiring at Vera Cruz," *Everybody's Magazine,* XXXI (July, 1914), 65–80.

Patton, 1st Lieut. George S. "Cavalry Work of the Punitive Expedition," *United States Cavalry Journal,* XXVII (Jan., 1917), 426–433.

Perrenot, E. E. "The National Guard Fiasco," *Out West Magazine,* XLVI (Aug., 1916), 79.

"Personal Glimpses: Entrenched with Villa," *Literary Digest,* L (June 19, 1915), 1485–1488.

Pickering, Col. Abner. "The Battle of Agua Prieta," *United States Infantry Journal,* XII (Jan., 1916), 707–710.

Rippy, J. Fred. "Border Troubles along the Rio Grande, 1848–1860," *Southwestern Historical Quarterly,* XXIII (July, 1919), 91–111.

———. "Some Precedents of the Pershing Expedition into Mexico," *Southwestern Historical Quarterly,* XXIII (Oct., 1919), 91–112.

"Rise of Villa's Star, The," *Literary Digest,* XLVIII (April 18, 1914), 889.

S., W. B. "Pershing on the Trail," *Review of Reviews,* LIII (April, 1916), 419–421.

"Shall We Join Hands with Villa?" *Literary Digest,* XLVIII (May 23, 1914), 1235–1238.

Shannon, Capt. James A. "With the Apache Scouts in Mexico," *United States Cavalry Journal,* XXVII (April, 1917), 839–857.

"Siege of Torreon, The," *World's Work,* CVI (April 4, 1914), 734–735.

Splitstone, F. J. "Fire and Blood in Mexico," *Leslie's Illustrated Weekly Newspaper,* CXVIII (June 23, 1914), 619; CXIX (July 2 and 9, 1914), 7 and 35.

———. "Looking Ahead in Mexico—A Forecast," *Leslie's Illustrated Weekly Newspaper,* CXIX (July 9, 1914), 33.

Steffens, Lincoln. "Making Friends with Mexico," *Collier's Magazine,* LVIII (Nov. 25, 1916), 5.

Stivison, Dr. Roy E., with Della Mavity McDonnell. "When Villa Raided Columbus," *New Mexico Magazine,* XXVIII (Dec., 1950), 17–19.

"Story of the Week, The," *Independent,* LXXXV (March 27, 1916), 440.

Tarbell, Ida M. "A Talk with the President of the United States," *Collier's Magazine,* LVIII (Oct. 28, 1916), 5.

Taylor, Joseph Rogers. "Pancho Villa at First Hand," *World's Work,* XXVIII (July, 1914), 265–269.

Troxel, Capt. C. C. "The Tenth Cavalry in Mexico," *United States Cavalry Journal,* XXVIII (Oct., 1917), 199–208.

Turner, John Kenneth. "What Is the Matter with Mexico?" *Metropolitan Magazine,* XXXVII (May, 1913), 7.

"Venustiano Carranza, Leader of the Most Respectable Revolution in Mexico," *Current Opinion*, LV (Oct., 1913), 243–244.

"Villa as a Socialist," *Literary Digest*, XLVIII (Jan. 24, 1914), 170–174.

"Villa-Carranza Break, The," *Literary Digest*, XLIX (Oct. 3, 1914), 619–620.

"Villa Now and Villa Then," *Collier's Magazine*, LIII (Sept. 12, 1914), 16.

"Villa's American Allies," *Literary Digest*, LII (April 8, 1916), 951–952.

"Villa's Style of War," *Literary Digest*, XLVIII (June 27, 1914), 1537–1538.

"Villa, the Ex-Bandit," *World's Work*, CVI (Jan. 10, 1914), 59–60.

Whelpley, John Davenport. "The Injustice of War on Mexico," *Living Age*, 7th ser., CCLXXXI (May, 1914), 323–329.

"Where Villa Crossed the Border: Crime and Punishment at Columbus," *Harper's Weekly*, LXII (April 1, 1916), 336–337.

"Why Mexico Hates Spaniards," *Literary Digest*, L (March 27, 1915), 679.

"Why We Heckle Huerta," *Literary Digest*, XLVII (Nov. 22, 1913), 998.

Wilkes, Allene Tupper. "Villa Enters Mexico City," *Harper's Weekly*, LX (Jan. 16, 1915), 57.

Williamson, Alice M. "My Attempt to Be a War Correspondent—Being the Confessions of a Coward," *McClure's Magazine*, XLIII (Sept., 1914), 66–76.

Wilson, Henry Lane. "Errors with Reference to Mexico," *Annals of the American Academy of Political Science*, LIV (July, 1914), 148–161.

——. "The Latest Phase of the Mexican Situation," *Independent*, LXXVI (Nov. 13, 1913), 297–298.

Wilson, Pres. Woodrow. "The Mexican Question," *Ladies' Home Journal*, XXXIII (Oct., 1916), 9.

"Wilson and Mexico," *Collier's Magazine*, LIII (June 13, 1914), 17.

Winton, George D. "The Present Situation in Mexico," *Proceedings of the Mississippi Valley Historical Association*, IX (1915–1916), 125–134.

6. *Periodicals*

Collier's Magazine, 1912–1916, New York.

Current Opinion, 1912–1916, New York.

Forum, 1916, New York.

Independent, 1912–1916, New York.

Information Quarterly, 1915–1917, New York.

Leslie's Illustrated Weekly Newspaper, 1914–1916, New York.

Literary Digest, 1911–1917, New York.

Living Age, 1912–1915, London.

Outlook, 1912–1916, New York.
Review of Reviews, 1913–1917, New York.
United States Cavalry Journal, 1916–1917, Washington, D.C.
United States Infantry Journal, 1915, Washington, D.C.

7. Newspapers

Acción Mundial, Jan.–July, 1916, Mexico City.
Berliner Börsen Zeitung, June 2, 1916, Berlin.
Christian Science Monitor, March–April, 1916, Boston.
Continental Times, May–June, 1916, Berlin.
Hannover Anzeiger, March 25, 1916, Hanover, Germany.
Leipziger Neueste Nachrichten, March–June, 1916, Leipzig.
London *Times,* Jan.–March, 1914; March, 1916; London.
New York *Times,* 1912–1916, New York.
Sacramento *Union,* 1913–1916, Sacramento, Calif.
San Francisco *Chronicle,* May–July, 1914, San Francisco.
San Francisco *Examiner,* May, 1914, San Francisco.
Täglische Rundschau, March–June, 1916, Berlin.
Vorwärts, March–June, 1916, Berlin.
Vossische Zeitung, March–June, 1916, Berlin.

8. Handbooks and Encyclopaedias

Democratic National Committee. *Democratic Campaign Text Book, 1916.*
Mexican Year Book. *A Statistical, Financial, and Economic Annual, Compiled from Official and Other Returns, 1909–1910.* London, 1911.
Pan-American Union. *Mexico: A General Sketch.* Washington, 1911.
Republican National Committee. *Republican Campaign Text Book, 1916.*
Rouaix, Ing. Pastor. *Diccionario geográfico, histórico y biográfico del Estado de Durango.* Mexico City, 1946.

Index

Acuña, Jesús: snubs Latin American diplomats, 254; statement on U.S. note on reciprocal permission, 188

Adair, Lieut. Henry R., killed at Carrizal, 281

Agua Prieta: battle of, 210-211; Carranzista garrison reinforced through U.S., 208-209; held by Carranzistas under Pact of Naco, 142; Villa charges Carranzistas violate agreement, 181

Aguascalientes convention: arrival of Zapatista delegates, 130; Carranza refers to for decision on Veracruz, 127; Carranza's speech, 124; designates Villa as Commander in Chief, 130; dispute over delegates to, 117; first session at Mexico City, reconvenes at Aguascalientes, 124-125; interest of U.S. in, 125-126; Luis Cabrera's speech, 125; orders Carranza to yield to Gutiérrez, 130; second Mexico City session, 143, 144, 146; Villa's speech before, 129-130

Aguilar, Gen.: designated to take over Veracruz, 127; issues proclamation embodying U.S. demands, U.S. rejects, 127-128

Alfonso XIII, requests U.S. protection for Spaniards, 63

Alger, Consul William C., 172

Alvarado Mining Co.: Cobb urges complaint be disregarded, 215; evacuates employees, 228

American Smelting & Refining Co.: loss of coal by reported, 55; resumes operations, 73-74

American Society of Mexico, 172

Angeles, Gen. Felipe: accused of causing trouble, 93; captured and shot, 312; heads commission to divide estates, 106-107; interview with Gen. Erwin, 312; joins Villa, 73; letter to Pres. Wilson, 179; meets Fuller at Chihuahua, 104; rumors of execution by Villa, 94; second in command in attack on Parral, 309-310; visits U.S., 178-179

Annapolis, U.S.S., fired upon at Mazatlán, 283

Anti-American feeling, 135

Antonio, employee of Palomas Land and Cattle Co., 238

Apache Indians, expeditions against, 5-6

Apache Indian Scouts, 264; accused of atrocities, 283

Arango, Doroteo (Villa's baptismal name), birth of, early life, 10-12

Arbitration and end of war, 1910 belief, 14

Arredondo: reads Carranza's reply to Secretary of State, 252; submits brief to Washington diplomats, 190; submits complaints about alleged Ameri-

342

Arredondo (*cont.*)
can atrocities, 283; transmits note
demanding withdrawal of Pun. Exp.,
267

Asama, Japanese cruiser, aground at
Turtle Bay, 156

Ashurst, Sen. Henry F., discusses border
conditions, 248

Associated Press: manager vetoes plan
for Villa to come to U.S., 236; quotes
Villa as threatening Spaniards, 65

Atrocities, Mexicans charge Americans
with, 282-283

Aviation in Villa's Torreón campaign,
71-72

Avila, gov. of Chihuahua, on asylum in
U.S. for Villa, 222

Avila, Gen. Fidel, attempts to extradite
Huerta, 182-183

Ayala, Zapata's Plan of, 107, 108, 130

Baker, Sec. of War Newton D., on orders for Pun. Exp., 251-252

Barnes, R. L., special agent, Dept. of
Justice, 199

Bell, Gen. J. F., reports removal of locomotives from Juárez, 265

Belt, Theodore, 256; designated as assistant to Silliman, 117; directed to
ascertain Carranza's attitude on Pun.
Exp., 255-256; forwards pronouncement by Carranza, 118; informs U.S.
of favorable impression in Mexico,
254; telegraphs Carranza's threatening proclamation, 252-253

Benton, William S.: disappearance and
death of, 65-66; Letcher assists Benton's widow, 159; ranch occupied by
squatters, 107

Berlin newspapers, statements on Mexico, 299-300

Bernstorff, Count Johann von: estimate
of U.S. resources for war, 301; final
decision on submarine warfare, 302

"Big business," and Mexican troubles,
90-91

Blatchford, Col. Richard M., 111

Bliss, Gen. Tasker H.: in command at
Naco, 142; telegram from Villa about
internees, 119n

Blocker, vice-consul, 265

Bonillas, Ignacio, Mexican commissioner
at New London, 284

Borah, Sen. William, attacks administration on Santa Ysabel, 232

Boyd, Capt. Charles T.: killed at Carrizal, 280; receives orders from Pershing, 279

Breceda, Capt. Alfredo, accuses Angeles
of fomenting trouble, 93

Brooklyn Eagle, 61

Brouch, Gustave, accused of spying, 65,
69

Brownsville, Tex.: attacked by Cor-
tina, Mexican troops restore order, 2;
Union and Confederate forces enter
Mexico, 3

Bryan, Sec. William Jennings: congrat-
ulates Villa and Obregón, 110; directs
Carothers to protect foreigners, 39,
to reconcile Villa and Carranza, 94;
gratified at Villa's attitude on Veracruz, 84-85; holds Villa responsible
for safety of Americans, 53; refers to
Villa as "Sir Galahad," 89; resigns as
Secretary of State, 176; responsibility
for foreigners in Mexico, 67; urges
negotiations between Carranza and
Carbajal, 98

Buford, U.S. Army transport, 177

Burleson, Postmaster General, suggests
mission for DuVal West, 308

Bush, Dr. Ira Jefferson: believes Villa
did not lead raid, 243; informed by
Villa of plans, 30; promised investigation of Harle case, 33

Cabrera, Luis: interview with DuVal
West, 291; Mexican commissioner at
New London, 284

Calles, Gen. Plutarco: appealed to on
behalf of Chinese, 160; in command
at Agua Prieta, 209; leaves Scott-
Obregón conference, 273; seizes
Naco, moves on Nogales, 181

Cananea Consolidated Copper Co.,
Villa accepts Scott's suggestions on,
158-159

Canova, Leon J.: as assistant to Carothers, reports failure of Carranza agents
to Zapata, 108; assists Iturbide to
escape, becomes *persona non grata* to
Villa, 137-138; assured by Villa as
to rights of foreigners, 120; chief of
Division of Mexican Affairs, State
Dept., 206; intervenes with Villa to
save Obregón, 116; recommends protest against executions, 136; reports
Villa's accumulation of supplies, 131;

Gillette, Maj. Cassius E., 49
Glover, Col. Francis W., 311
Gómez, Gen. Arnulfo, 273
Gómez, Gen. Felix U., killed at Carrizal, 278, 280
Gompers, Samuel, endorses Carranza, 205
González, Don Abrán: and Villa, 15, 26; assassinated by Huertistas, 29
González, Gen. Francisco, protests U.S. intervention at Juárez, 312
González, Gen. Pablo: occupation of Mexico City, 177, 178; occupies Tampico, 92
González Garza, Gen. Roque: issues statement on recognition of Carranza, 192; named Prov. President, 144; requests offices of U.S. to communicate with Villa, 171-172; resigns as Prov. President, 177
Gray, George, 284
Grey, Sir Edward: opinion of Villa, 71; replies in Parliament on Benton case, 67
Guadalupe, Plan of, 29, 32
Guanaceví mine, 64
Guerrero, fight with Villistas near, 264
Gutiérrez, Gen. Eulalio: as Prov. President, 128, 130, 143; orders to Maytorena on Naco, 142
Gutiérrez, Gen. Luis, 249; leaves Scott-Obregón conference, 273; on better relations with U.S., 268

Hague Tribunal, 82
Hall, named as envoy to Zapata, 107
Hall, F., questions in Parliament on Benton case, 70
Hall, Adm. Sir Reginald, intercepts Bernstorff message, 301
Hamm, Consul Theodore C.: intervenes in Douglas case, 97; reports on Villa's attitude toward foreigners, 77, 80
Hanna, Consul General Philip: entertains Villa and officers, 167; informed by Carranza of pact of Torreón, 97; recommends evacuation of Americans, 228; recommends withdrawal of Pun. Exp., 293; reports on occupation of Monterrey by Angeles, 146
Harle, Dr., imprisonment and release of, 33, 213
Harper's Weekly, 43, 89, 135
Hart, Albert Bushnell, on Villa and Carranza, 132

Hart, Capt. Juan, 17
Harvey, George, 291
Hayden, Frank, killed by Villa, 237
Hearst, William Randolph, owner of Mexican lands, 8
Hearst newspapers, on Villa, 89
Hearst ranch, evacuates American employees, 228
Hearst's International News Service, experiences of correspondent, 169-170
Heintzelman, Maj. Samuel P., attacks Cortina, 2
Hermosillo, disaster to Villa, 214
Hernandez, Gen., killed near Guerrero, 264
Herrera, Gen. Maclovio, 32, 135
Herron, Maj. Gen. F. J., sends U.S. troops to Matamoros, 3
Hill, Gen. Benjamin: besieged at Naco, 141; reported as Obregón's successor, 170
Hindenburg, Field Marshal von, 302
Holland, Consul Philip E., estimate of Carranza, 28
Hollis, Sen. Henry F., 266
Holmes, Thomas R., escapes from Santa Ysabel massacre, 226
Hopkins, Sherburne: and Cobb, 203; papers stolen from, 95
Hostetter, Consul Louis, instructions on protection for Spaniards, 40, 63, 65
House, Col. Edward M., receives letters from Steffens, 201, 291
Howze, Maj. Robert L.: attacked at San José del Sitio, 270; surprises Villistas at Ojos Azules, 275; threatened at San Borja, 271
Hudson, Paul, 49
Huerta, Gen. Victoriano: arrested in U.S. and extradition refused, 182-183; becomes dictator, 41; commands forces against Orozco, 23; in *coup d'état* seizes government, 28-30; refuses U.S. demands after Tampico incident, 82; relations with Villa, 23; resigns and leaves Mexico, 98; responsibility for death of Madero, 28
Hunt, Frazier, interview with Villa, 313

Iglesias Calderón, Fernando, 114
Immanuel, Col. Friedrich, estimate on war between Mexico and U.S., 301
Independent, 43
Indian raids on lower Rio Grande, 3-4
Industrial Workers of the World, 165

43480